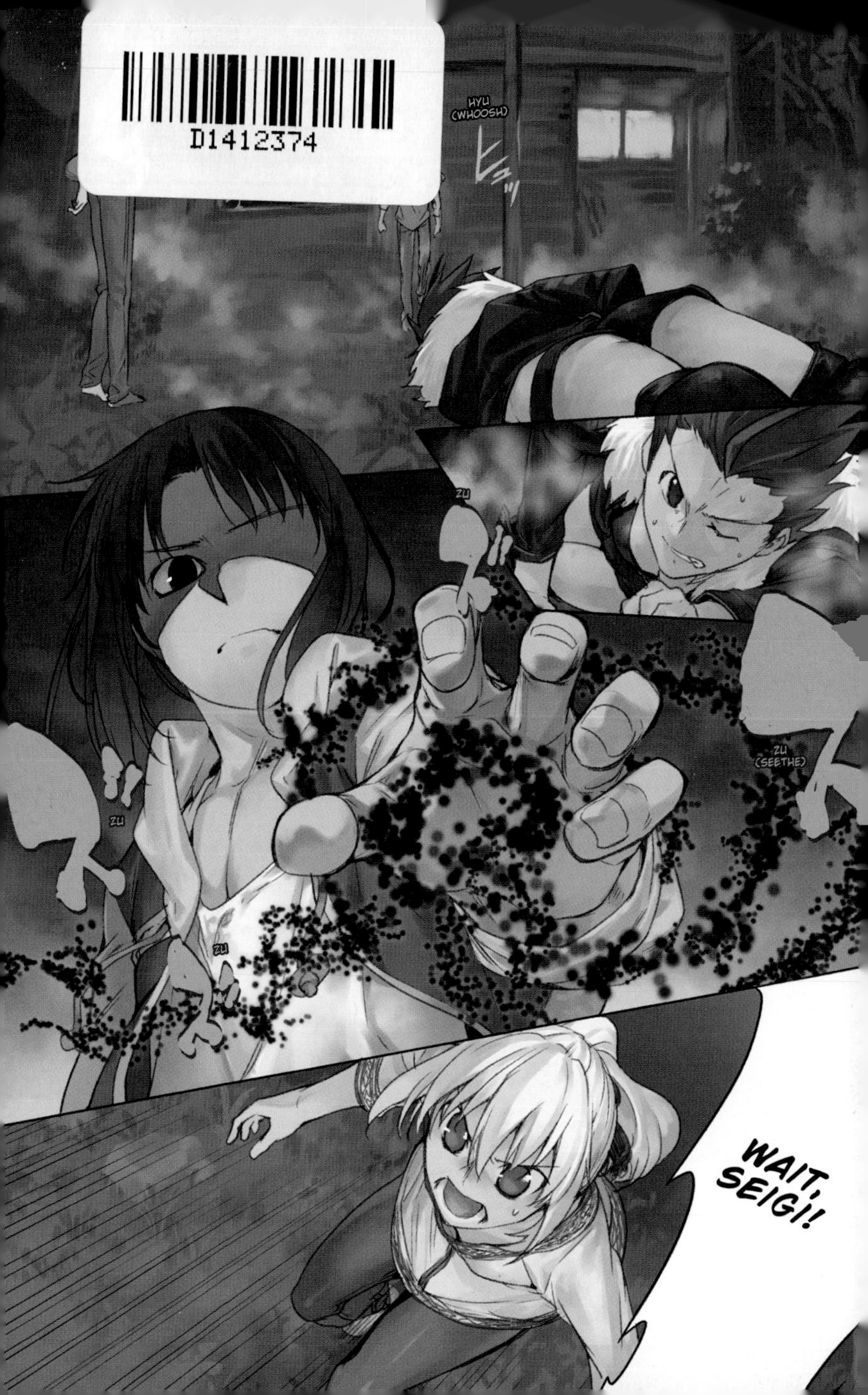
HYU
(WHOOSH)
ZU
ZU
(SEETHE)
ZU
ZU
WAIT, SEIGI!

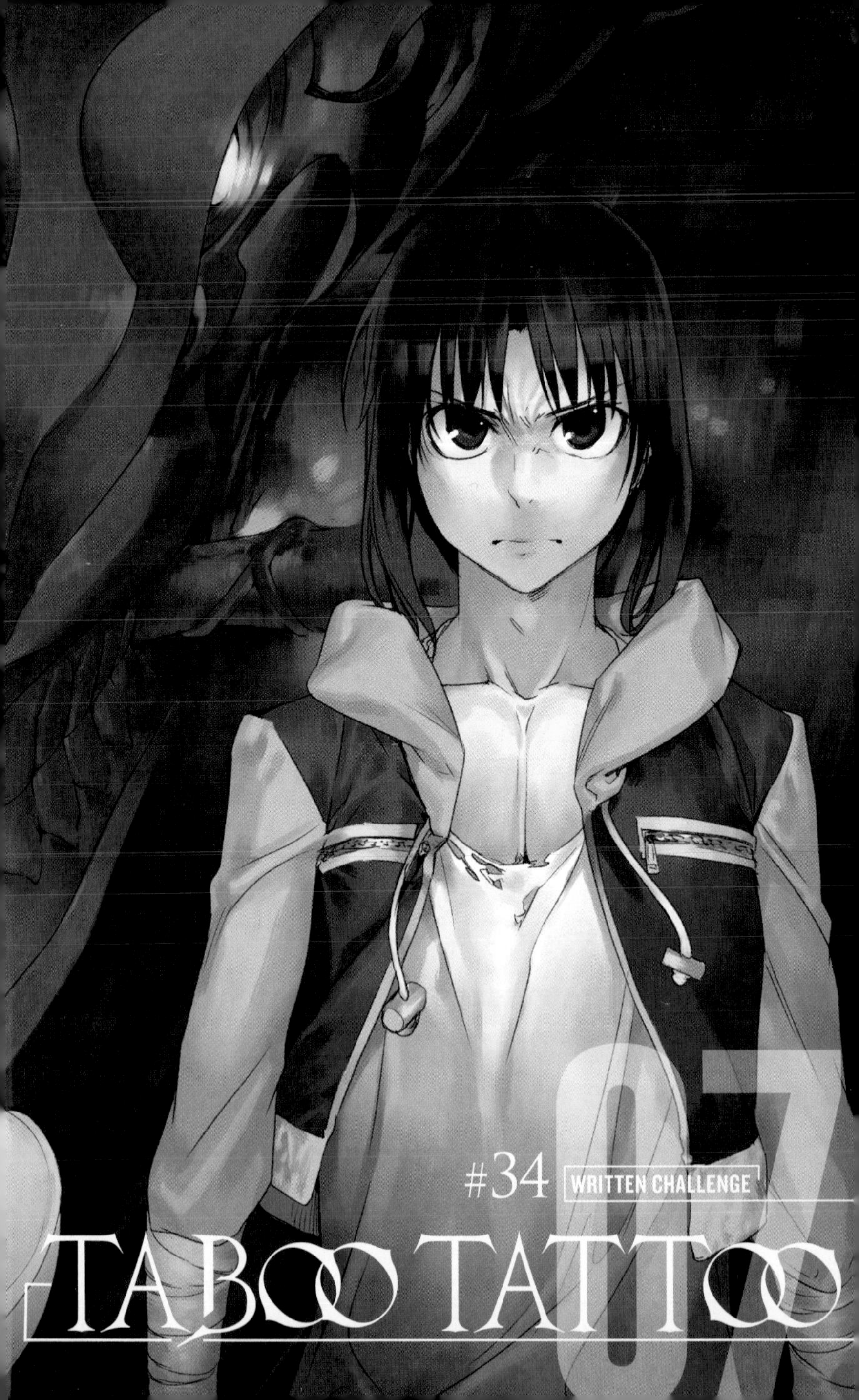

#34 WRITTEN CHALLENGE
TABOO TATTOO
07

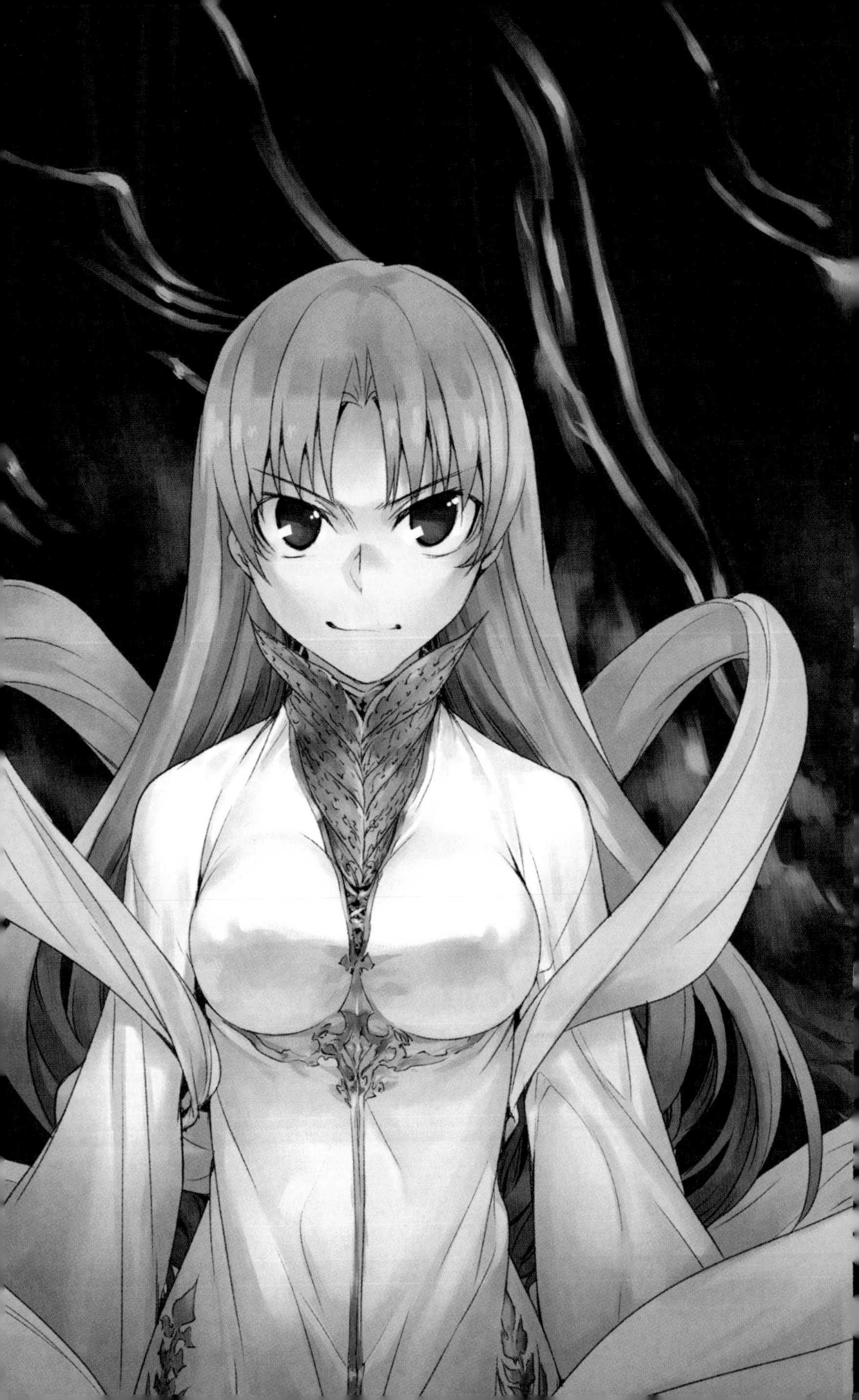

TABOO TATTOO

07

CONTENTS

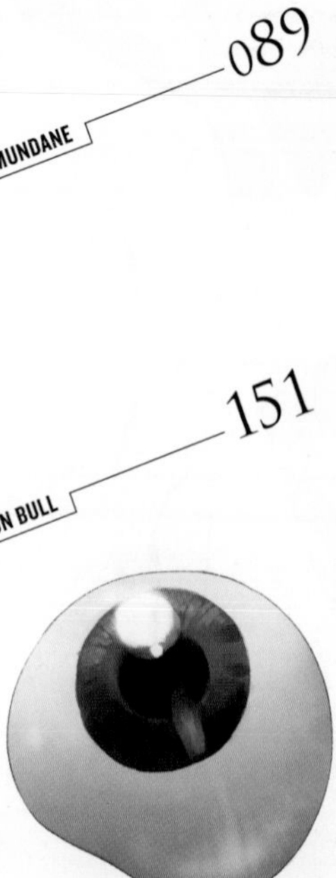

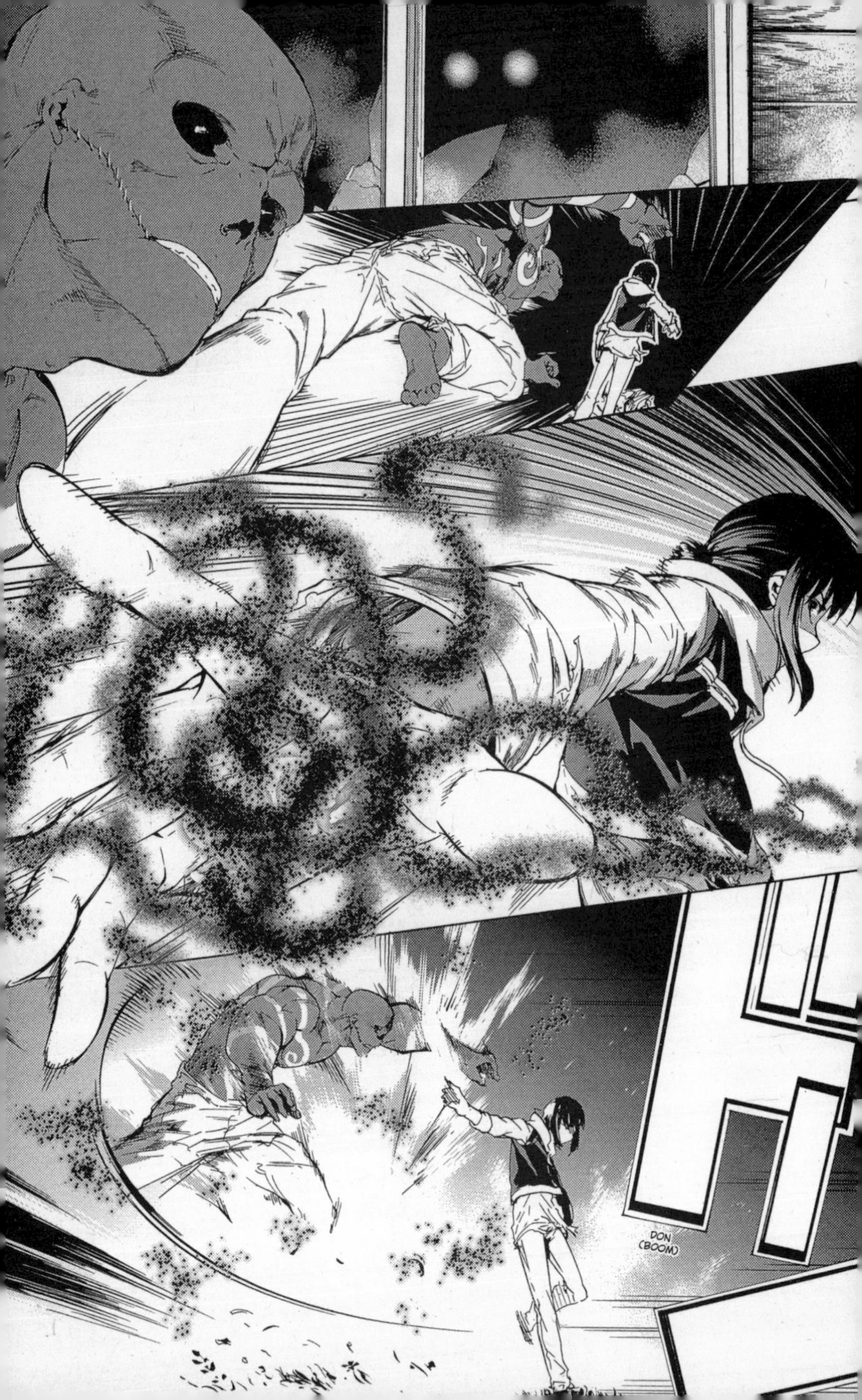
DON
(BOOM)

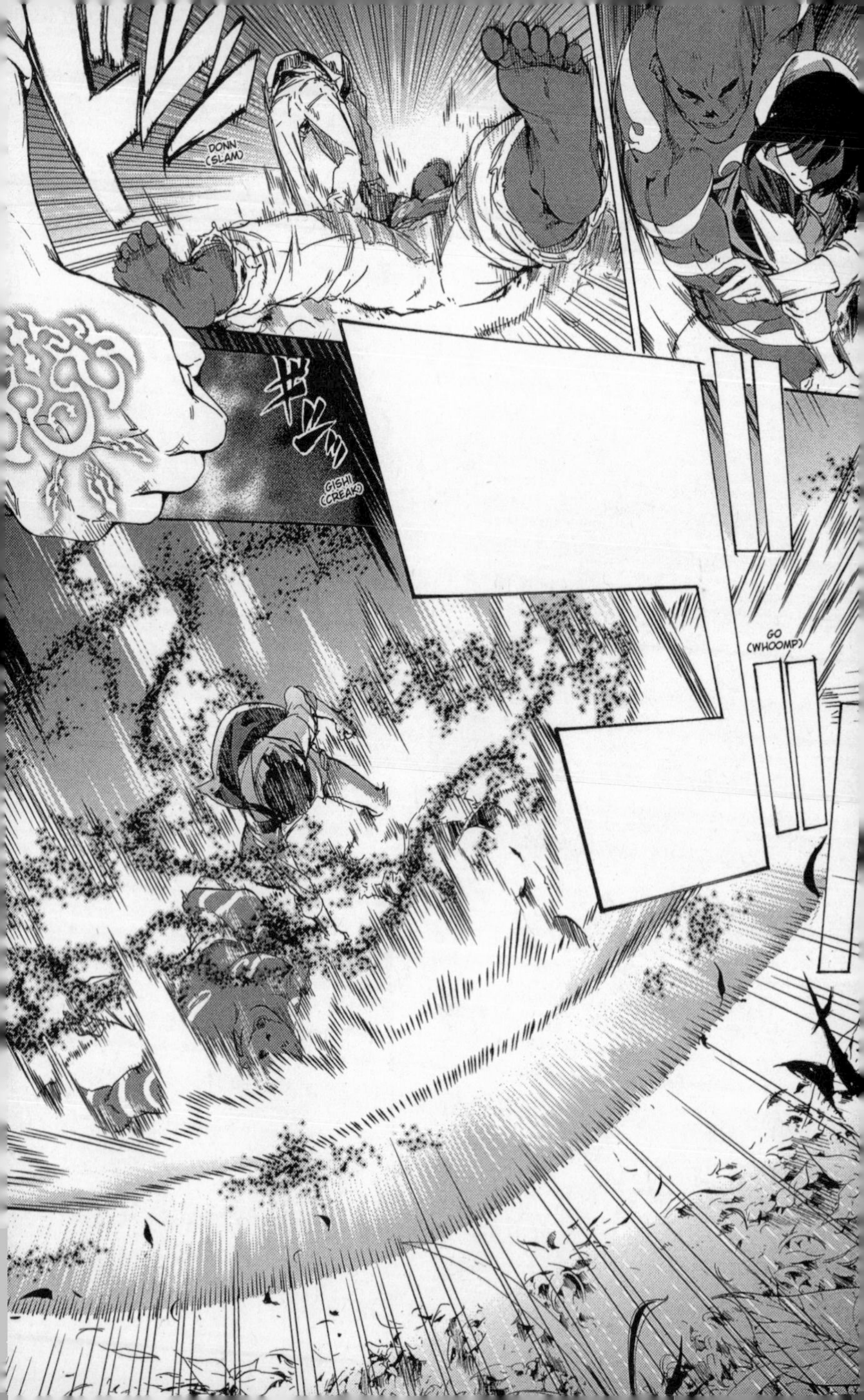
DONN (SLAM)
GISHI (CREAK)
GO (WHOOMP)

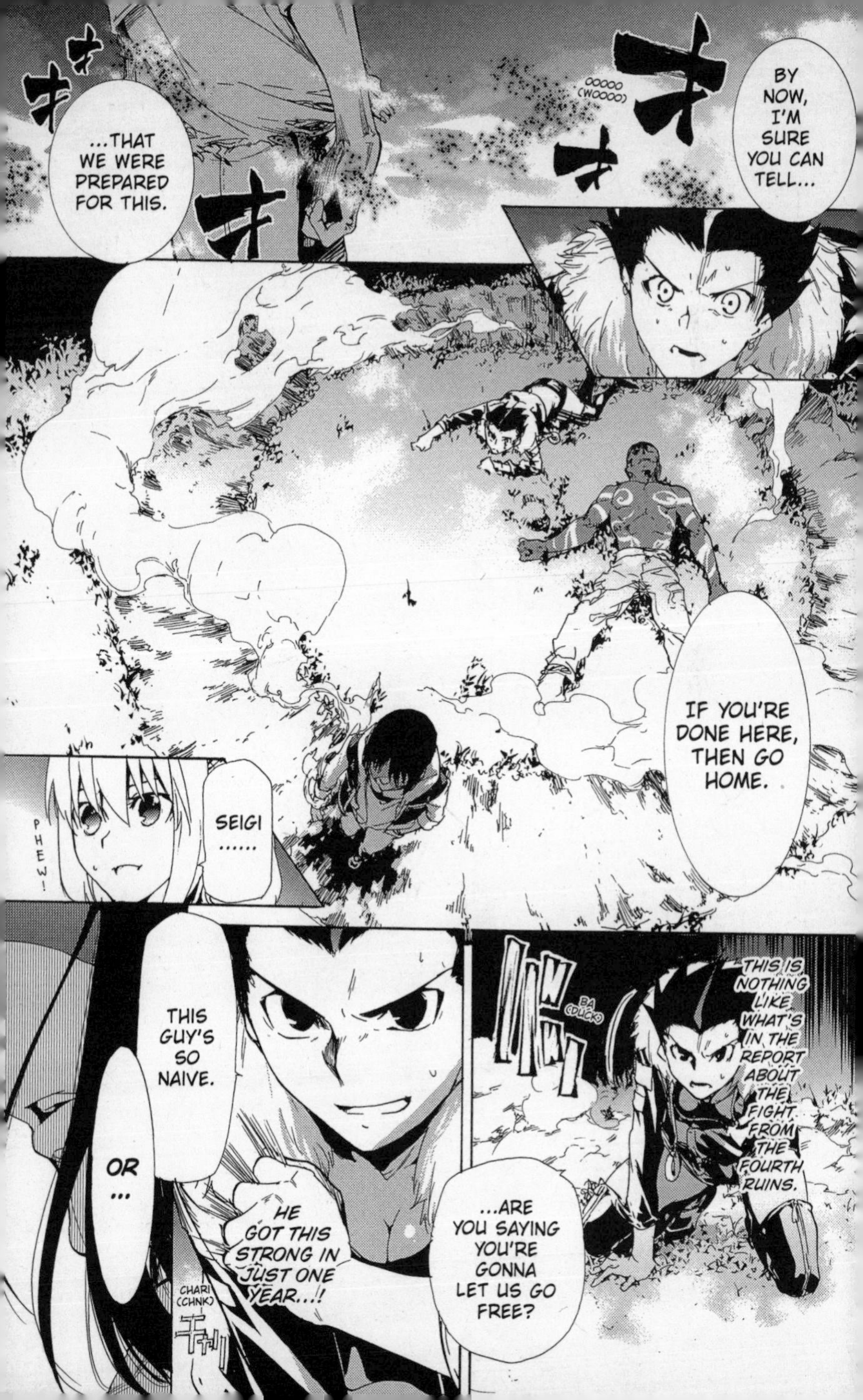
OOOOO (WOOOOO)
BY NOW, I'M SURE YOU CAN TELL...
...THAT WE WERE PREPARED FOR THIS.
IF YOU'RE DONE HERE, THEN GO HOME.
SEIGI ......
PHEW!
BA (DUCK)
THIS IS NOTHING LIKE WHAT'S IN THE REPORT ABOUT THE FIGHT FROM THE FOURTH RUINS.
...ARE YOU SAYING YOU'RE GONNA LET US GO FREE?
THIS GUY'S SO NAIVE.
OR ...
HE GOT THIS STRONG IN JUST ONE YEAR...!
CHARI (CHNK)

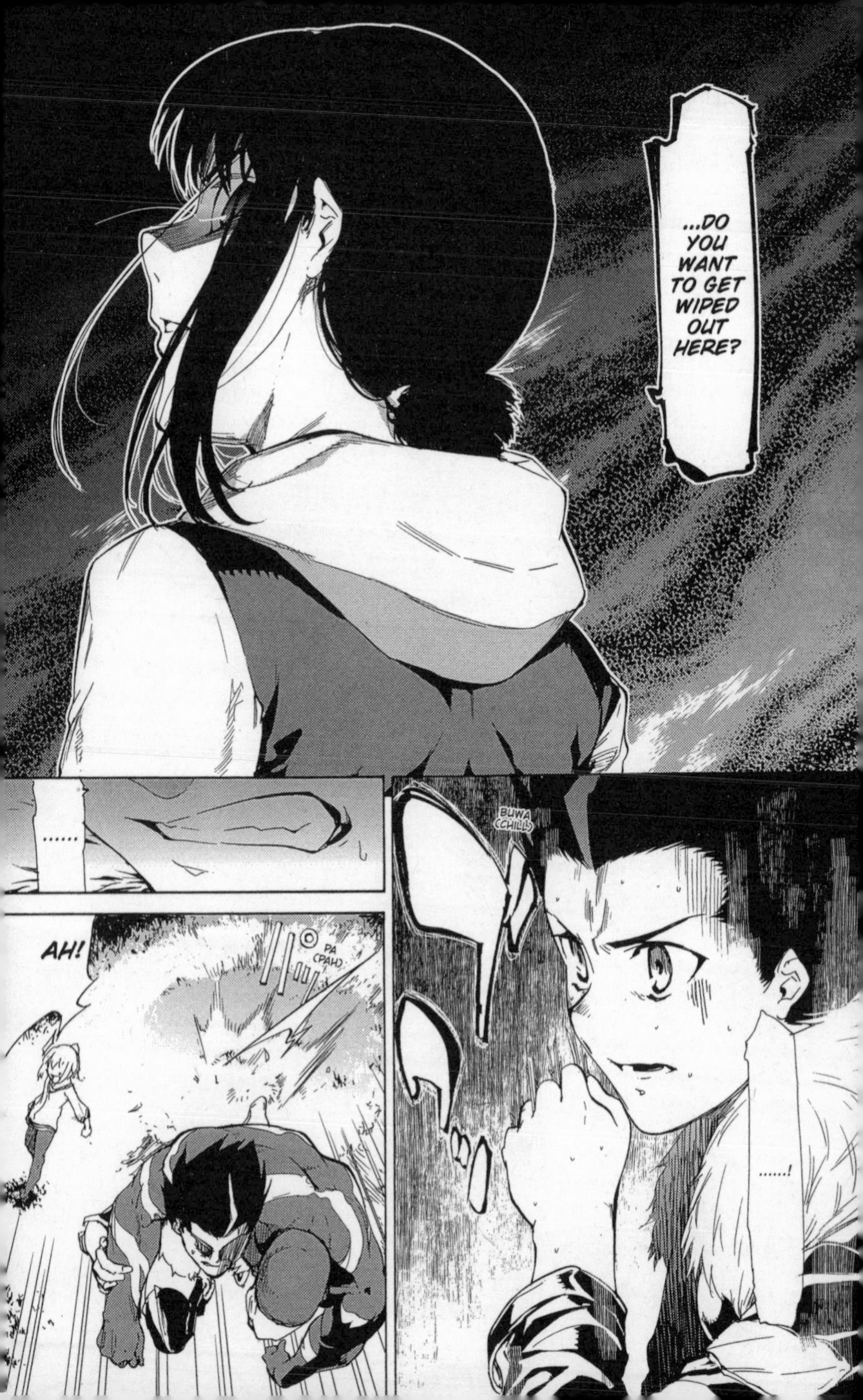
...DO YOU WANT TO GET WIPED OUT HERE?
BUWA (CHILL)
......!
......
AH!
PA (PAH)

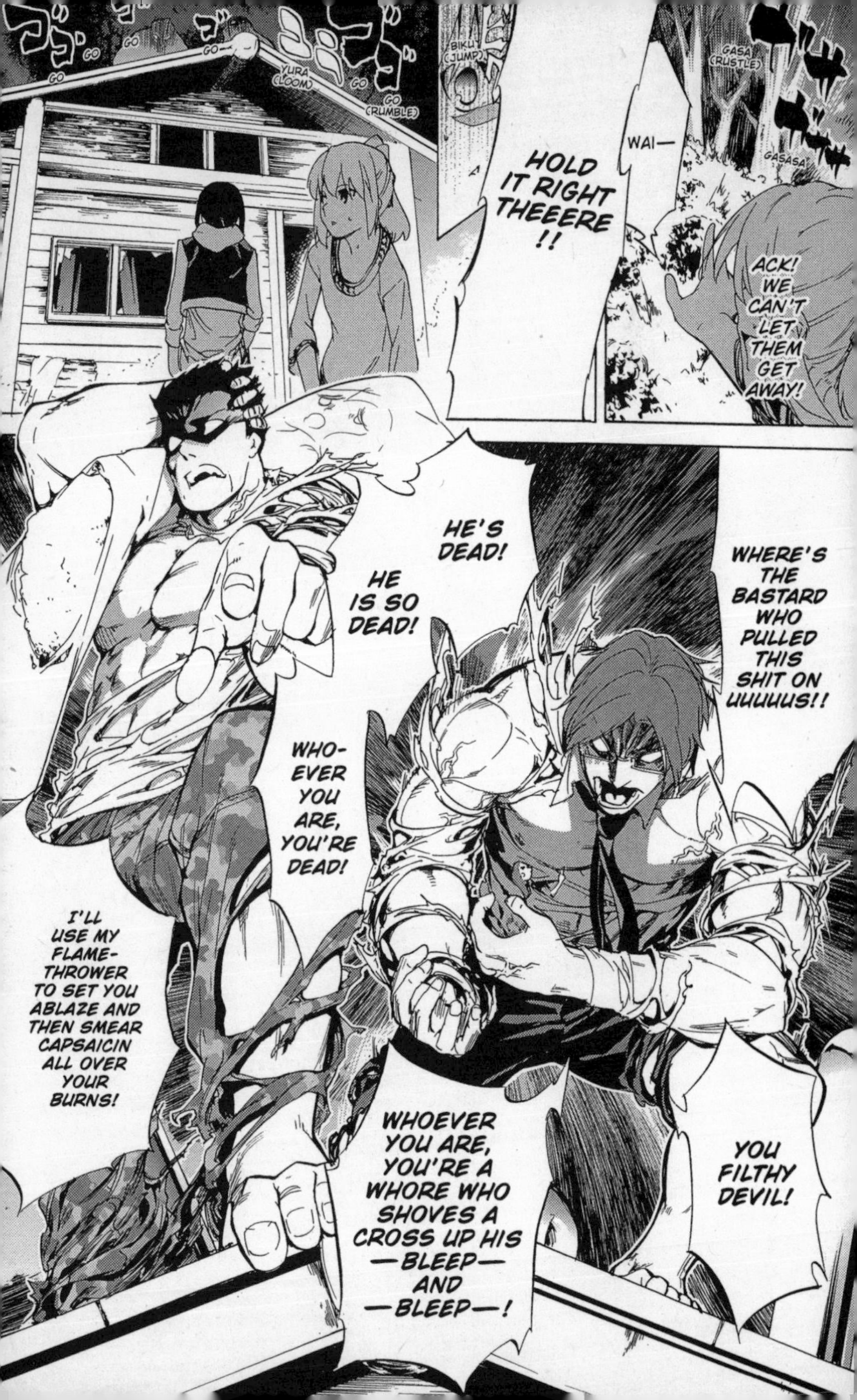
GASA (RUSTLE)
GASASA
ACK! WE CAN'T LET THEM GET AWAY!
BIKU (JUMP)
WAI—
HOLD IT RIGHT THEEERE!!
GO
GO
GO
GO
YURA (LOOM)
GO
GO (RUMBLE)
WHERE'S THE BASTARD WHO PULLED THIS SHIT ON UUUUUS!!
HE'S DEAD!
HE IS SO DEAD!
WHO-EVER YOU ARE, YOU'RE DEAD!
I'LL USE MY FLAME-THROWER TO SET YOU ABLAZE AND THEN SMEAR CAPSAICIN ALL OVER YOUR BURNS!
YOU FILTHY DEVIL!
WHOEVER YOU ARE, YOU'RE A WHORE WHO SHOVES A CROSS UP HIS —BLEEP— AND —BLEEP—!

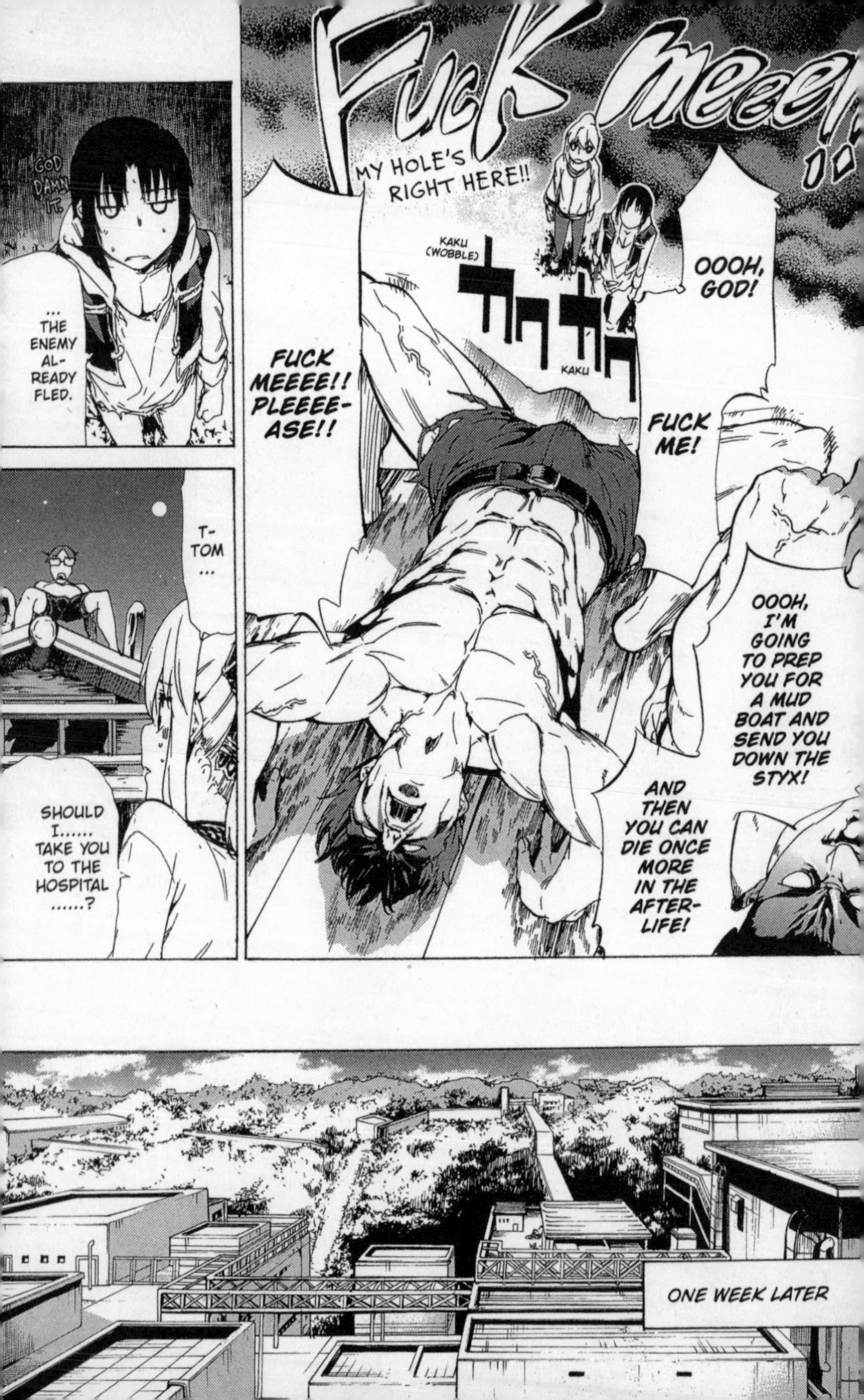
FUCK MEEEE!!
MY HOLE'S RIGHT HERE!!
OOOH, GOD!
KAKU (WOBBLE)
KAKU
FUCK ME!
FUCK MEEEE!! PLEEEE-ASE!!
OOOH, I'M GOING TO PREP YOU FOR A MUD BOAT AND SEND YOU DOWN THE STYX!
AND THEN YOU CAN DIE ONCE MORE IN THE AFTER-LIFE!
GOD DAMN IT
... THE ENEMY AL-READY FLED.
T-TOM ...
SHOULD I...... TAKE YOU TO THE HOSPITAL ......?
ONE WEEK LATER

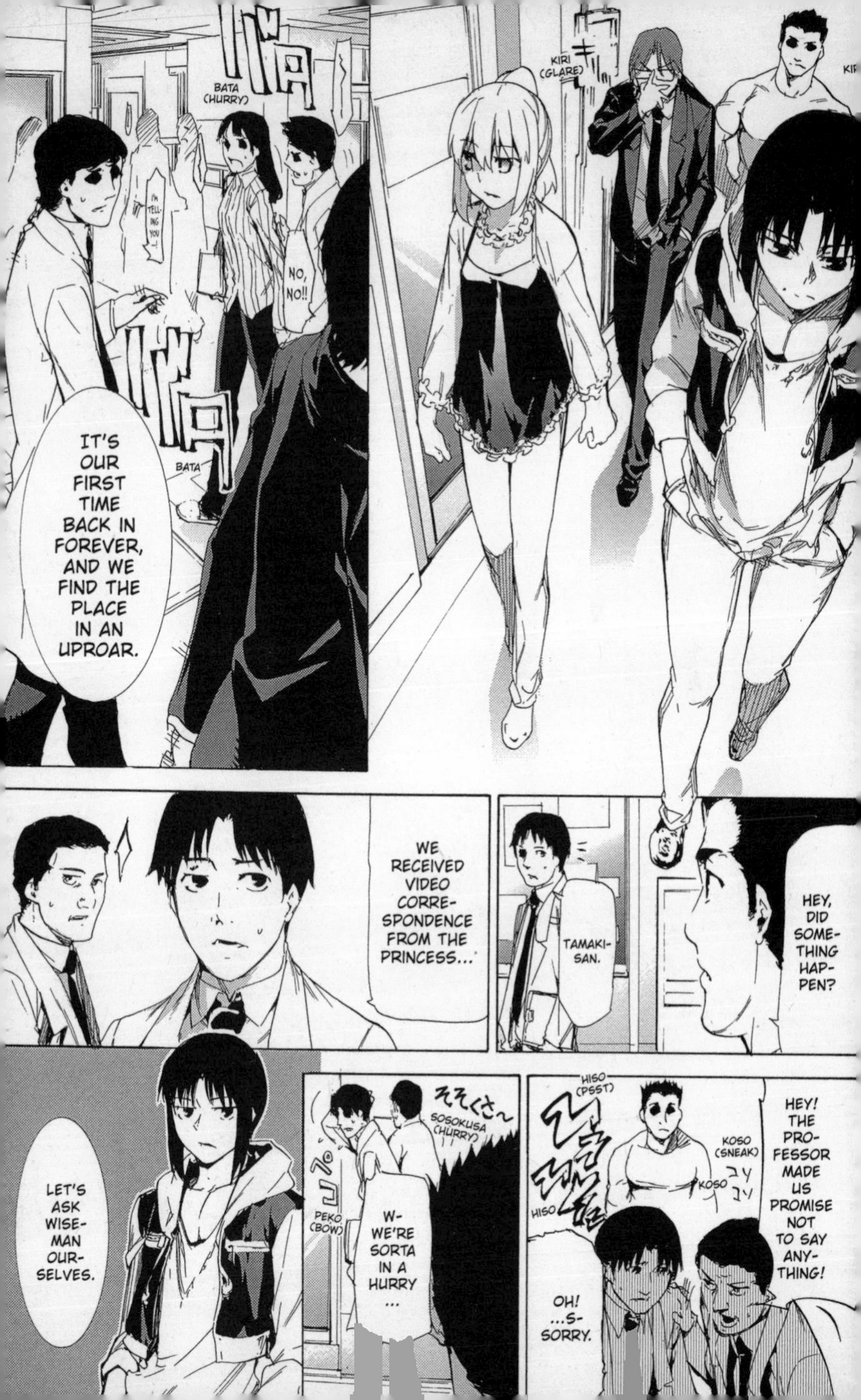
KIRI (GLARE)
KIRI
BATA (HURRY)
I'M TELLING YOU—!
NO, NO!!
BATA
IT'S OUR FIRST TIME BACK IN FOREVER, AND WE FIND THE PLACE IN AN UPROAR.
HEY, DID SOMETHING HAPPEN?
TAMAKI-SAN.
WE RECEIVED VIDEO CORRESPONDENCE FROM THE PRINCESS...
HISO (PSST)
HISO
KOSO (SNEAK)
KOSO
HEY! THE PROFESSOR MADE US PROMISE NOT TO SAY ANYTHING!
OH! ...S-SORRY.
そそくさ~
SOSOKUSA (HURRY)
PEKO (BOW)
W-WE'RE SORTA IN A HURRY...
LET'S ASK WISEMAN OURSELVES.

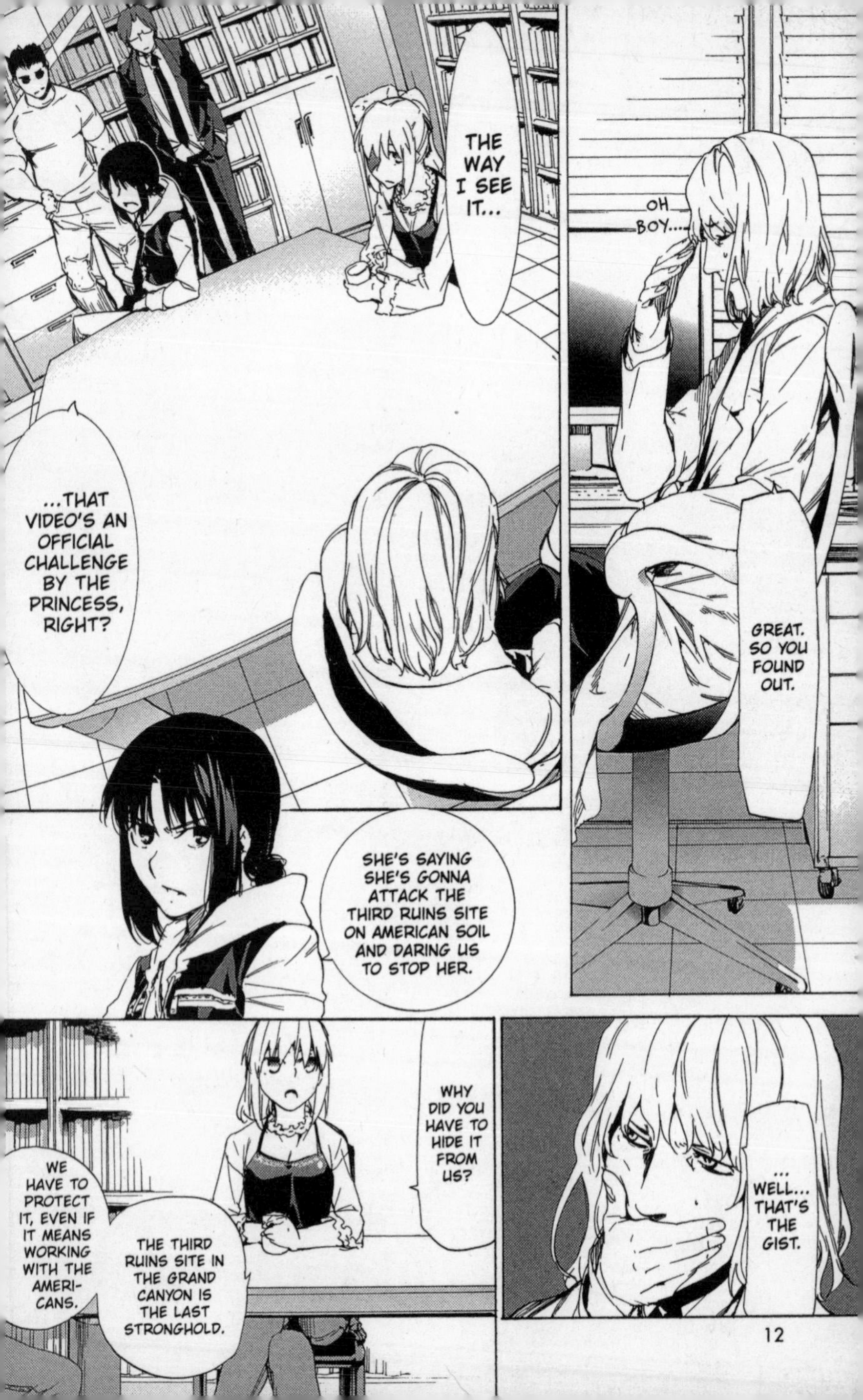
OH BOY....
GREAT. SO YOU FOUND OUT.
THE WAY I SEE IT...
...THAT VIDEO'S AN OFFICIAL CHALLENGE BY THE PRINCESS, RIGHT?
SHE'S SAYING SHE'S GONNA ATTACK THE THIRD RUINS SITE ON AMERICAN SOIL AND DARING US TO STOP HER.
... WELL... THAT'S THE GIST.
WHY DID YOU HAVE TO HIDE IT FROM US?
THE THIRD RUINS SITE IN THE GRAND CANYON IS THE LAST STRONGHOLD.
WE HAVE TO PROTECT IT, EVEN IF IT MEANS WORKING WITH THE AMERI-CANS.

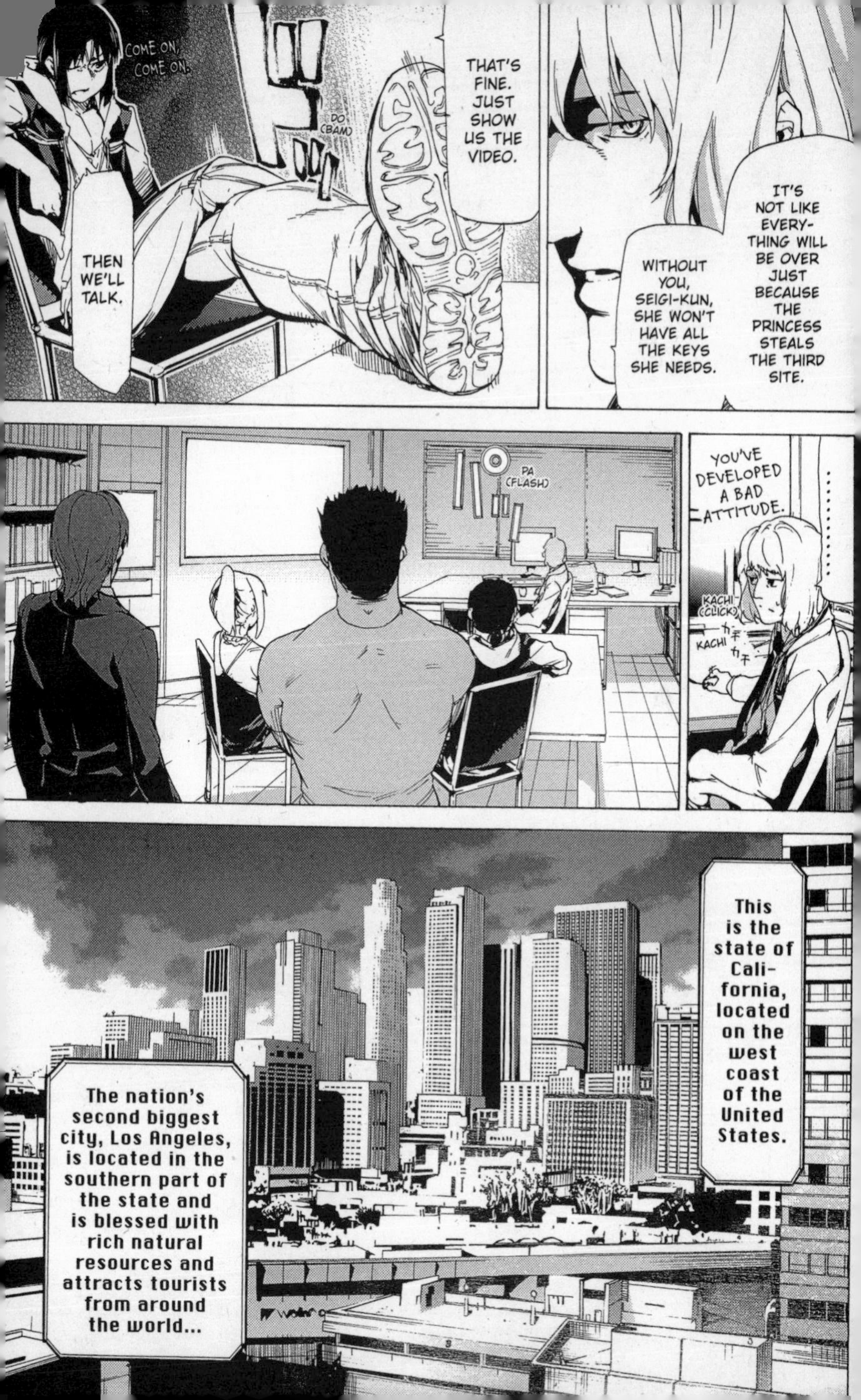
IT'S NOT LIKE EVERYTHING WILL BE OVER JUST BECAUSE THE PRINCESS STEALS THE THIRD SITE.
WITHOUT YOU, SEIGI-KUN, SHE WON'T HAVE ALL THE KEYS SHE NEEDS.
THAT'S FINE. JUST SHOW US THE VIDEO.
DO (BAM)
COME ON, COME ON.
THEN WE'LL TALK.
.....
YOU'VE DEVELOPED A BAD ATTITUDE.
KACHI (CLICK)
KACHI
PA (FLASH)
This is the state of California, located on the west coast of the United States.
The nation's second biggest city, Los Angeles, is located in the southern part of the state and is blessed with rich natural resources and attracts tourists from around the world...

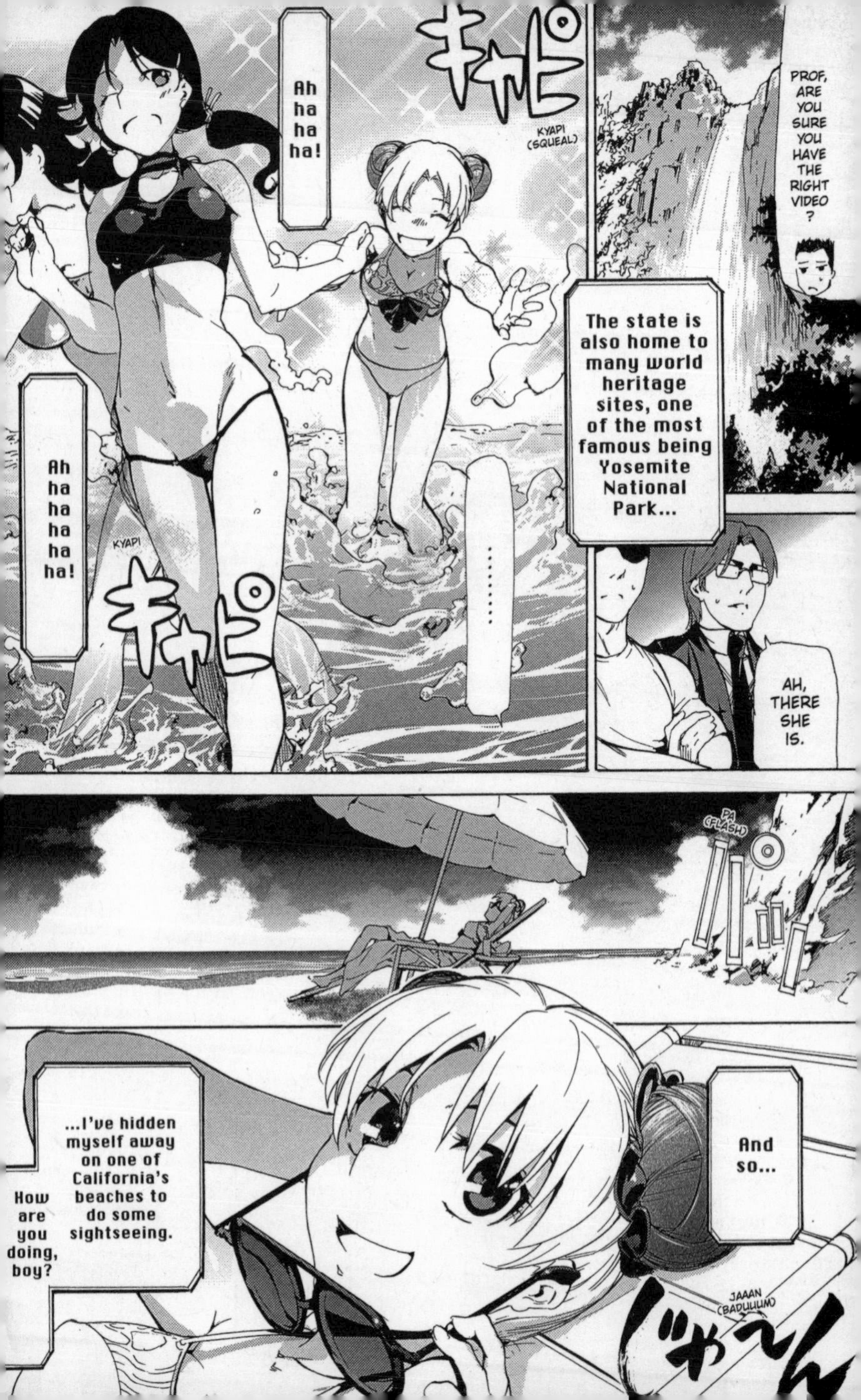
PROF, ARE YOU SURE YOU HAVE THE RIGHT VIDEO ?
The state is also home to many world heritage sites, one of the most famous being Yosemite National Park...
AH, THERE SHE IS.
キャピ
KYAPI (SQUEAL)
Ah ha ha ha!
......
Ah ha ha ha ha ha!
KYAPI
キャピ
PA (FLASH)
And so...
...I've hidden myself away on one of California's beaches to do some sightseeing.
How are you doing, boy?
JAAAN (BADUUUM)
じゃ〜ん

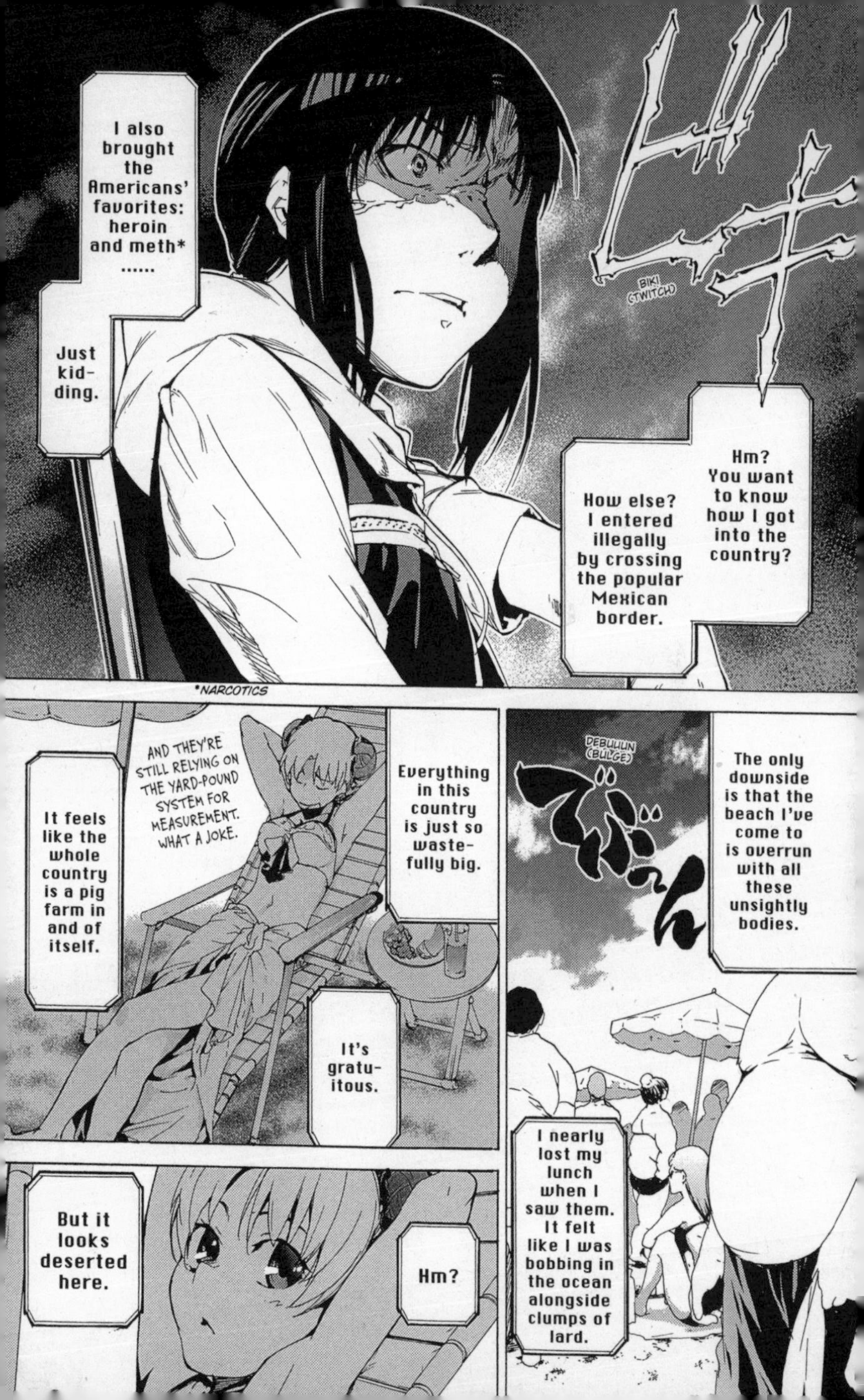
BIKI (TWITCH)
Hm? You want to know how I got into the country?
How else? I entered illegally by crossing the popular Mexican border.
I also brought the Americans' favorites: heroin and meth* ......
Just kid-ding.
*NARCOTICS
DEBUUUN (BULGE)
The only downside is that the beach I've come to is overrun with all these unsightly bodies.
I nearly lost my lunch when I saw them. It felt like I was bobbing in the ocean alongside clumps of lard.
Everything in this country is just so waste-fully big.
AND THEY'RE STILL RELYING ON THE YARD-POUND SYSTEM FOR MEASUREMENT. WHAT A JOKE.
It feels like the whole country is a pig farm in and of itself.
It's gratu-itous.
Hm?
But it looks deserted here.

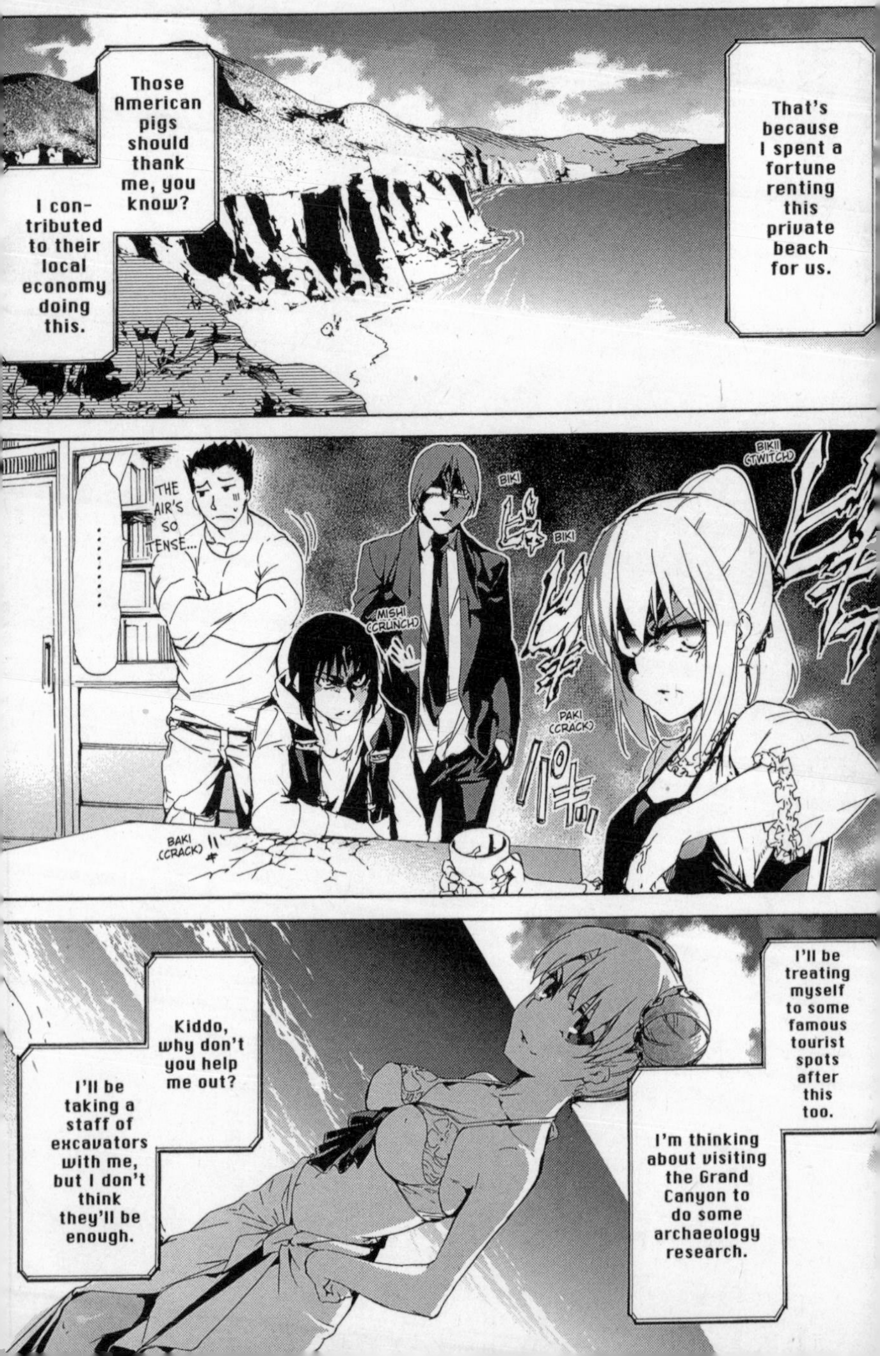
That's because I spent a fortune renting this private beach for us.
Those American pigs should thank me, you know?
I contributed to their local economy doing this.
BIKII (TWITCH)
BIKI
BIKI
PAKI (CRACK)
MISHI (CRUNCH)
THE AIR'S SO TENSE...
......
BAKI (CRACK)
I'll be treating myself to some famous tourist spots after this too.
I'm thinking about visiting the Grand Canyon to do some archaeology research.
Kiddo, why don't you help me out?
I'll be taking a staff of excavators with me, but I don't think they'll be enough.

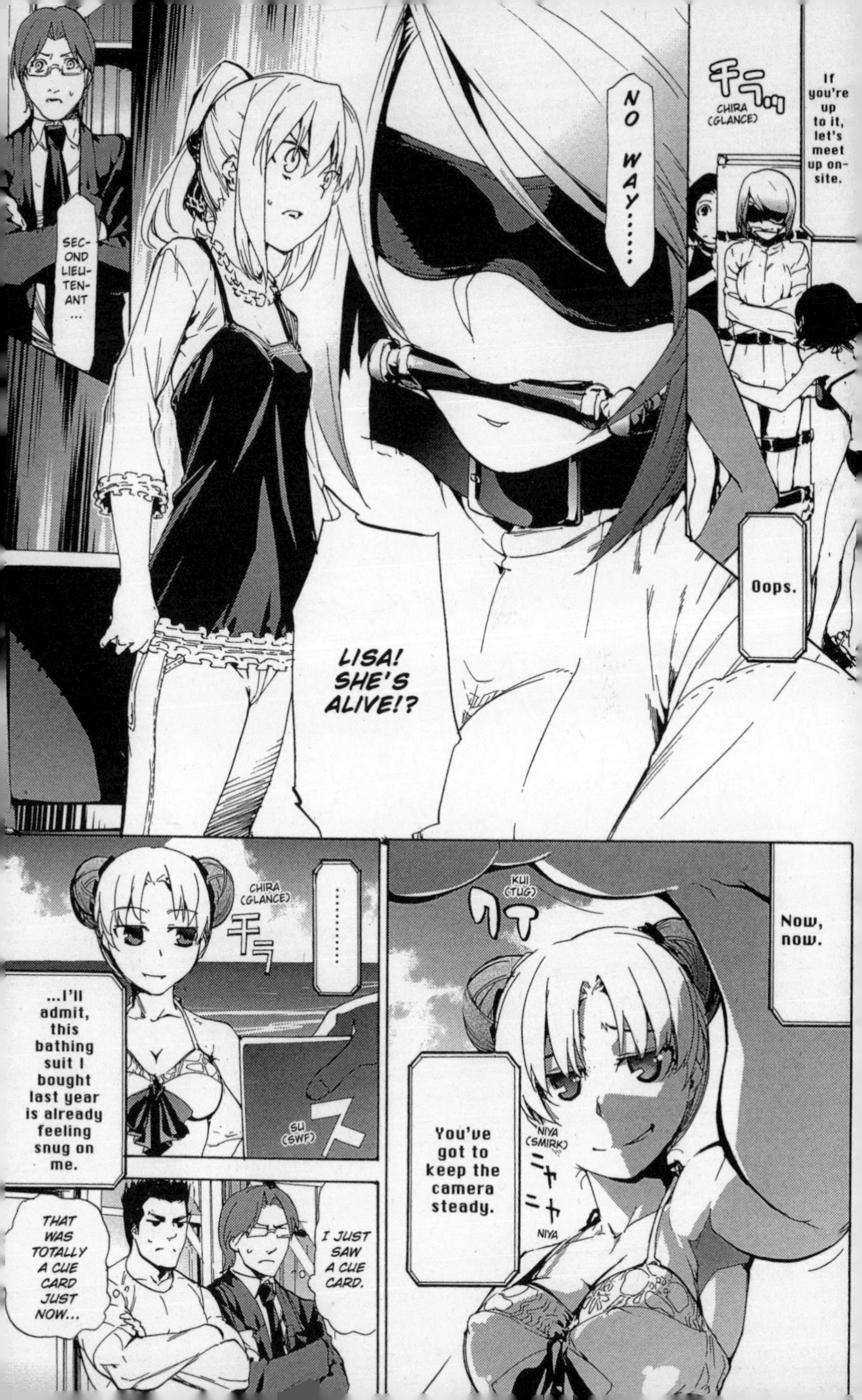

チラッ
CHIRA (GLANCE)
If you're up to it, let's meet up on-site.
Oops.
NO WAY......
SECOND LIEUTENANT...
LISA! SHE'S ALIVE!?
Now, now.
クイ
KUI (TUG)
You've got to keep the camera steady.
ニヤニヤ
NIYA (SMIRK)
NIYA
....
チラ
CHIRA (GLANCE)
...I'll admit, this bathing suit I bought last year is already feeling snug on me.
ス
SU (SWF)
I JUST SAW A CUE CARD.
THAT WAS TOTALLY A CUE CARD JUST NOW...

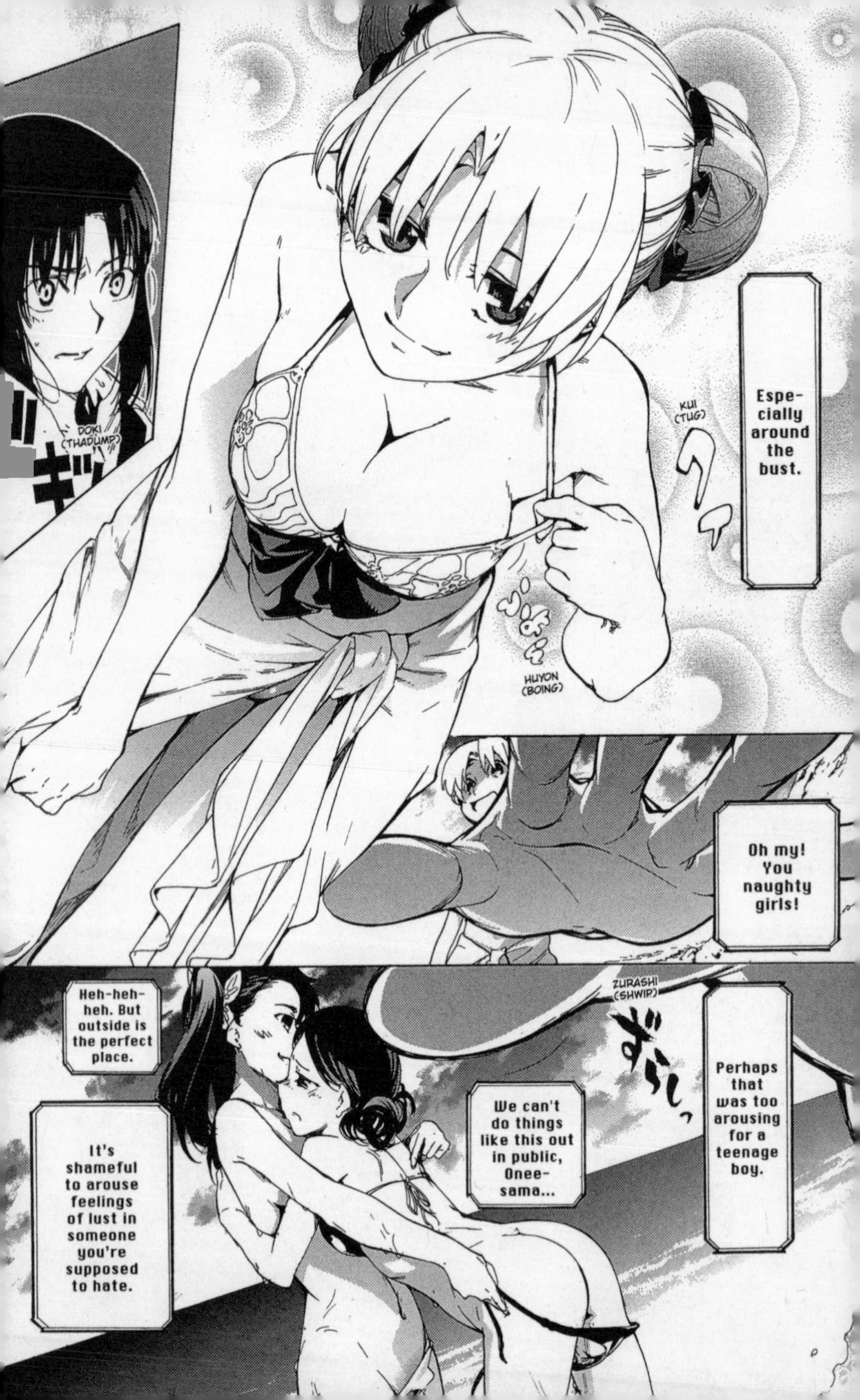
Espe-cially around the bust.
KUI (TUG)
HUYON (BOING)
DOKI (THADUMP)
Oh my! You naughty girls!
ZURASHI (SHWIP)
Perhaps that was too arousing for a teenage boy.
We can't do things like this out in public, Onee-sama...
Heh-heh-heh. But outside is the perfect place.
It's shameful to arouse feelings of lust in someone you're supposed to hate.

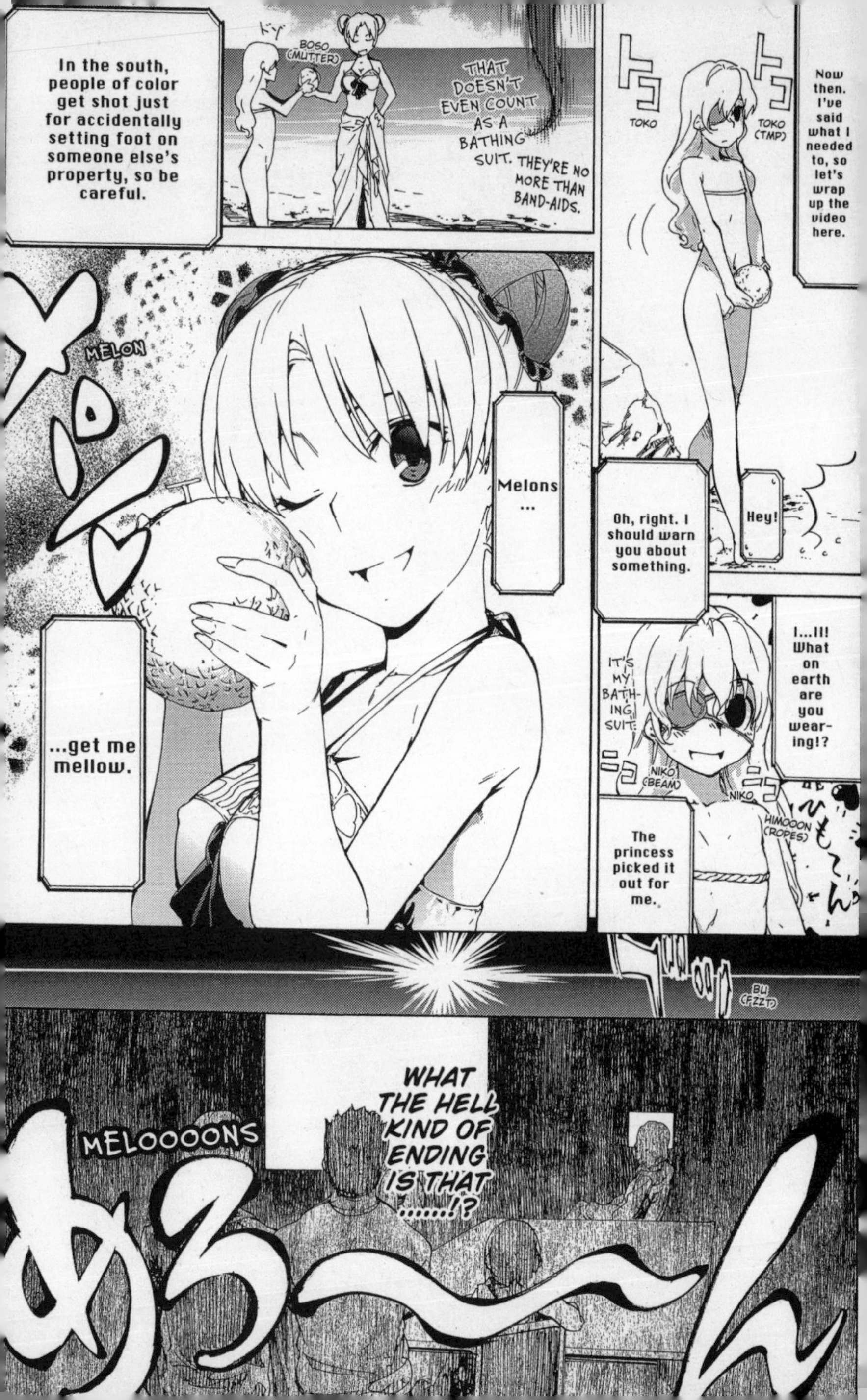
TOKO
TOKO (TMP)
Now then. I've said what I needed to, so let's wrap up the video here.
BOSO (MUTTER)
THAT DOESN'T EVEN COUNT AS A BATHING SUIT. THEY'RE NO MORE THAN BAND-AIDS.
In the south, people of color get shot just for accidentally setting foot on someone else's property, so be careful.
Hey!
Oh, right. I should warn you about something.
I...I! What on earth are you wearing!?
IT'S MY BATHING SUIT
NIKO (BEAM)
NIKO
HIMOOON (ROPES)
The princess picked it out for me.
Melons...
MELON
...get me mellow.
BU (FZZT)
WHAT THE HELL KIND OF ENDING IS THAT......!?
MELOOOONS

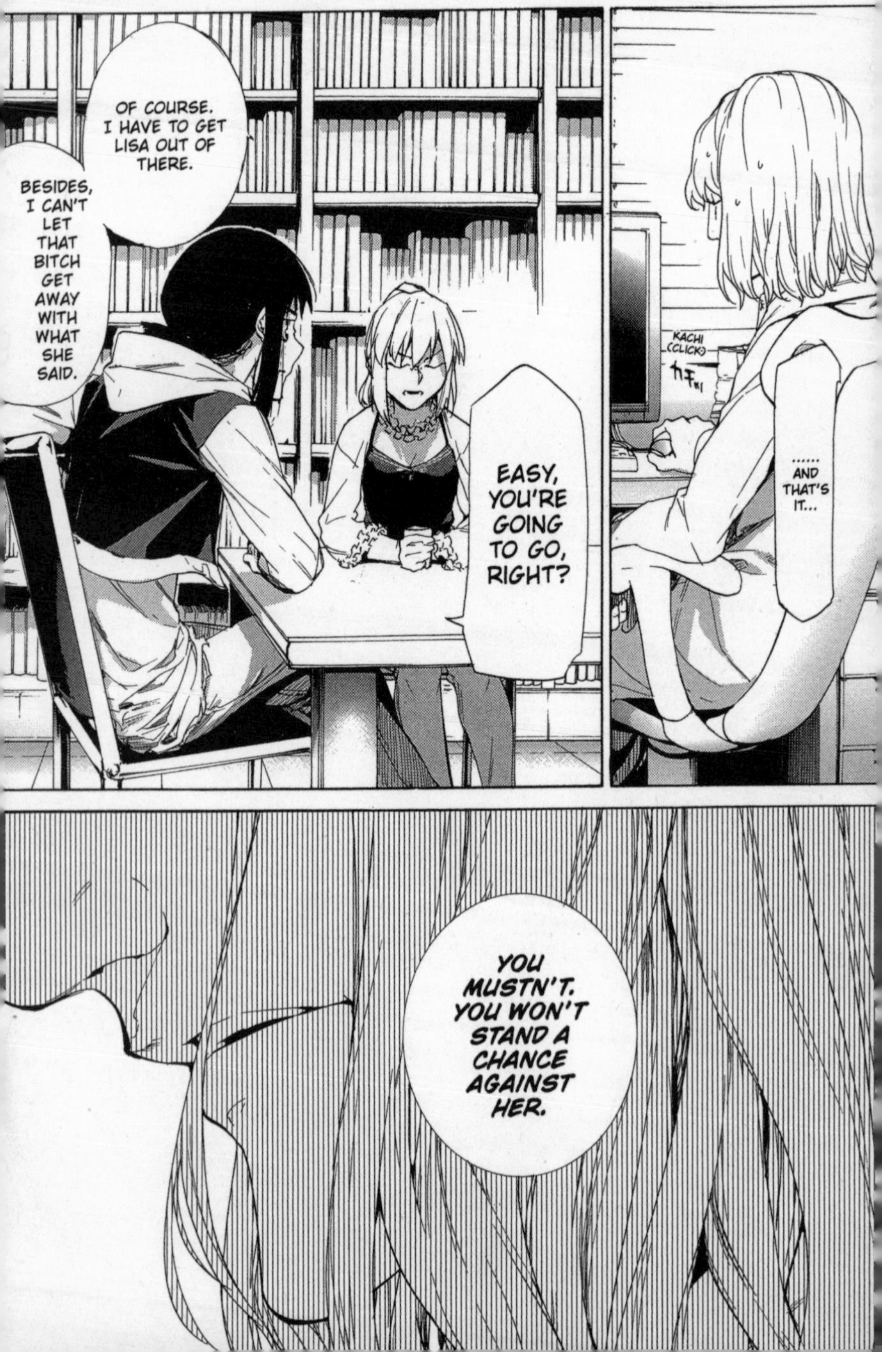
KACHI (CLICK)
...... AND THAT'S IT...
EASY, YOU'RE GOING TO GO, RIGHT?
OF COURSE. I HAVE TO GET LISA OUT OF THERE.
BESIDES, I CAN'T LET THAT BITCH GET AWAY WITH WHAT SHE SAID.
YOU MUSTN'T. YOU WON'T STAND A CHANCE AGAINST HER.

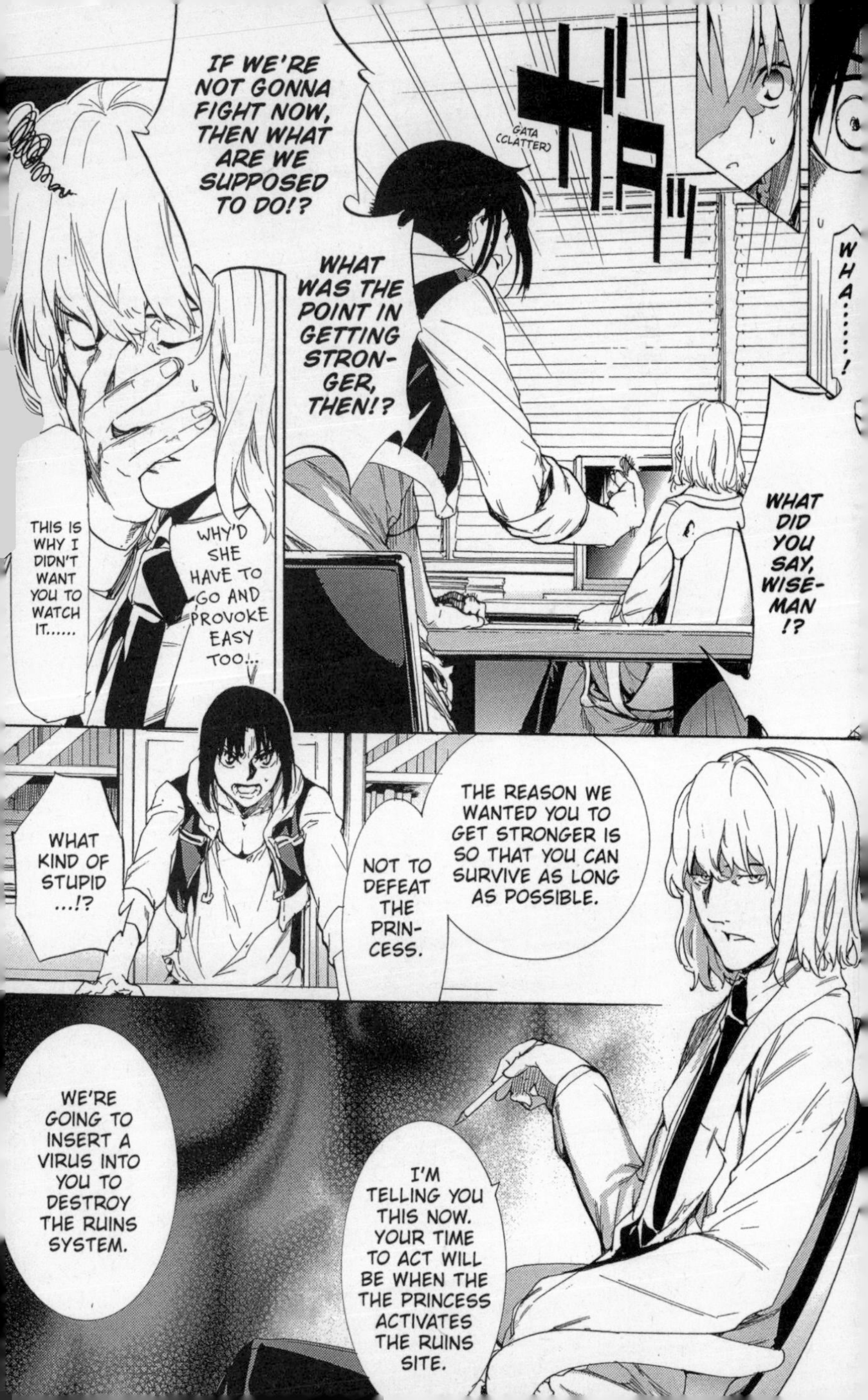
GATA (CLATTER)
WHA......!
IF WE'RE NOT GONNA FIGHT NOW, THEN WHAT ARE WE SUPPOSED TO DO!?
WHAT WAS THE POINT IN GETTING STRONGER, THEN!?
WHAT DID YOU SAY, WISEMAN!?
WHY'D SHE HAVE TO GO AND PROVOKE EASY TOO...
THIS IS WHY I DIDN'T WANT YOU TO WATCH IT......
THE REASON WE WANTED YOU TO GET STRONGER IS SO THAT YOU CAN SURVIVE AS LONG AS POSSIBLE.
NOT TO DEFEAT THE PRINCESS.
WHAT KIND OF STUPID ...!?
I'M TELLING YOU THIS NOW. YOUR TIME TO ACT WILL BE WHEN THE THE PRINCESS ACTIVATES THE RUINS SITE.
WE'RE GOING TO INSERT A VIRUS INTO YOU TO DESTROY THE RUINS SYSTEM.

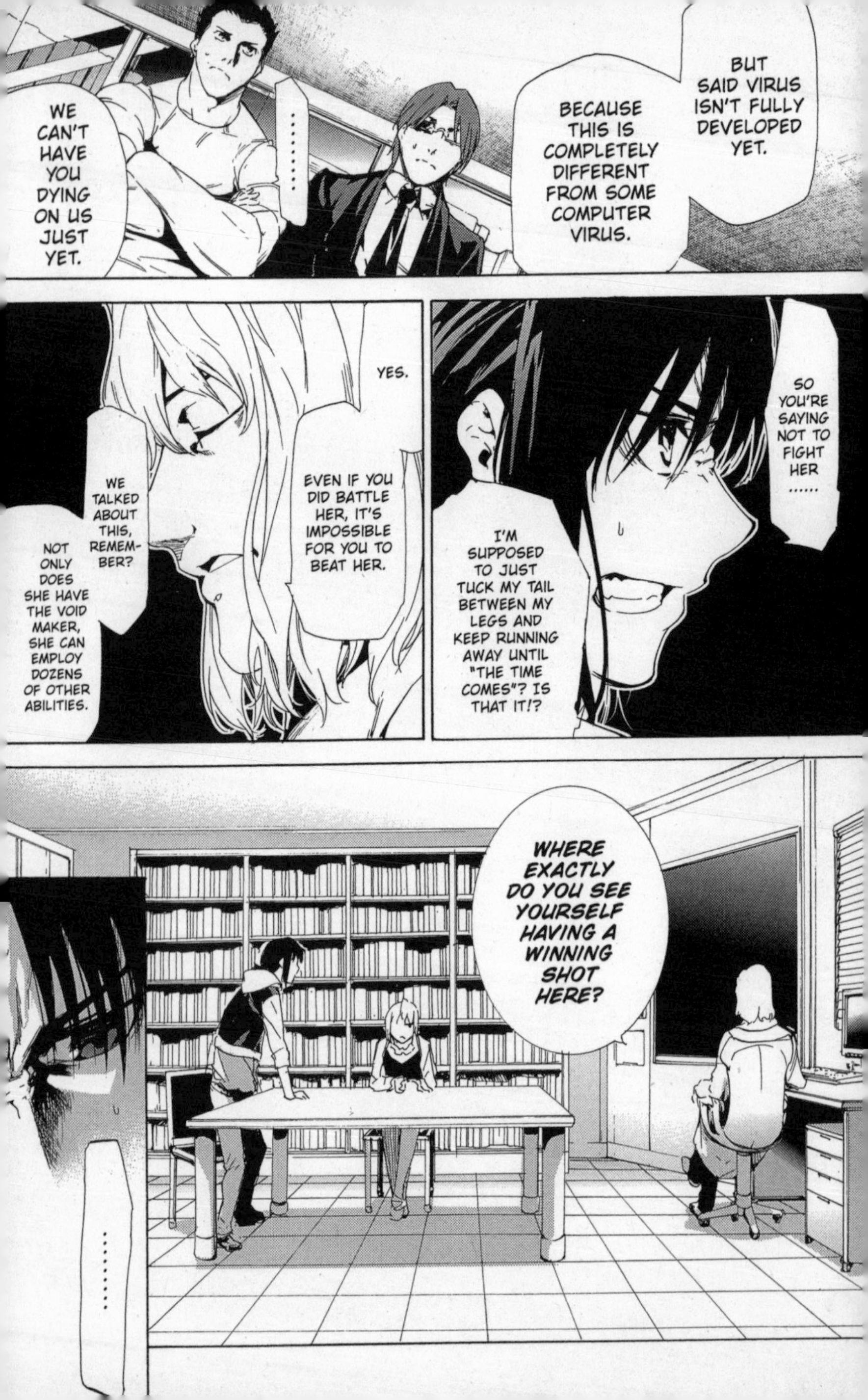
BUT SAID VIRUS ISN'T FULLY DEVELOPED YET.
BECAUSE THIS IS COMPLETELY DIFFERENT FROM SOME COMPUTER VIRUS.
......
WE CAN'T HAVE YOU DYING ON US JUST YET.
SO YOU'RE SAYING NOT TO FIGHT HER ......
I'M SUPPOSED TO JUST TUCK MY TAIL BETWEEN MY LEGS AND KEEP RUNNING AWAY UNTIL "THE TIME COMES"? IS THAT IT!?
YES.
EVEN IF YOU DID BATTLE HER, IT'S IMPOSSIBLE FOR YOU TO BEAT HER.
WE TALKED ABOUT THIS, REMEMBER?
NOT ONLY DOES SHE HAVE THE VOID MAKER, SHE CAN EMPLOY DOZENS OF OTHER ABILITIES.
WHERE EXACTLY DO YOU SEE YOURSELF HAVING A WINNING SHOT HERE?
......

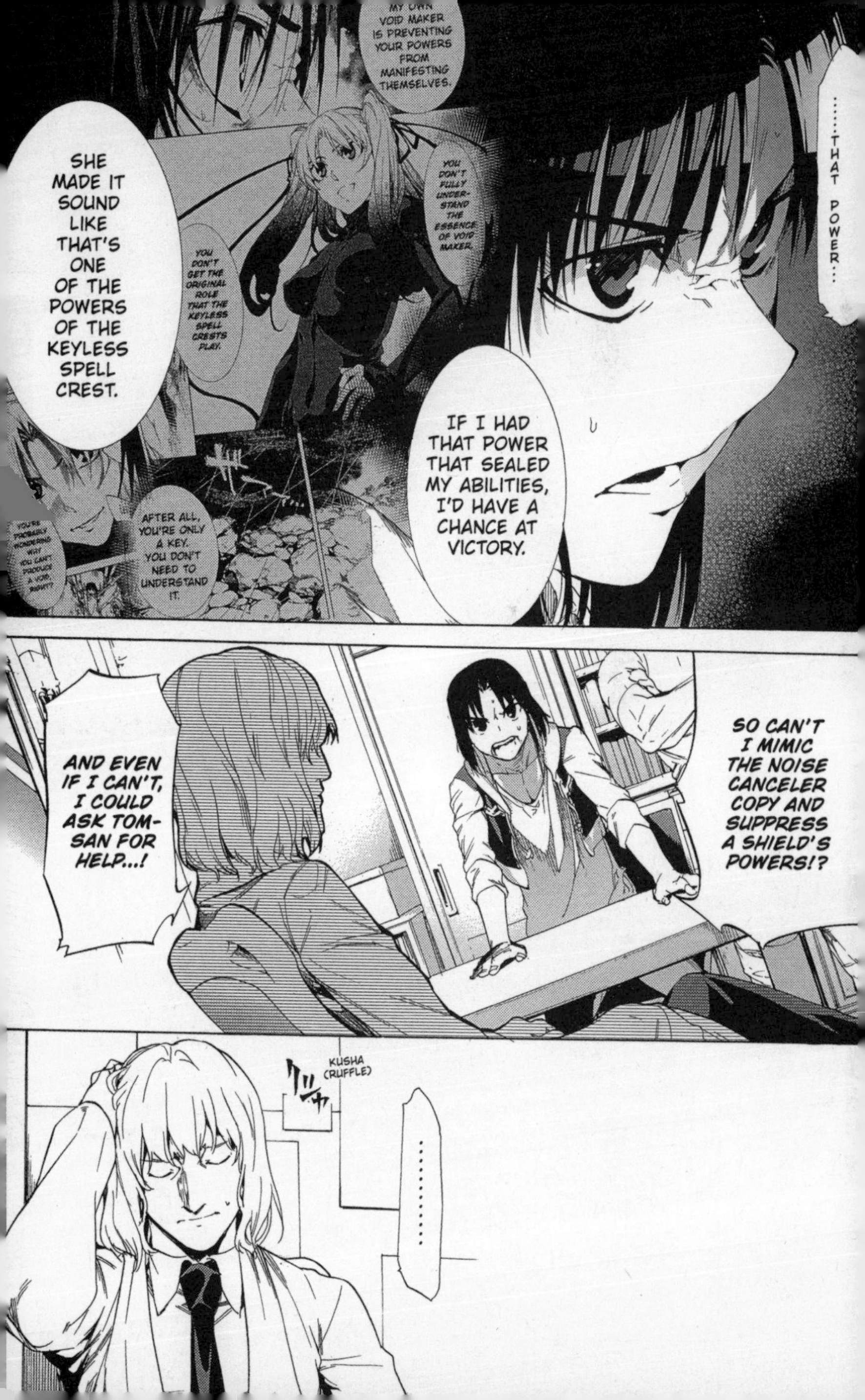

.....THAT POWER...
IF I HAD THAT POWER THAT SEALED MY ABILITIES, I'D HAVE A CHANCE AT VICTORY.
MY OWN VOID MAKER IS PREVENTING YOUR POWERS FROM MANIFESTING THEMSELVES.
YOU DON'T FULLY UNDERSTAND THE ESSENCE OF VOID MAKER.
YOU DON'T GET THE ORIGINAL ROLE THAT THE KEYLESS SPELL CRESTS PLAY.
SHE MADE IT SOUND LIKE THAT'S ONE OF THE POWERS OF THE KEYLESS SPELL CREST.
AFTER ALL, YOU'RE ONLY A KEY. YOU DON'T NEED TO UNDERSTAND IT.
YOU'RE PROBABLY WONDERING WHY YOU CAN'T PRODUCE A VOID, RIGHT?
SO CAN'T I MIMIC THE NOISE CANCELER COPY AND SUPPRESS A SHIELD'S POWERS!?
AND EVEN IF I CAN'T, I COULD ASK TOM-SAN FOR HELP...!
KUSHA (RUFFLE)
....

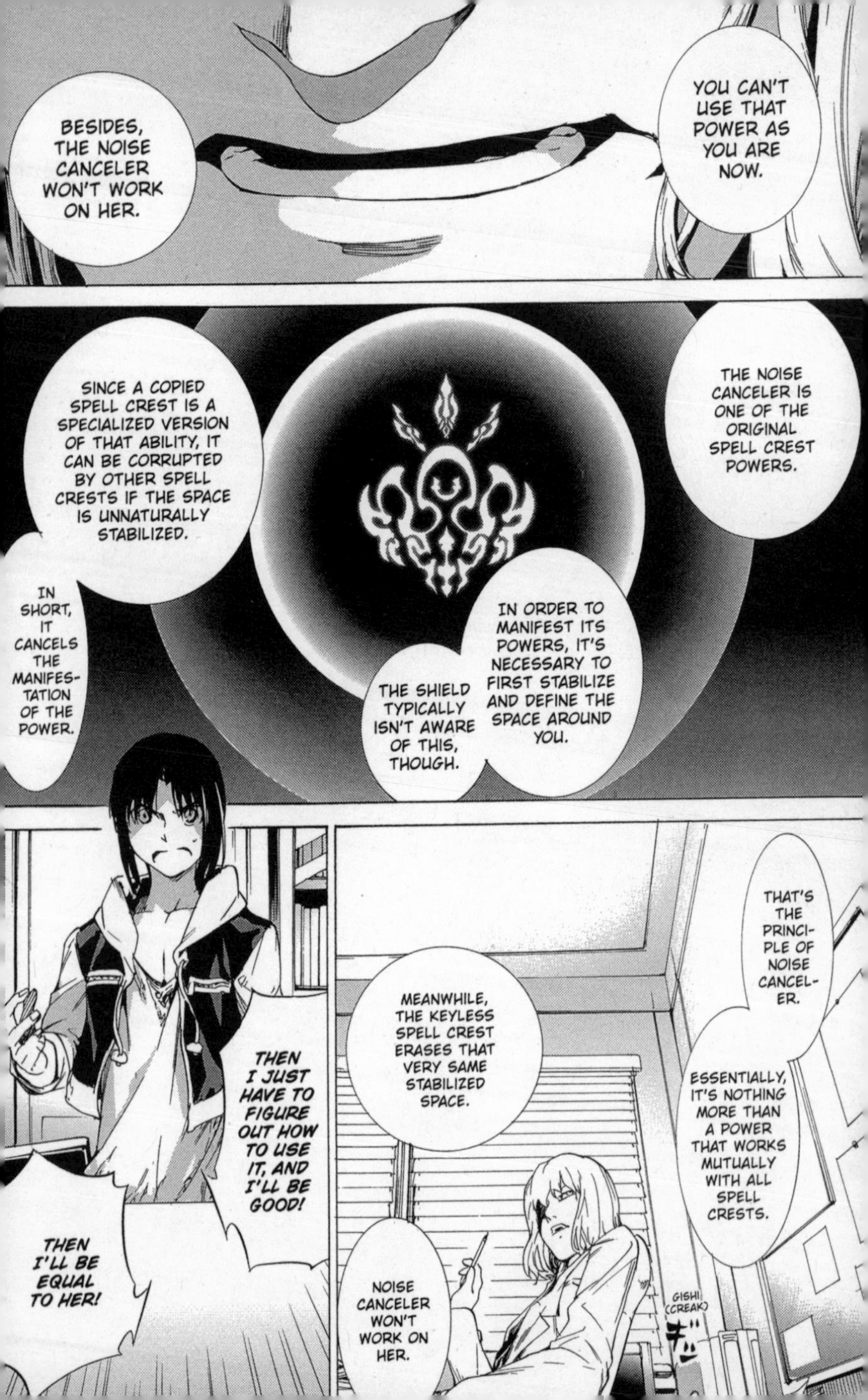
YOU CAN'T USE THAT POWER AS YOU ARE NOW.
BESIDES, THE NOISE CANCELER WON'T WORK ON HER.
THE NOISE CANCELER IS ONE OF THE ORIGINAL SPELL CREST POWERS.
IN ORDER TO MANIFEST ITS POWERS, IT'S NECESSARY TO FIRST STABILIZE AND DEFINE THE SPACE AROUND YOU.
THE SHIELD TYPICALLY ISN'T AWARE OF THIS, THOUGH.
SINCE A COPIED SPELL CREST IS A SPECIALIZED VERSION OF THAT ABILITY, IT CAN BE CORRUPTED BY OTHER SPELL CRESTS IF THE SPACE IS UNNATURALLY STABILIZED.
IN SHORT, IT CANCELS THE MANIFES-TATION OF THE POWER.
THAT'S THE PRINCI-PLE OF NOISE CANCEL-ER.
ESSENTIALLY, IT'S NOTHING MORE THAN A POWER THAT WORKS MUTUALLY WITH ALL SPELL CRESTS.
MEANWHILE, THE KEYLESS SPELL CREST ERASES THAT VERY SAME STABILIZED SPACE.
NOISE CANCELER WON'T WORK ON HER.
GISHI (CREAK)
THEN I JUST HAVE TO FIGURE OUT HOW TO USE IT, AND I'LL BE GOOD!
THEN I'LL BE EQUAL TO HER!

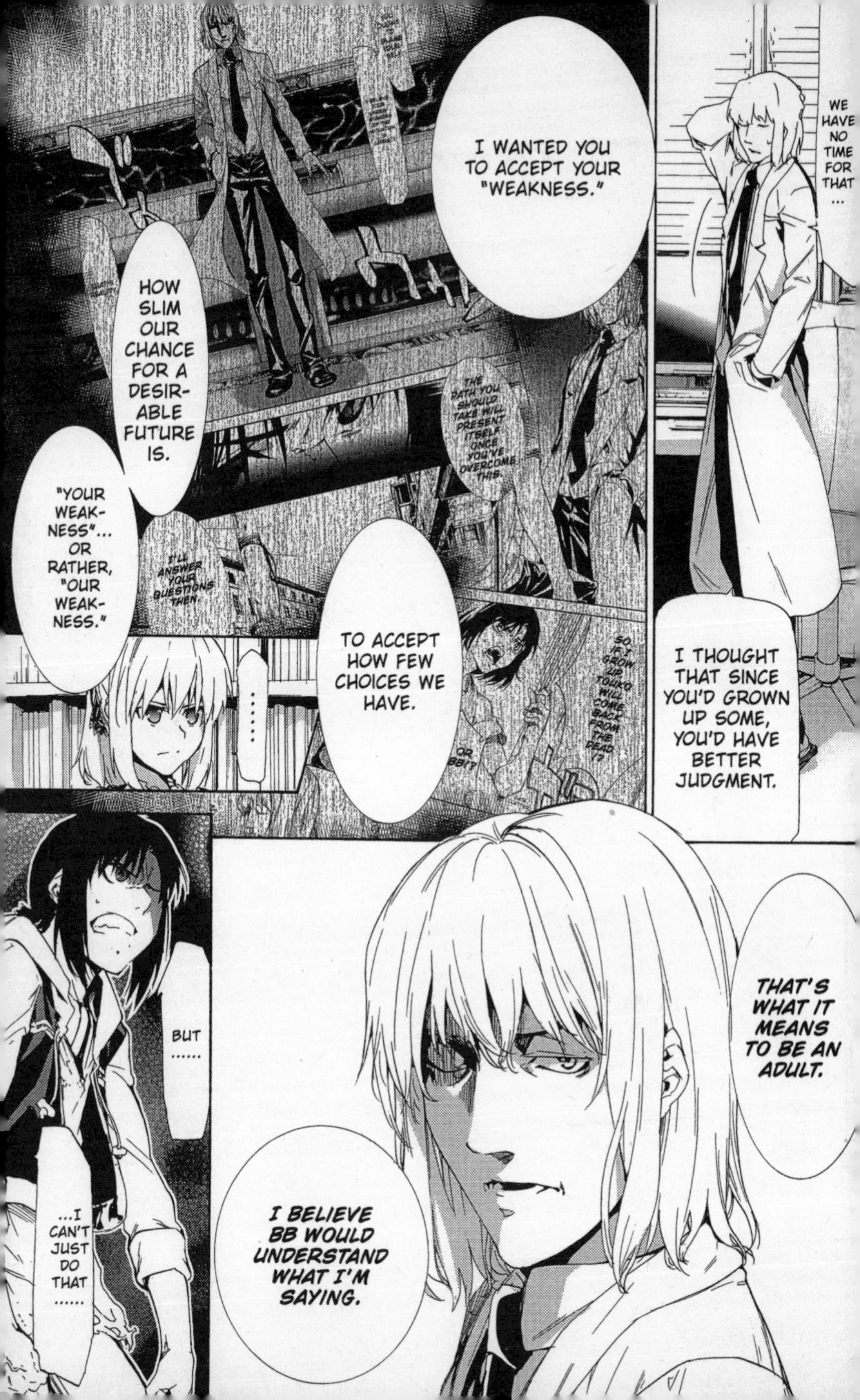
WE HAVE NO TIME FOR THAT...
I THOUGHT THAT SINCE YOU'D GROWN UP SOME, YOU'D HAVE BETTER JUDGMENT.
I WANTED YOU TO ACCEPT YOUR "WEAKNESS."
HOW SLIM OUR CHANCE FOR A DESIRABLE FUTURE IS.
THE PATH YOU SHOULD TAKE WILL PRESENT ITSELF ONCE YOU'VE OVERCOME THIS.
"YOUR WEAKNESS"... OR RATHER, "OUR WEAKNESS."
I'LL ANSWER YOUR QUESTIONS THEN.
TO ACCEPT HOW FEW CHOICES WE HAVE.
SO IF I GROW UP TOUKO WILL COME BACK FROM THE DEAD!?
OR BB!?
......
THAT'S WHAT IT MEANS TO BE AN ADULT.
I BELIEVE BB WOULD UNDERSTAND WHAT I'M SAYING.
BUT......
...I CAN'T JUST DO THAT......

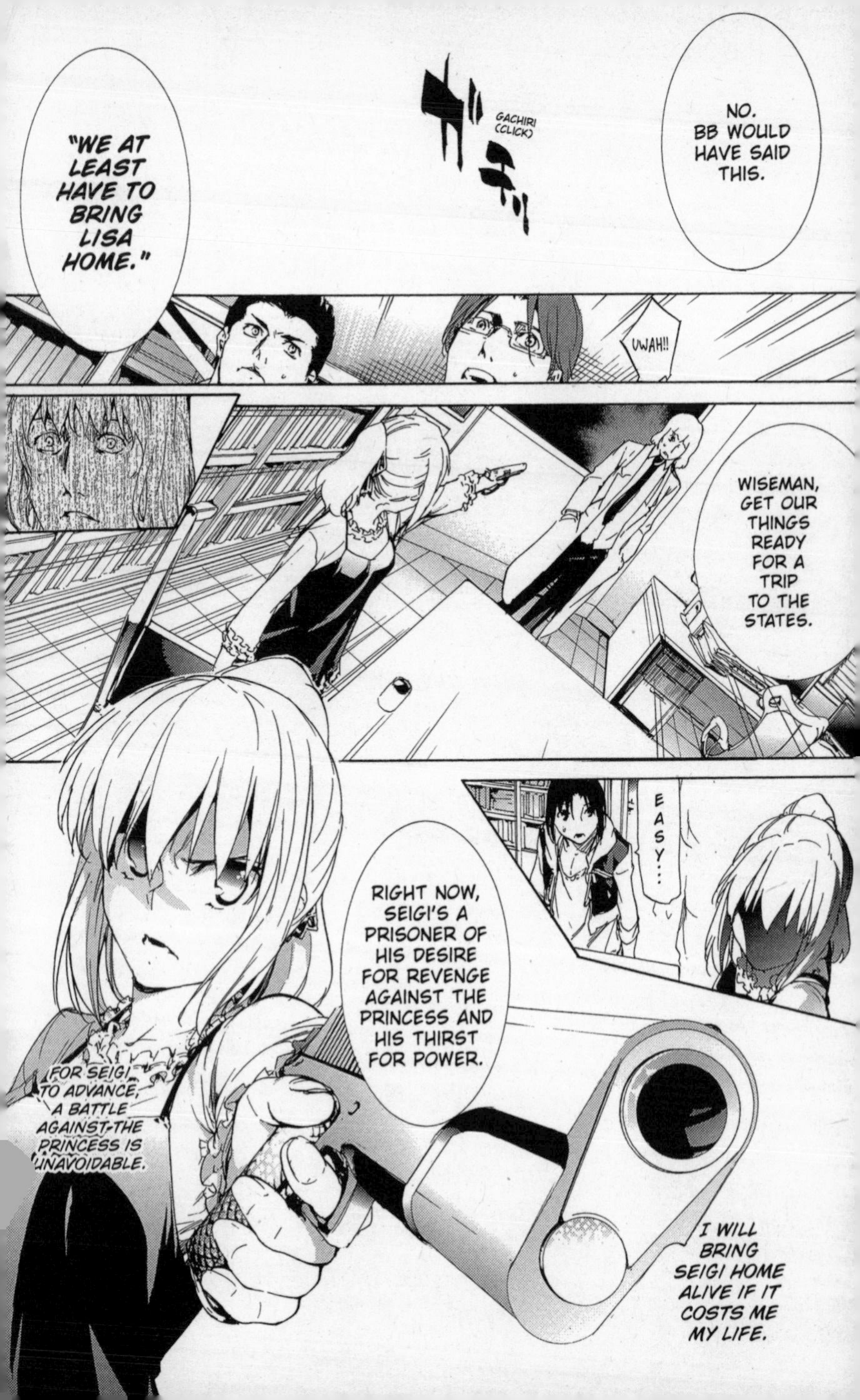
NO. BB WOULD HAVE SAID THIS.
GACHIRI (CLICK)
"WE AT LEAST HAVE TO BRING LISA HOME."
UWAH!!
WISEMAN, GET OUR THINGS READY FOR A TRIP TO THE STATES.
EASY...
RIGHT NOW, SEIGI'S A PRISONER OF HIS DESIRE FOR REVENGE AGAINST THE PRINCESS AND HIS THIRST FOR POWER.
FOR SEIGI TO ADVANCE, A BATTLE AGAINST THE PRINCESS IS UNAVOIDABLE.
I WILL BRING SEIGI HOME ALIVE IF IT COSTS ME MY LIFE.

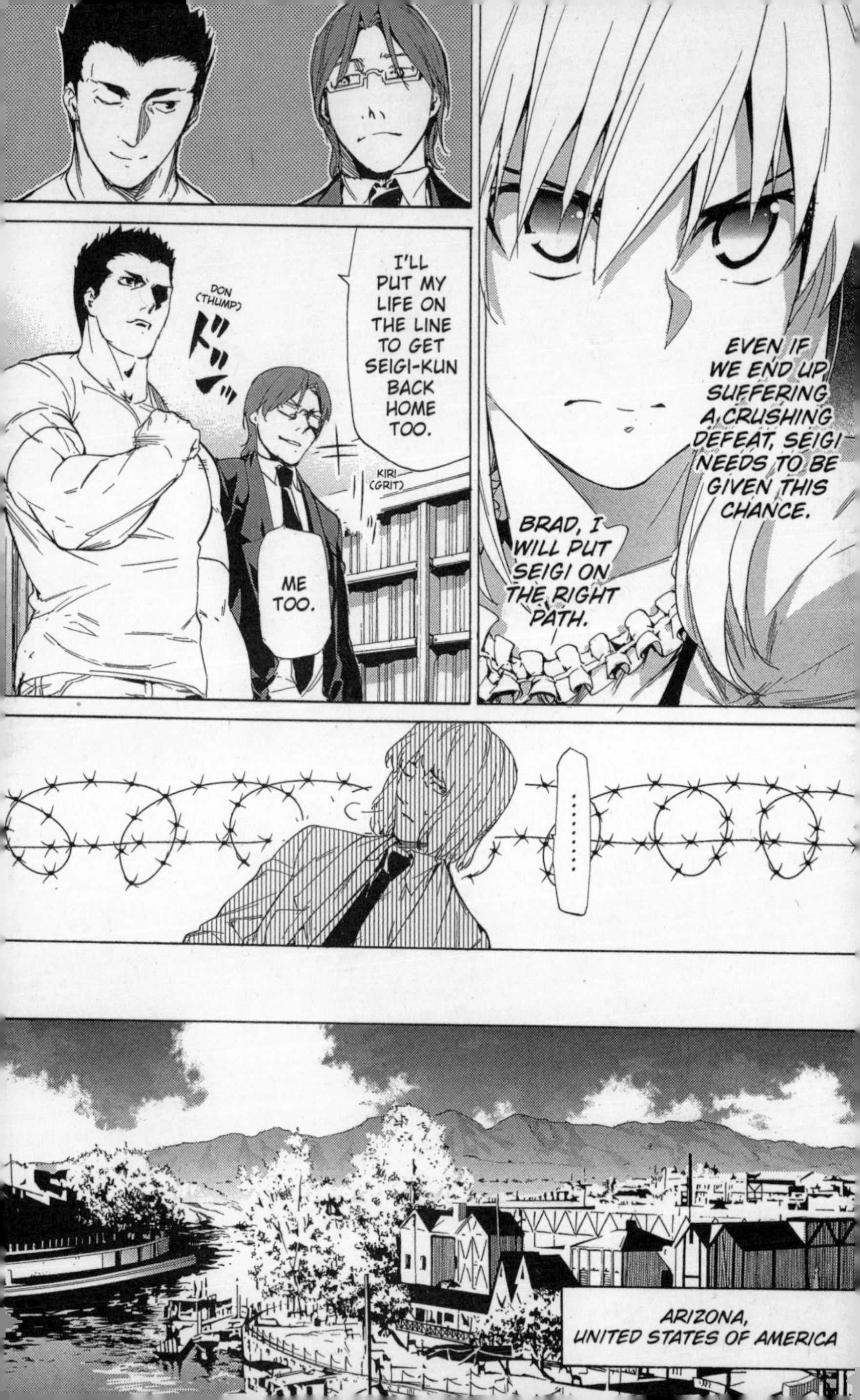
EVEN IF WE END UP SUFFERING A CRUSHING DEFEAT, SEIGI NEEDS TO BE GIVEN THIS CHANCE.
BRAD, I WILL PUT SEIGI ON THE RIGHT PATH.
I'LL PUT MY LIFE ON THE LINE TO GET SEIGI-KUN BACK HOME TOO.
DON (THUMP)
ドッ
KIRI (GRIT)
ME TOO.
......
ARIZONA, UNITED STATES OF AMERICA

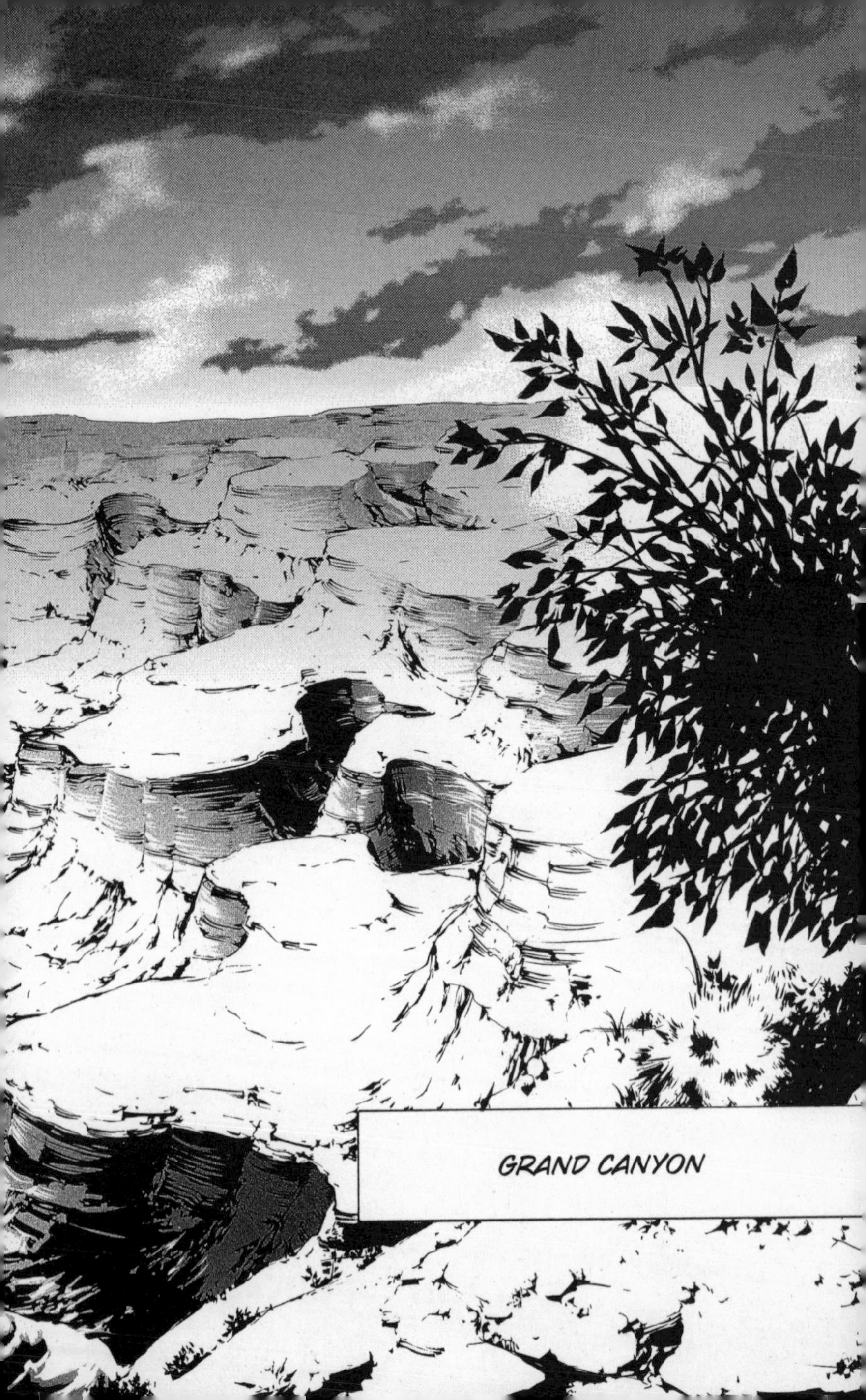
GRAND CANYON

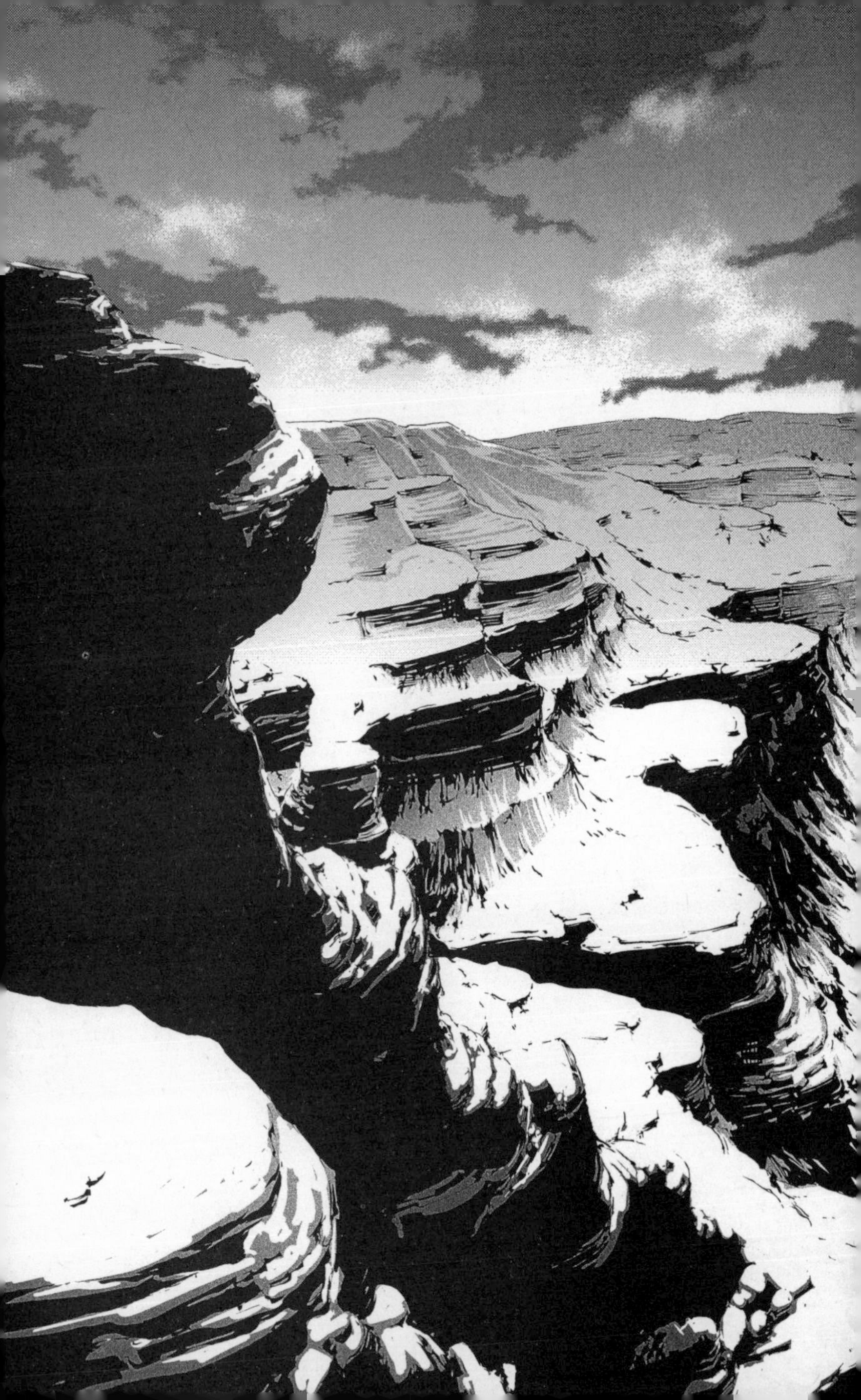

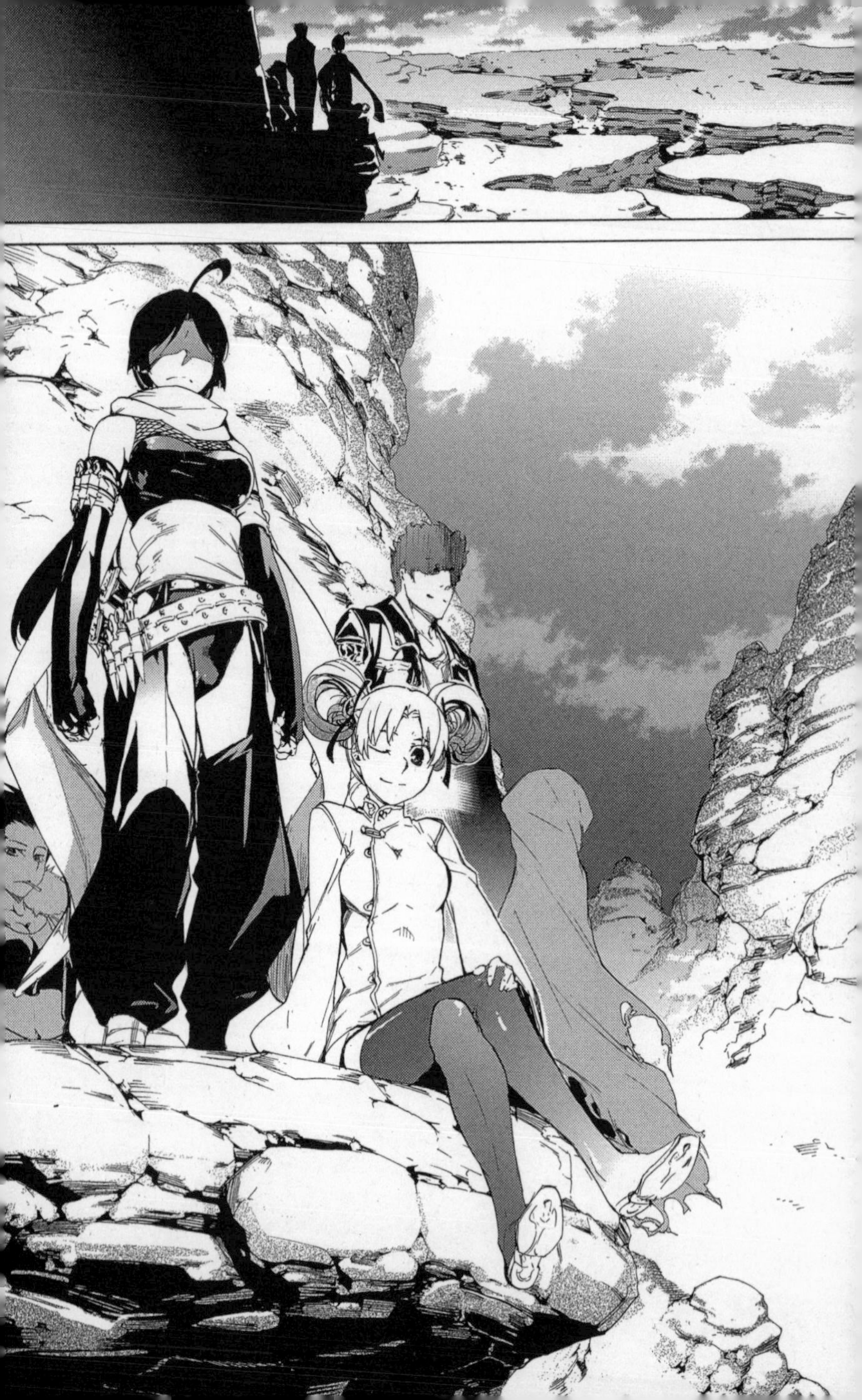

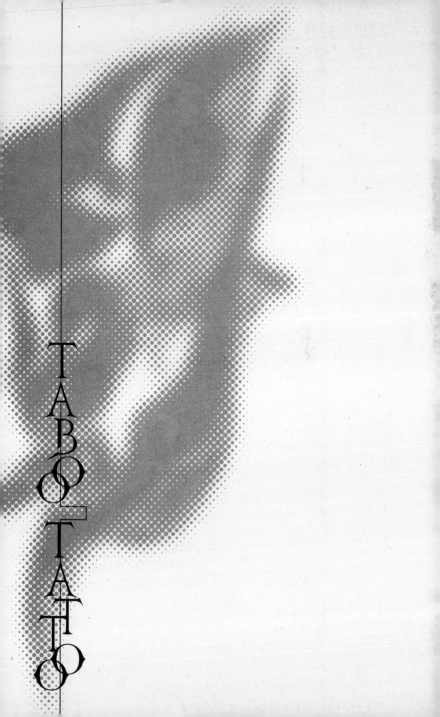

TABOO TATTOO

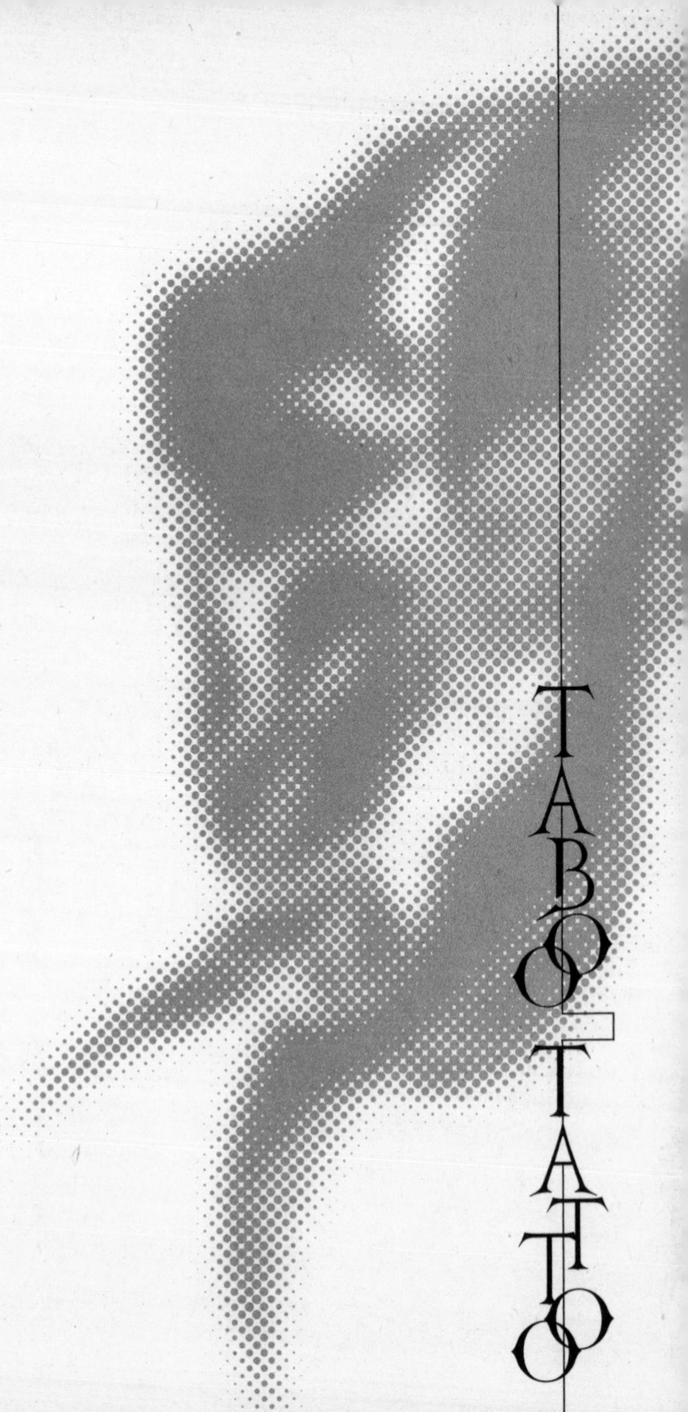

TABOO TATTOO

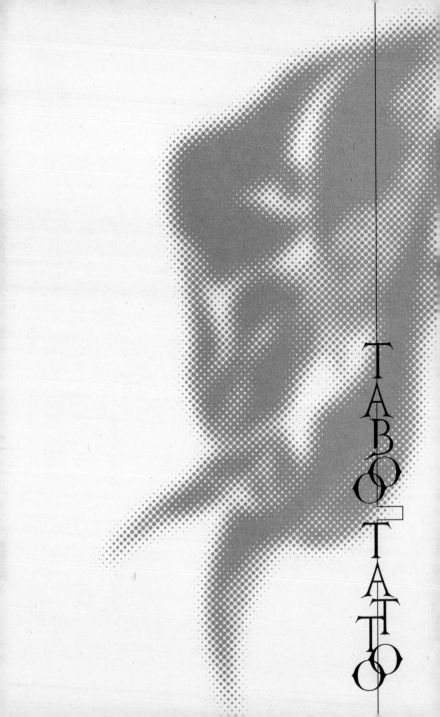

#35 OPEN HOSTILITIES

TABOO TATTOO

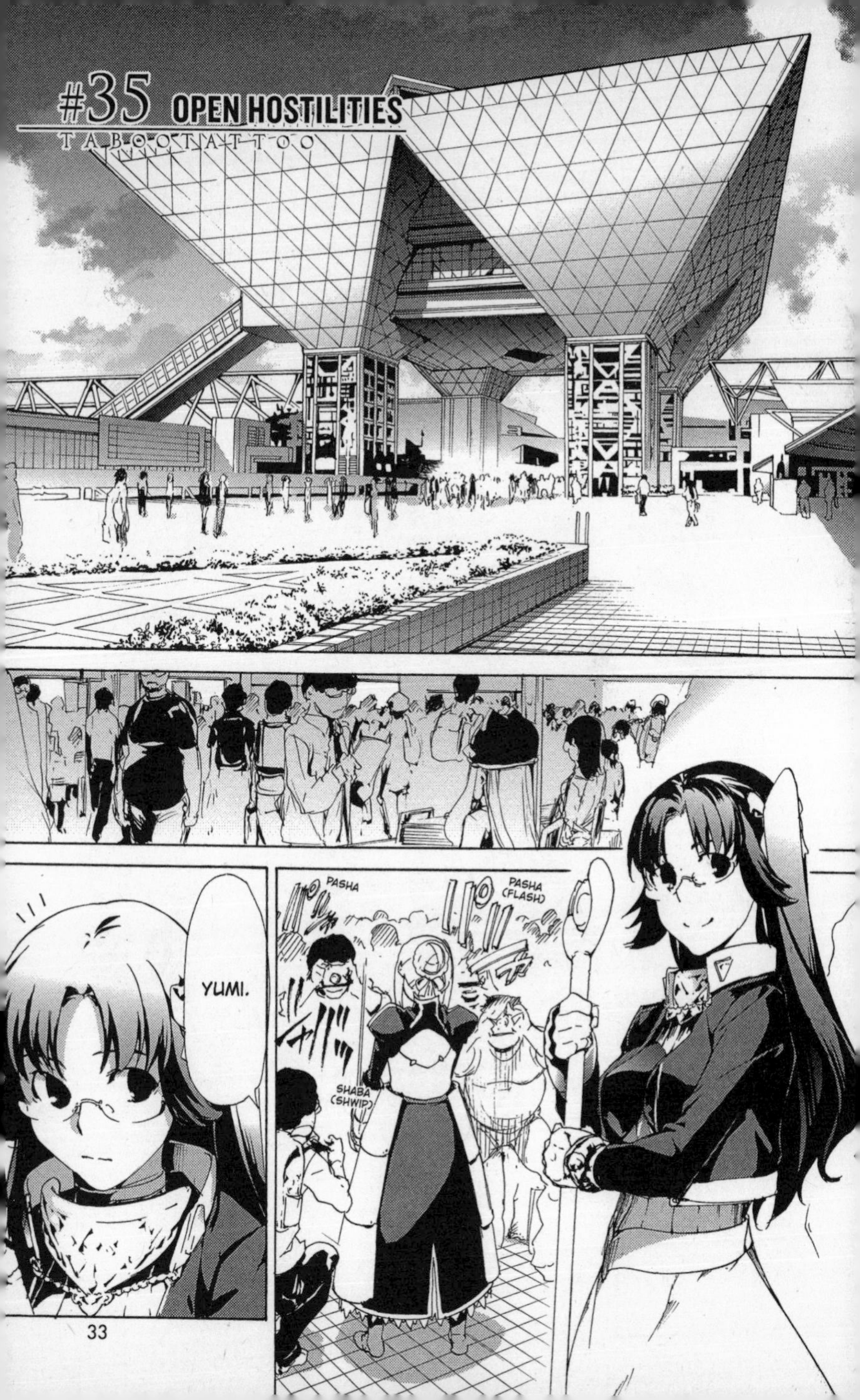

PASHA (FLASH)
PASHA
SHABA (SHWIP)
YUMI.

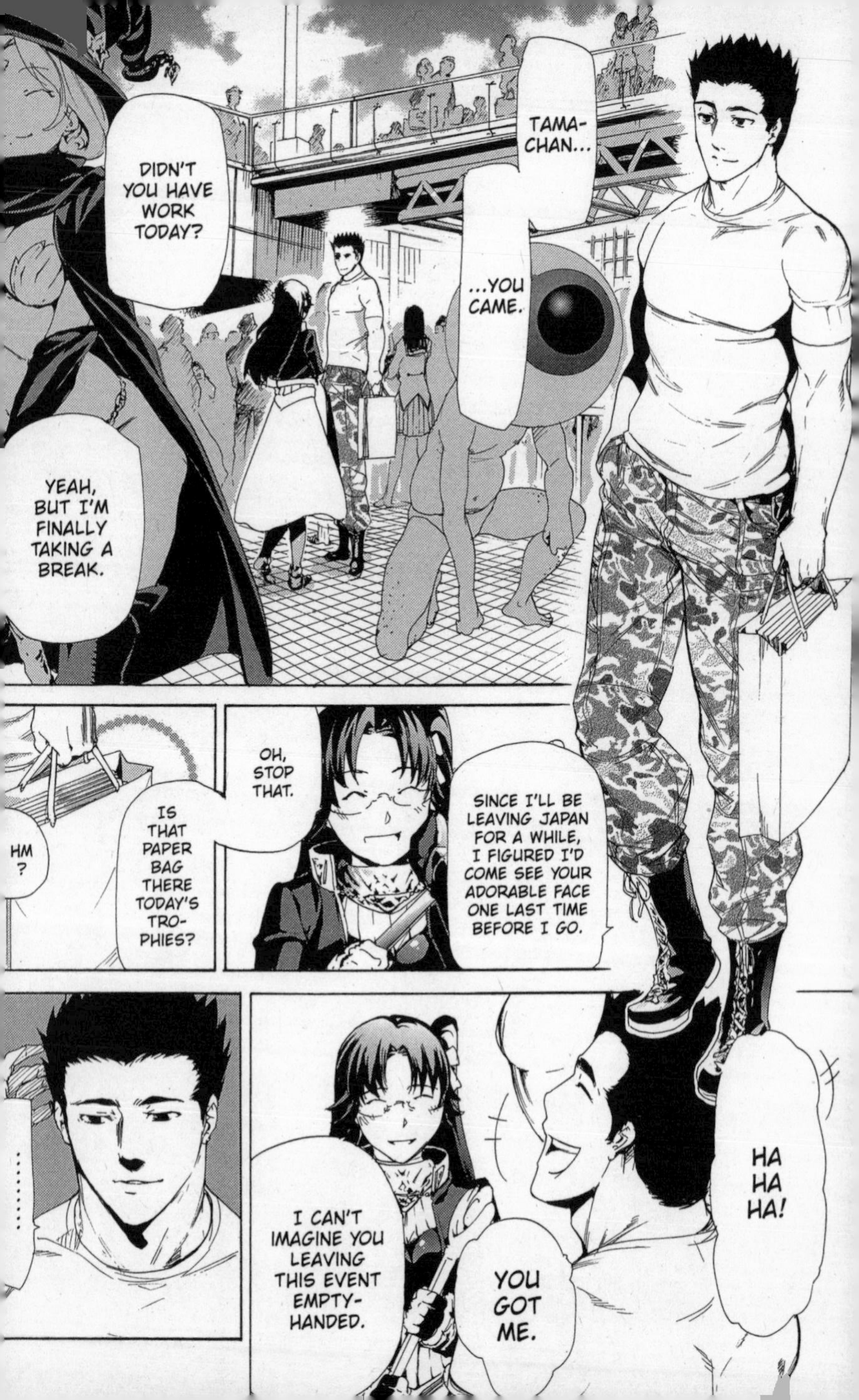

TAMA-CHAN...
...YOU CAME.
DIDN'T YOU HAVE WORK TODAY?
YEAH, BUT I'M FINALLY TAKING A BREAK.
SINCE I'LL BE LEAVING JAPAN FOR A WHILE, I FIGURED I'D COME SEE YOUR ADORABLE FACE ONE LAST TIME BEFORE I GO.
OH, STOP THAT.
HM?
IS THAT PAPER BAG THERE TODAY'S TRO-PHIES?
I CAN'T IMAGINE YOU LEAVING THIS EVENT EMPTY-HANDED.
YOU GOT ME.
HA HA HA!
......

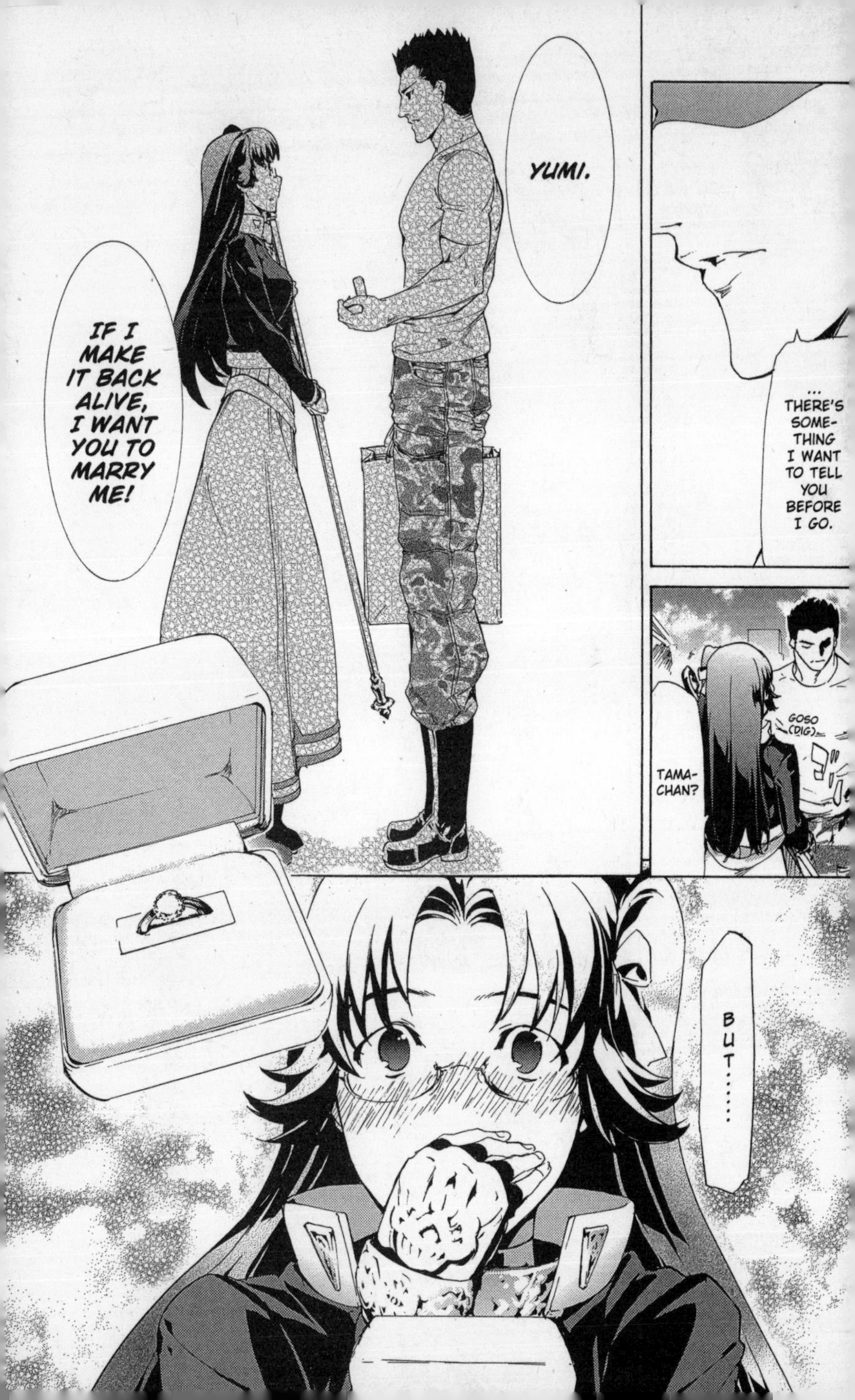

...THERE'S SOMETHING I WANT TO TELL YOU BEFORE I GO.
GOSO (DIG)
TAMA-CHAN?
YUMI.
IF I MAKE IT BACK ALIVE, I WANT YOU TO MARRY ME!
BUT......

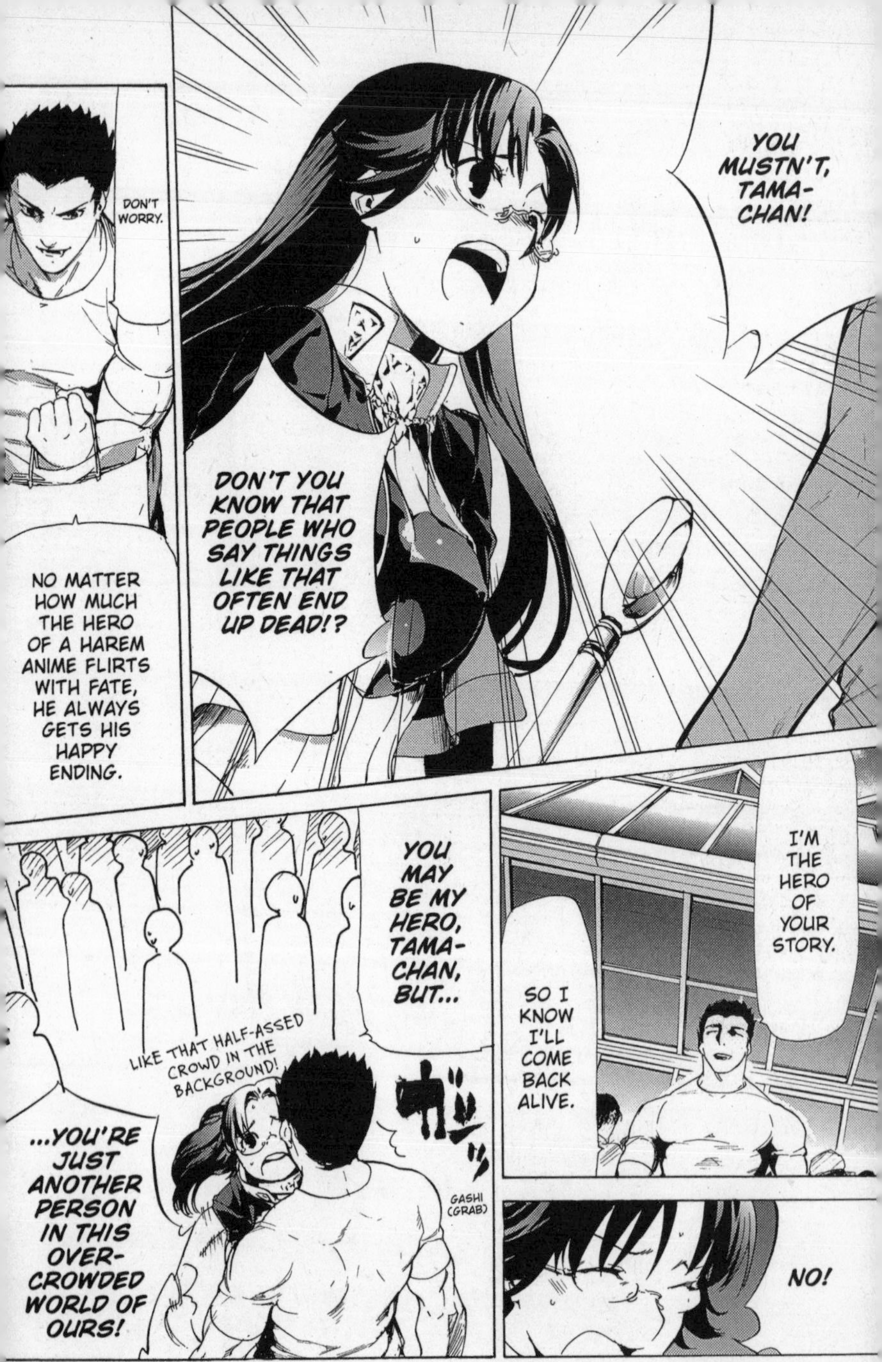
YOU MUSTN'T, TAMA-CHAN!
DON'T YOU KNOW THAT PEOPLE WHO SAY THINGS LIKE THAT OFTEN END UP DEAD!?
DON'T WORRY.
NO MATTER HOW MUCH THE HERO OF A HAREM ANIME FLIRTS WITH FATE, HE ALWAYS GETS HIS HAPPY ENDING.
I'M THE HERO OF YOUR STORY.
SO I KNOW I'LL COME BACK ALIVE.
NO!
YOU MAY BE MY HERO, TAMA-CHAN, BUT...
GASHI (GRAB)
LIKE THAT HALF-ASSED CROWD IN THE BACKGROUND!
...YOU'RE JUST ANOTHER PERSON IN THIS OVER-CROWDED WORLD OF OURS!

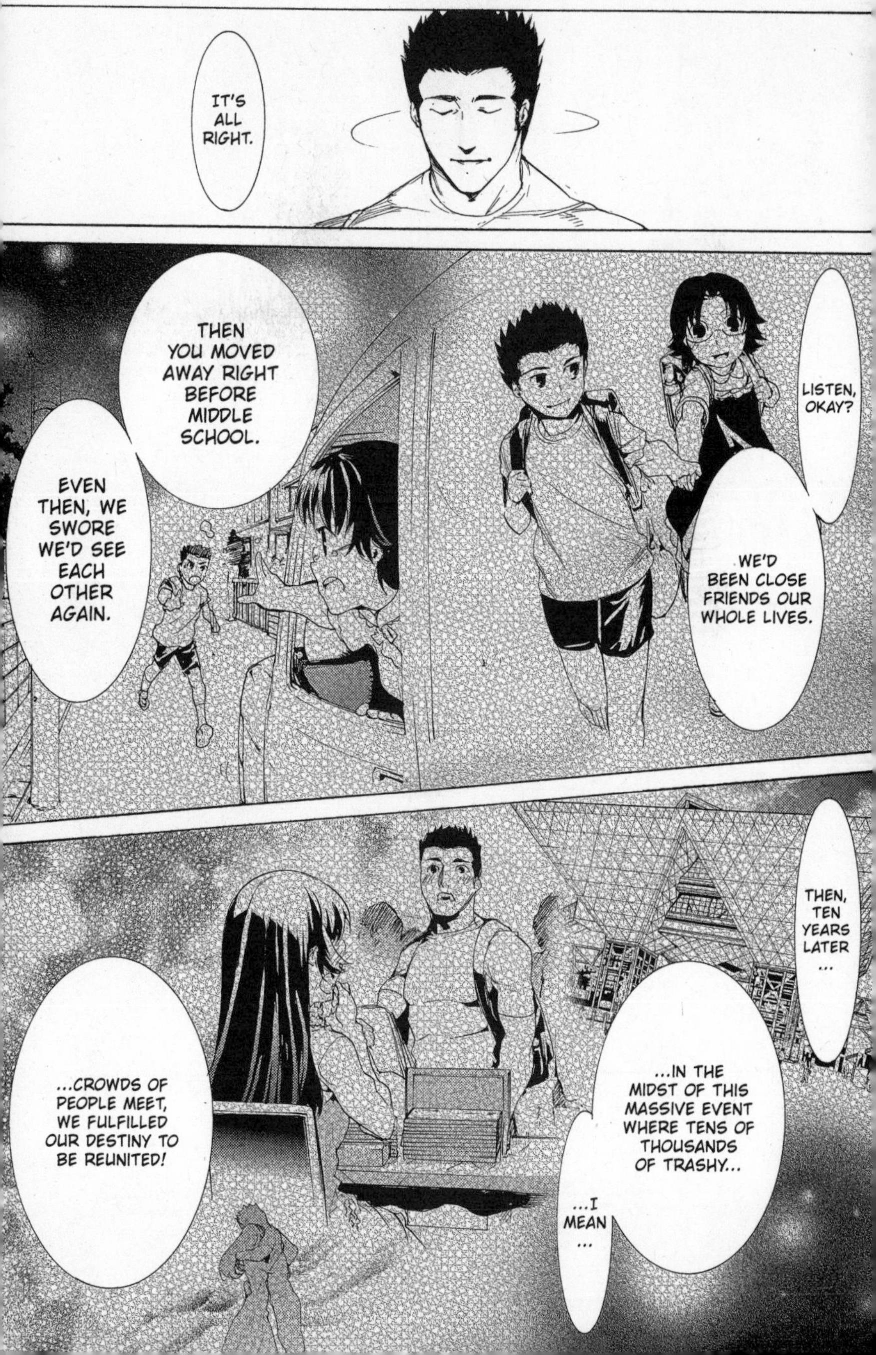
IT'S ALL RIGHT.
LISTEN, OKAY?
WE'D BEEN CLOSE FRIENDS OUR WHOLE LIVES.
THEN YOU MOVED AWAY RIGHT BEFORE MIDDLE SCHOOL.
EVEN THEN, WE SWORE WE'D SEE EACH OTHER AGAIN.
THEN, TEN YEARS LATER...
...IN THE MIDST OF THIS MASSIVE EVENT WHERE TENS OF THOUSANDS OF TRASHY...
...I MEAN...
...CROWDS OF PEOPLE MEET, WE FULFILLED OUR DESTINY TO BE REUNITED!

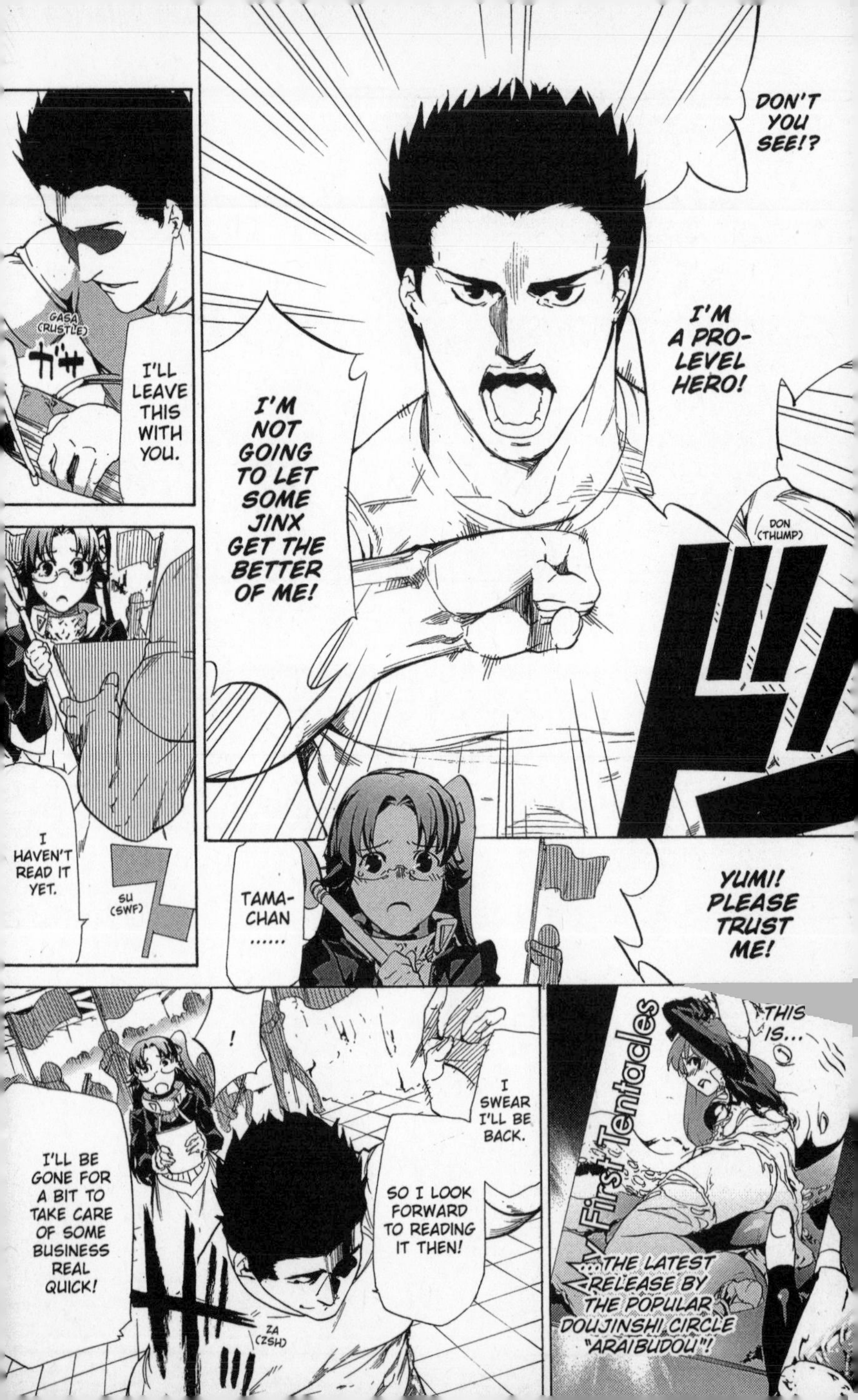
DON'T YOU SEE!?
I'M A PRO-LEVEL HERO!
I'M NOT GOING TO LET SOME JINX GET THE BETTER OF ME!
DON (THUMP)
YUMI! PLEASE TRUST ME!
TAMA-CHAN ......
GASA (RUSTLE)
I'LL LEAVE THIS WITH YOU.
I HAVEN'T READ IT YET.
SU (SWF)
THIS IS...
My First Tentacles
...THE LATEST RELEASE BY THE POPULAR DOUJINSHI CIRCLE "ARAIBUDOU"!
!
I SWEAR I'LL BE BACK.
SO I LOOK FORWARD TO READING IT THEN!
I'LL BE GONE FOR A BIT TO TAKE CARE OF SOME BUSINESS REAL QUICK!
ZA (ZSH)

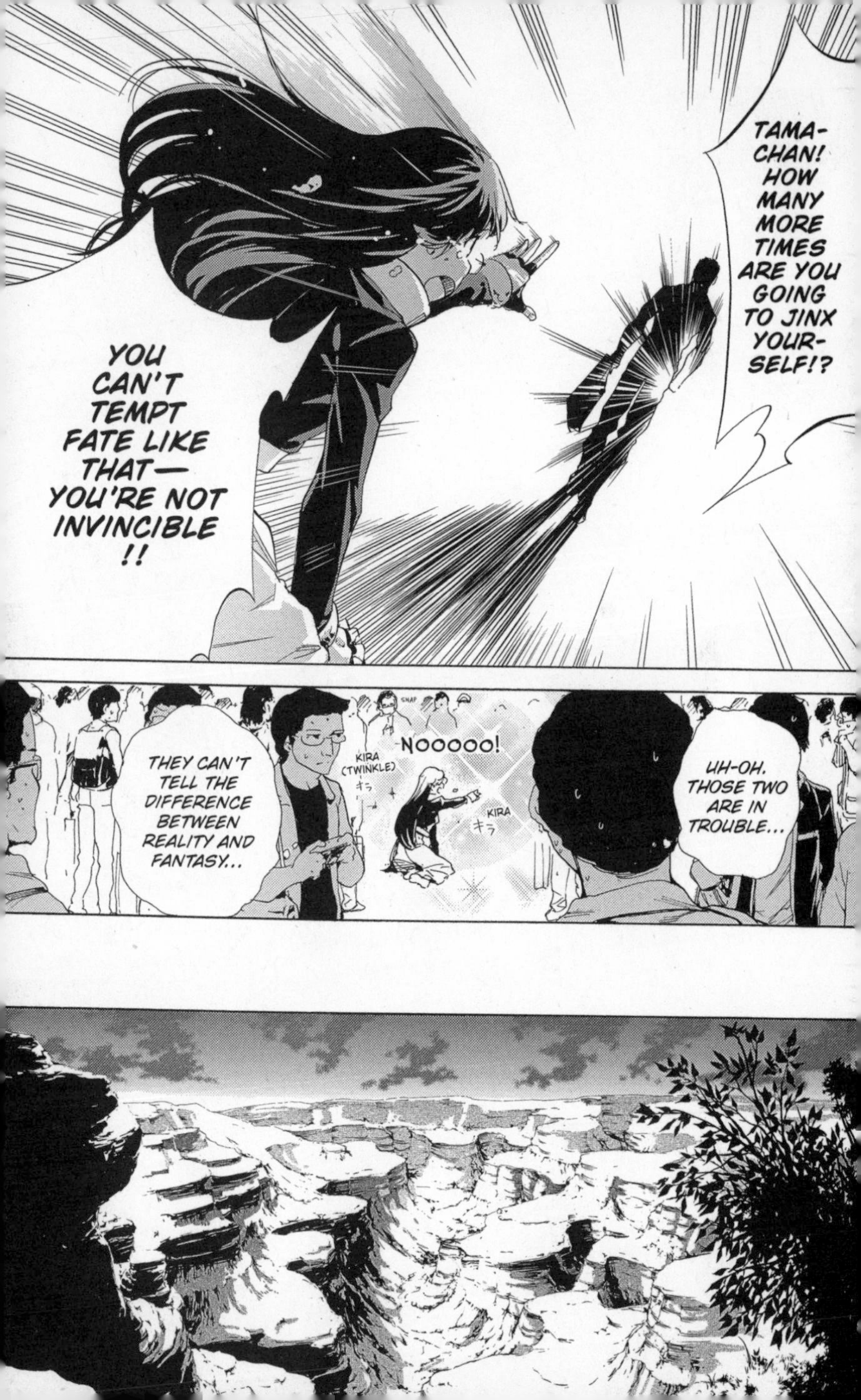
TAMA-CHAN! HOW MANY MORE TIMES ARE YOU GOING TO JINX YOUR-SELF!?
YOU CAN'T TEMPT FATE LIKE THAT— YOU'RE NOT INVINCIBLE!!
UH-OH. THOSE TWO ARE IN TROUBLE...
KIRA キラ
NOOOOO!
SNAP
KIRA (TWINKLE) キラ
THEY CAN'T TELL THE DIFFERENCE BETWEEN REALITY AND FANTASY...

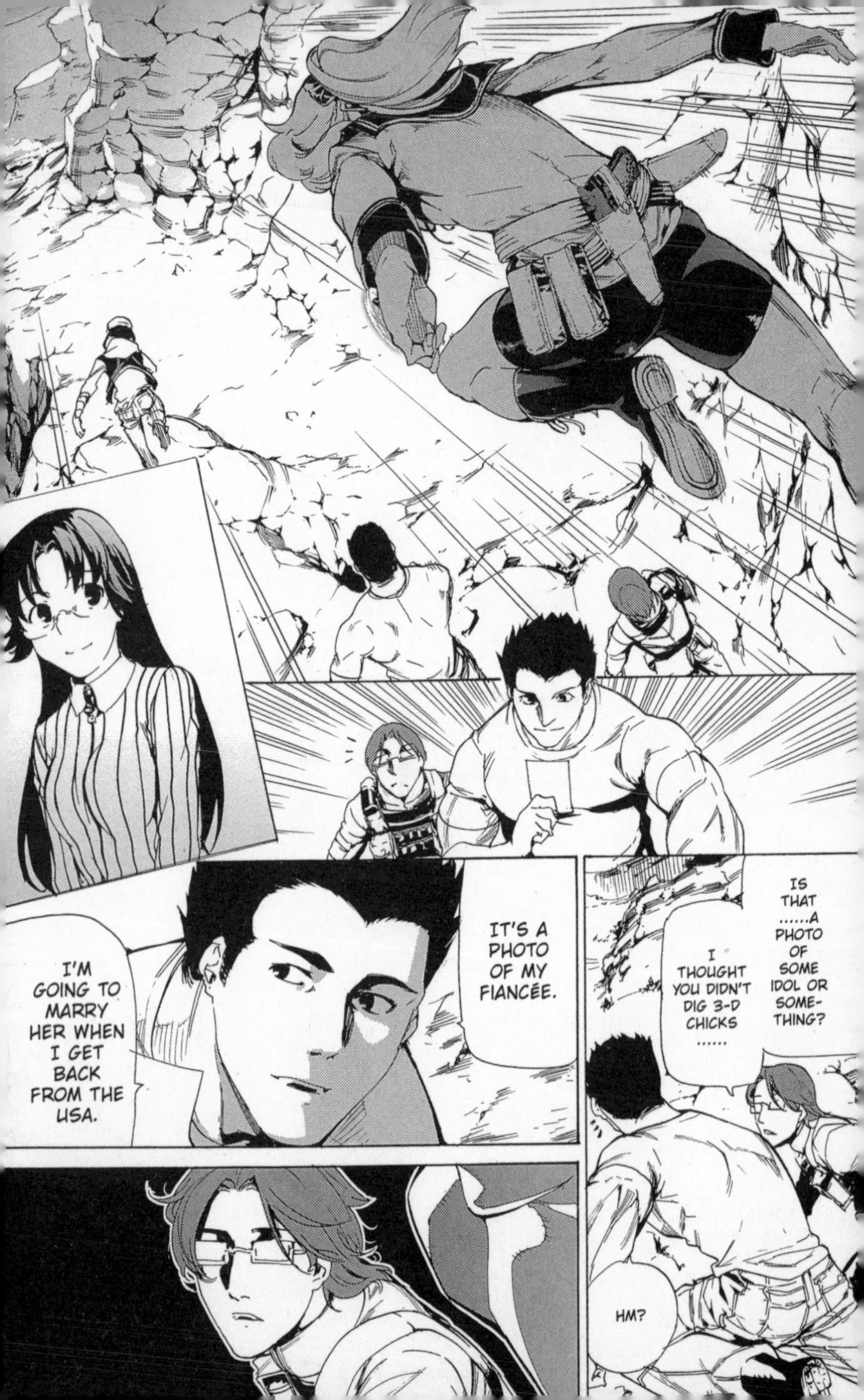
IS THAT ......A PHOTO OF SOME IDOL OR SOME-THING?
I THOUGHT YOU DIDN'T DIG 3-D CHICKS ......
IT'S A PHOTO OF MY FIANCÉE.
I'M GOING TO MARRY HER WHEN I GET BACK FROM THE USA.
HM?

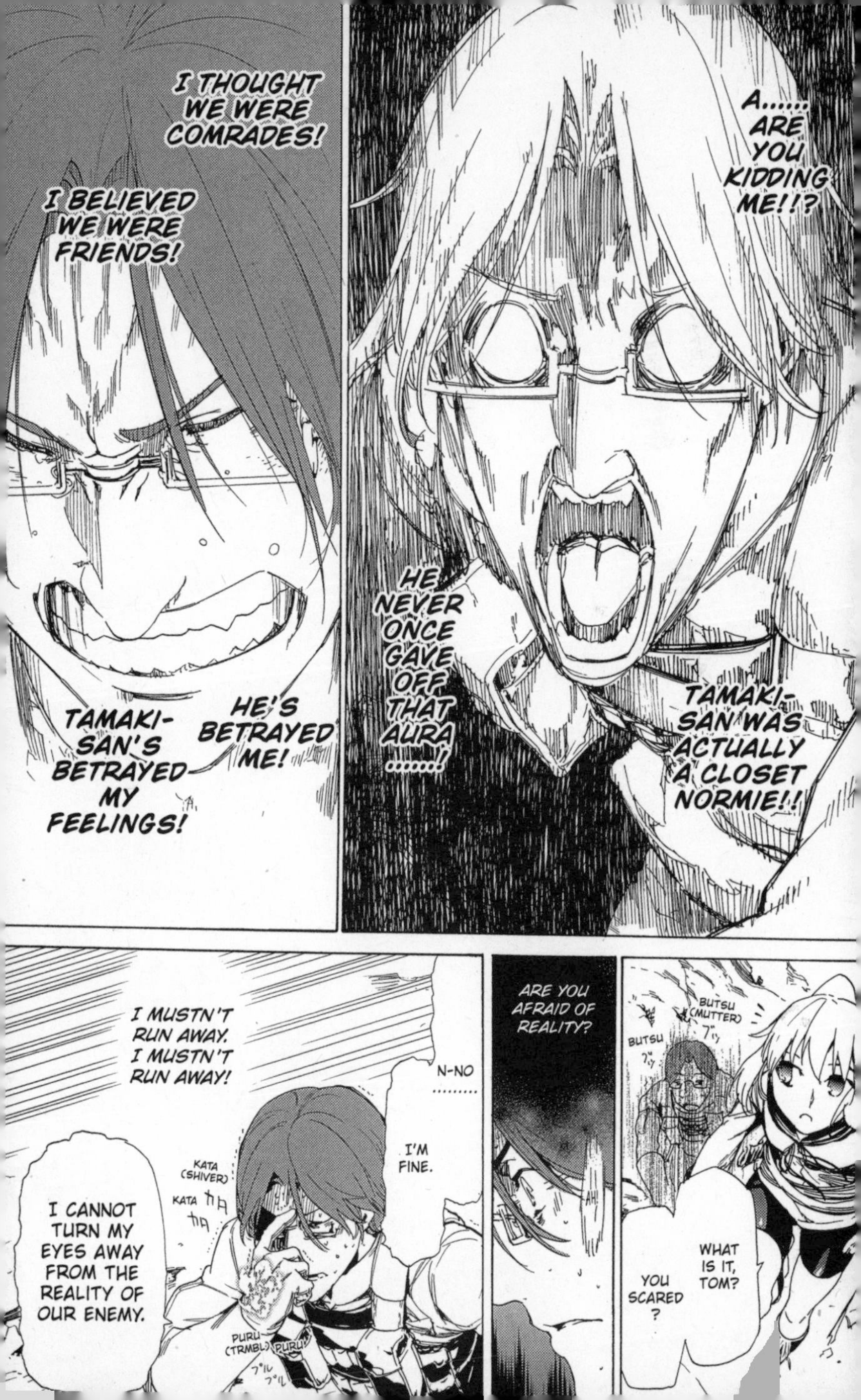
A...... ARE YOU KIDDING ME!!?
TAMAKI-SAN WAS ACTUALLY A CLOSET NORMIE!!
HE NEVER ONCE GAVE OFF THAT AURA......!
I THOUGHT WE WERE COMRADES!
I BELIEVED WE WERE FRIENDS!
HE'S BETRAYED ME!
TAMAKI-SAN'S BETRAYED MY FEELINGS!
BUTSU (MUTTER)
BUTSU
WHAT IS IT, TOM?
YOU SCARED?
ARE YOU AFRAID OF REALITY?
AH!
N-NO......
I'M FINE.
I MUSTN'T RUN AWAY. I MUSTN'T RUN AWAY!
KATA (SHIVER)
KATA
I CANNOT TURN MY EYES AWAY FROM THE REALITY OF OUR ENEMY.
PURU (TRMBL) PURU

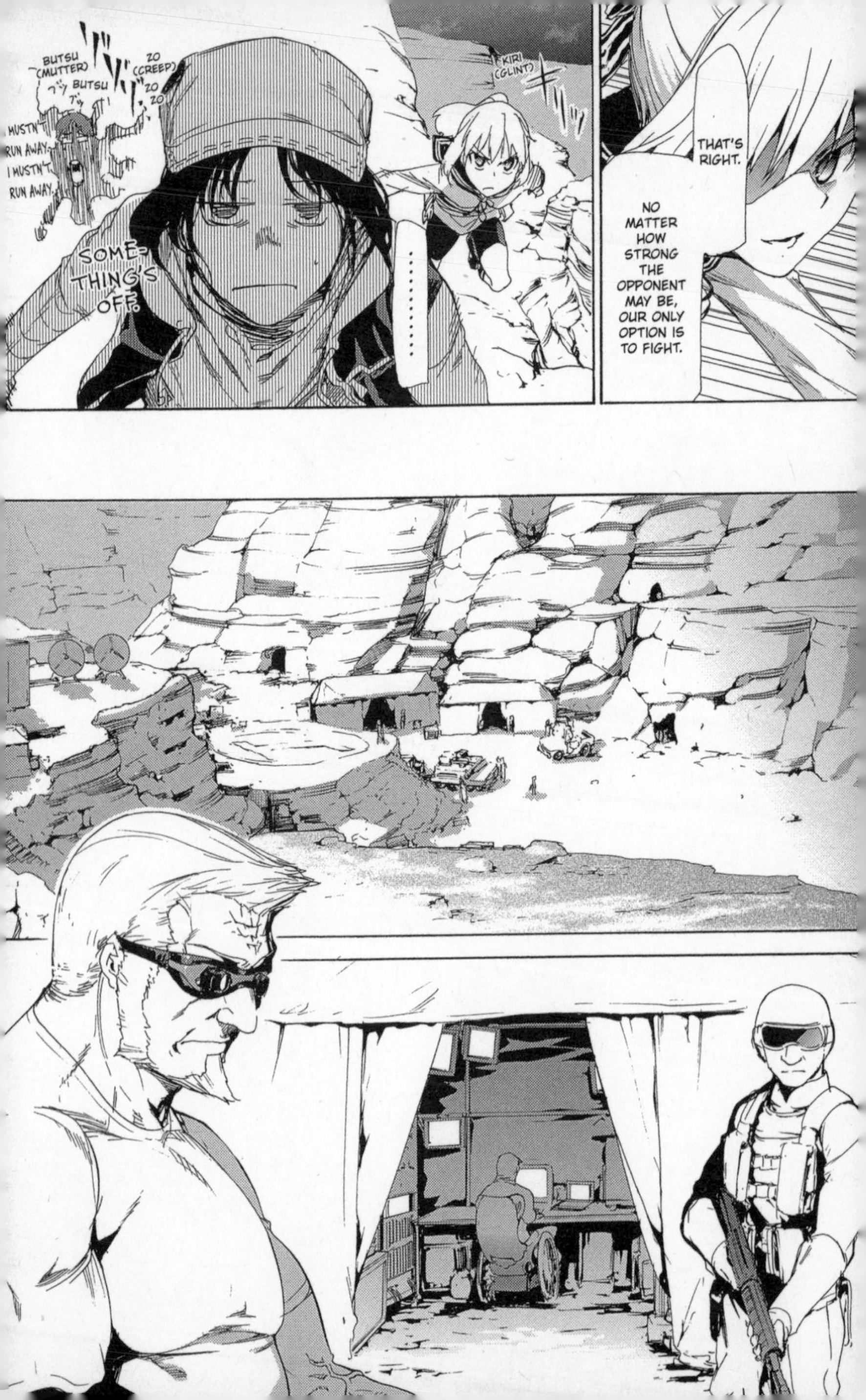
THAT'S RIGHT.
NO MATTER HOW STRONG THE OPPONENT MAY BE, OUR ONLY OPTION IS TO FIGHT.
KIRI (GLINT)
ZO (CREEP) ZO ZO
BUTSU (MUTTER) BUTSU
I MUSTN'T RUN AWAY. I MUSTN'T RUN AWAY.
SOME-THING'S OFF.
......

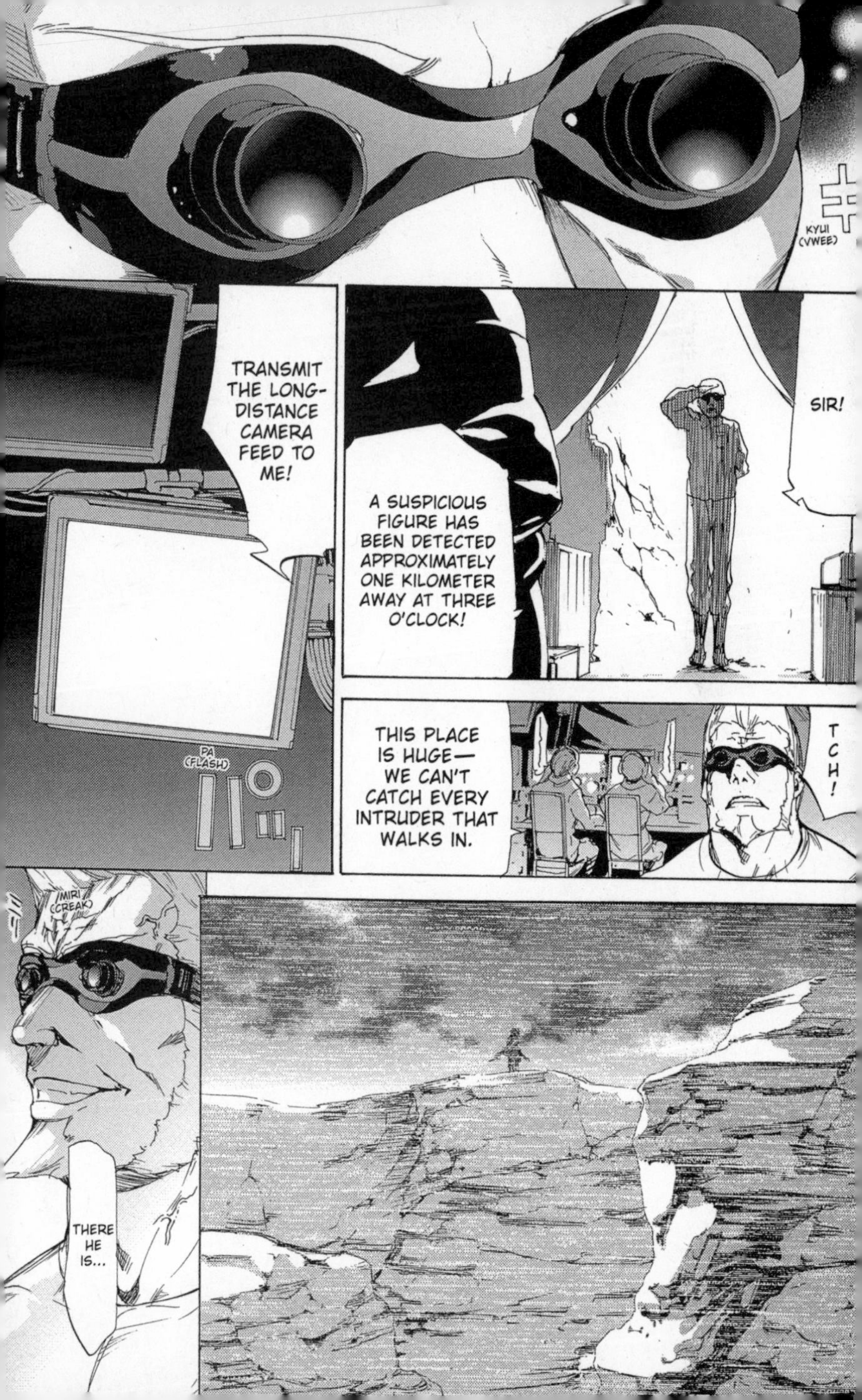
KYUI
(VWEE)
SIR!
A SUSPICIOUS FIGURE HAS BEEN DETECTED APPROXIMATELY ONE KILOMETER AWAY AT THREE O'CLOCK!
TCH!
THIS PLACE IS HUGE—WE CAN'T CATCH EVERY INTRUDER THAT WALKS IN.
TRANSMIT THE LONG-DISTANCE CAMERA FEED TO ME!
PA
(FLASH)
MIRI
(CREAK)
THERE HE IS...

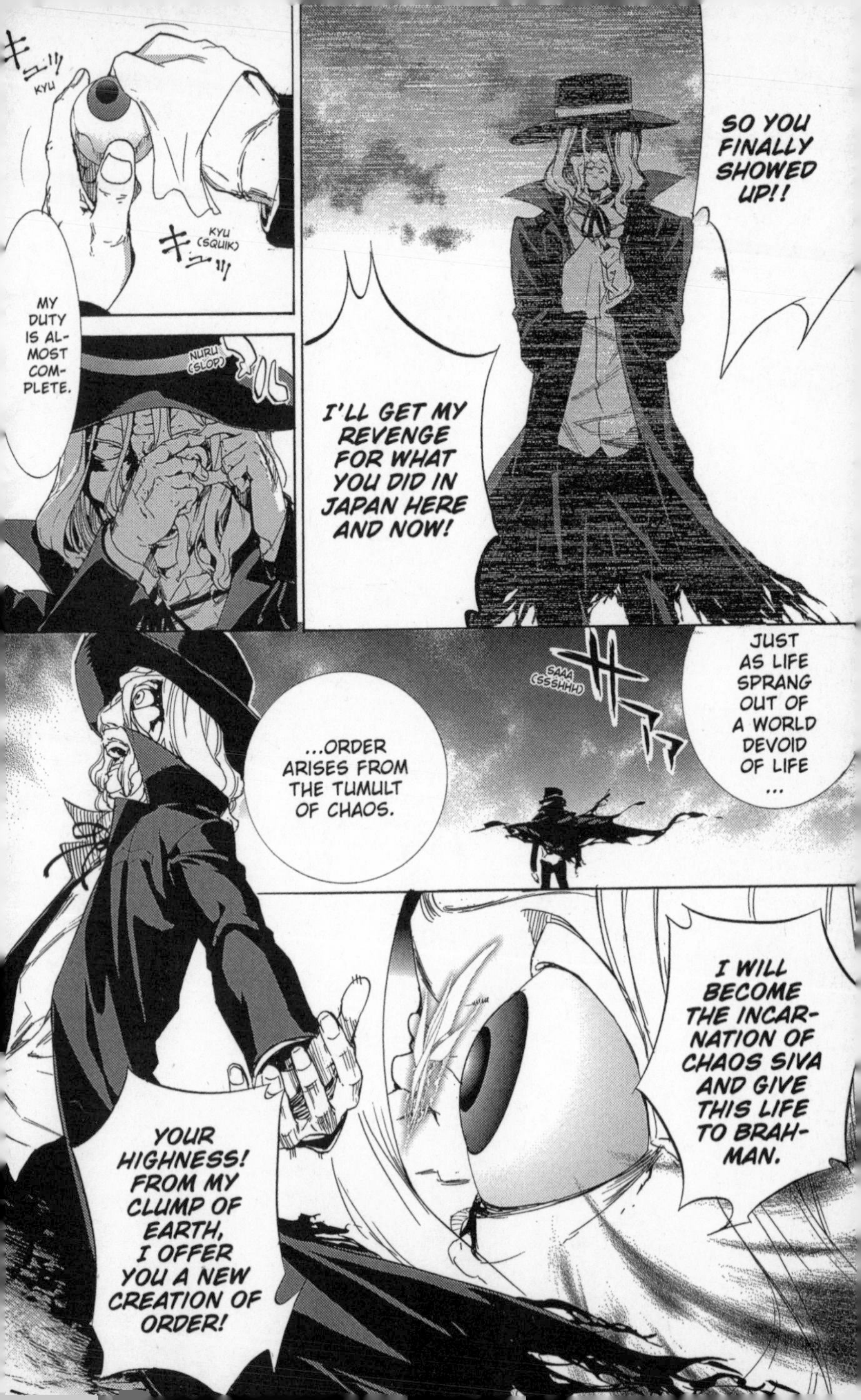
SO YOU FINALLY SHOWED UP!!
I'LL GET MY REVENGE FOR WHAT YOU DID IN JAPAN HERE AND NOW!
KYU
KYU (SQUIK)
MY DUTY IS AL-MOST COM-PLETE.
NURU (SLOP)
SAAA (SSSHHH)
JUST AS LIFE SPRANG OUT OF A WORLD DEVOID OF LIFE ...
...ORDER ARISES FROM THE TUMULT OF CHAOS.
I WILL BECOME THE INCAR-NATION OF CHAOS SIVA AND GIVE THIS LIFE TO BRAH-MAN.
YOUR HIGHNESS! FROM MY CLUMP OF EARTH, I OFFER YOU A NEW CREATION OF ORDER!

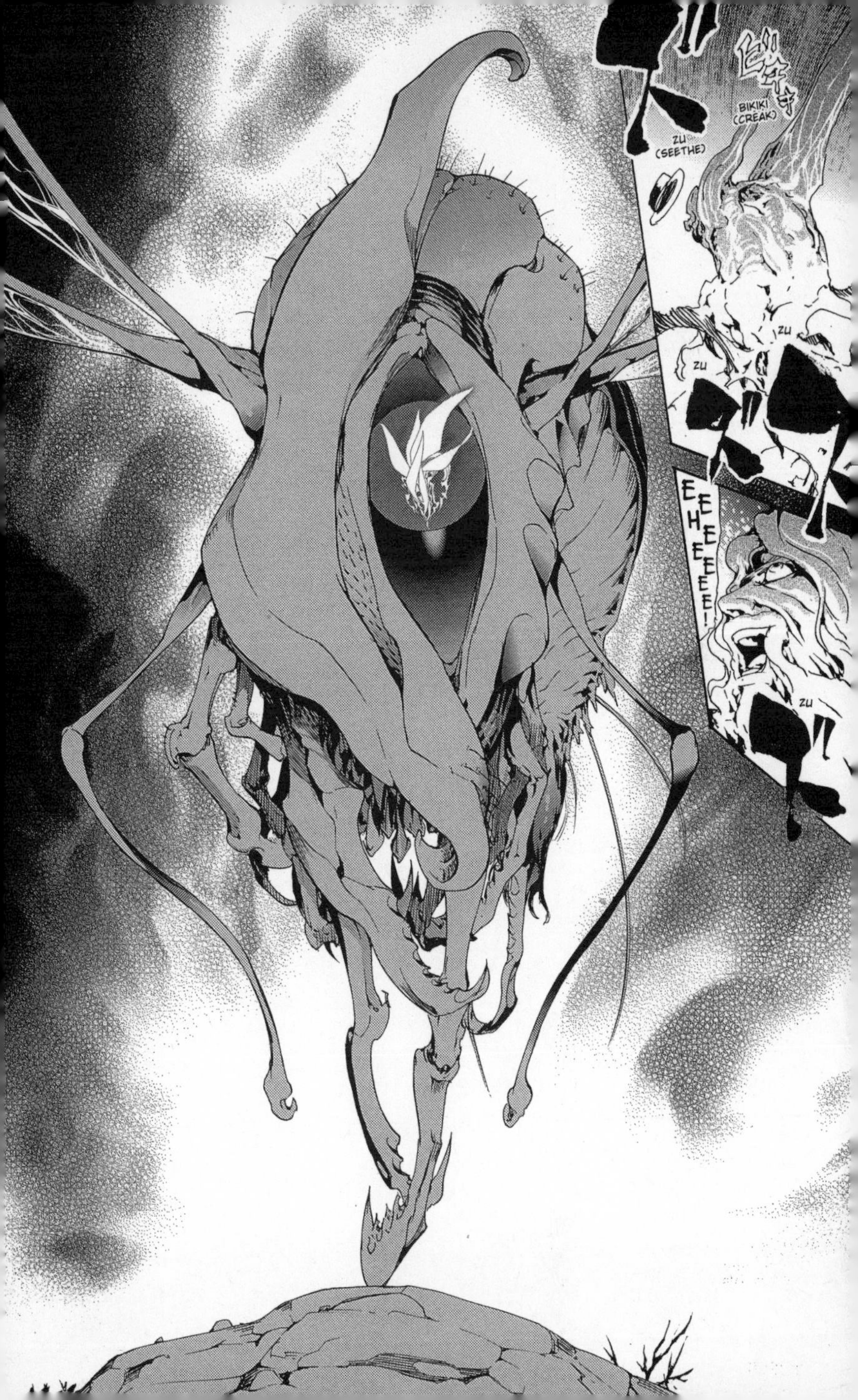
BIKIKI (CREAK)
ZU (SEETHE)
ZU
ZU
EHEEEEEE!
ZU

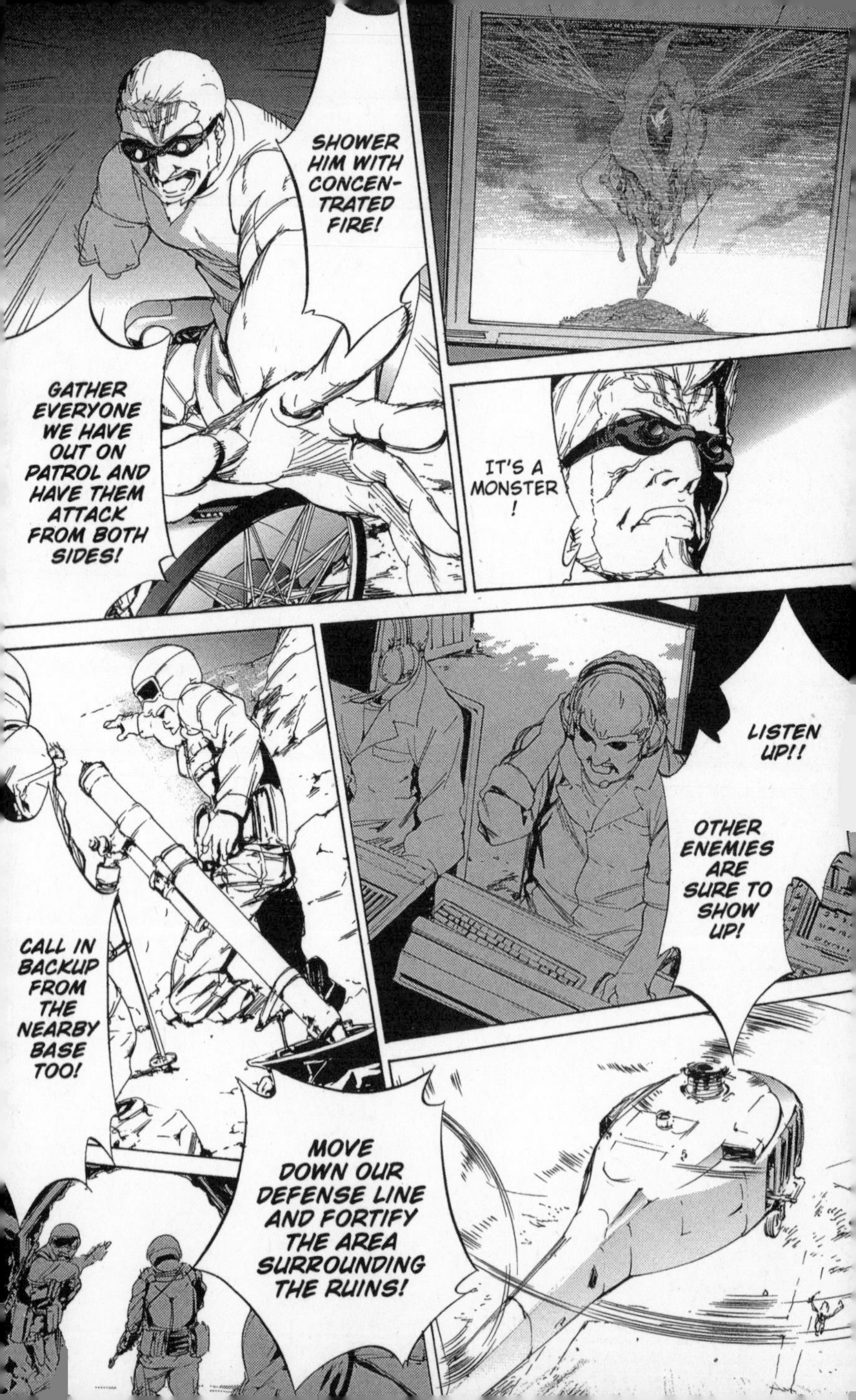
IT'S A MONSTER!
SHOWER HIM WITH CONCEN-TRATED FIRE!
GATHER EVERYONE WE HAVE OUT ON PATROL AND HAVE THEM ATTACK FROM BOTH SIDES!
LISTEN UP!!
OTHER ENEMIES ARE SURE TO SHOW UP!
CALL IN BACKUP FROM THE NEARBY BASE TOO!
MOVE DOWN OUR DEFENSE LINE AND FORTIFY THE AREA SURROUNDING THE RUINS!

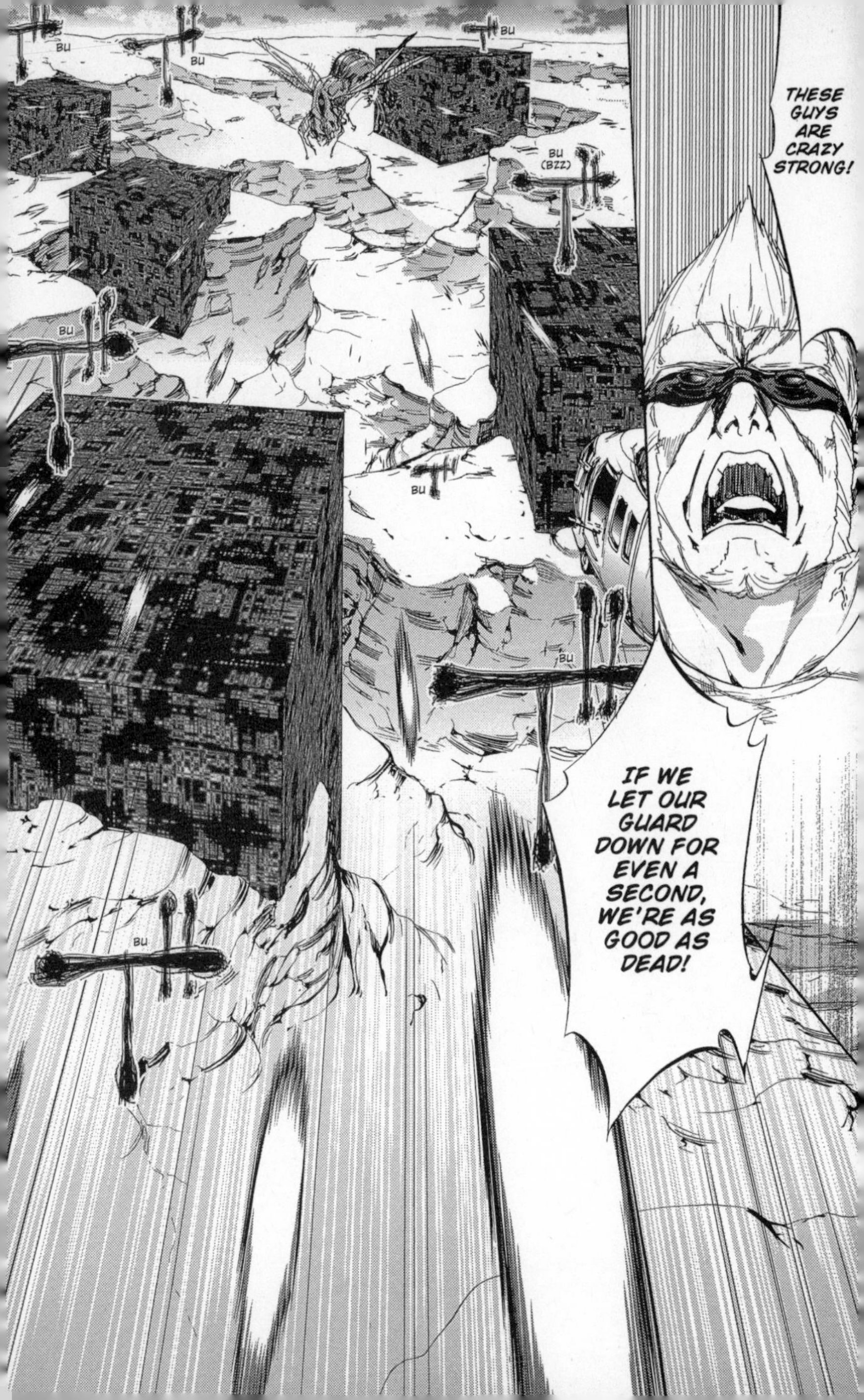
THESE GUYS ARE CRAZY STRONG!
BU
BU
BU
BU (BZZ)
IF WE LET OUR GUARD DOWN FOR EVEN A SECOND, WE'RE AS GOOD AS DEAD!
BU
BU
BU
BU

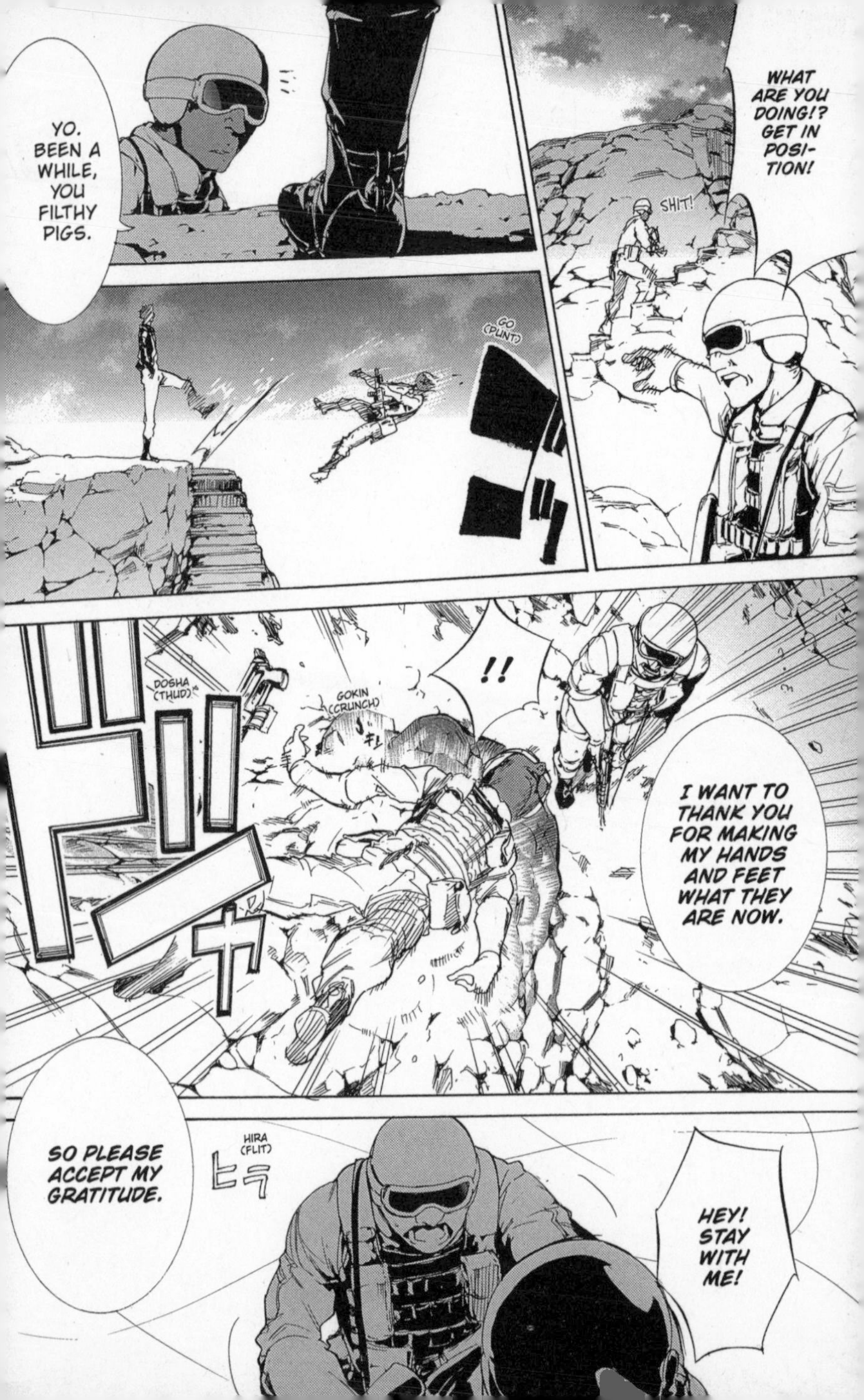
WHAT ARE YOU DOING!? GET IN POSI-TION!
SHIT!
YO. BEEN A WHILE, YOU FILTHY PIGS.
GO (PUNT)
I WANT TO THANK YOU FOR MAKING MY HANDS AND FEET WHAT THEY ARE NOW.
!!
GOKIN (CRUNCH)
DOSHA (THUD)
HEY! STAY WITH ME!
HIRA (FLIT)
SO PLEASE ACCEPT MY GRATITUDE.

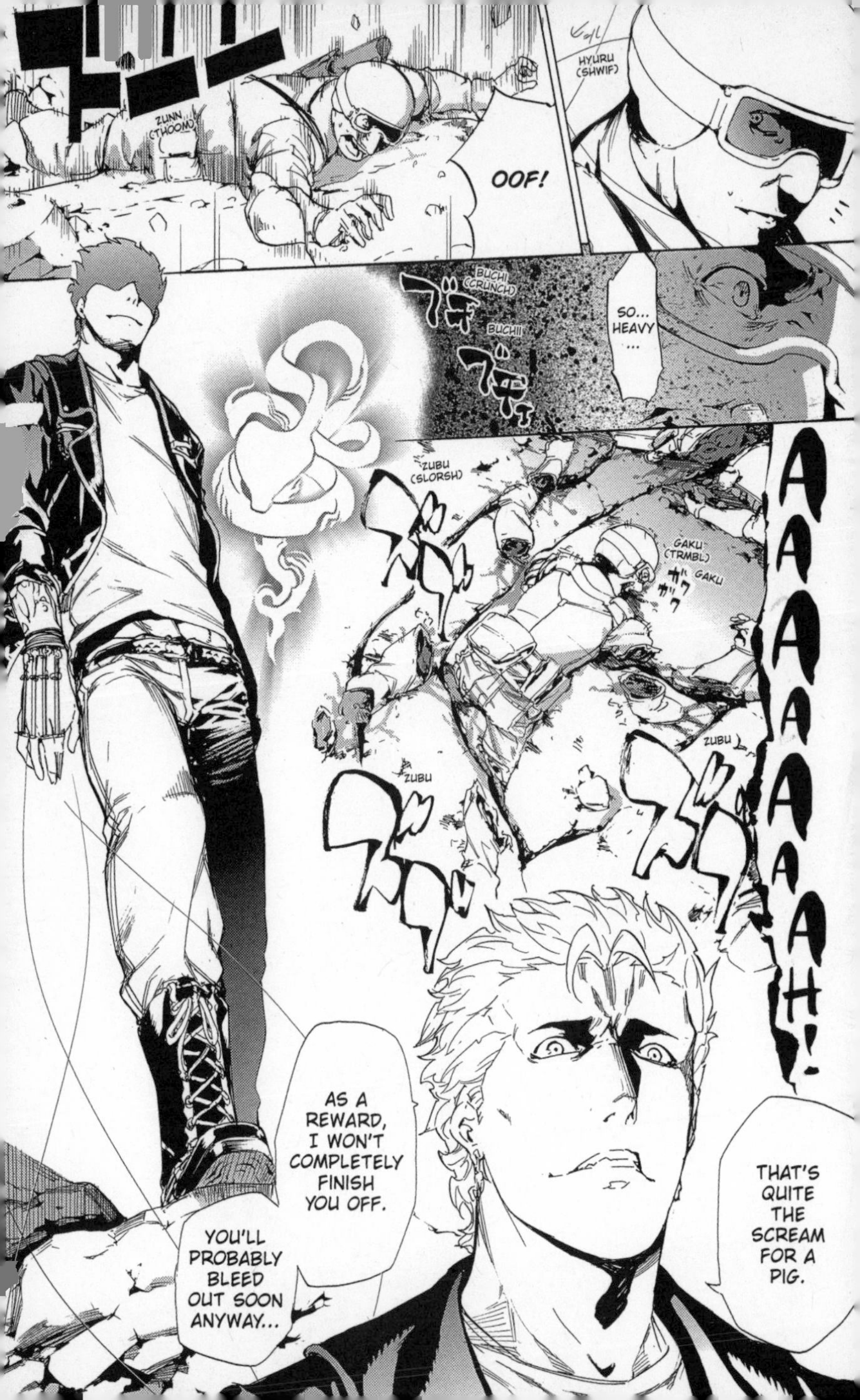
HYURU (SHWIF)
ZUNN (THOOM)
OOF!
SO... HEAVY...
BUCHI (CRUNCH)
BUCHI
AAAAAAAH!
ZUBU (SLORSH)
GAKU (TRMBL) GAKU
ZUBU
ZUBU
THAT'S QUITE THE SCREAM FOR A PIG.
AS A REWARD, I WON'T COMPLETELY FINISH YOU OFF.
YOU'LL PROBABLY BLEED OUT SOON ANYWAY...

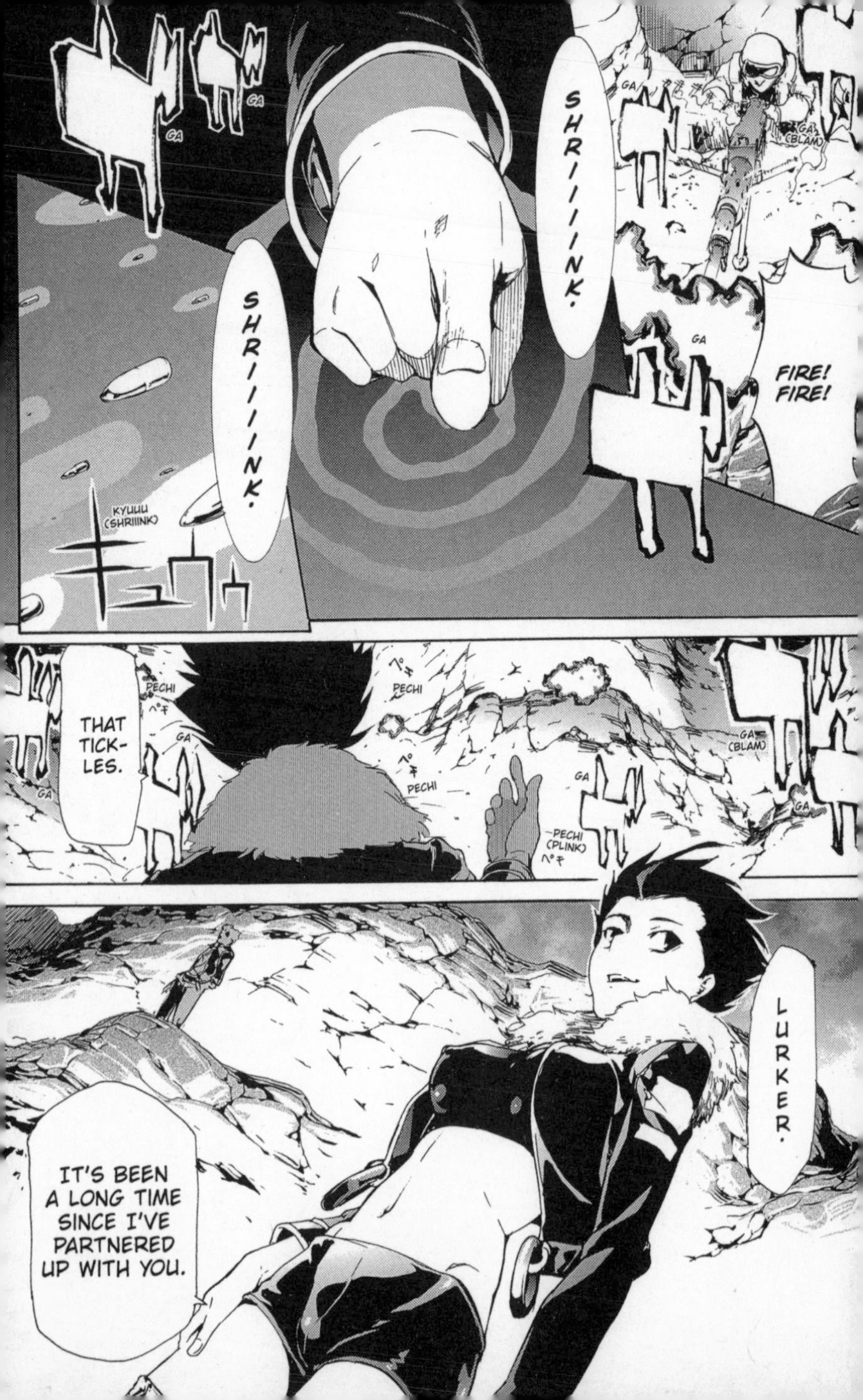
SHRIIIIINK.
GA
GA
GA (BLAM)
GA
FIRE! FIRE!
SHRIIIIINK.
KYUUU (SHRIIINK)
GA
GA
GA (BLAM)
GA
GA
PECHI (PLINK)
PECHI
PECHI
PECHI
THAT TICKLES.
GA
GA
LURKER.
IT'S BEEN A LONG TIME SINCE I'VE PARTNERED UP WITH YOU.

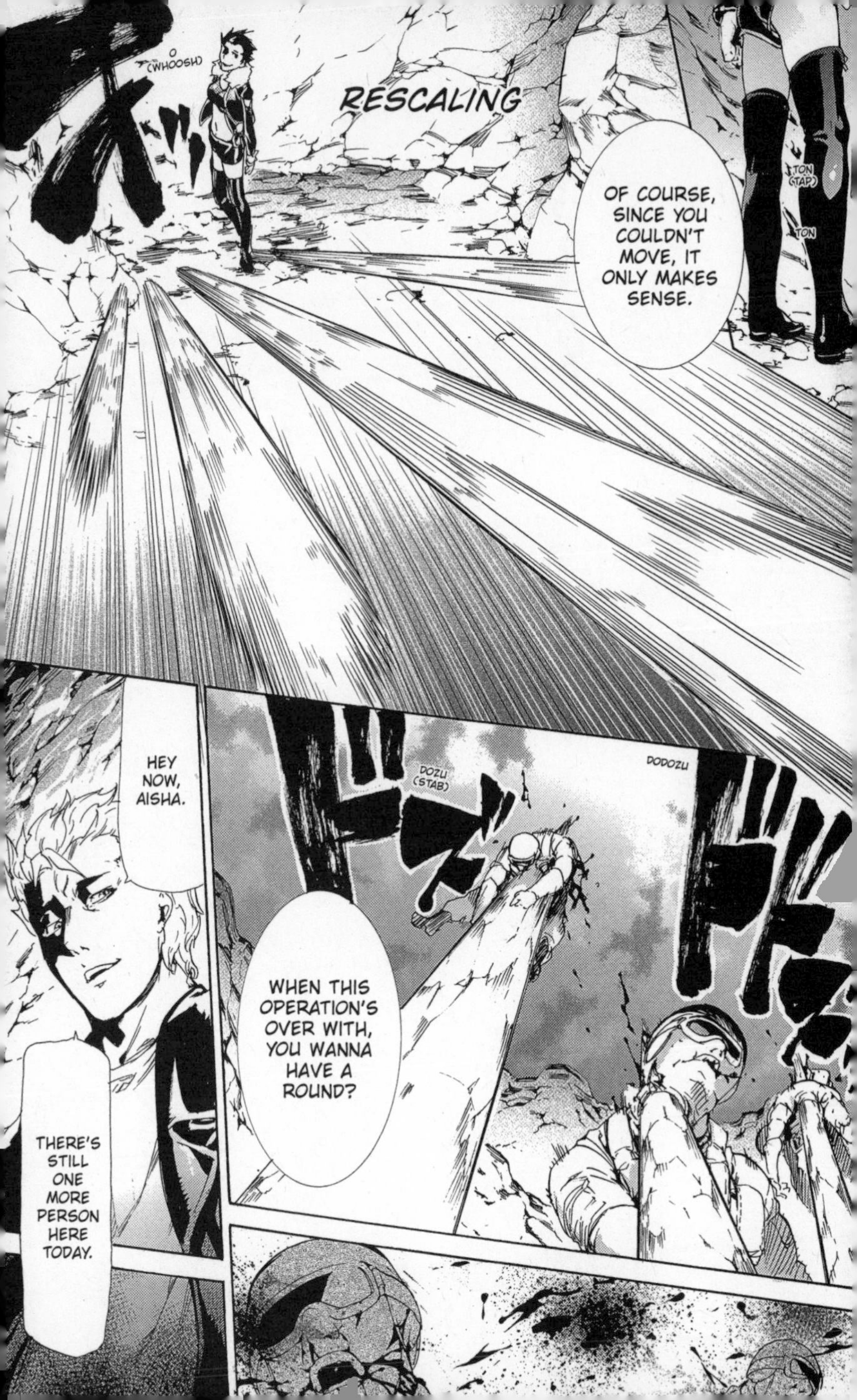
TON (TAP)
TON
OF COURSE, SINCE YOU COULDN'T MOVE, IT ONLY MAKES SENSE.
RESCALING
O (WHOOSH)
DODOZU
DOZU (STAB)
WHEN THIS OPERATION'S OVER WITH, YOU WANNA HAVE A ROUND?
HEY NOW, AISHA.
THERE'S STILL ONE MORE PERSON HERE TODAY.

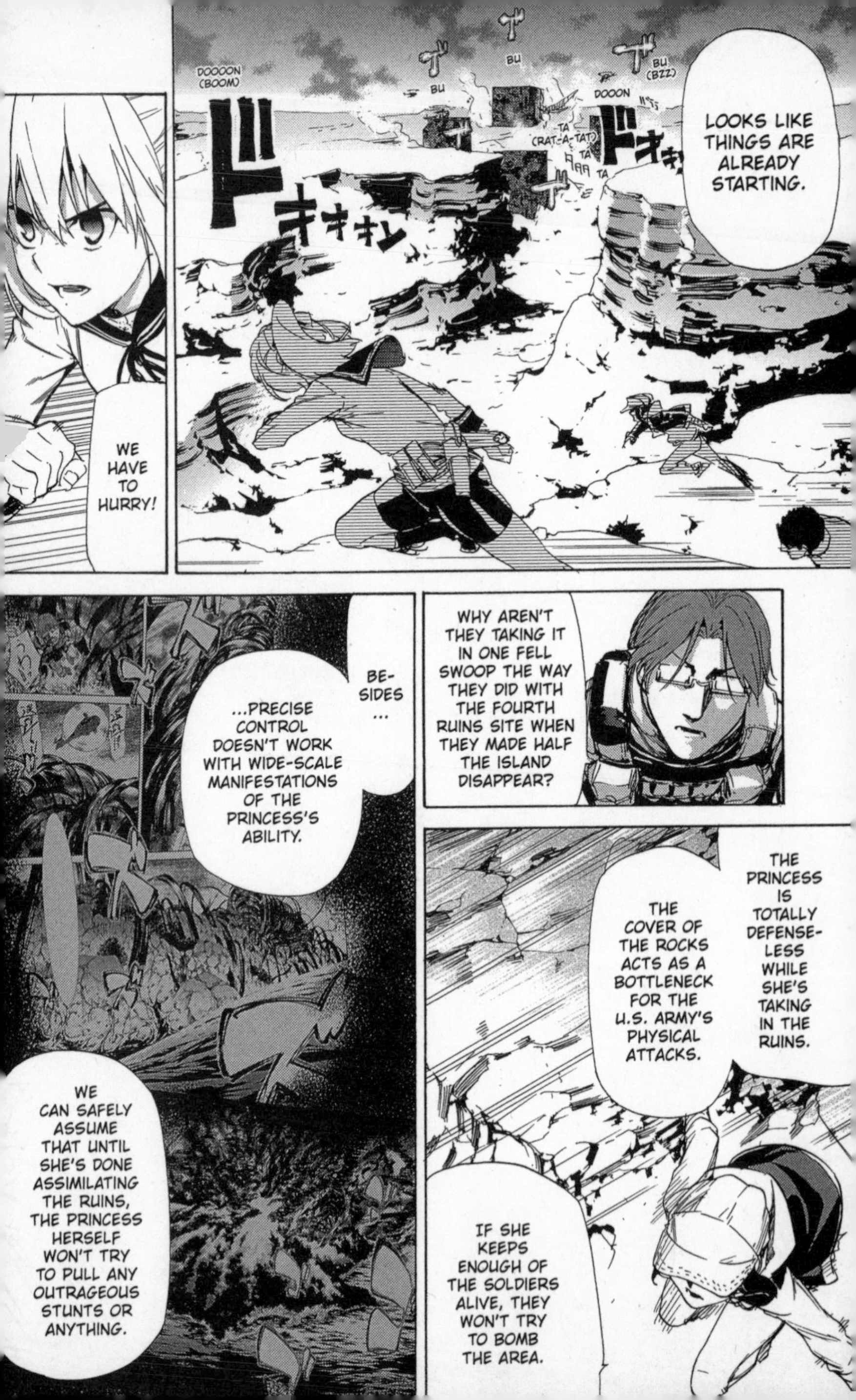
DOOOON (BOOM)
BU
BU
BU (BZZ)
DOOON
TA (RAT-A-TAT)
TA
TA
LOOKS LIKE THINGS ARE ALREADY STARTING.
WE HAVE TO HURRY!
WHY AREN'T THEY TAKING IT IN ONE FELL SWOOP THE WAY THEY DID WITH THE FOURTH RUINS SITE WHEN THEY MADE HALF THE ISLAND DISAPPEAR?
THE PRINCESS IS TOTALLY DEFENSELESS WHILE SHE'S TAKING IN THE RUINS.
THE COVER OF THE ROCKS ACTS AS A BOTTLENECK FOR THE U.S. ARMY'S PHYSICAL ATTACKS.
IF SHE KEEPS ENOUGH OF THE SOLDIERS ALIVE, THEY WON'T TRY TO BOMB THE AREA.
BESIDES...
...PRECISE CONTROL DOESN'T WORK WITH WIDE-SCALE MANIFESTATIONS OF THE PRINCESS'S ABILITY.
WE CAN SAFELY ASSUME THAT UNTIL SHE'S DONE ASSIMILATING THE RUINS, THE PRINCESS HERSELF WON'T TRY TO PULL ANY OUTRAGEOUS STUNTS OR ANYTHING.

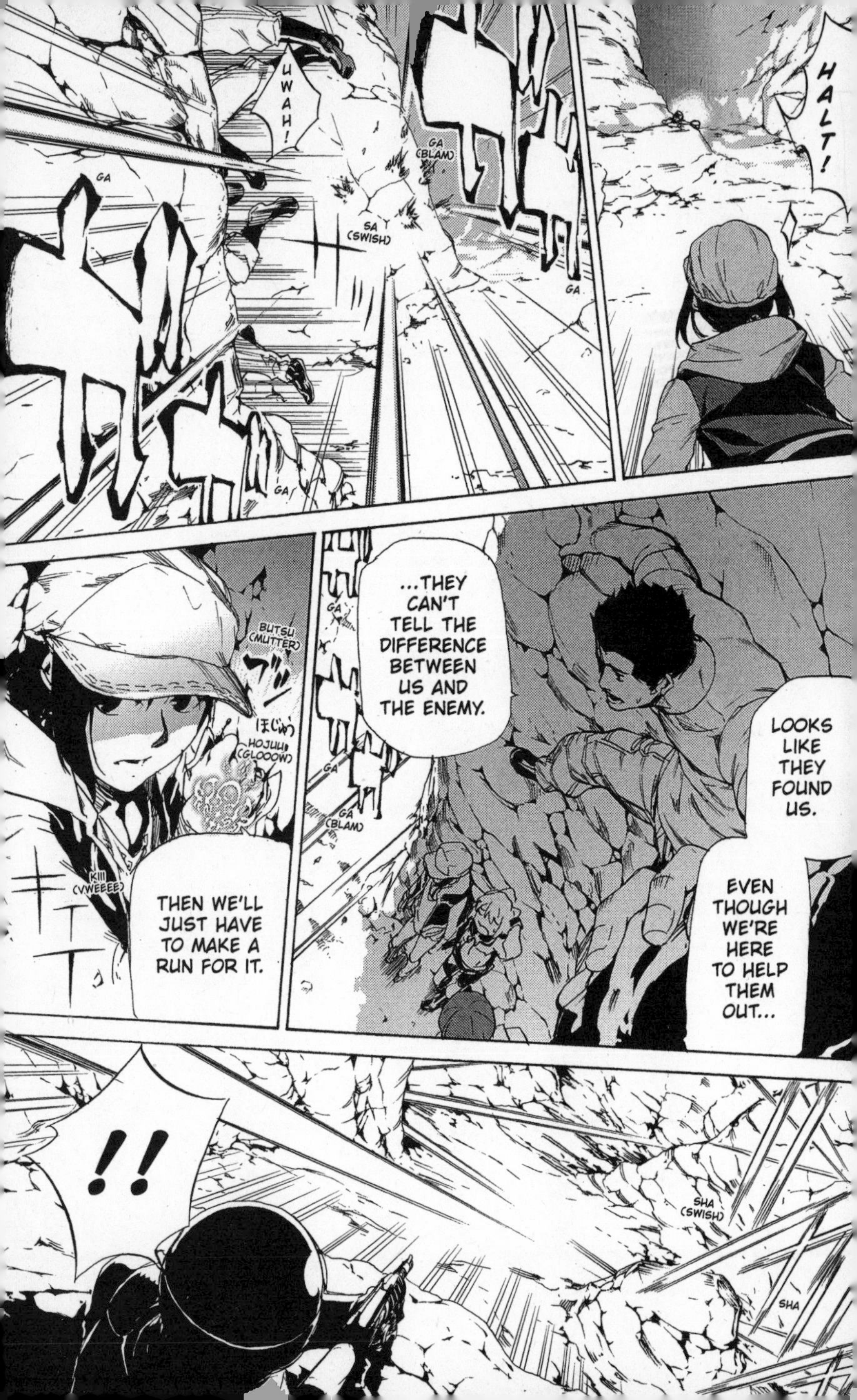
HALT!
GA
GA (BLAM)
SA (SWISH)
UWAH!
GA
GA!
LOOKS LIKE THEY FOUND US.
EVEN THOUGH WE'RE HERE TO HELP THEM OUT...
...THEY CAN'T TELL THE DIFFERENCE BETWEEN US AND THE ENEMY.
GA
GA
GA (BLAM)
BUTSU (MUTTER)
ブツ
ほじゅ
HOJUU (GLOOOW)
THEN WE'LL JUST HAVE TO MAKE A RUN FOR IT.
KIII (VWEEEE)
SHA (SWISH)
SHA
!!

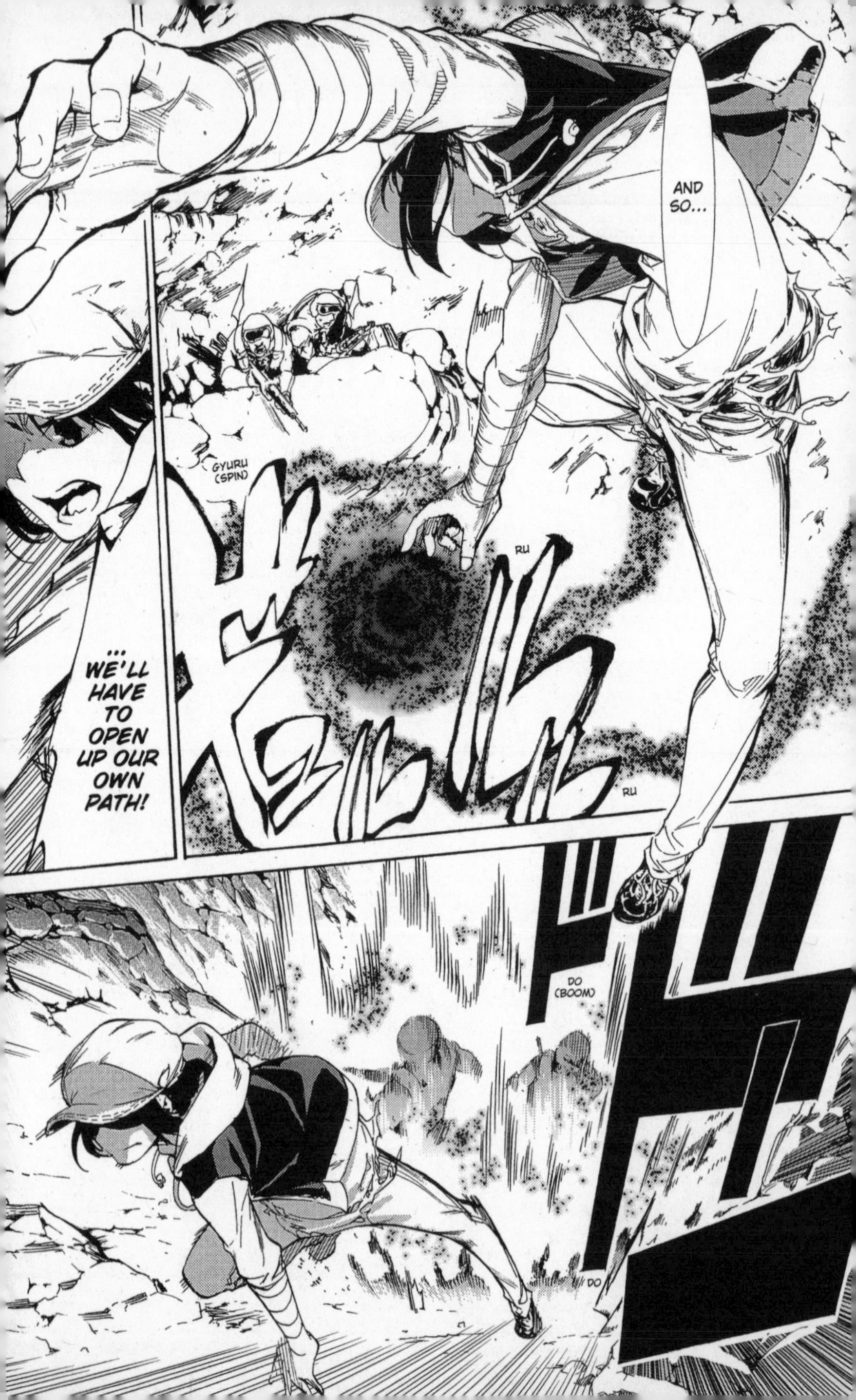

AND SO...
...WE'LL HAVE TO OPEN UP OUR OWN PATH!
GYURU (SPIN)
RU
RU
DO (BOOM)
DO

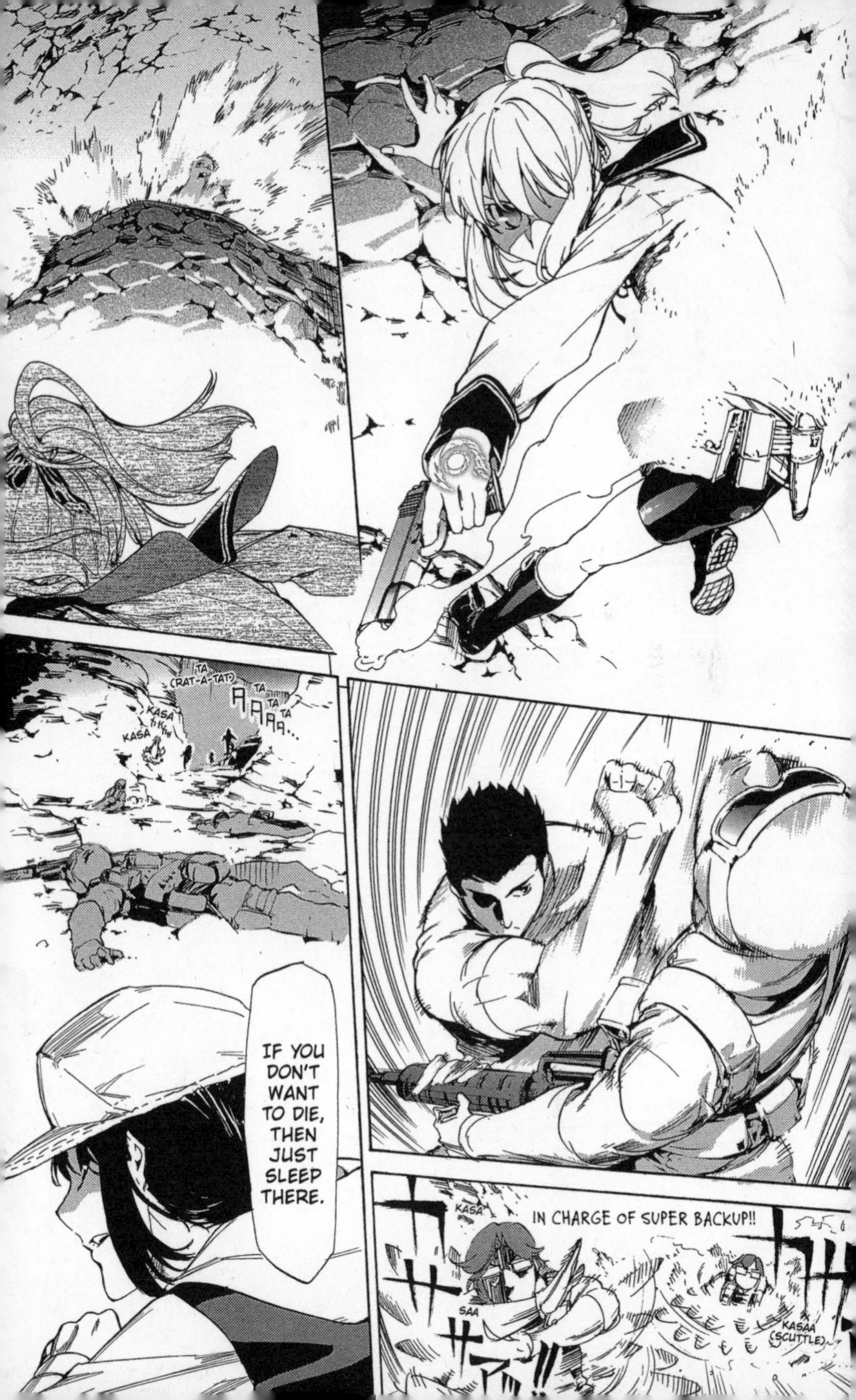
TA
(RAT-A-TAT)
TA TA TA
KASA
KASA
KASA
IN CHARGE OF SUPER BACKUP!!
SAA
KASAA
(SCUTTLE)
IF YOU DON'T WANT TO DIE, THEN JUST SLEEP THERE.

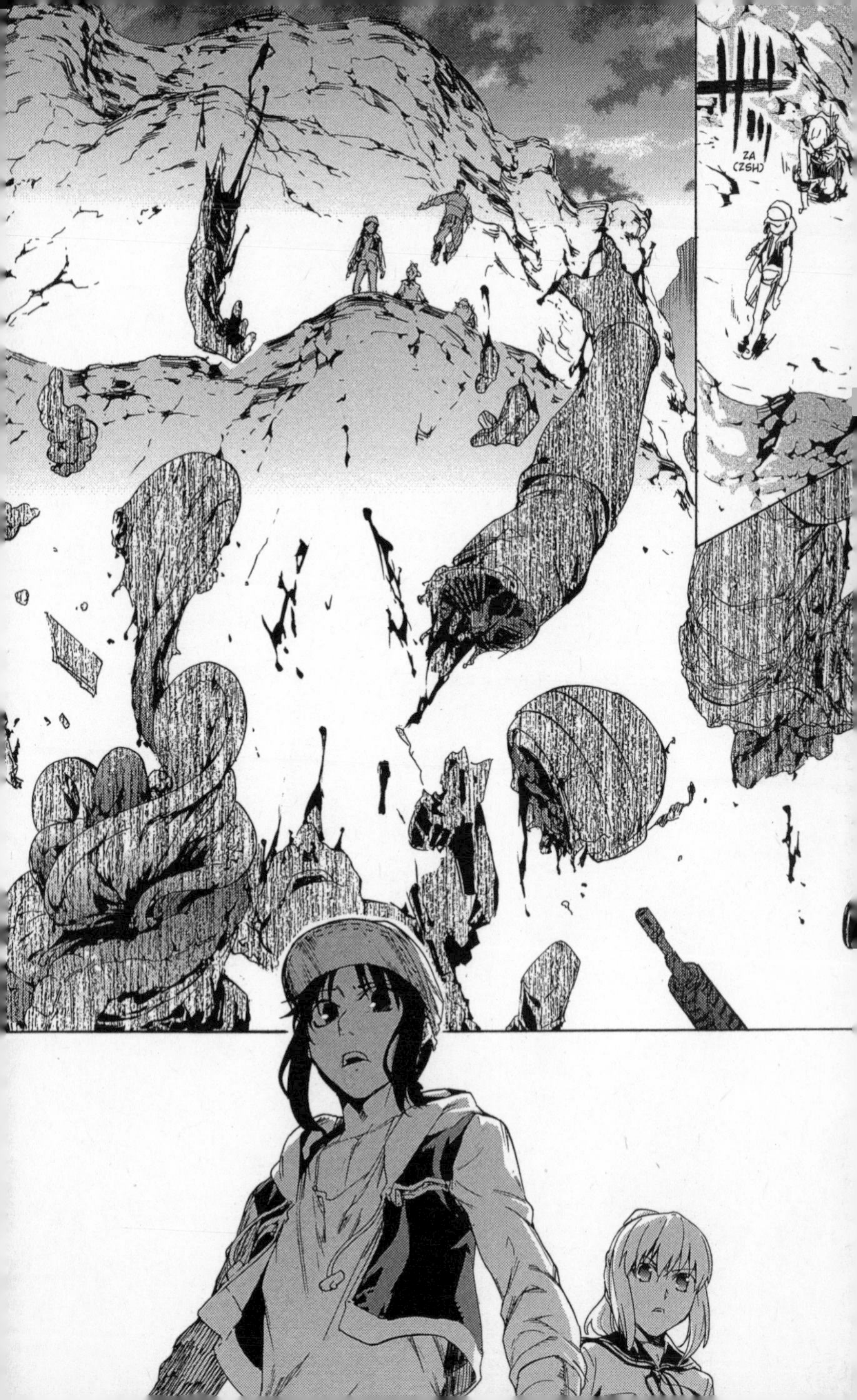
ZA
(ZSH)

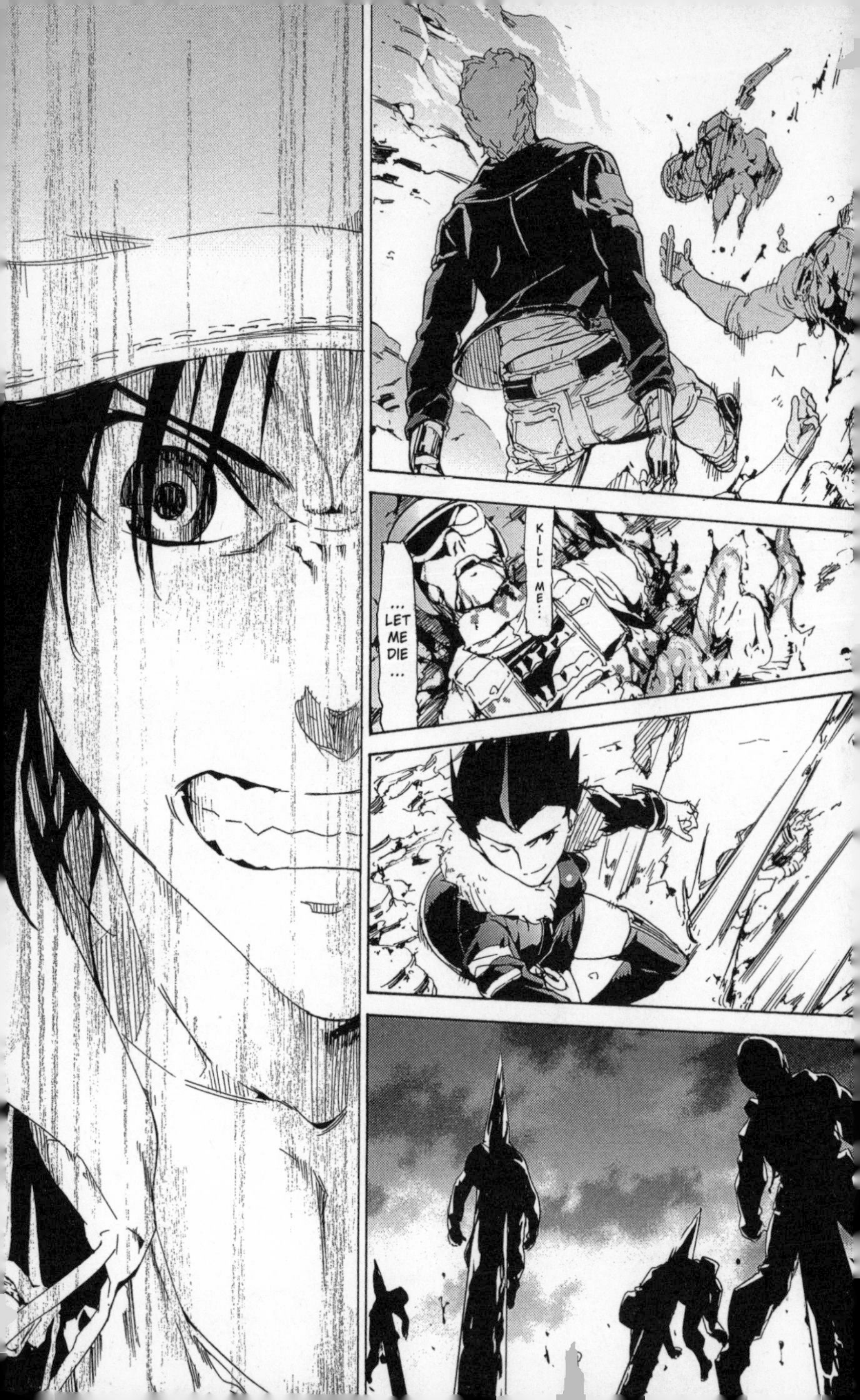
KILL ME...
...LET ME DIE...

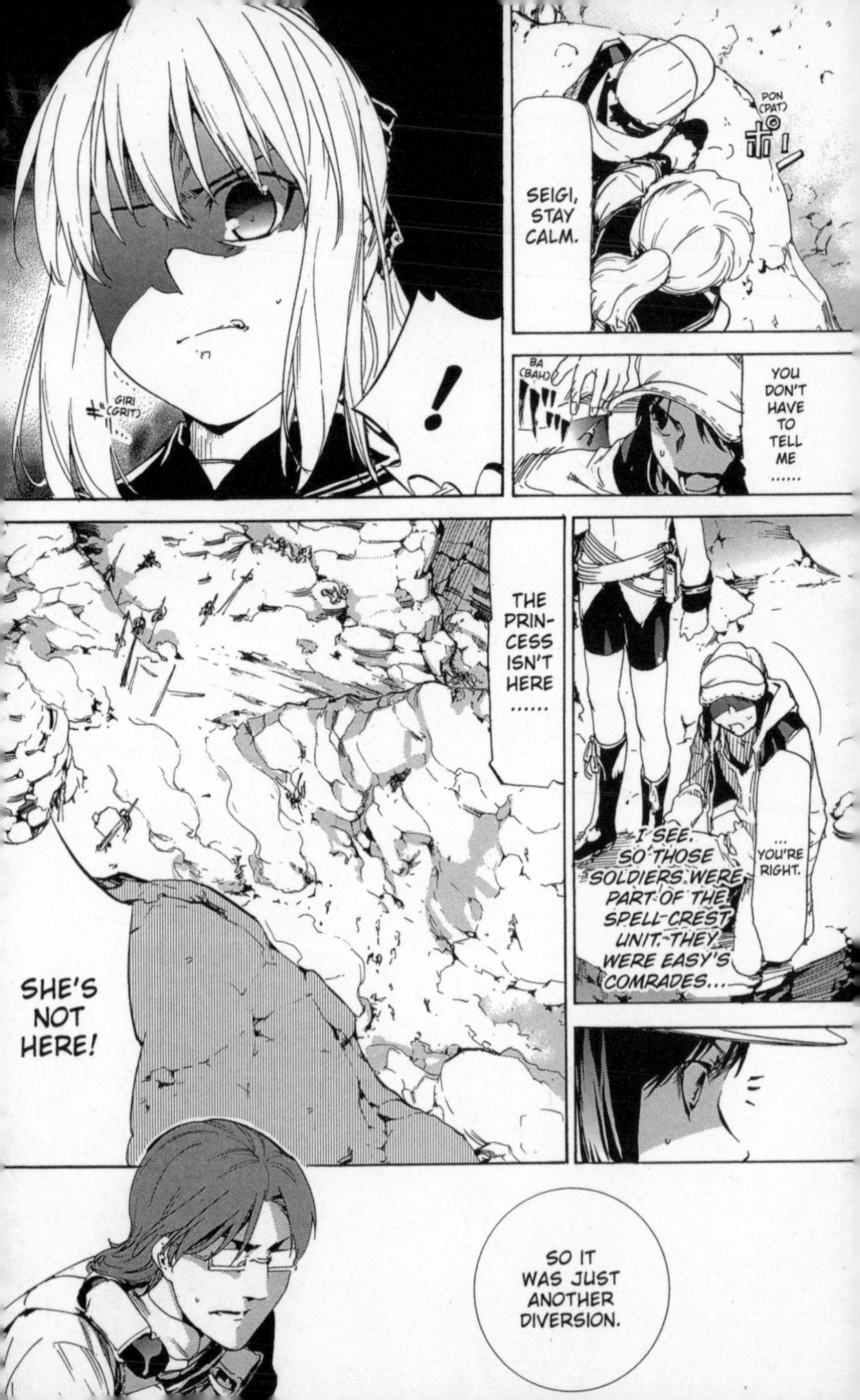
PON (PAT)
SEIGI, STAY CALM.
BA (BAH)
YOU DON'T HAVE TO TELL ME ......
GIRI (GRIT)
!
...YOU'RE RIGHT.
I SEE. SO THOSE SOLDIERS WERE PART OF THE SPELL-CREST UNIT. THEY WERE EASY'S COMRADES...
THE PRINCESS ISN'T HERE ......
SHE'S NOT HERE!
SO IT WAS JUST ANOTHER DIVERSION.

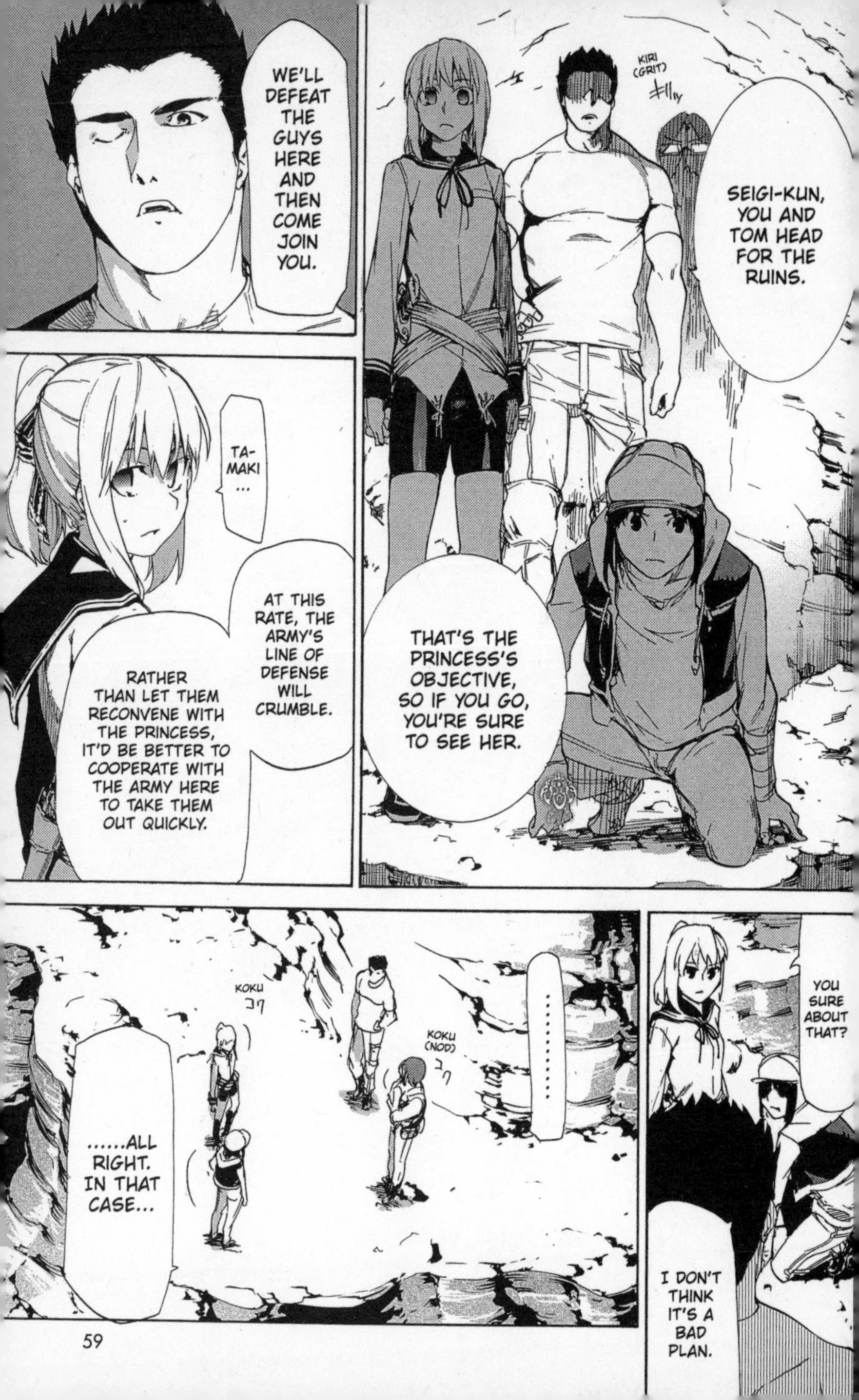
KIRI (GRIT)
SEIGI-KUN, YOU AND TOM HEAD FOR THE RUINS.
THAT'S THE PRINCESS'S OBJECTIVE, SO IF YOU GO, YOU'RE SURE TO SEE HER.
WE'LL DEFEAT THE GUYS HERE AND THEN COME JOIN YOU.
TA-MAKI ...
AT THIS RATE, THE ARMY'S LINE OF DEFENSE WILL CRUMBLE.
RATHER THAN LET THEM RECONVENE WITH THE PRINCESS, IT'D BE BETTER TO COOPERATE WITH THE ARMY HERE TO TAKE THEM OUT QUICKLY.
YOU SURE ABOUT THAT?
I DON'T THINK IT'S A BAD PLAN.
....
KOKU (NOD)
KOKU
......ALL RIGHT. IN THAT CASE...

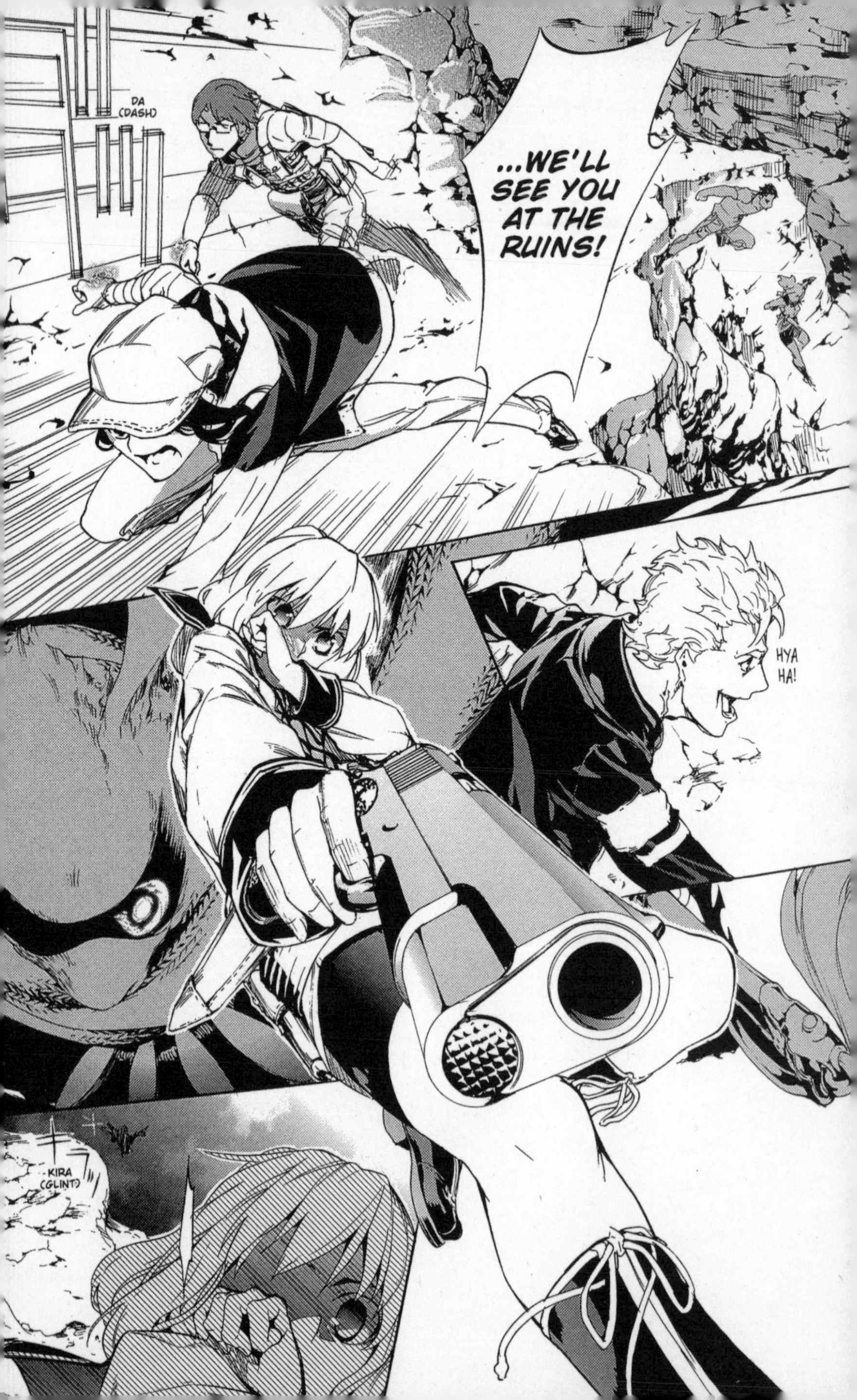
...WE'LL SEE YOU AT THE RUINS!
DA (DASH)
HYA HA!
KIRA (GLINT)

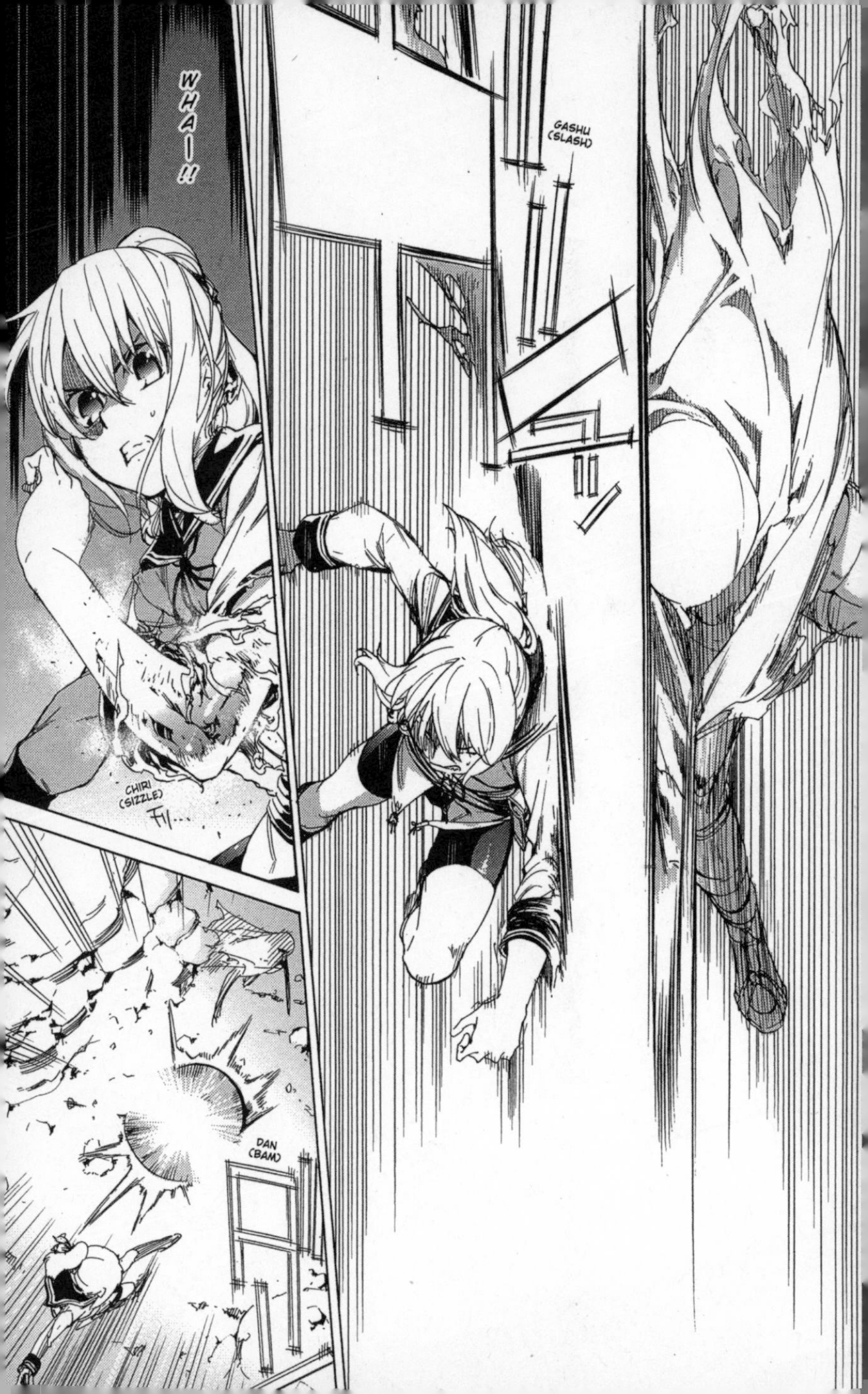
GASHU (SLASH)
WHA-!!
CHIRI (SIZZLE)
チリ...
DAN (BAM)

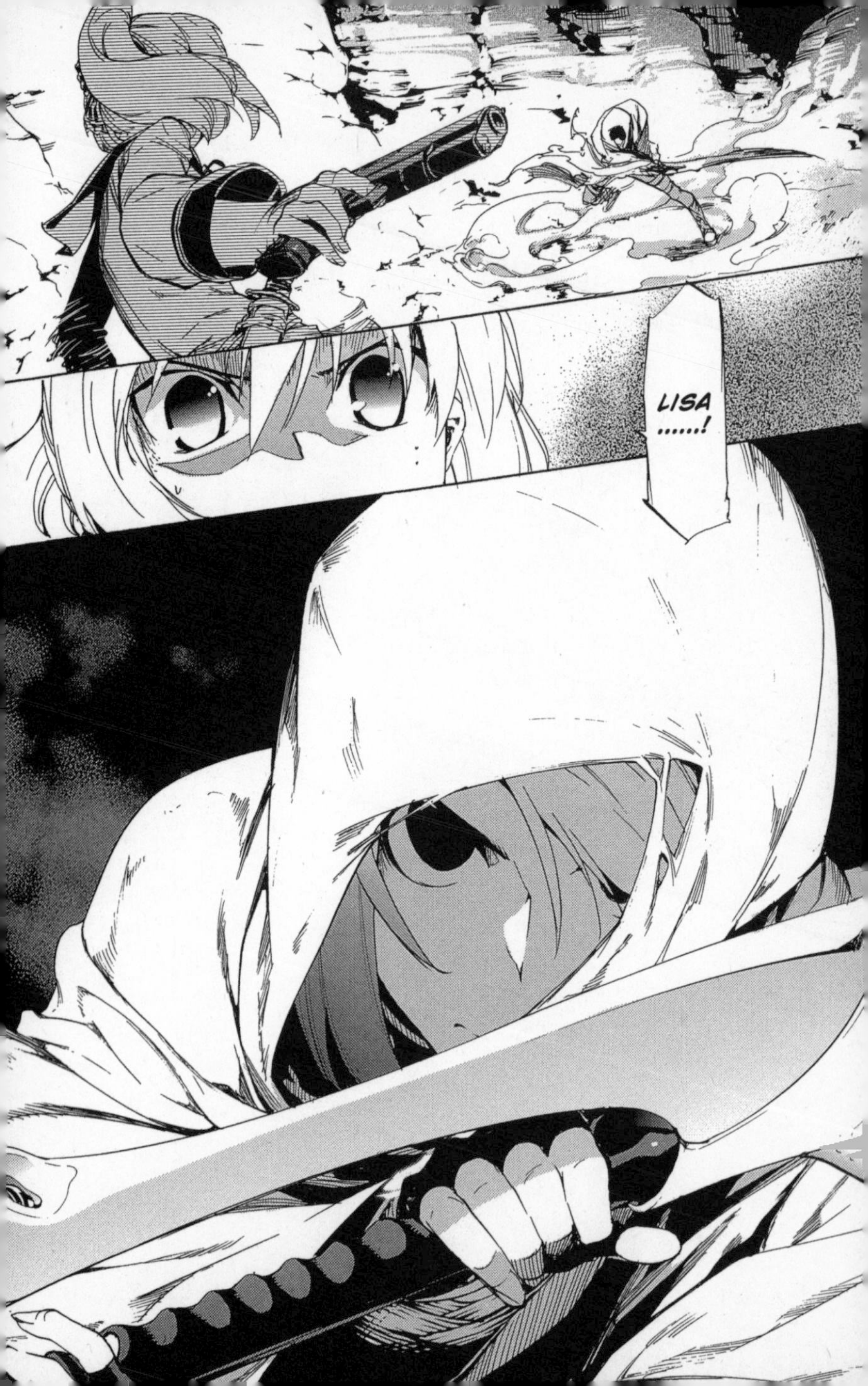
LISA
......!

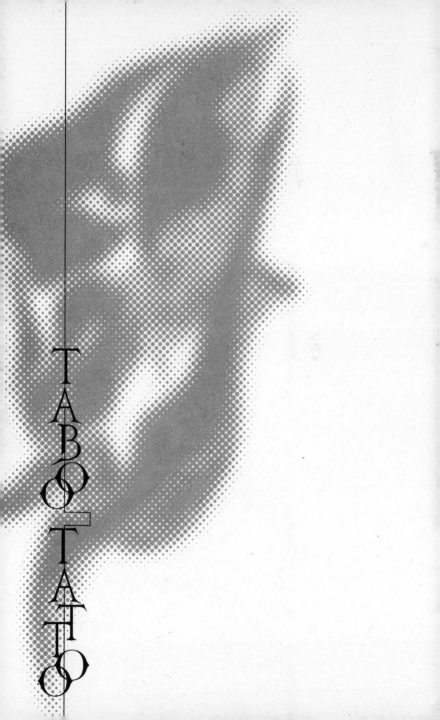

TABOO TATTOO

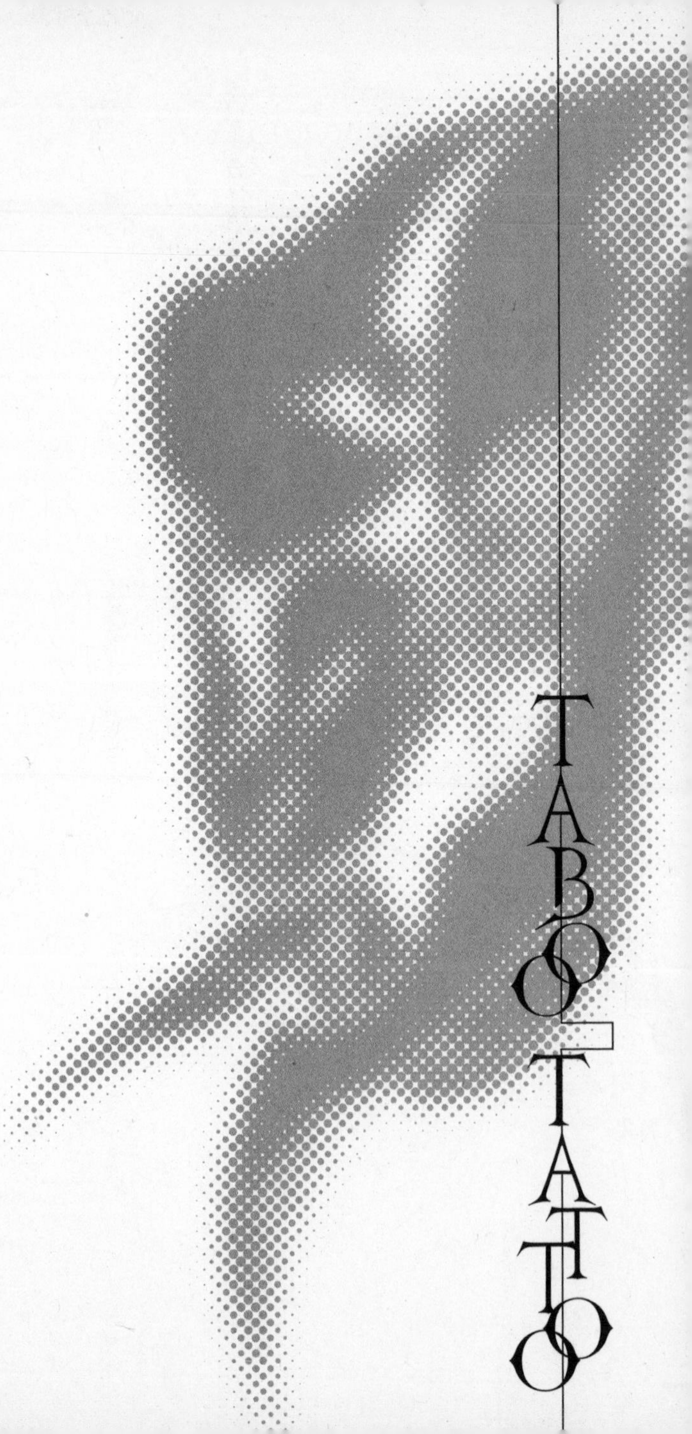
TABOO TATTOO

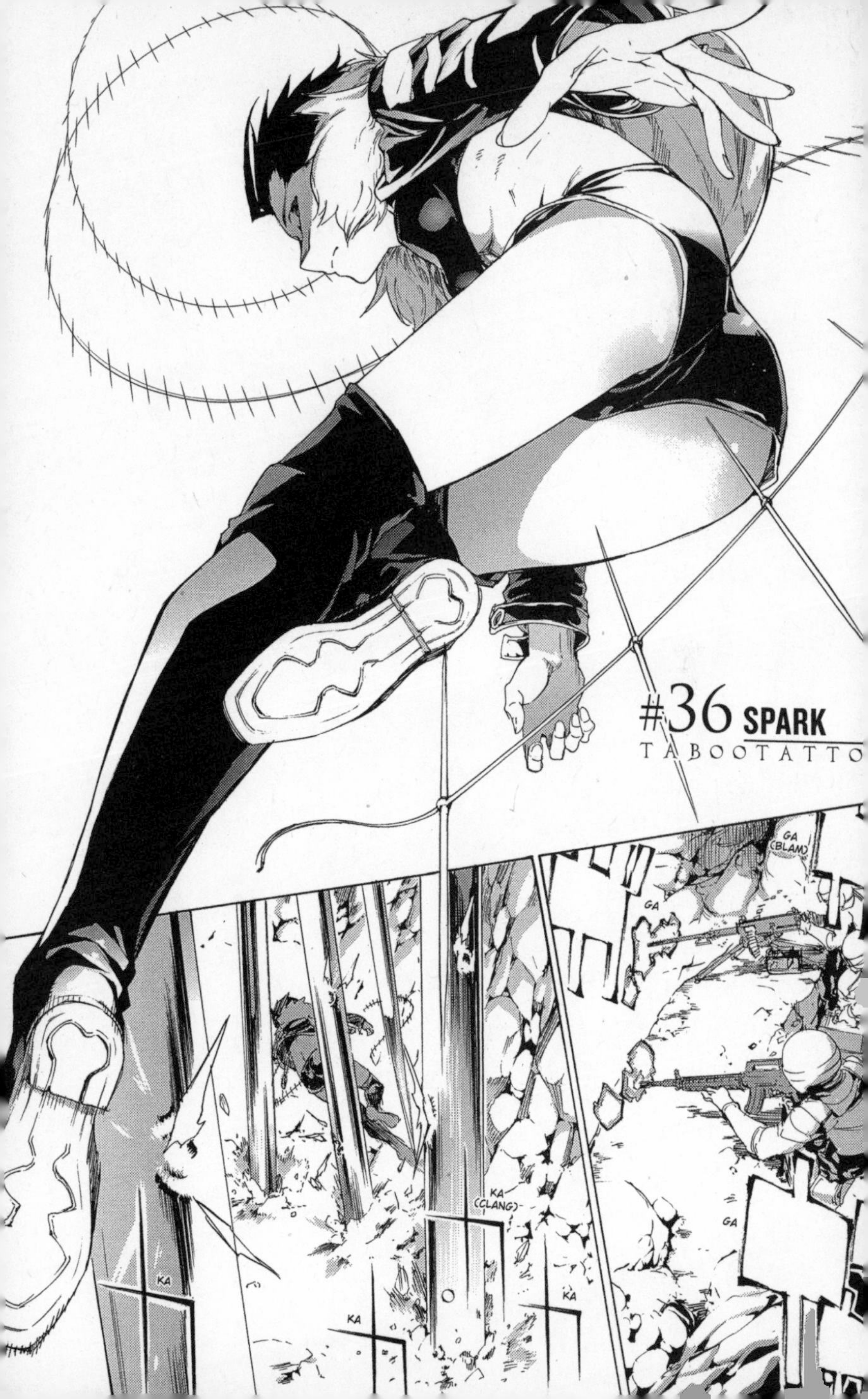
#36 SPARK
TABOOTATTO
GA (BLAM)
GA
GA
KA (CLANG)
KA
KA
KA

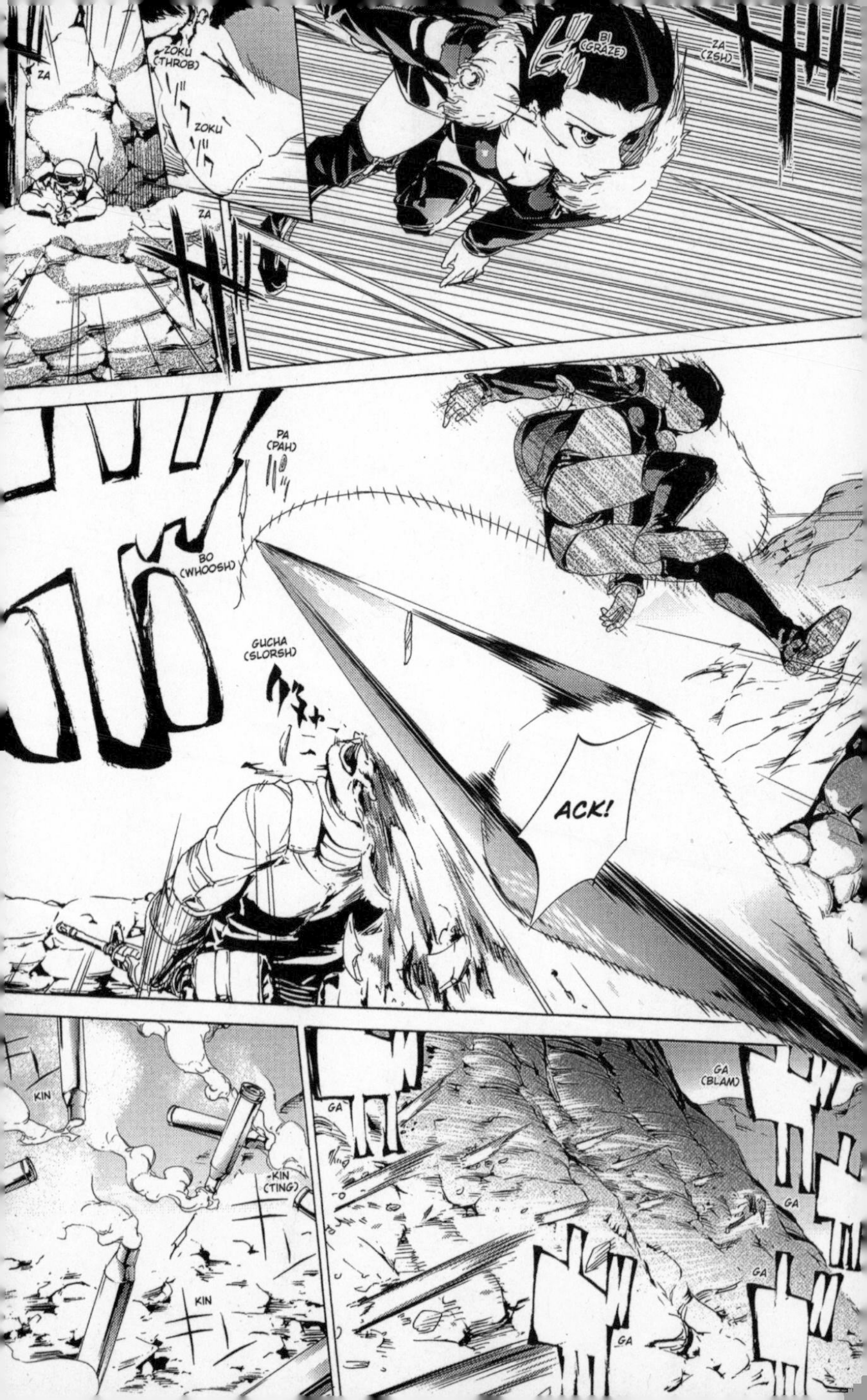
ZA
(ZSH)
BI
(GRAZE)
ZOKU
(THROB)
ZOKU
ZA
ZA
PA
(PAH)
BO
(WHOOSH)
GUCHA
(SLORSH)
ACK!
GA
(BLAM)
GA
GA
GA
GA
-KIN
(TING)
KIN
KIN

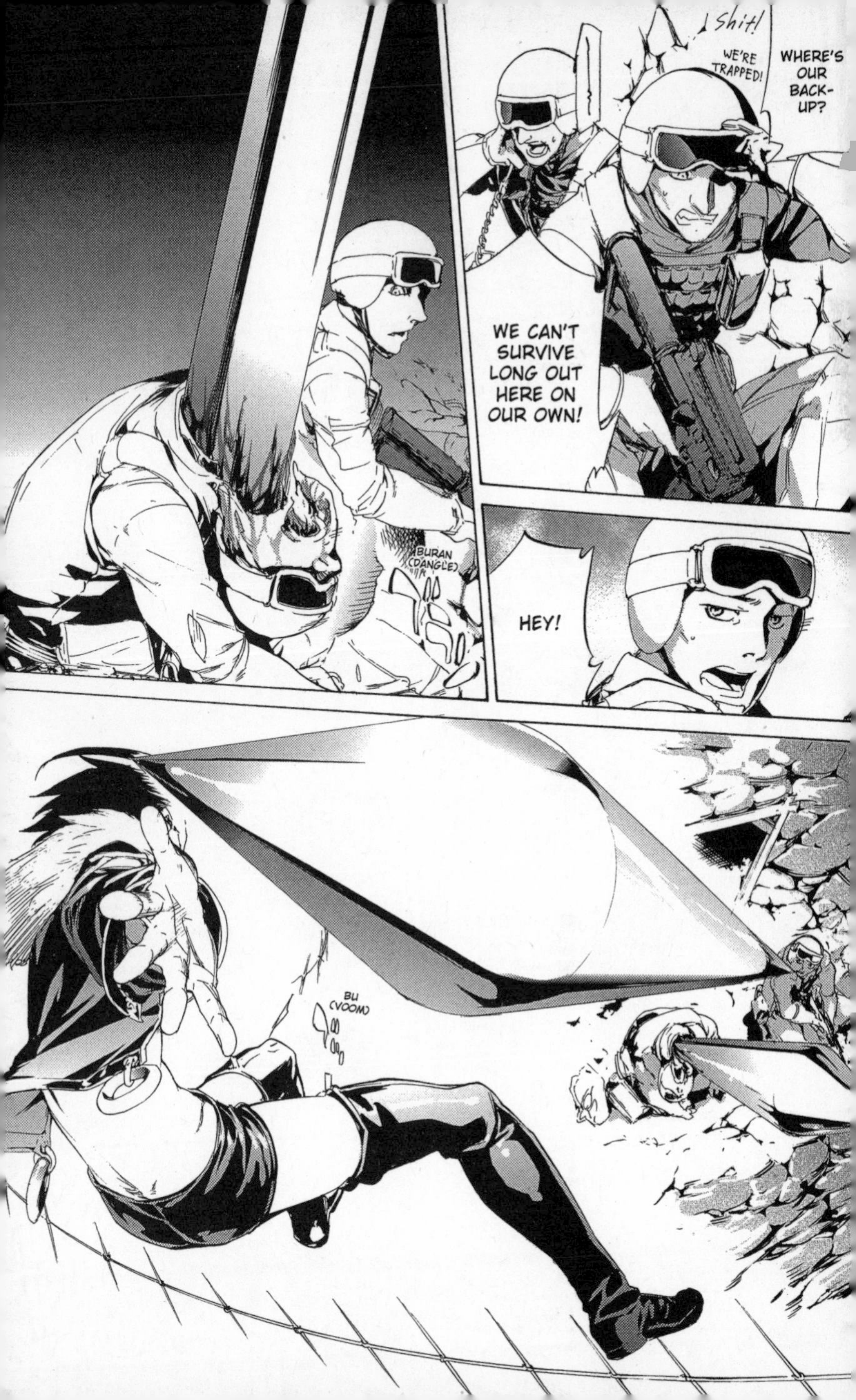
WHERE'S OUR BACK-UP?
WE'RE TRAPPED!
Shit!
WE CAN'T SURVIVE LONG OUT HERE ON OUR OWN!
HEY!
BURAN (DANGLE)
BU (VOOM)

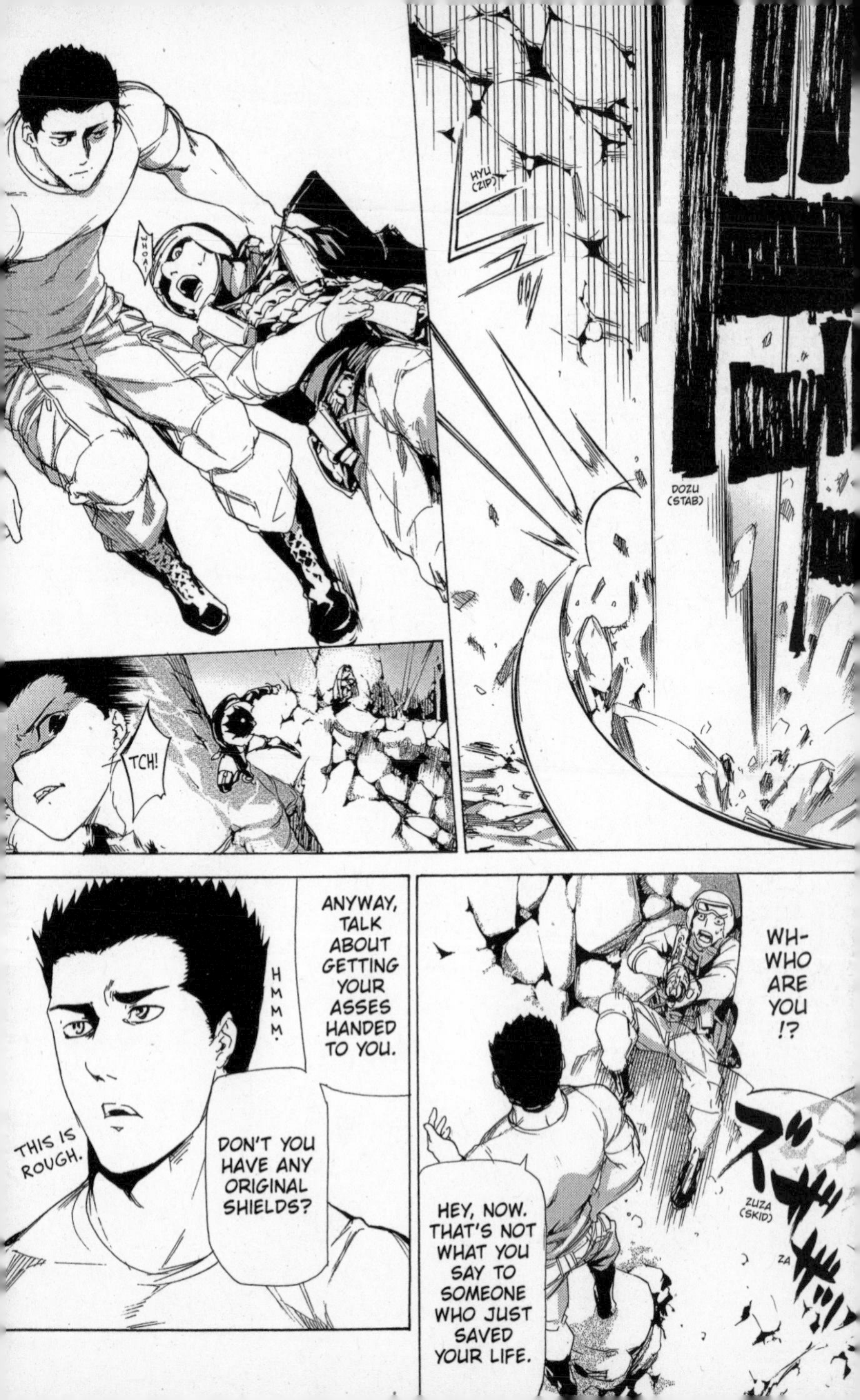
HYU (ZIP)
DOZU (STAB)
WHOA!
TCH!
WH-WHO ARE YOU!?
ZUZA (SKID)
ZA
HEY, NOW. THAT'S NOT WHAT YOU SAY TO SOMEONE WHO JUST SAVED YOUR LIFE.
ANYWAY, TALK ABOUT GETTING YOUR ASSES HANDED TO YOU.
HMMM.
DON'T YOU HAVE ANY ORIGINAL SHIELDS?
THIS IS ROUGH.

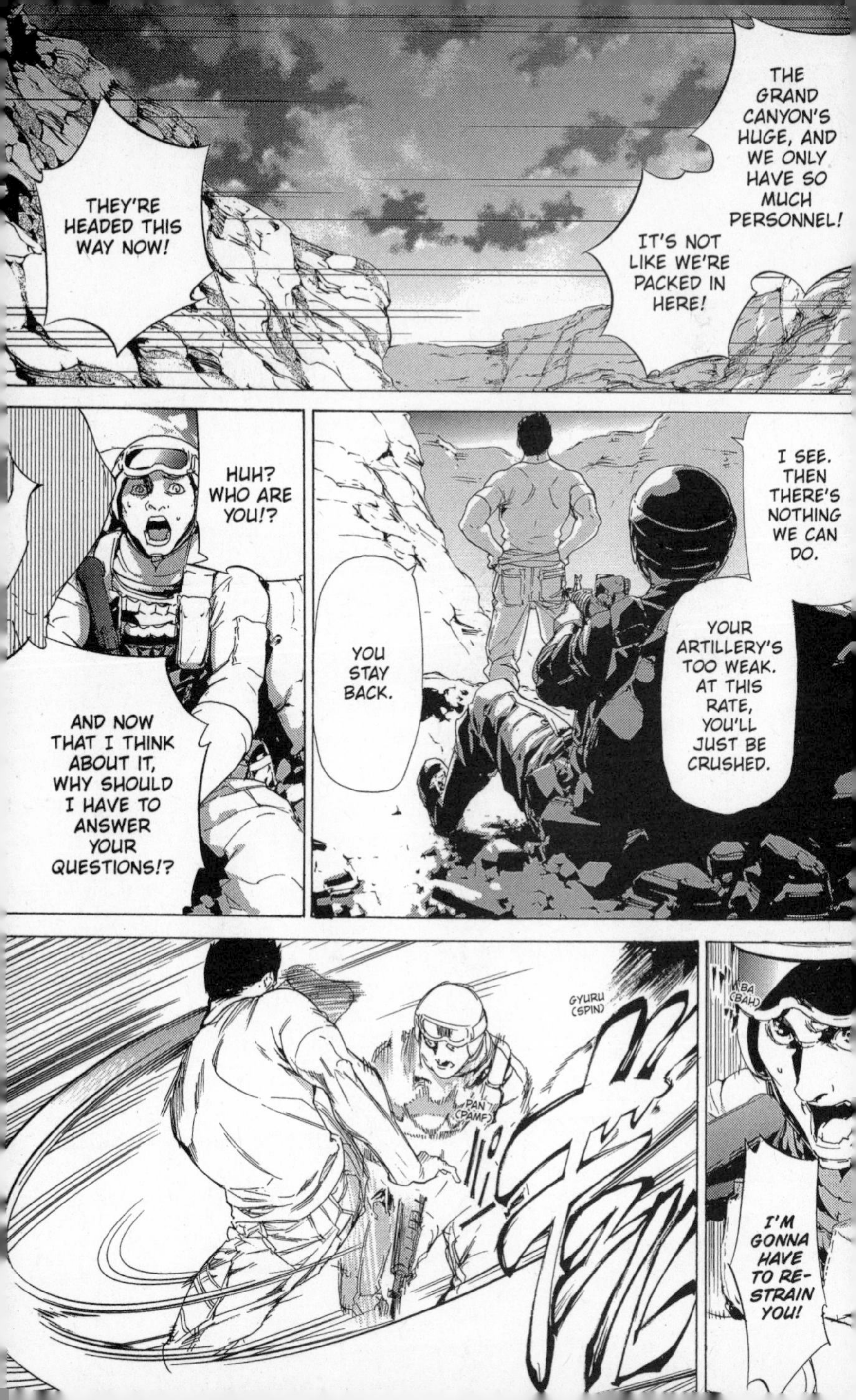
THE GRAND CANYON'S HUGE, AND WE ONLY HAVE SO MUCH PERSONNEL!
IT'S NOT LIKE WE'RE PACKED IN HERE!
THEY'RE HEADED THIS WAY NOW!
I SEE. THEN THERE'S NOTHING WE CAN DO.
YOUR ARTILLERY'S TOO WEAK. AT THIS RATE, YOU'LL JUST BE CRUSHED.
YOU STAY BACK.
HUH? WHO ARE YOU!?
AND NOW THAT I THINK ABOUT IT, WHY SHOULD I HAVE TO ANSWER YOUR QUESTIONS!?
BA (BAH)
I'M GONNA HAVE TO RE-STRAIN YOU!
GYURU (SPIN)
PAN (PAMF)

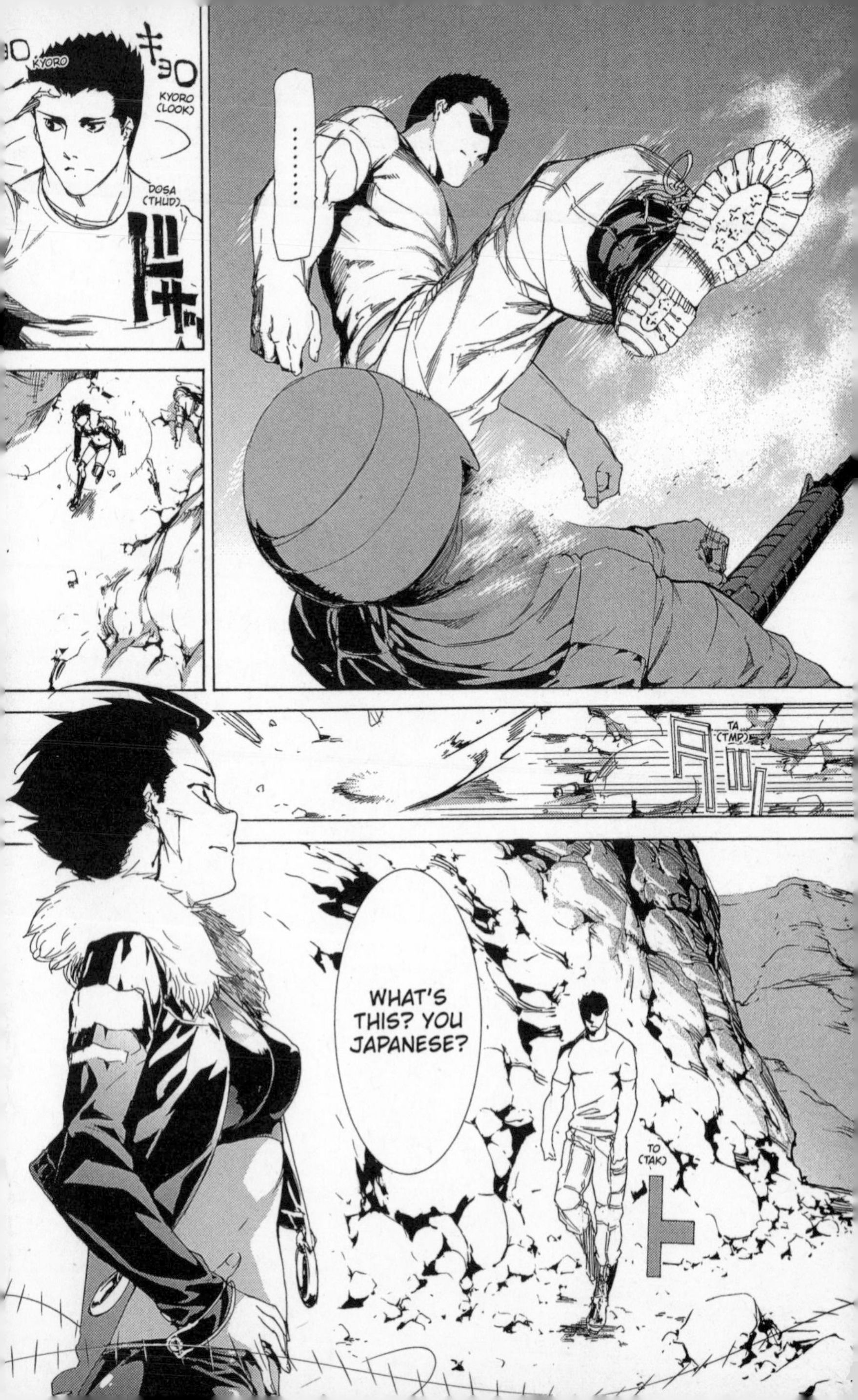
KYORO
KYORO (LOOK)
DOSA (THUD)
....
TA (TMP)
WHAT'S THIS? YOU JAPANESE?
TO (TAK)

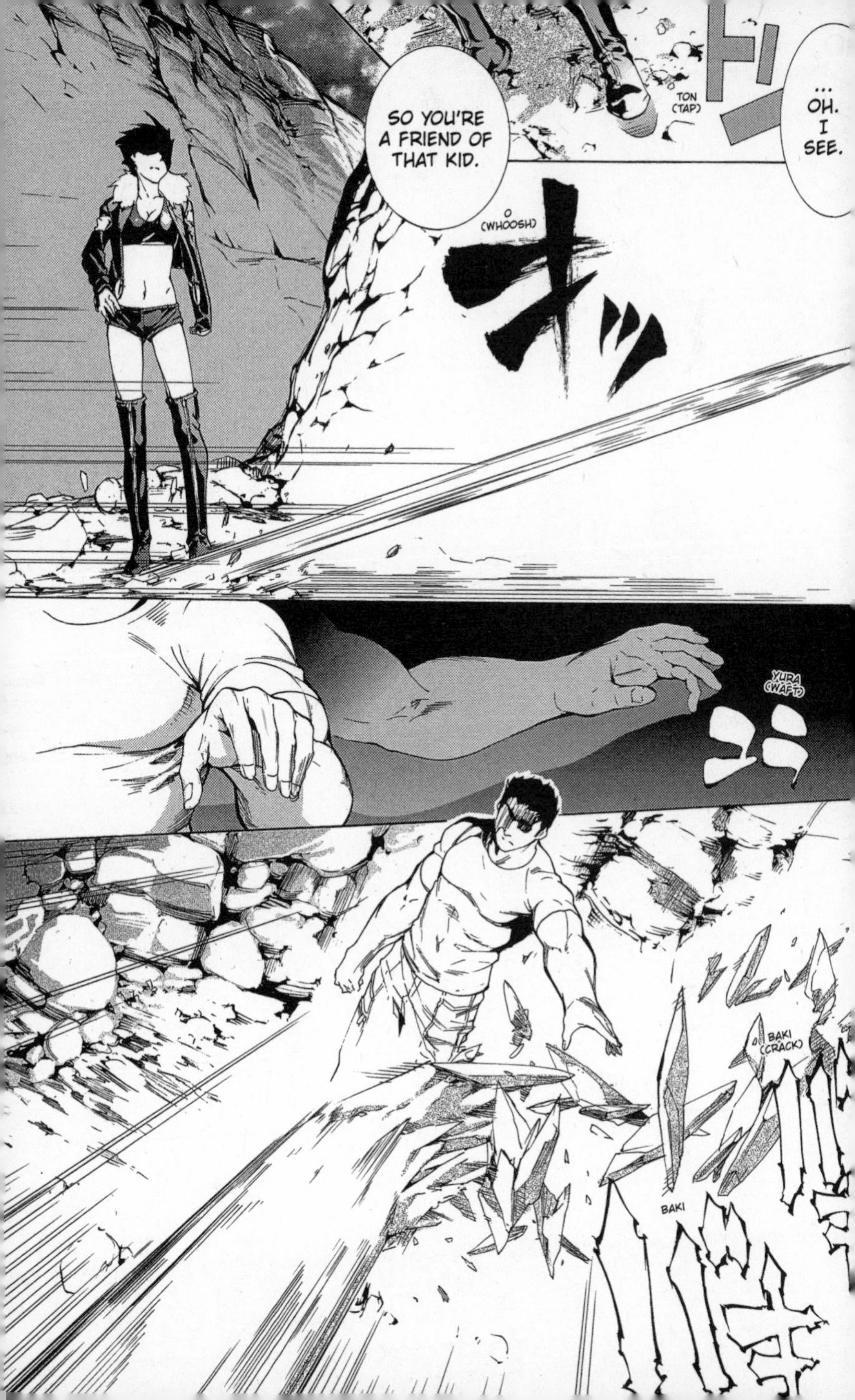

...OH. I SEE.
TON (TAP)
SO YOU'RE A FRIEND OF THAT KID.
O (WHOOSH)
YURA (WAFT)
BAKI (CRACK)
BAKI

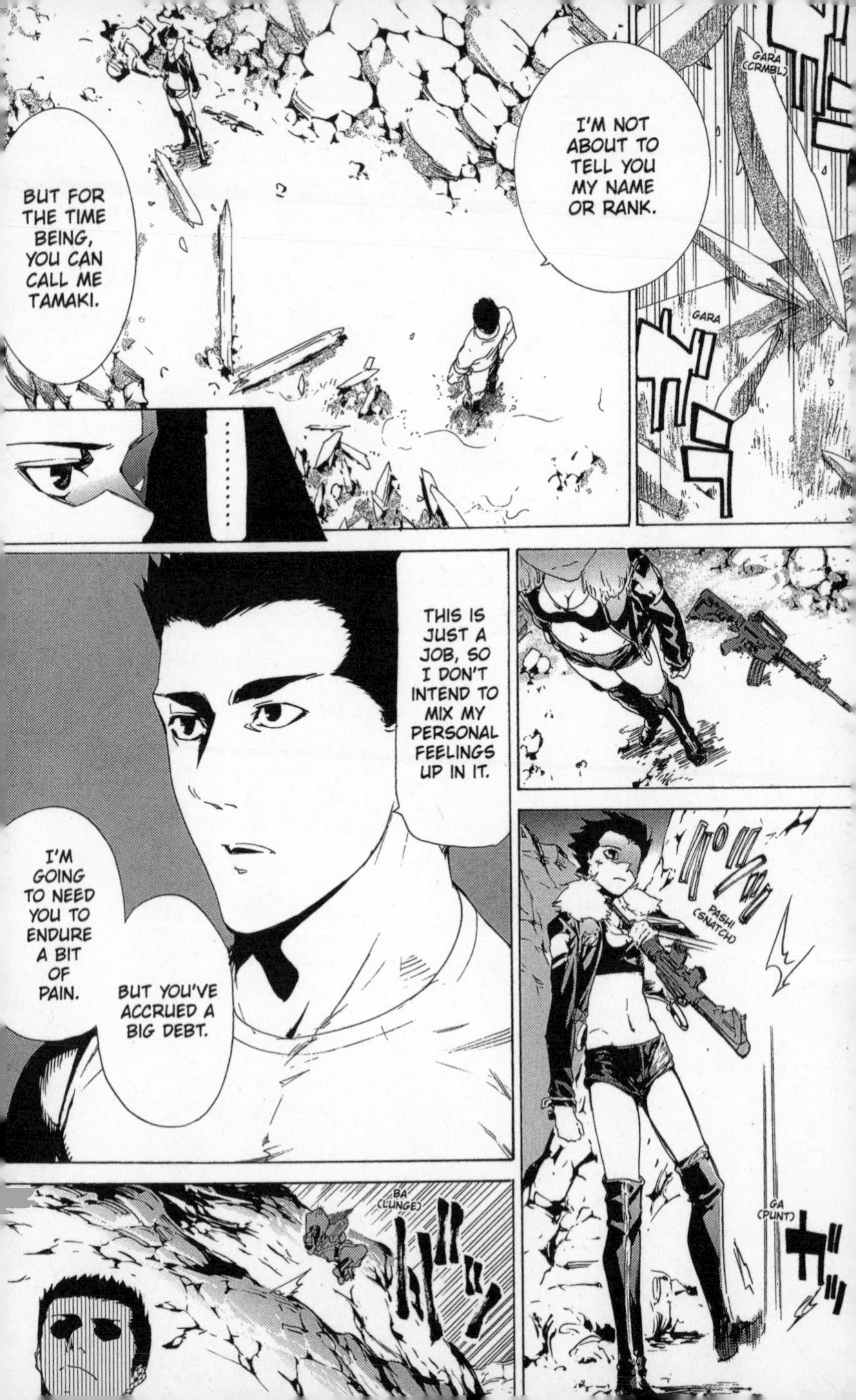
GARA (CRMBL)
GARA
I'M NOT ABOUT TO TELL YOU MY NAME OR RANK.
BUT FOR THE TIME BEING, YOU CAN CALL ME TAMAKI.
PASHI (SNATCH)
GA (PUNT)
THIS IS JUST A JOB, SO I DON'T INTEND TO MIX MY PERSONAL FEELINGS UP IN IT.
BUT YOU'VE ACCRUED A BIG DEBT.
I'M GOING TO NEED YOU TO ENDURE A BIT OF PAIN.
BA (LUNGE)

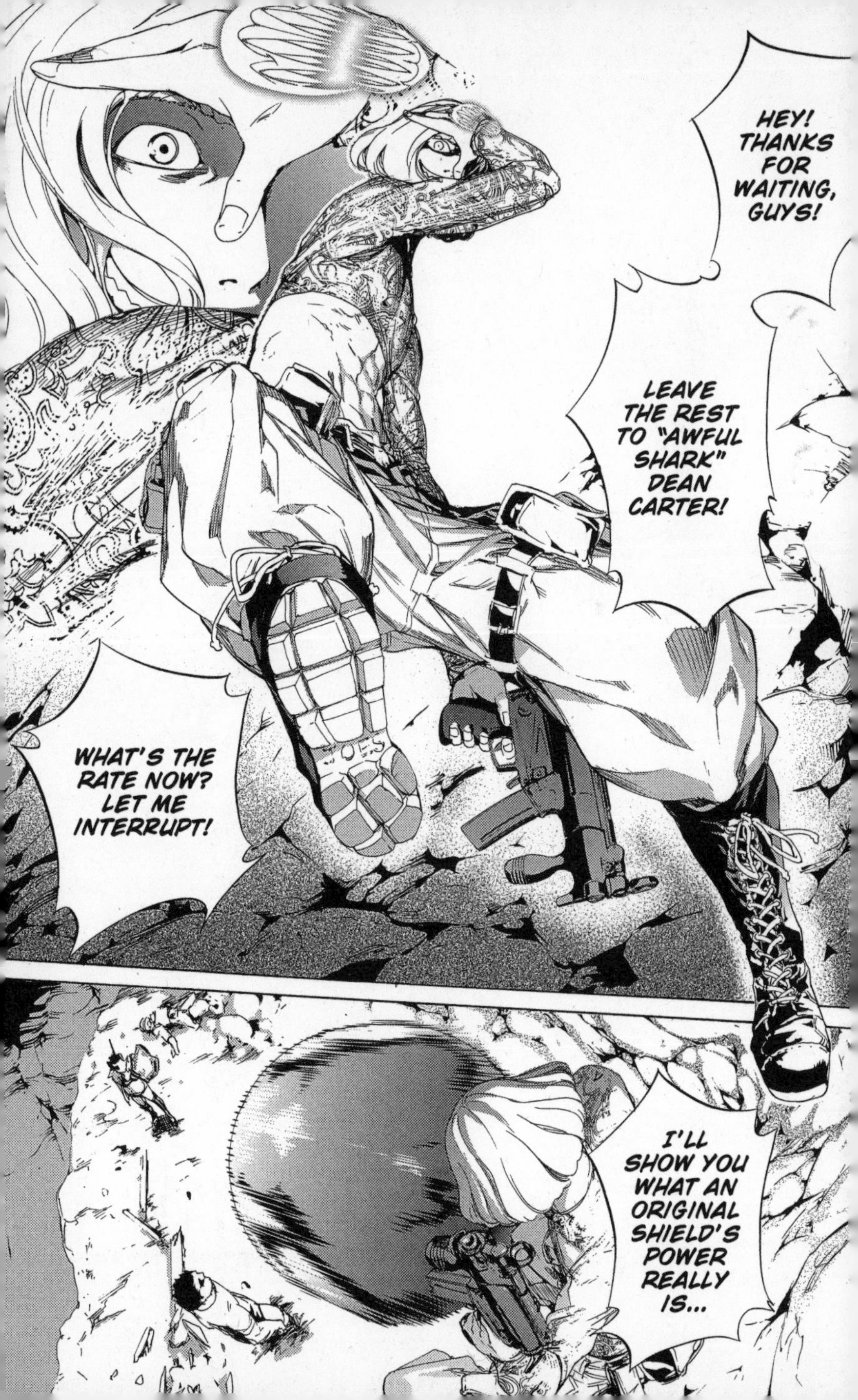
HEY! THANKS FOR WAITING, GUYS!
LEAVE THE REST TO "AWFUL SHARK" DEAN CARTER!
WHAT'S THE RATE NOW? LET ME INTERRUPT!
I'LL SHOW YOU WHAT AN ORIGINAL SHIELD'S POWER REALLY IS...

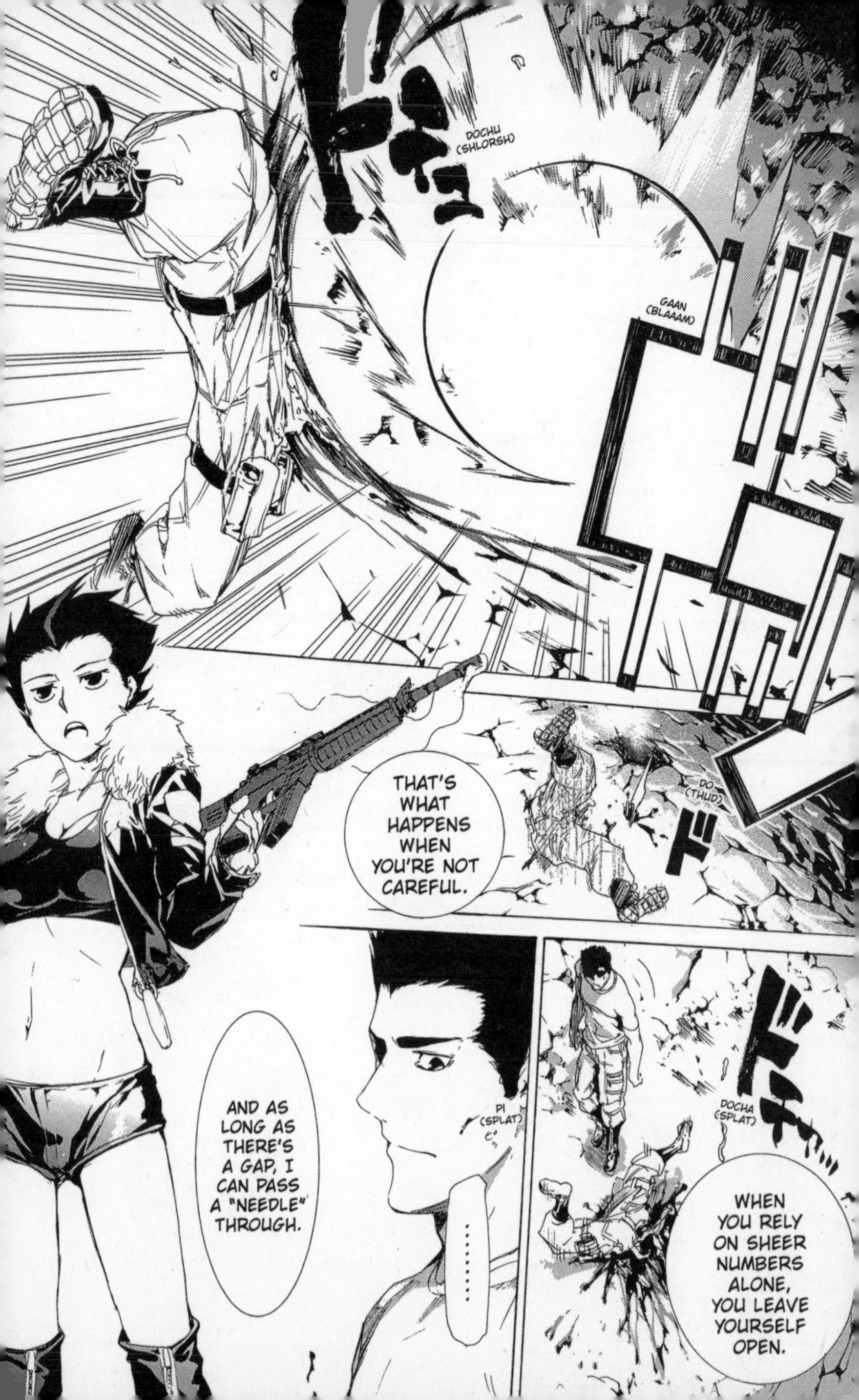
GAAN (BLAAAM)
DOCHU (SHLORSH)
DO (THUD)
THAT'S WHAT HAPPENS WHEN YOU'RE NOT CAREFUL.
DOCHA (SPLAT)
WHEN YOU RELY ON SHEER NUMBERS ALONE, YOU LEAVE YOURSELF OPEN.
PI (SPLAT)
......
AND AS LONG AS THERE'S A GAP, I CAN PASS A "NEEDLE" THROUGH.

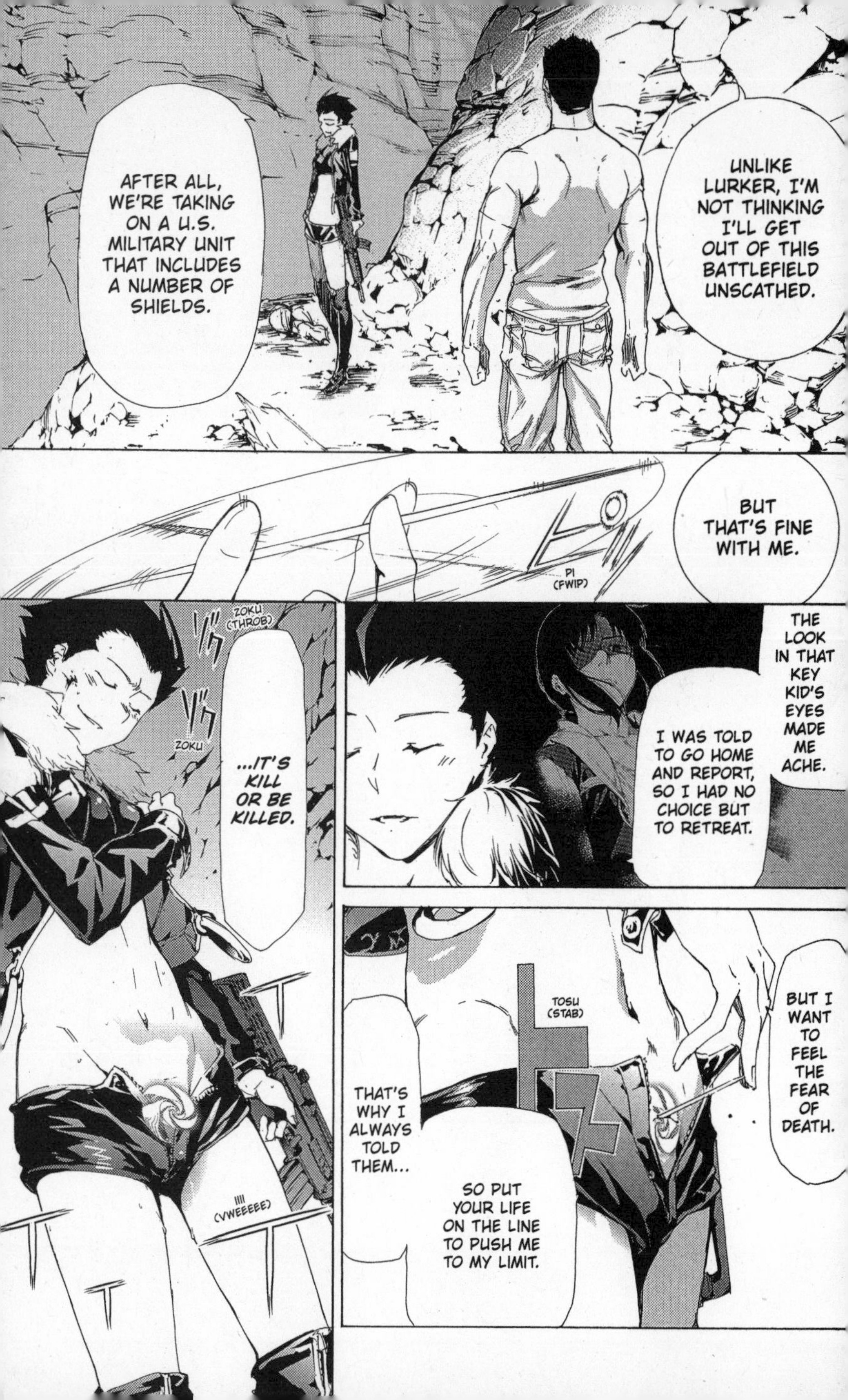
UNLIKE LURKER, I'M NOT THINKING I'LL GET OUT OF THIS BATTLEFIELD UNSCATHED.
AFTER ALL, WE'RE TAKING ON A U.S. MILITARY UNIT THAT INCLUDES A NUMBER OF SHIELDS.
BUT THAT'S FINE WITH ME.
PI (FWIP)
THE LOOK IN THAT KEY KID'S EYES MADE ME ACHE.
I WAS TOLD TO GO HOME AND REPORT, SO I HAD NO CHOICE BUT TO RETREAT.
BUT I WANT TO FEEL THE FEAR OF DEATH.
TOSU (STAB)
THAT'S WHY I ALWAYS TOLD THEM...
SO PUT YOUR LIFE ON THE LINE TO PUSH ME TO MY LIMIT.
ZOKU (THROB)
ZOKU
...IT'S KILL OR BE KILLED.
IIII (VWEEEEE)

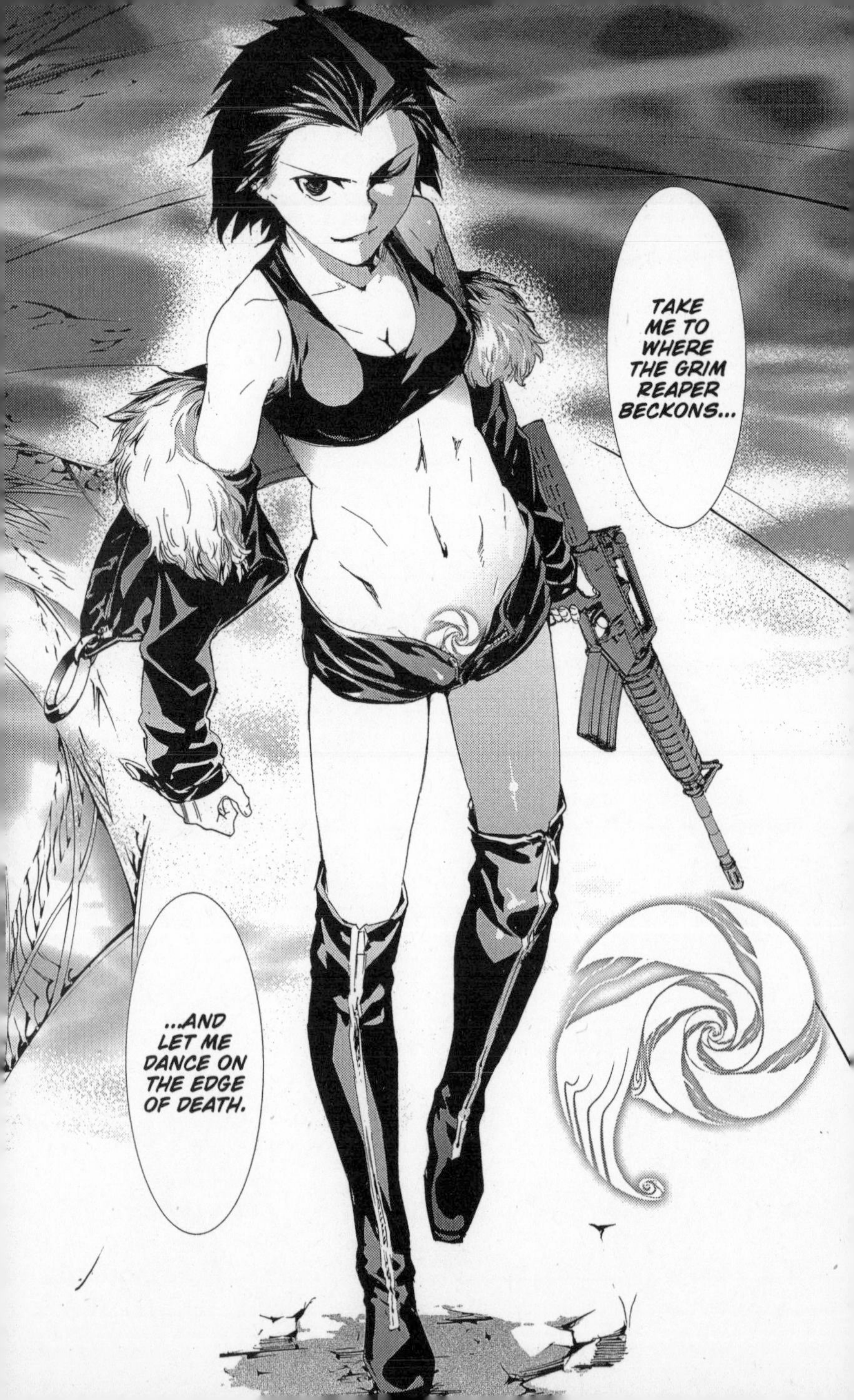
TAKE ME TO WHERE THE GRIM REAPER BECKONS...
...AND LET ME DANCE ON THE EDGE OF DEATH.

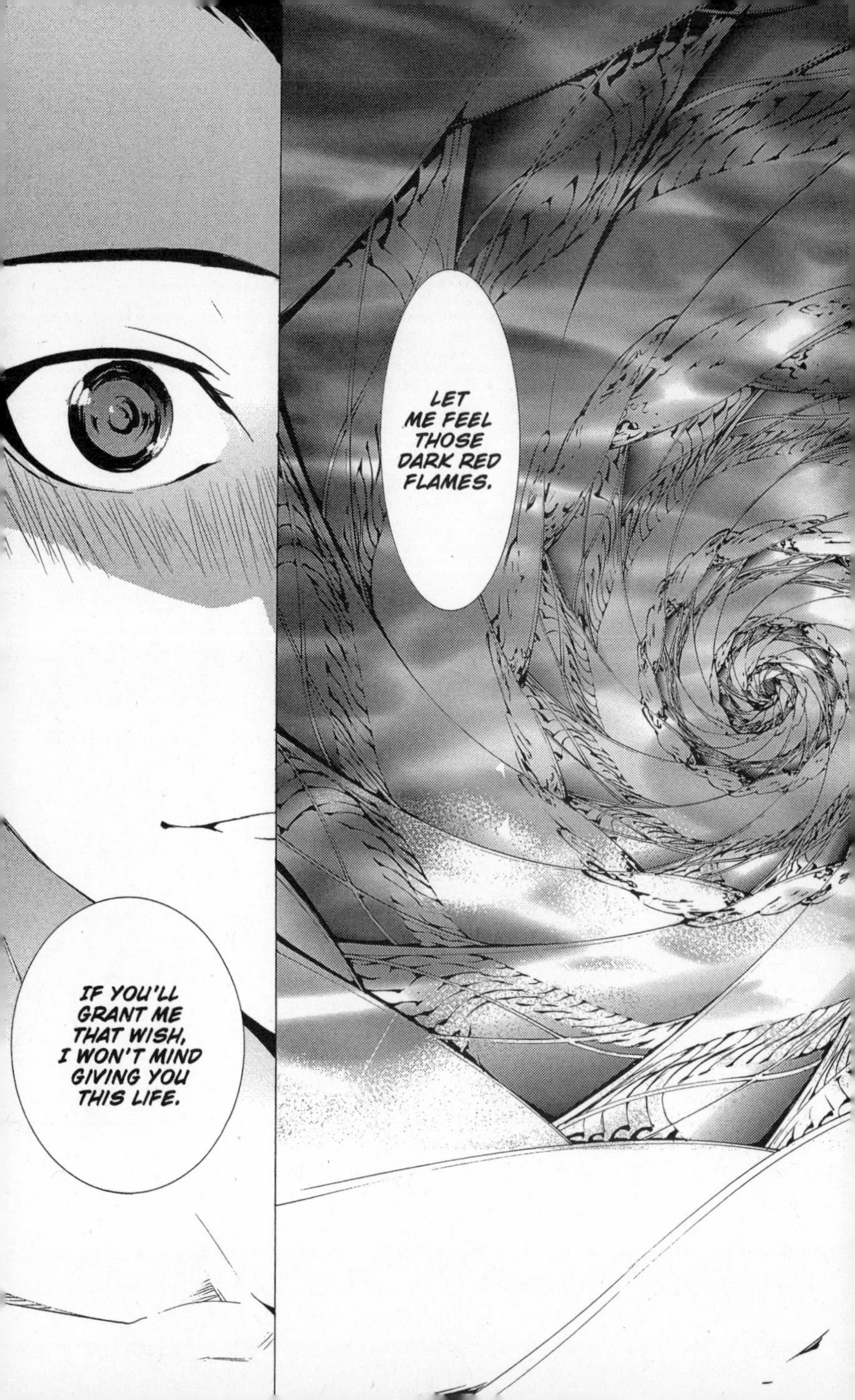
LET ME FEEL THOSE DARK RED FLAMES.
IF YOU'LL GRANT ME THAT WISH, I WON'T MIND GIVING YOU THIS LIFE.

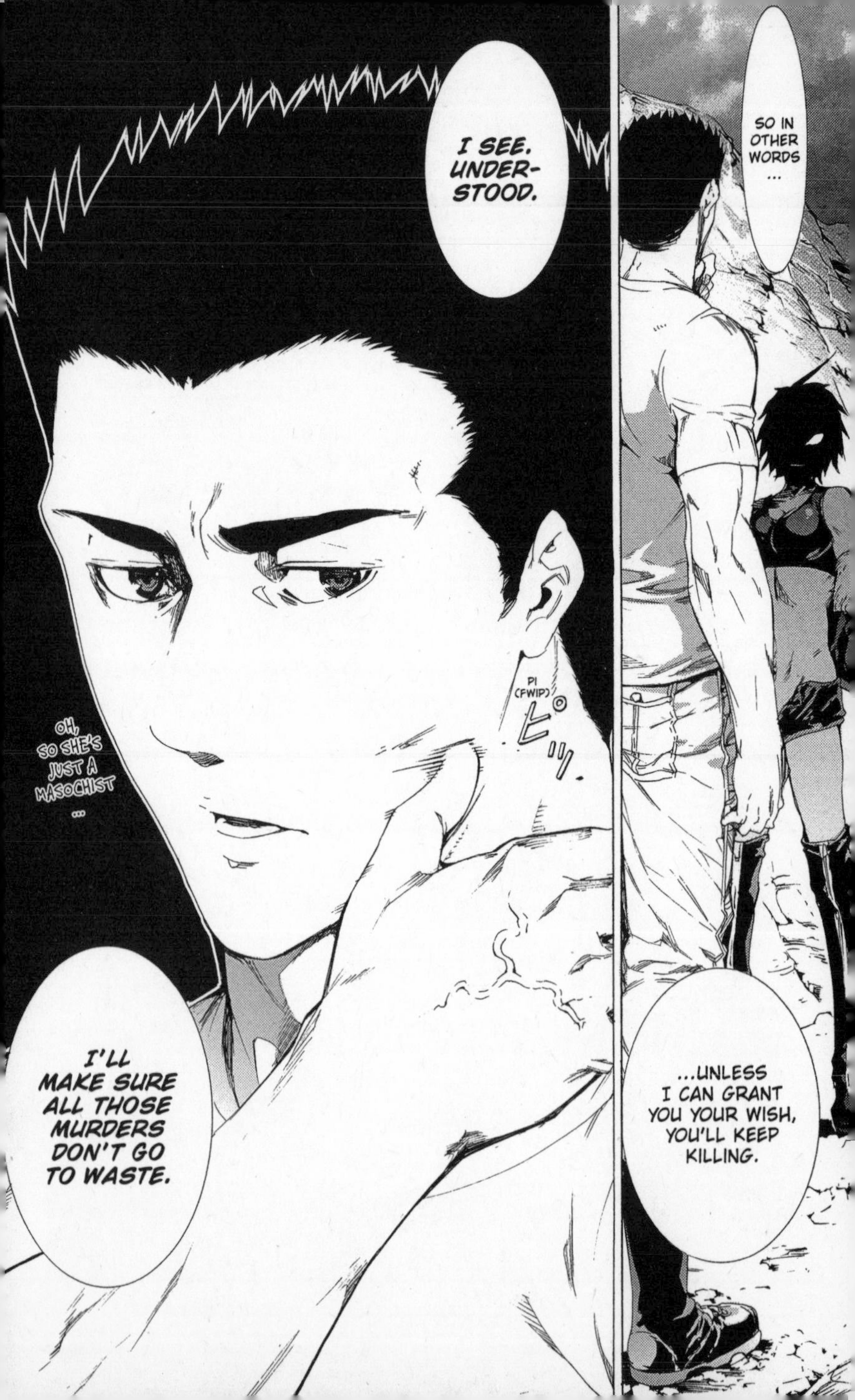
SO IN OTHER WORDS ...
...UNLESS I CAN GRANT YOU YOUR WISH, YOU'LL KEEP KILLING.
I SEE. UNDER-STOOD.
PI (FWIP)
OH, SO SHE'S JUST A MASOCHIST ...
I'LL MAKE SURE ALL THOSE MURDERS DON'T GO TO WASTE.

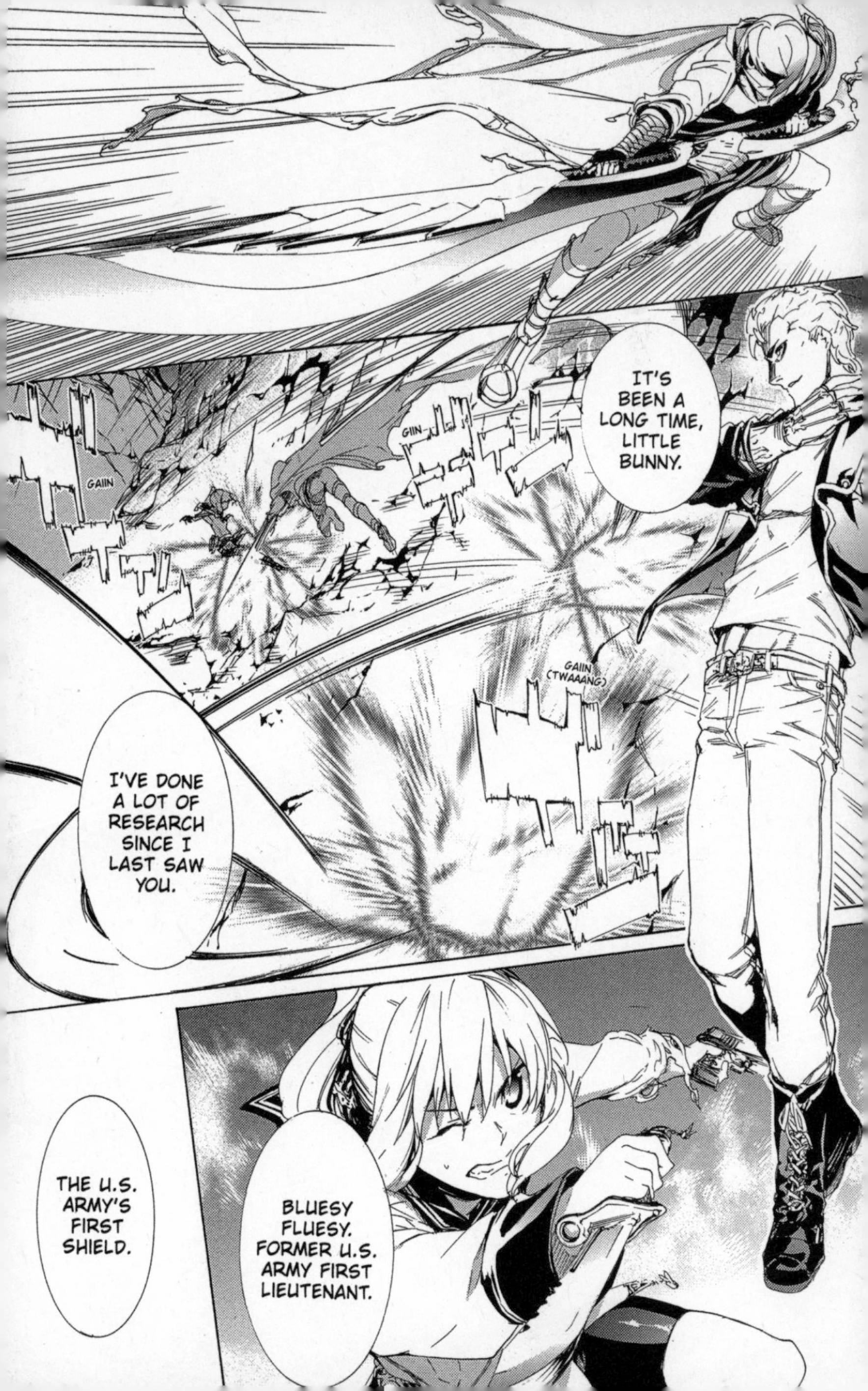
IT'S BEEN A LONG TIME, LITTLE BUNNY.
GIIN
GAIIN
GAIIN (TWAAANG)
I'VE DONE A LOT OF RESEARCH SINCE I LAST SAW YOU.
BLUESY FLUESY. FORMER U.S. ARMY FIRST LIEUTENANT.
THE U.S. ARMY'S FIRST SHIELD.

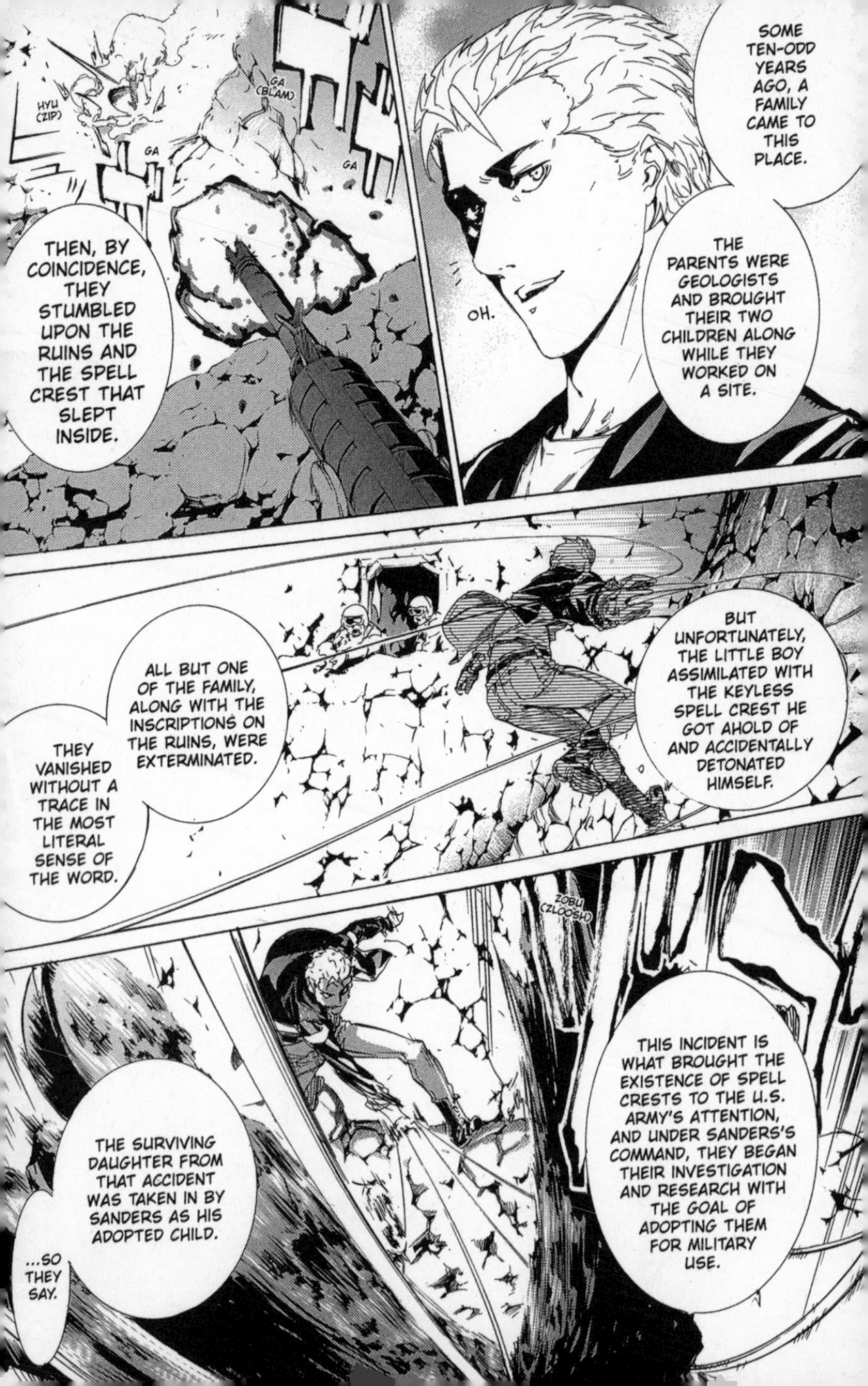
SOME TEN-ODD YEARS AGO, A FAMILY CAME TO THIS PLACE.
THE PARENTS WERE GEOLOGISTS AND BROUGHT THEIR TWO CHILDREN ALONG WHILE THEY WORKED ON A SITE.
OH.
GA (BLAM)
GA
HYU (ZIP)
GA
THEN, BY COINCIDENCE, THEY STUMBLED UPON THE RUINS AND THE SPELL CREST THAT SLEPT INSIDE.
BUT UNFORTUNATELY, THE LITTLE BOY ASSIMILATED WITH THE KEYLESS SPELL CREST HE GOT AHOLD OF AND ACCIDENTALLY DETONATED HIMSELF.
ALL BUT ONE OF THE FAMILY, ALONG WITH THE INSCRIPTIONS ON THE RUINS, WERE EXTERMINATED.
THEY VANISHED WITHOUT A TRACE IN THE MOST LITERAL SENSE OF THE WORD.
ZOBU (ZLOOSH)
THIS INCIDENT IS WHAT BROUGHT THE EXISTENCE OF SPELL CRESTS TO THE U.S. ARMY'S ATTENTION, AND UNDER SANDERS'S COMMAND, THEY BEGAN THEIR INVESTIGATION AND RESEARCH WITH THE GOAL OF ADOPTING THEM FOR MILITARY USE.
THE SURVIVING DAUGHTER FROM THAT ACCIDENT WAS TAKEN IN BY SANDERS AS HIS ADOPTED CHILD.
...SO THEY SAY.

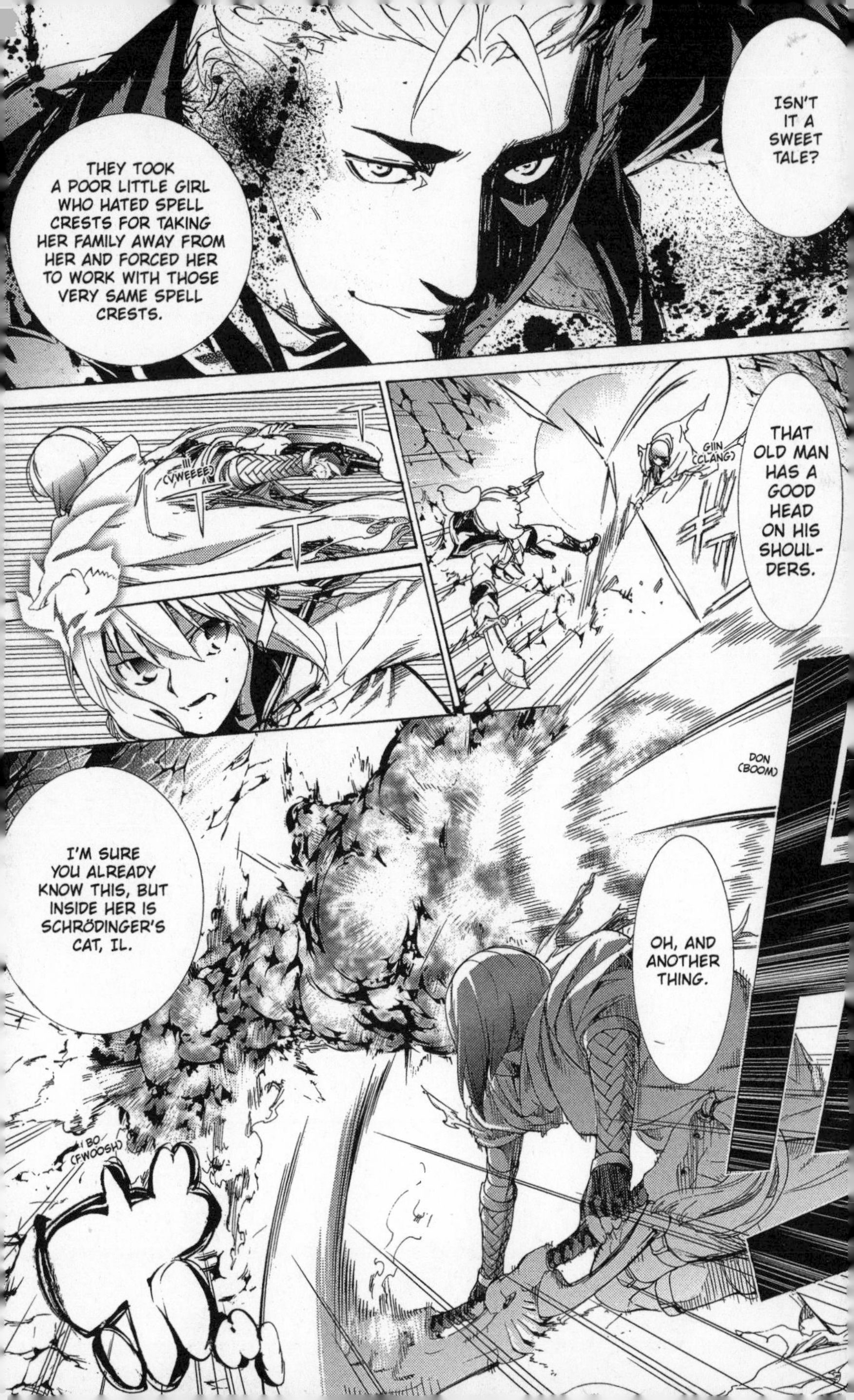
ISN'T IT A SWEET TALE?
THEY TOOK A POOR LITTLE GIRL WHO HATED SPELL CRESTS FOR TAKING HER FAMILY AWAY FROM HER AND FORCED HER TO WORK WITH THOSE VERY SAME SPELL CRESTS.
THAT OLD MAN HAS A GOOD HEAD ON HIS SHOULDERS.
GIIN (CLANG)
(VWEEEE)
DON (BOOM)
OH, AND ANOTHER THING.
I'M SURE YOU ALREADY KNOW THIS, BUT INSIDE HER IS SCHRÖDINGER'S CAT, IL.
BO (FWOOSH)

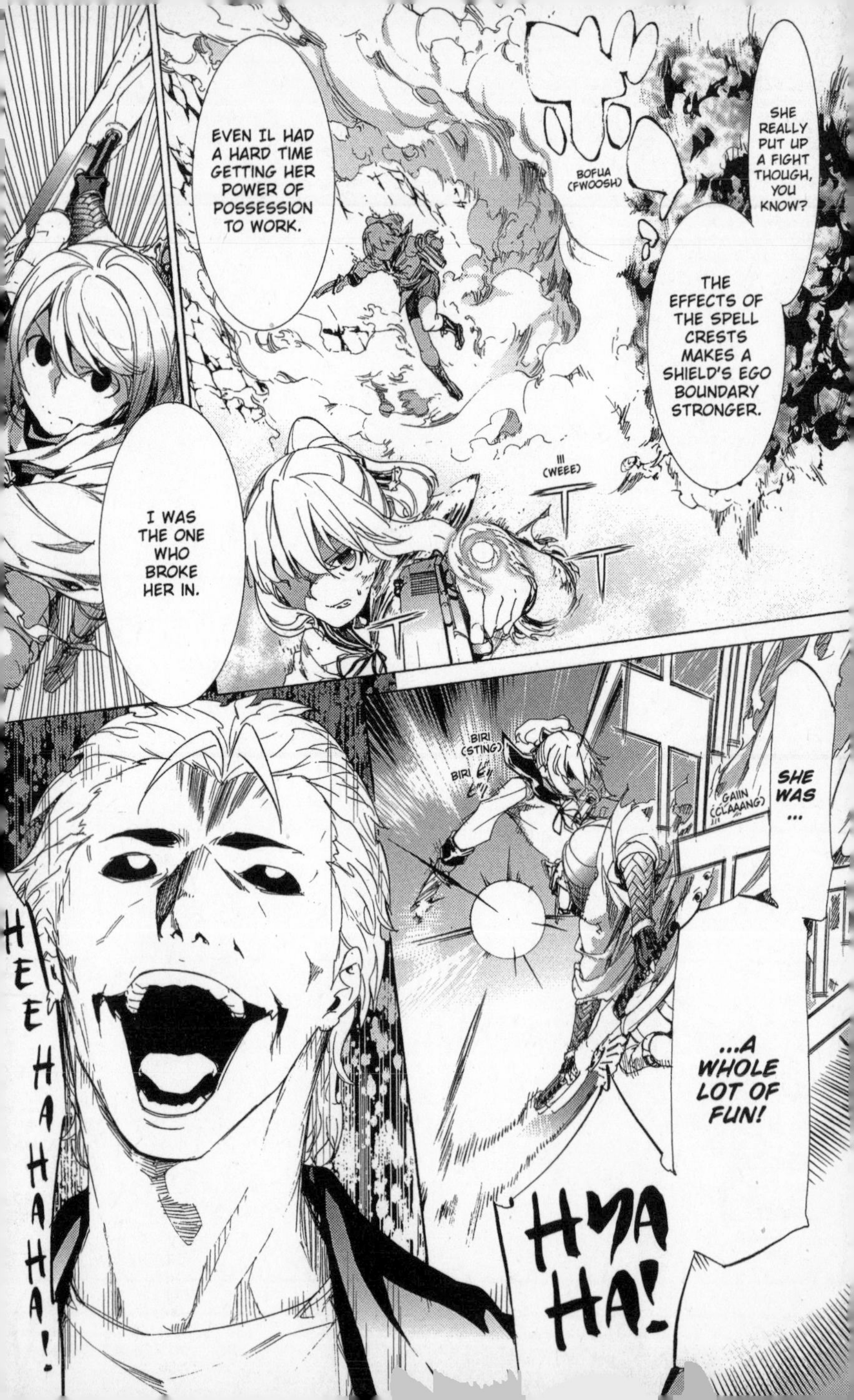

SHE REALLY PUT UP A FIGHT THOUGH, YOU KNOW?
BOFUA (FWOOSH)
THE EFFECTS OF THE SPELL CRESTS MAKES A SHIELD'S EGO BOUNDARY STRONGER.
EVEN IL HAD A HARD TIME GETTING HER POWER OF POSSESSION TO WORK.
III (WEEE)
I WAS THE ONE WHO BROKE HER IN.
SHE WAS ...
GAIIN (CLAAANG)
BIRI (STING)
BIRI
...A WHOLE LOT OF FUN!
HYA HA HA!
HEE HA HA HA HA HA!

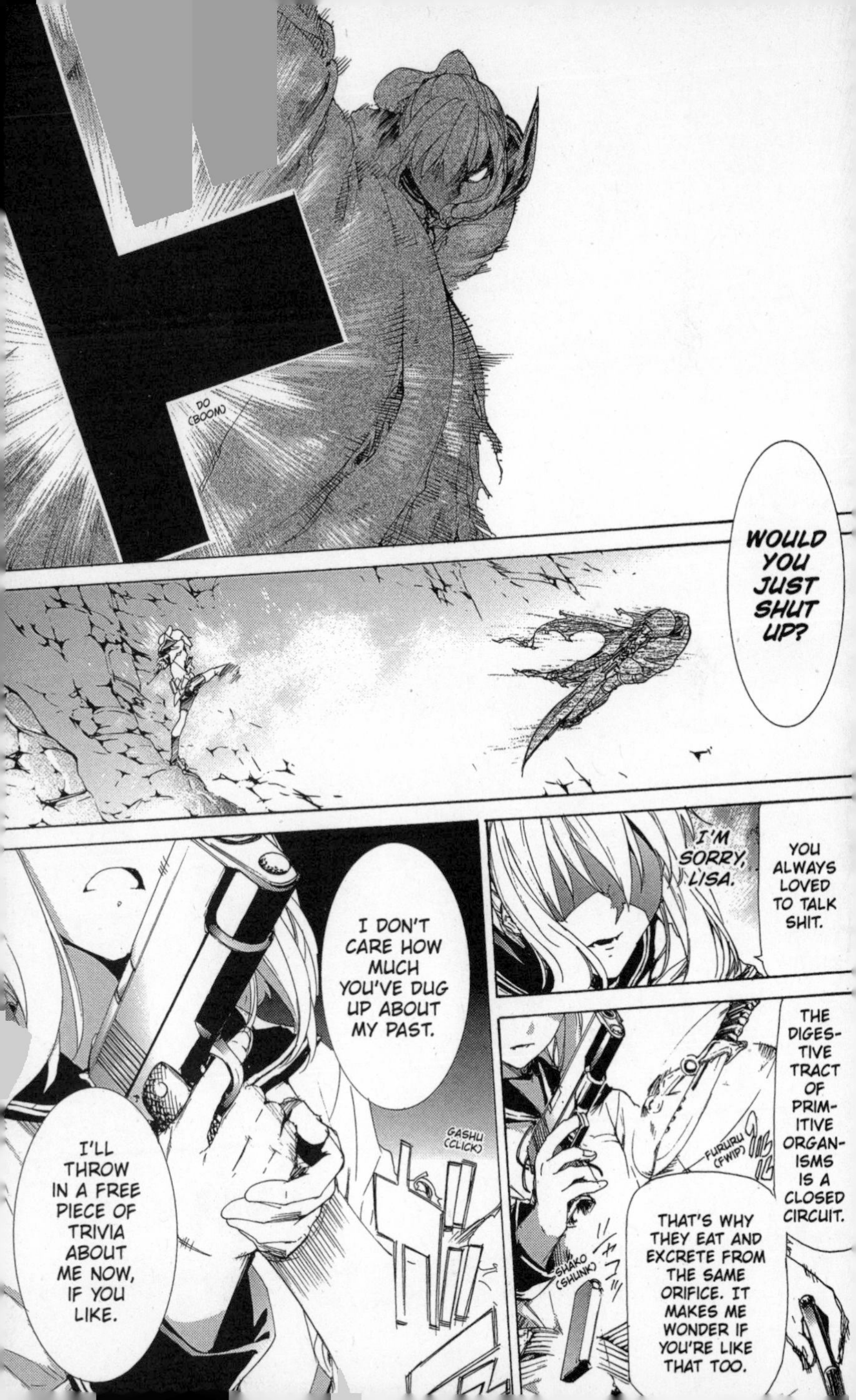
DO (BOOM)
WOULD YOU JUST SHUT UP?
YOU ALWAYS LOVED TO TALK SHIT.
I'M SORRY, LISA.
THE DIGESTIVE TRACT OF PRIMITIVE ORGANISMS IS A CLOSED CIRCUIT.
FURURU (FWIP)
THAT'S WHY THEY EAT AND EXCRETE FROM THE SAME ORIFICE. IT MAKES ME WONDER IF YOU'RE LIKE THAT TOO.
SHAKO (SHUNK)
I DON'T CARE HOW MUCH YOU'VE DUG UP ABOUT MY PAST.
GASHU (CLICK)
I'LL THROW IN A FREE PIECE OF TRIVIA ABOUT ME NOW, IF YOU LIKE.

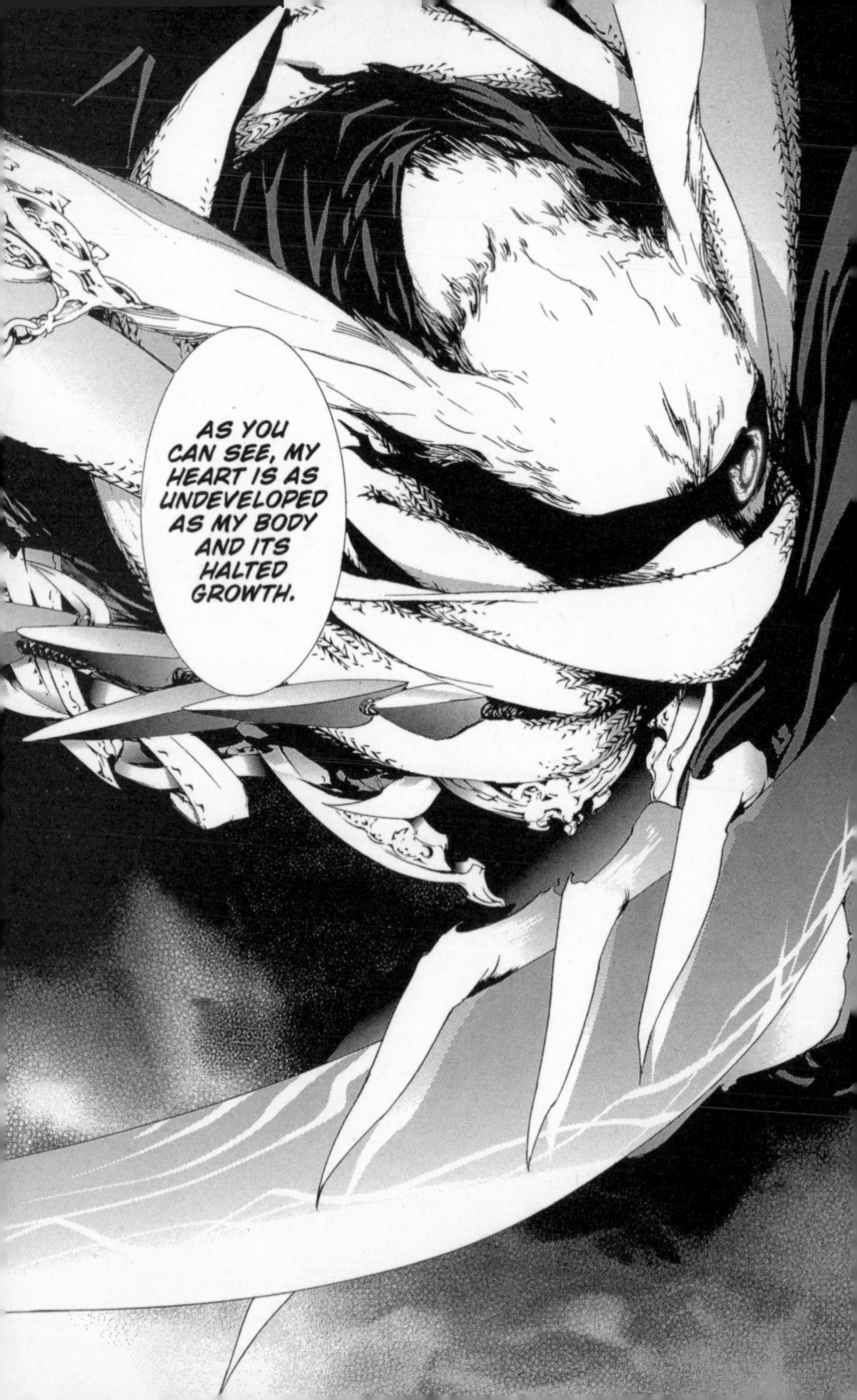
AS YOU CAN SEE, MY HEART IS AS UNDEVELOPED AS MY BODY AND ITS HALTED GROWTH.

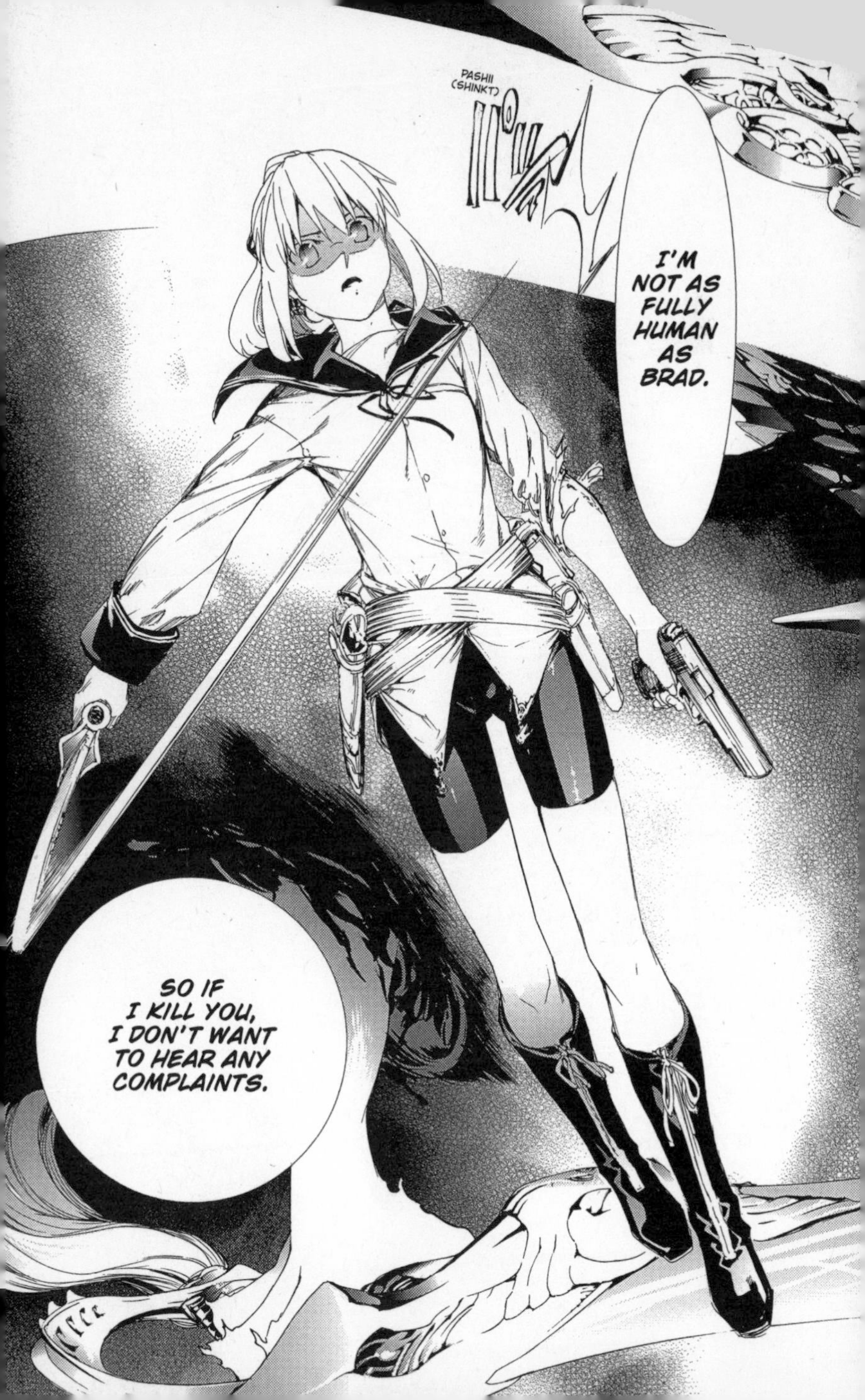
PASHII (SHINKT)
I'M NOT AS FULLY HUMAN AS BRAD.
SO IF I KILL YOU, I DON'T WANT TO HEAR ANY COMPLAINTS.

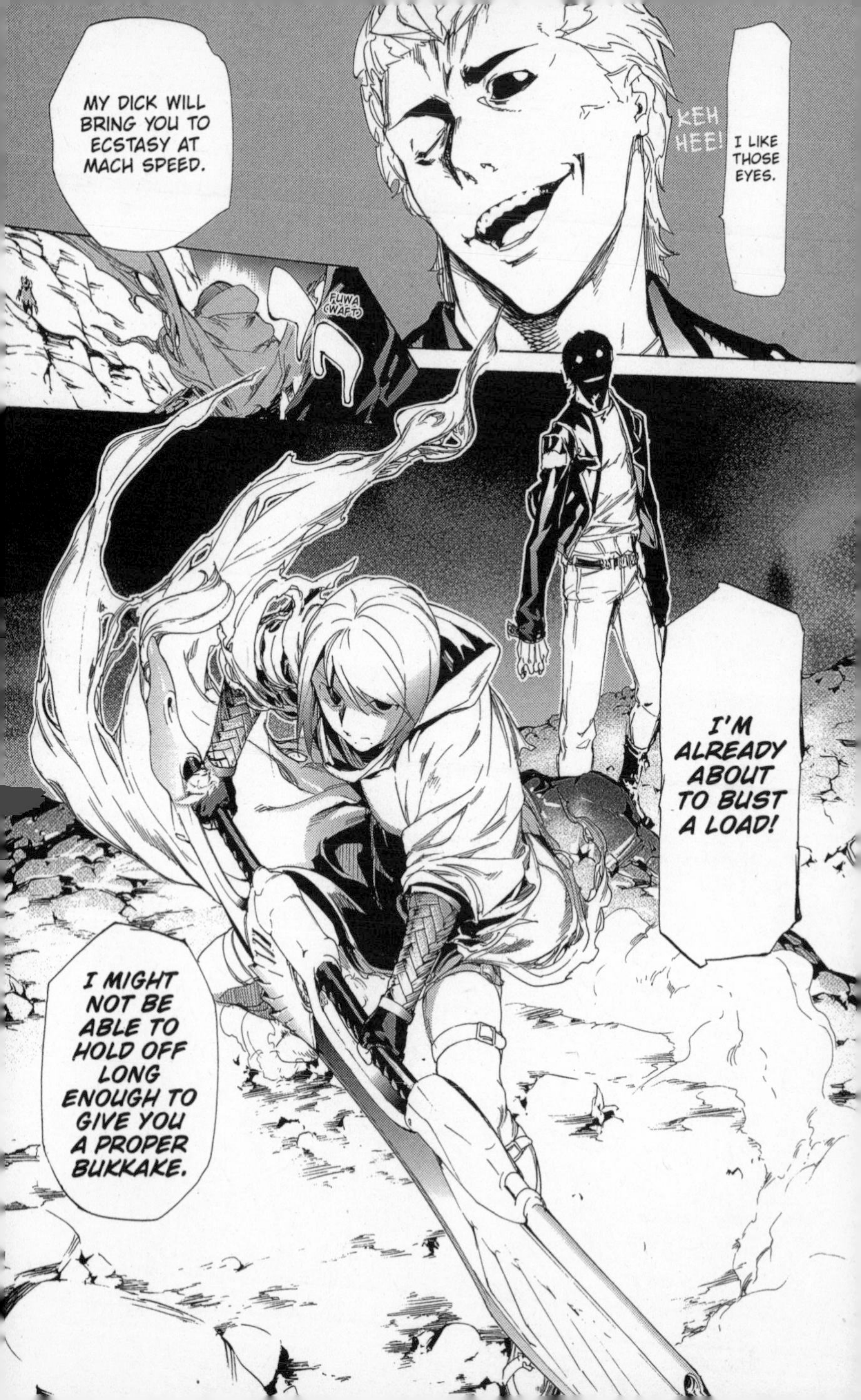
KEH HEE!
I LIKE THOSE EYES.
MY DICK WILL BRING YOU TO ECSTASY AT MACH SPEED.
FUWA (WAFT)
I'M ALREADY ABOUT TO BUST A LOAD!
I MIGHT NOT BE ABLE TO HOLD OFF LONG ENOUGH TO GIVE YOU A PROPER BUKKAKE.

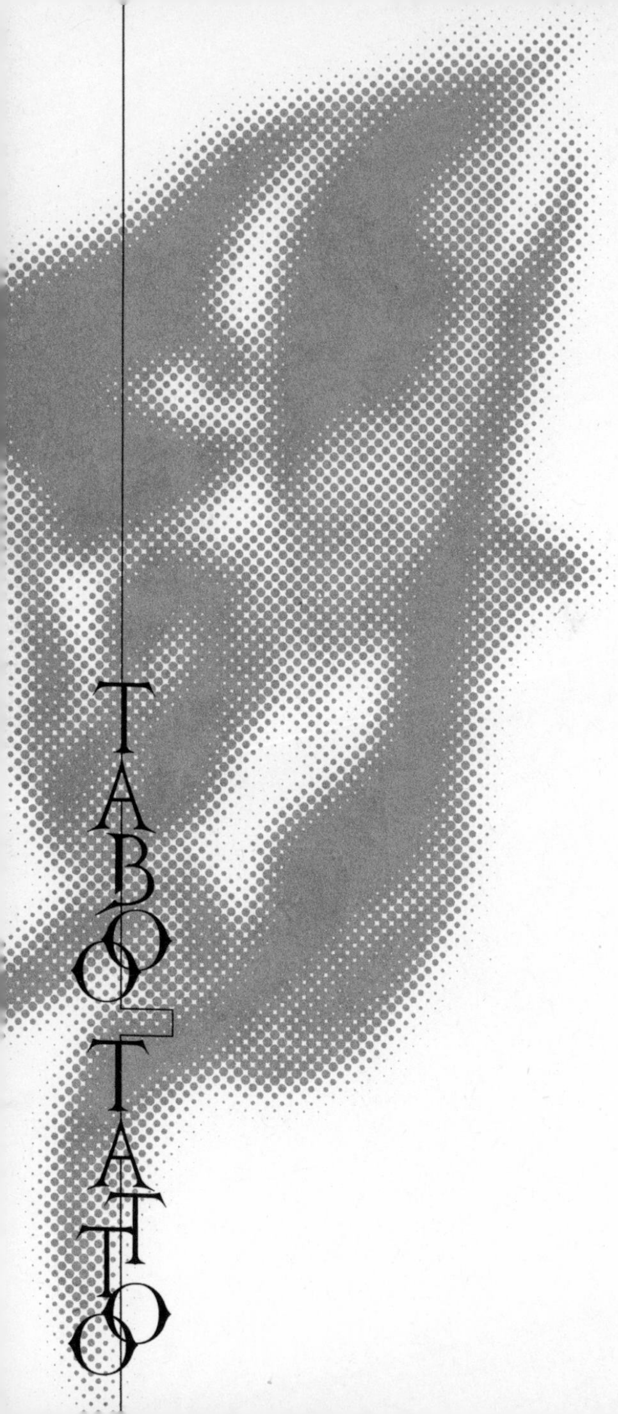

TABOO TATTOO

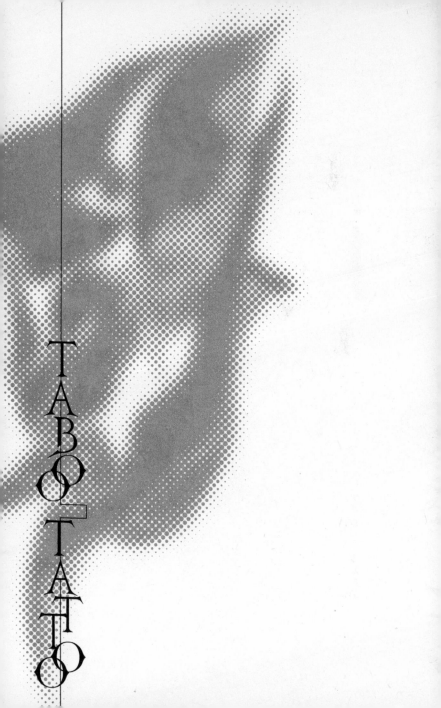

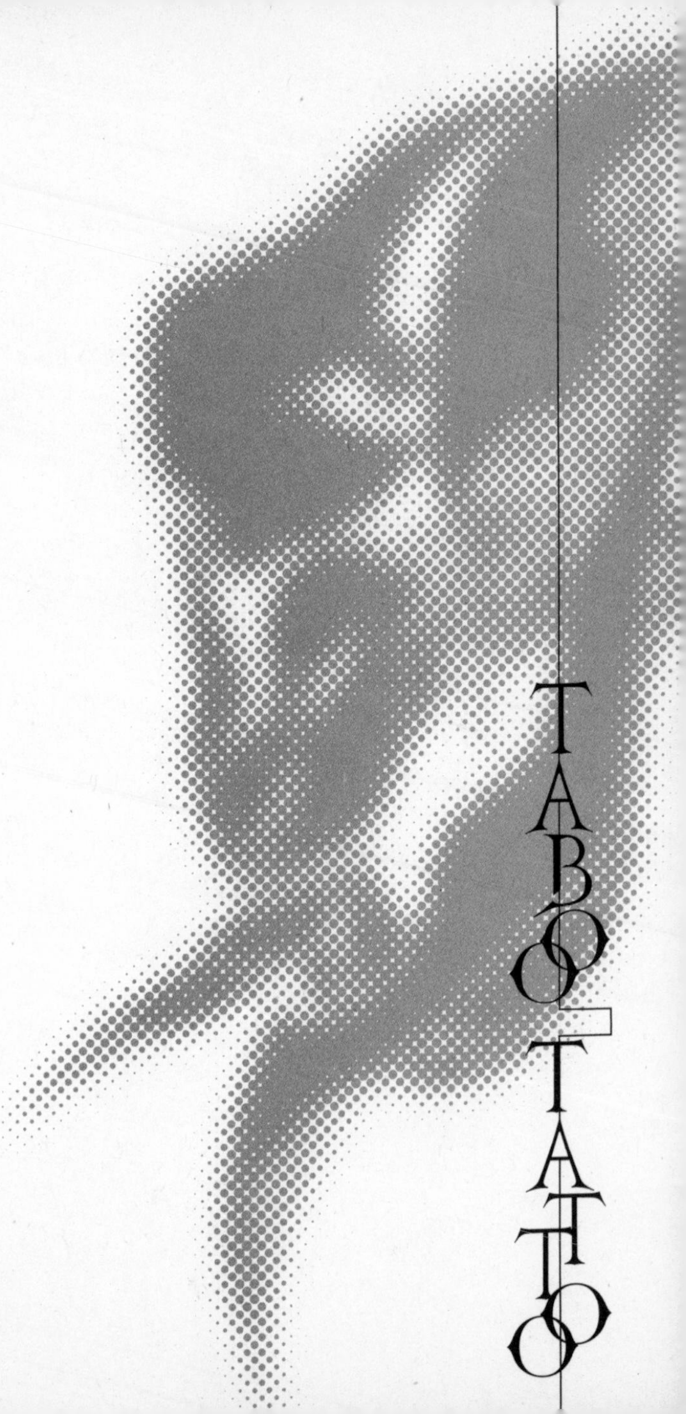
TABOO TATTOO

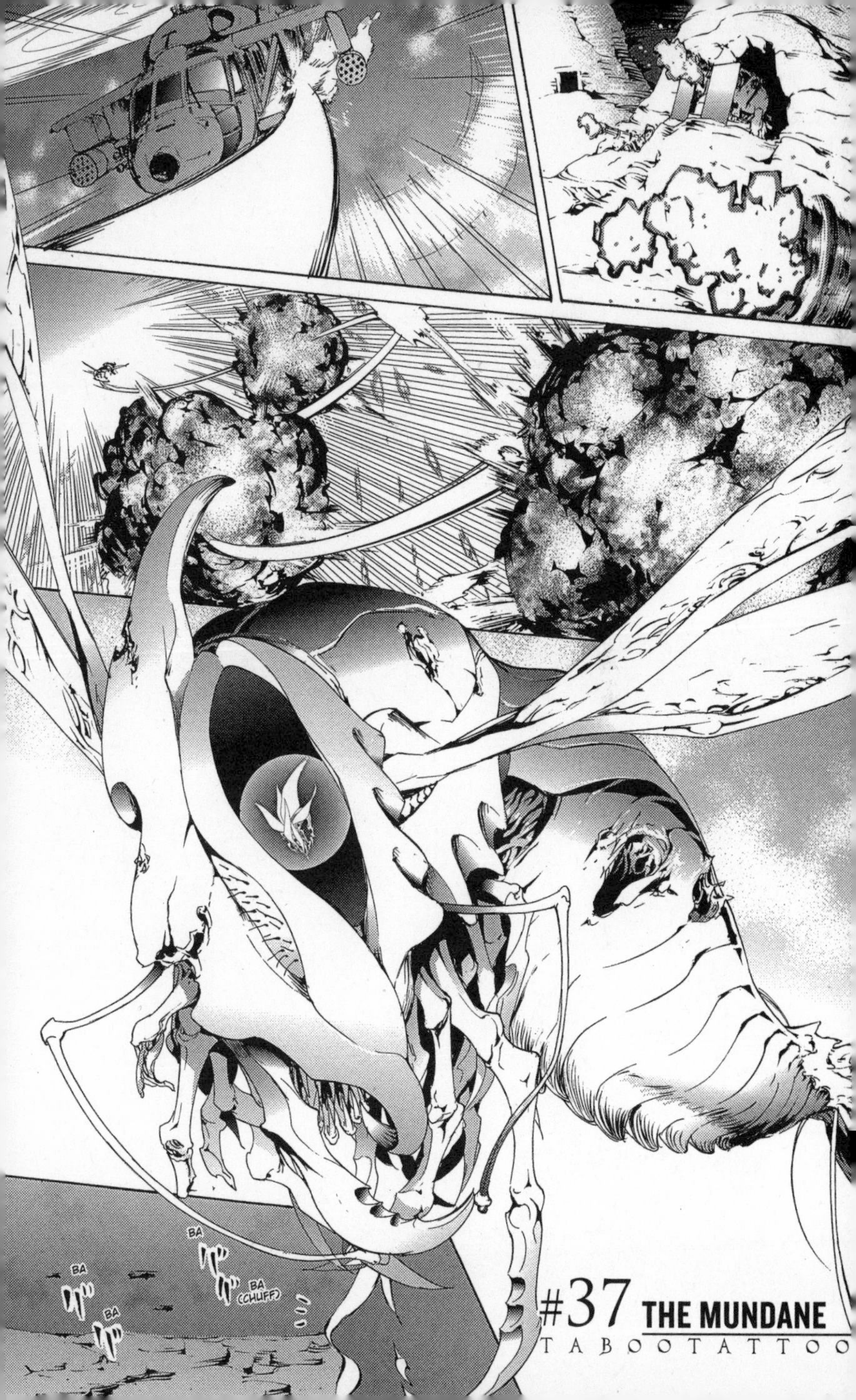
BA
BA (CHUFF)
BA
BA

#37 THE MUNDANE

TABOOTATTOO

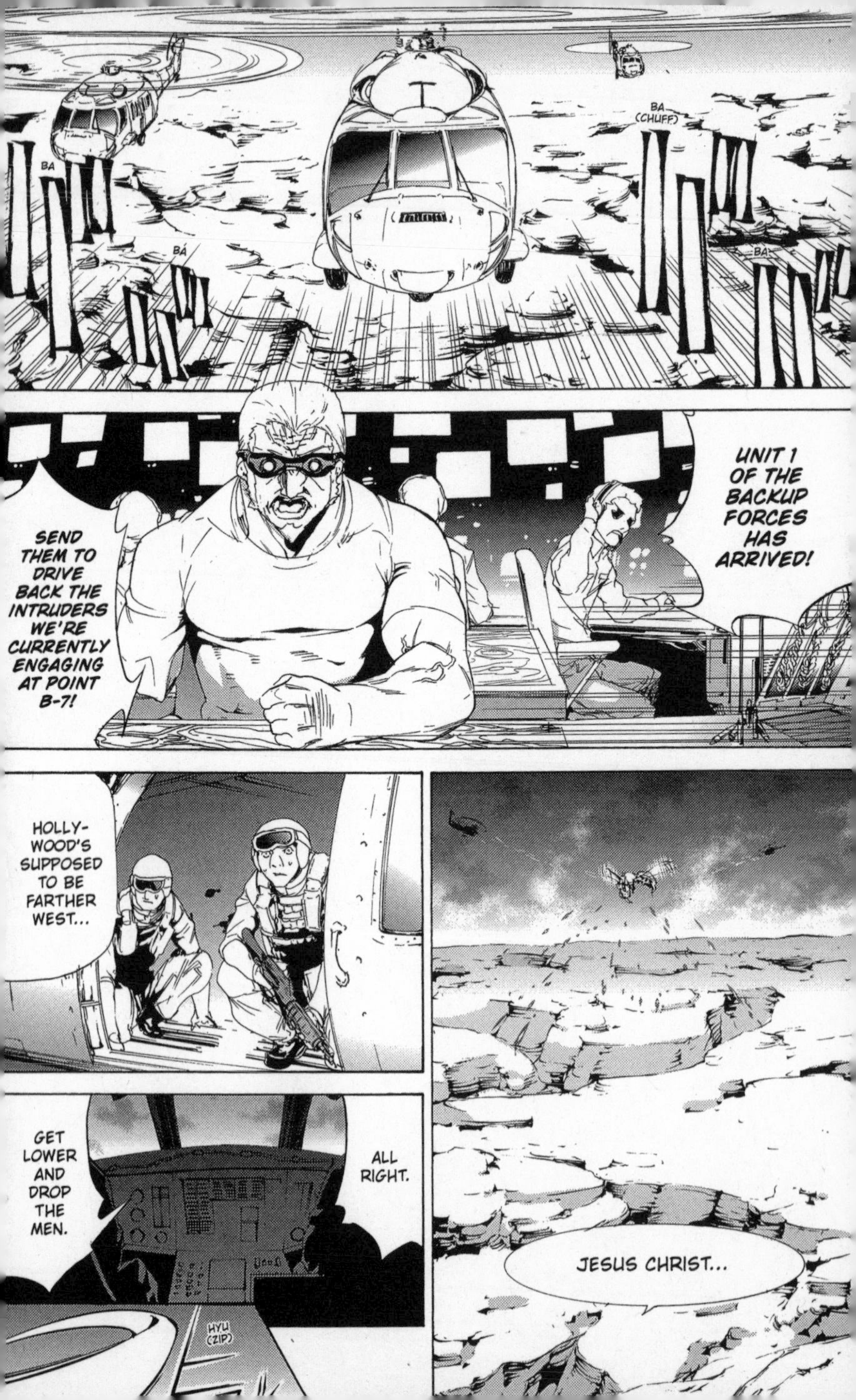
BA (CHUFF)
BA
BA
BÁ
UNIT 1 OF THE BACKUP FORCES HAS ARRIVED!
SEND THEM TO DRIVE BACK THE INTRUDERS WE'RE CURRENTLY ENGAGING AT POINT B-7!
JESUS CHRIST...
HOLLY-WOOD'S SUPPOSED TO BE FARTHER WEST...
GET LOWER AND DROP THE MEN.
ALL RIGHT.
HYU (ZIP)

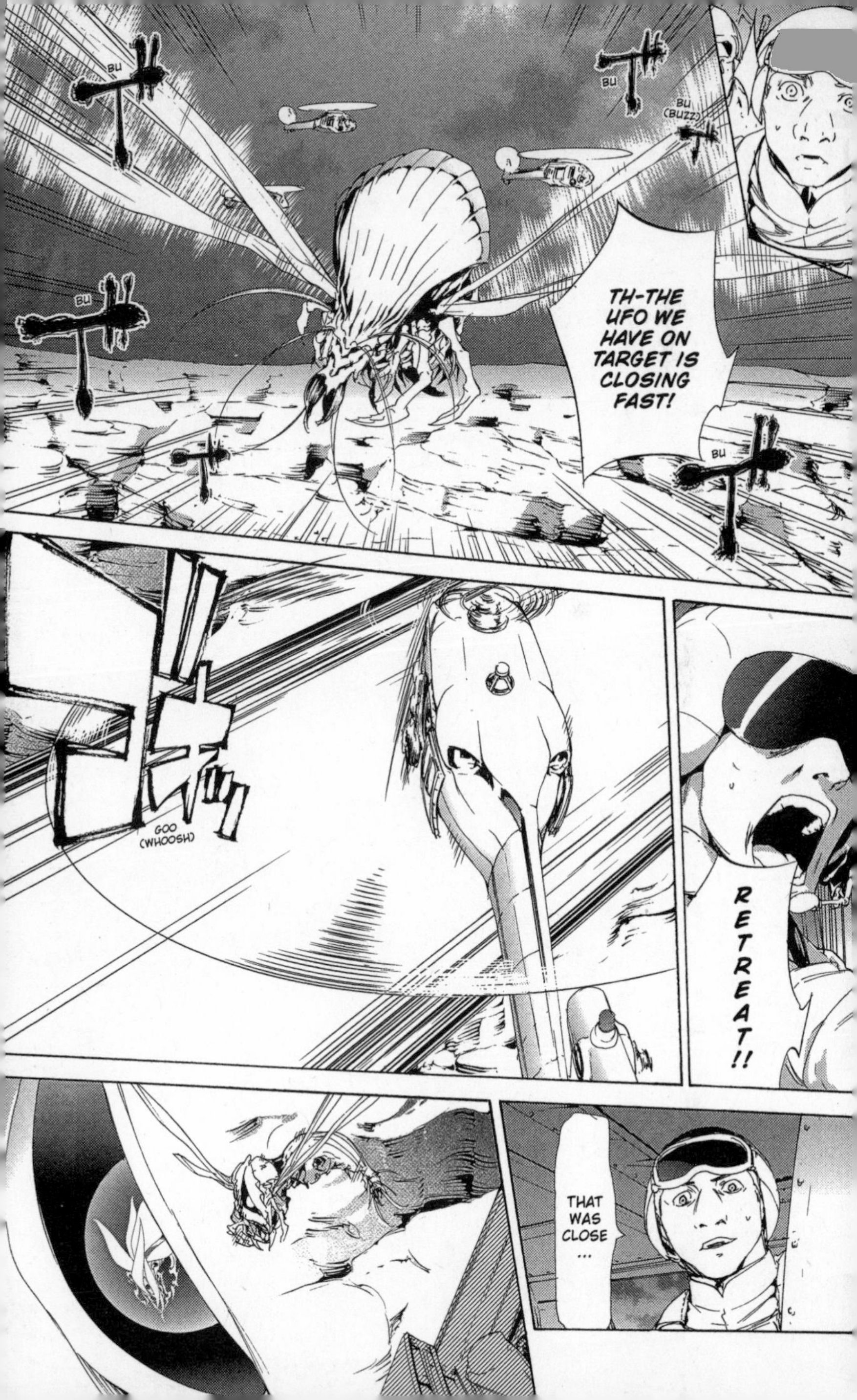
BU
BU (BUZZ)
TH-THE UFO WE HAVE ON TARGET IS CLOSING FAST!
BU
BU
BU
RETREAT!!
GOO (WHOOSH)
THAT WAS CLOSE ...

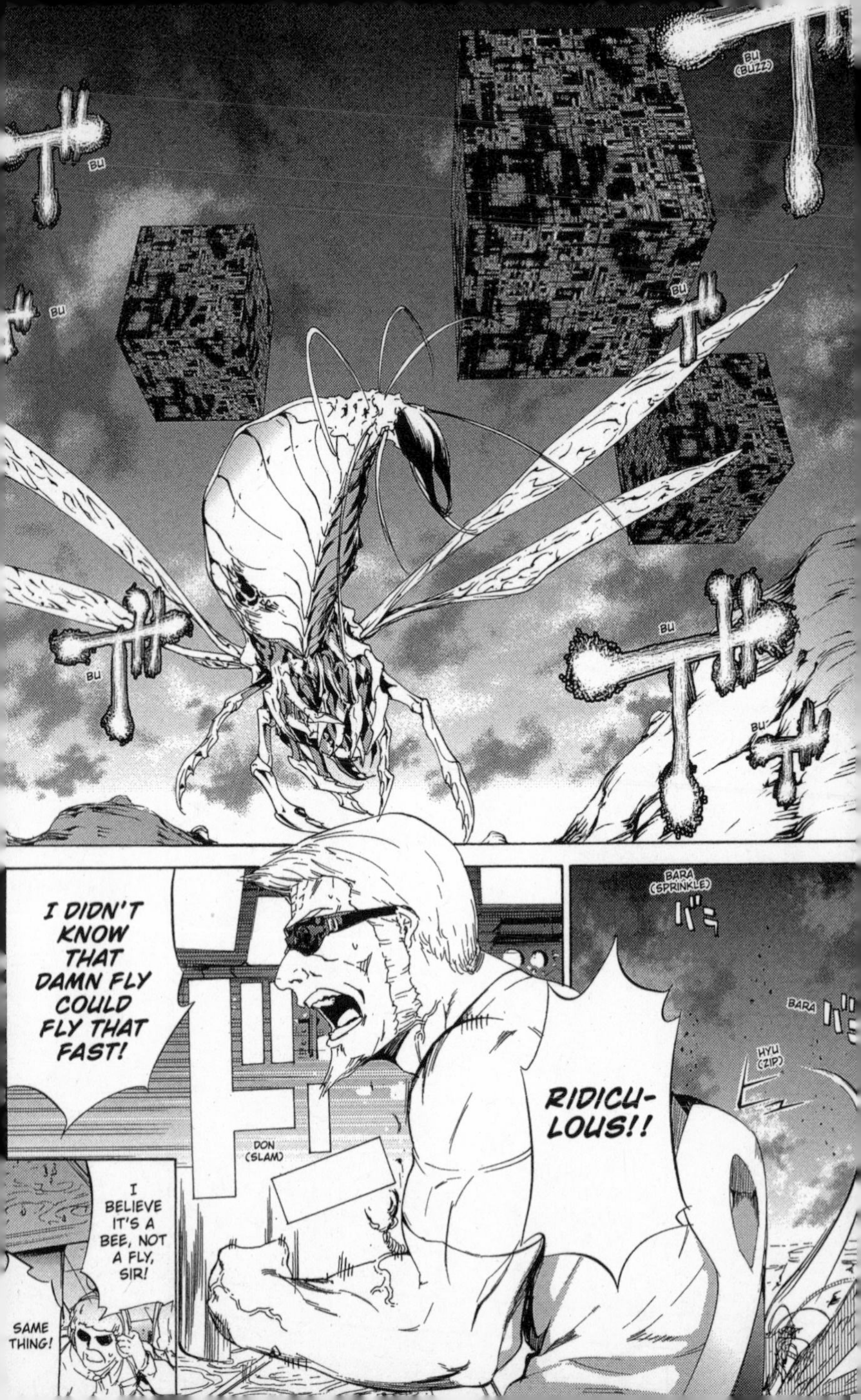

BU (BUZZ)
BU
BU
BU
BU
BU
BU
BARA (SPRINKLE)
BARA
HYU (ZIP)
RIDICU-LOUS!!
I DIDN'T KNOW THAT DAMN FLY COULD FLY THAT FAST!
DON (SLAM)
I BELIEVE IT'S A BEE, NOT A FLY, SIR!
SAME THING!

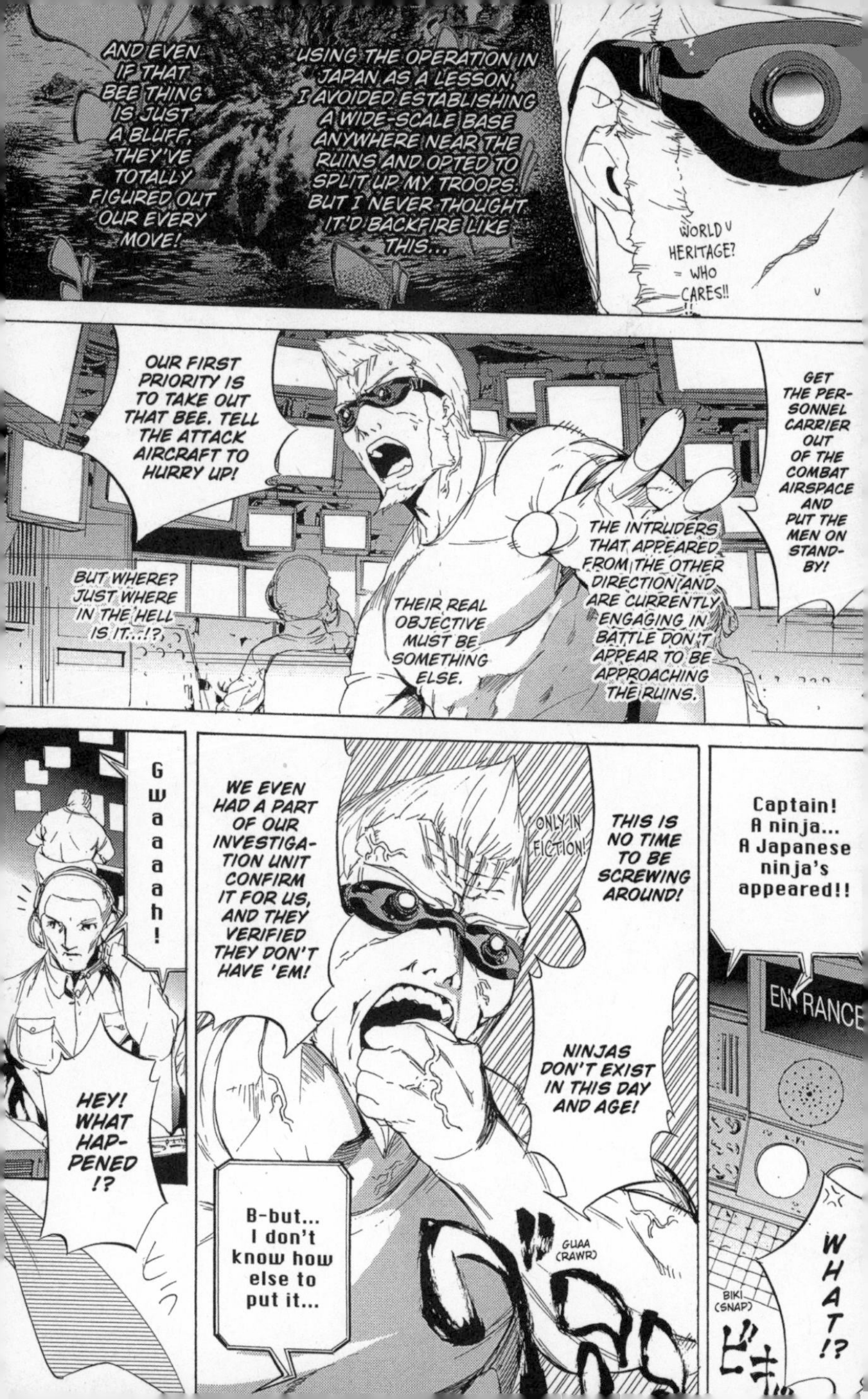
WORLD HERITAGE? WHO CARES!!
USING THE OPERATION IN JAPAN AS A LESSON, I AVOIDED ESTABLISHING A WIDE-SCALE BASE ANYWHERE NEAR THE RUINS AND OPTED TO SPLIT UP MY TROOPS. BUT I NEVER THOUGHT IT'D BACKFIRE LIKE THIS...
AND EVEN IF THAT BEE THING IS JUST A BLUFF, THEY'VE TOTALLY FIGURED OUT OUR EVERY MOVE!
GET THE PER-SONNEL CARRIER OUT OF THE COMBAT AIRSPACE AND PUT THE MEN ON STAND-BY!
OUR FIRST PRIORITY IS TO TAKE OUT THAT BEE. TELL THE ATTACK AIRCRAFT TO HURRY UP!
THE INTRUDERS THAT APPEARED FROM THE OTHER DIRECTION AND ARE CURRENTLY ENGAGING IN BATTLE DON'T APPEAR TO BE APPROACHING THE RUINS.
THEIR REAL OBJECTIVE MUST BE SOMETHING ELSE.
BUT WHERE? JUST WHERE IN THE HELL IS IT...!?
Captain! A ninja... A Japanese ninja's appeared!!
BIKI (SNAP)
WHAT!?
THIS IS NO TIME TO BE SCREWING AROUND!
ONLY IN FICTION!
WE EVEN HAD A PART OF OUR INVESTIGA-TION UNIT CONFIRM IT FOR US, AND THEY VERIFIED THEY DON'T HAVE 'EM!
NINJAS DON'T EXIST IN THIS DAY AND AGE!
B-but... I don't know how else to put it...
GUAA (RAWR)
Gwaaaaah!
HEY! WHAT HAP-PENED!?

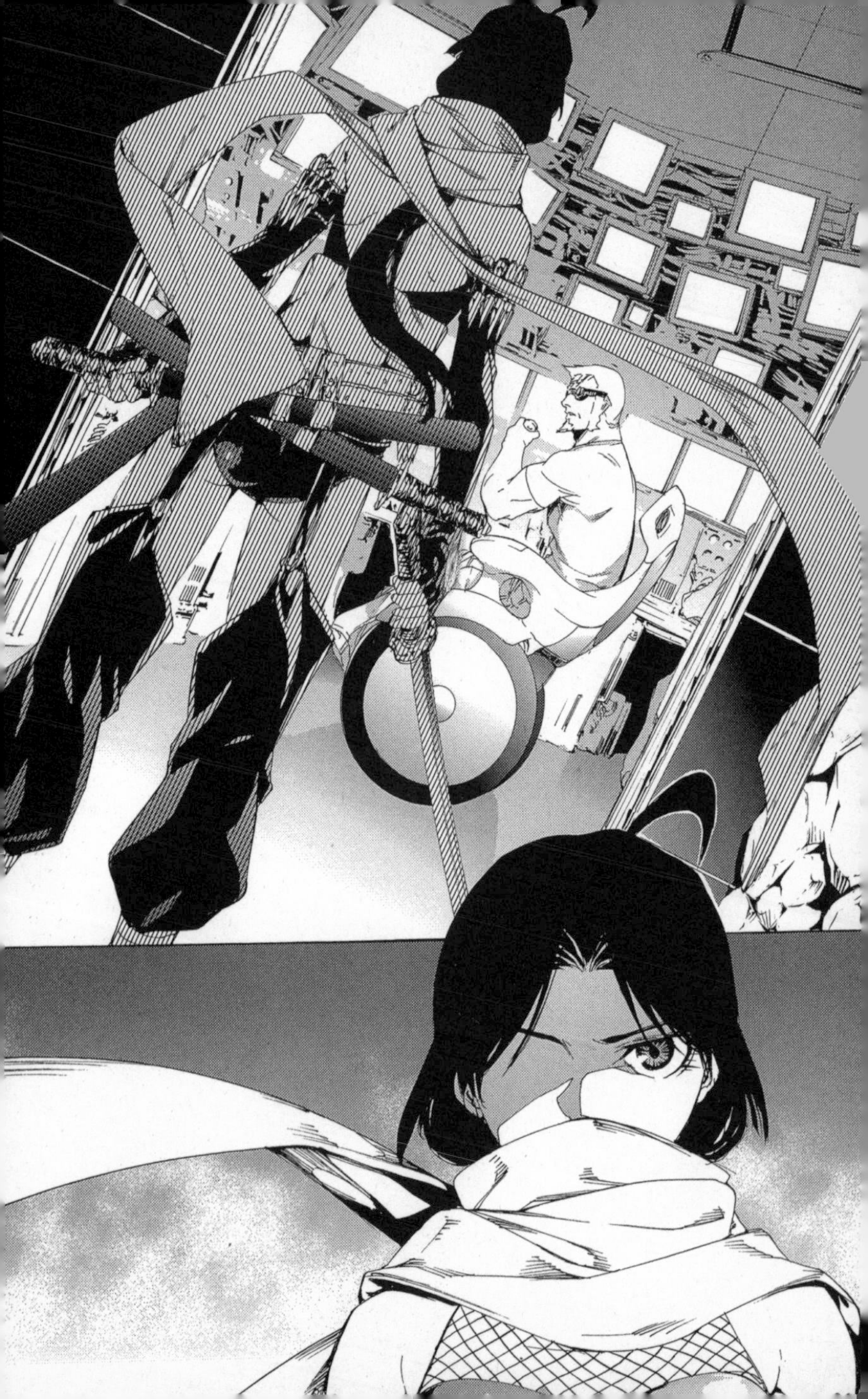

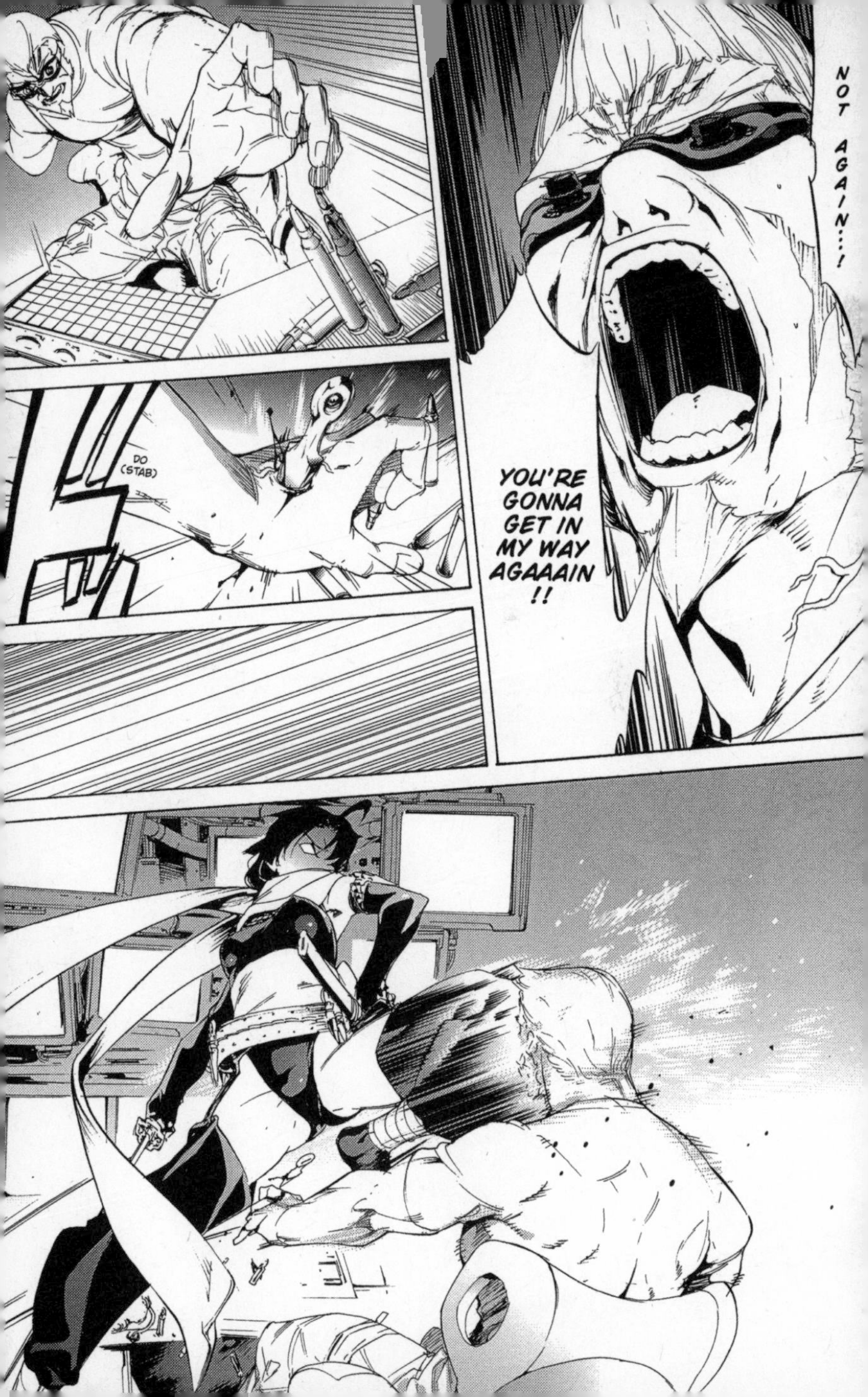
NOT AGAIN...!
YOU'RE GONNA GET IN MY WAY AGAAAIN!!
DO (STAB)

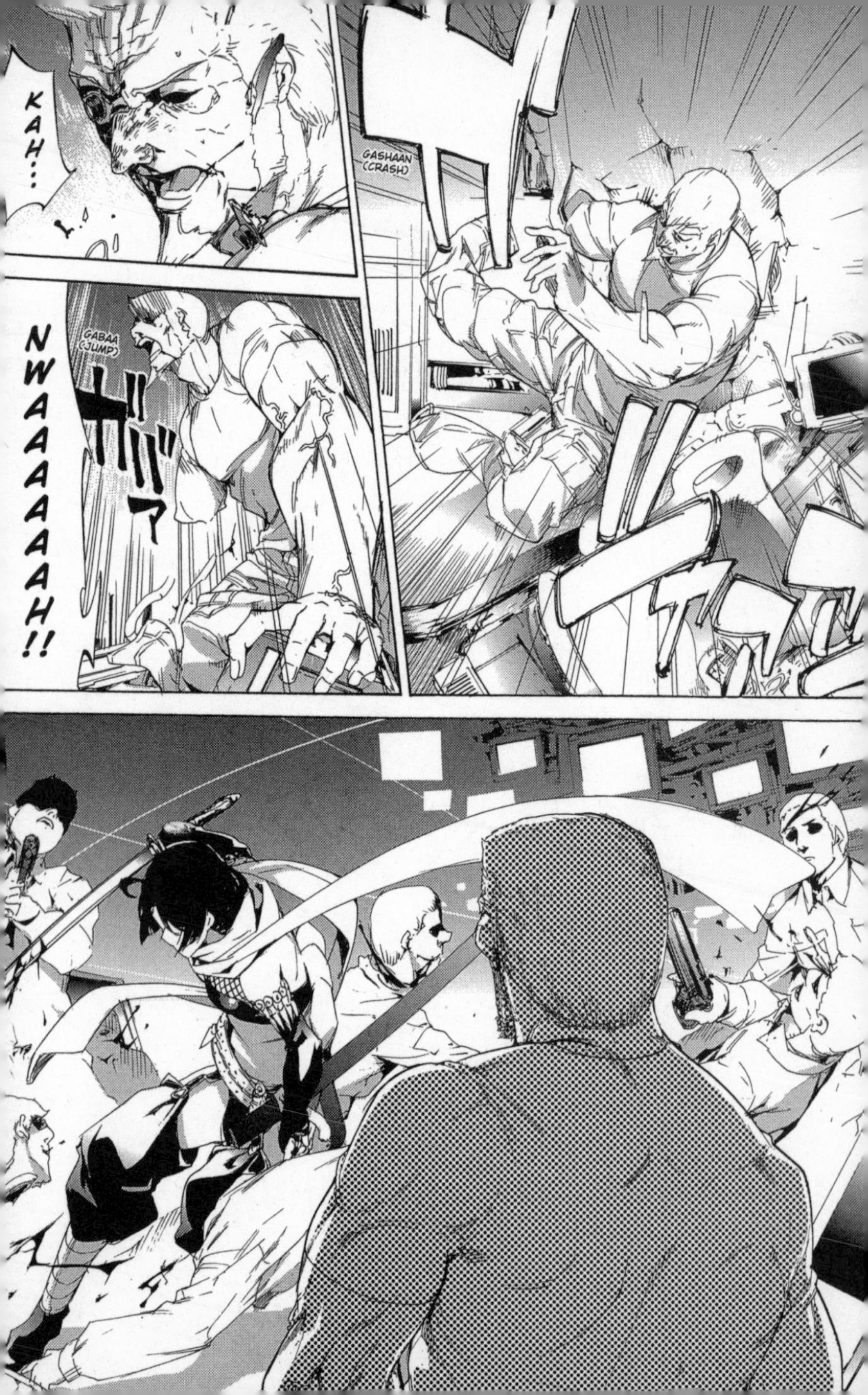
GASHAAN (CRASH)
KAH...
GABAA (JUMP)
NWAAAAAAAAAH!!

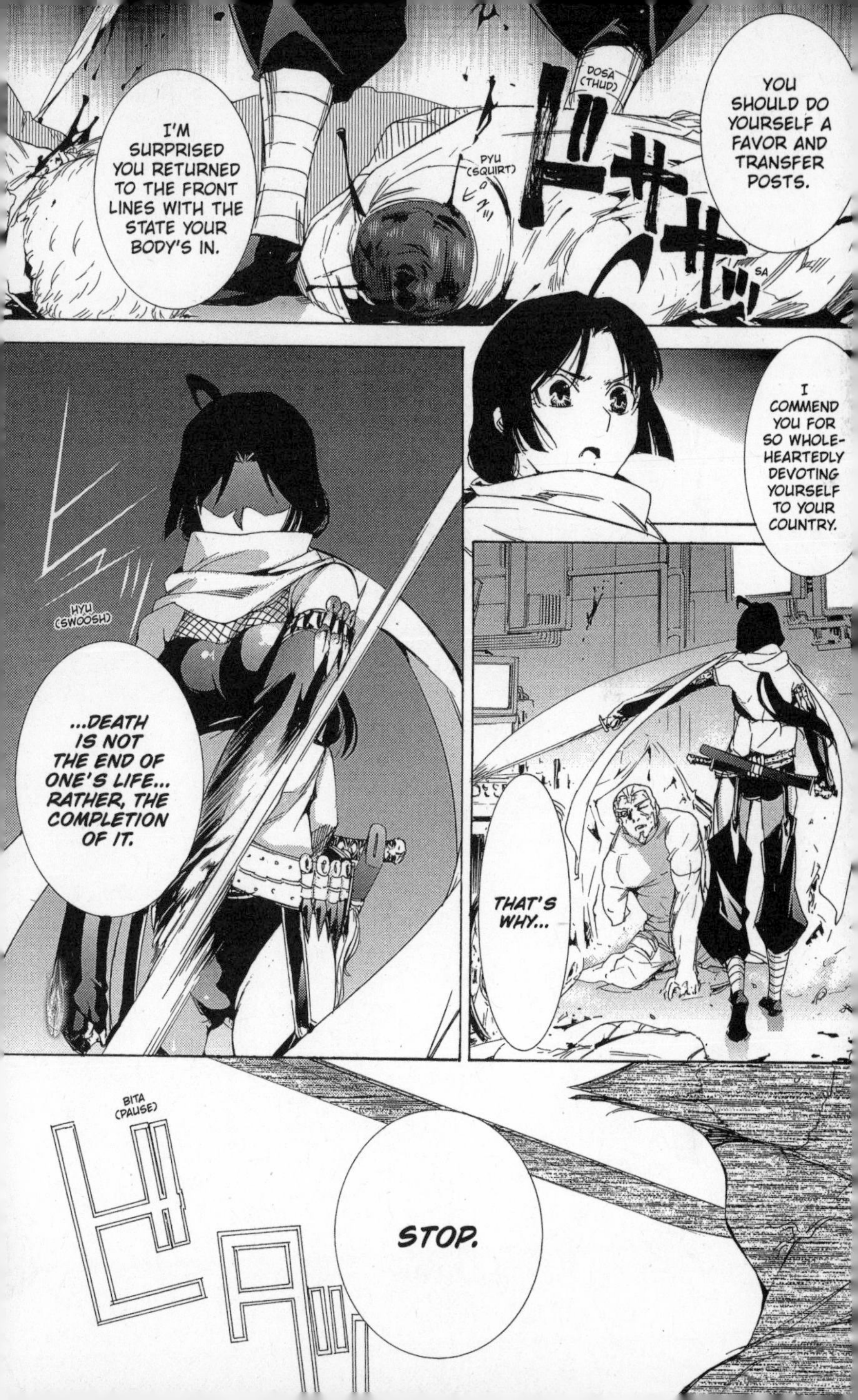
YOU SHOULD DO YOURSELF A FAVOR AND TRANSFER POSTS.
DOSA (THUD)
PYU (SQUIRT)
SA
I'M SURPRISED YOU RETURNED TO THE FRONT LINES WITH THE STATE YOUR BODY'S IN.
I COMMEND YOU FOR SO WHOLE-HEARTEDLY DEVOTING YOURSELF TO YOUR COUNTRY.
THAT'S WHY...
...DEATH IS NOT THE END OF ONE'S LIFE... RATHER, THE COMPLETION OF IT.
HYU (SWOOSH)
STOP.
BITA (PAUSE)

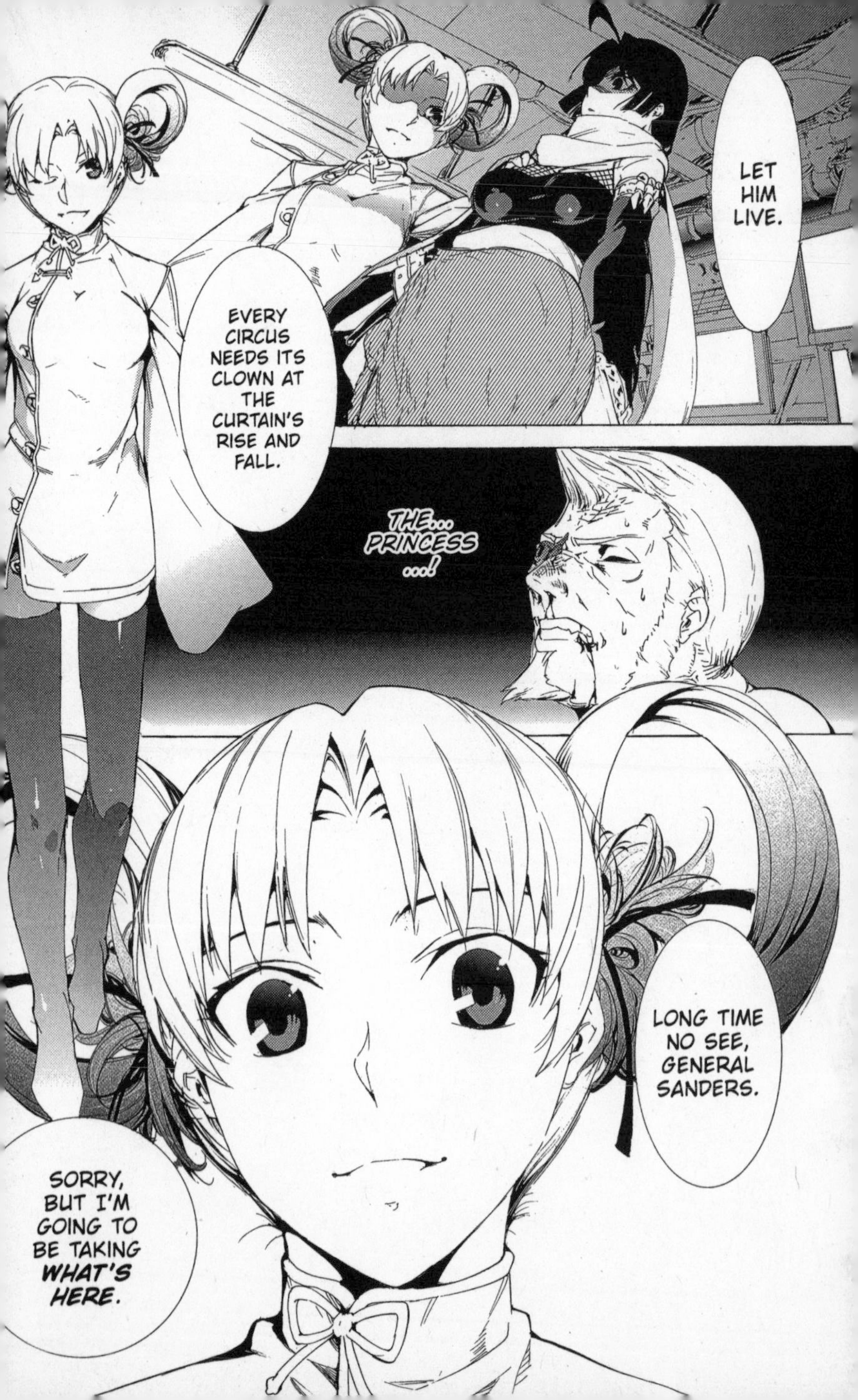
LET HIM LIVE.
EVERY CIRCUS NEEDS ITS CLOWN AT THE CURTAIN'S RISE AND FALL.
THE... PRINCESS ...!
LONG TIME NO SEE, GENERAL SANDERS.
SORRY, BUT I'M GOING TO BE TAKING **WHAT'S HERE**.

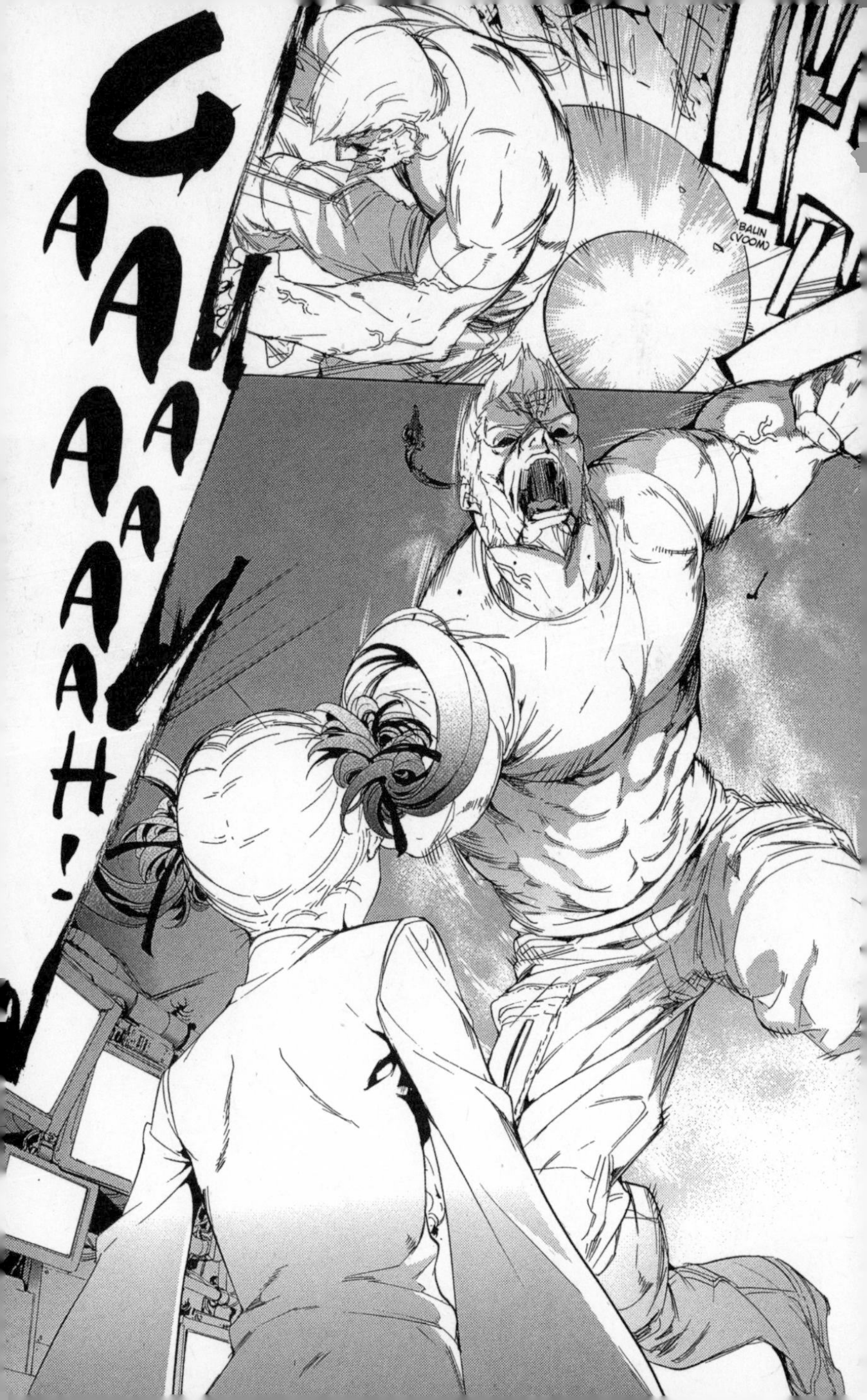
BAUN (VOOM)
GAAAAAAAH!

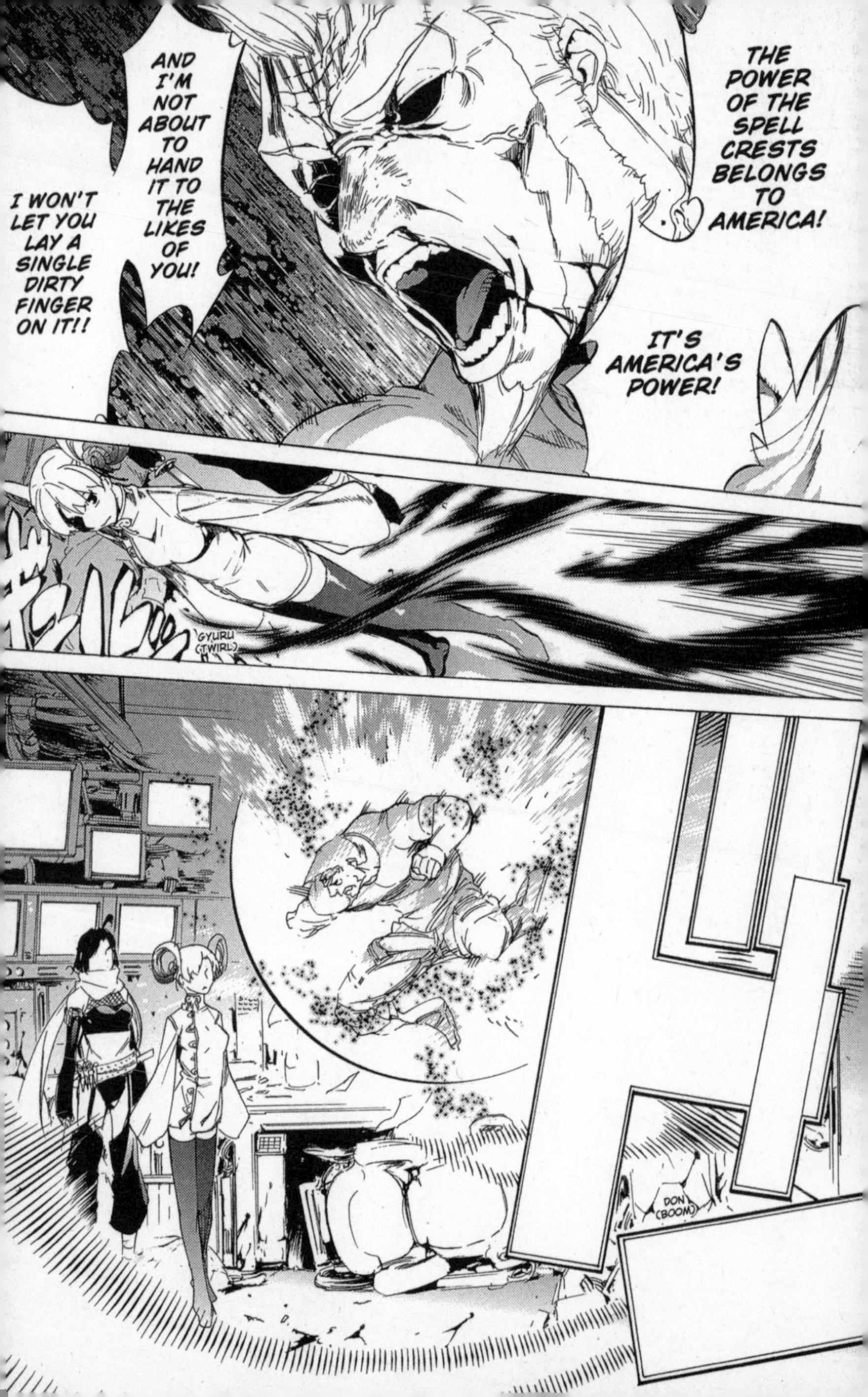
THE POWER OF THE SPELL CRESTS BELONGS TO AMERICA!
IT'S AMERICA'S POWER!
AND I'M NOT ABOUT TO HAND IT TO THE LIKES OF YOU!
I WON'T LET YOU LAY A SINGLE DIRTY FINGER ON IT!!
GYURU (TWIRL)
DON (BOOM)

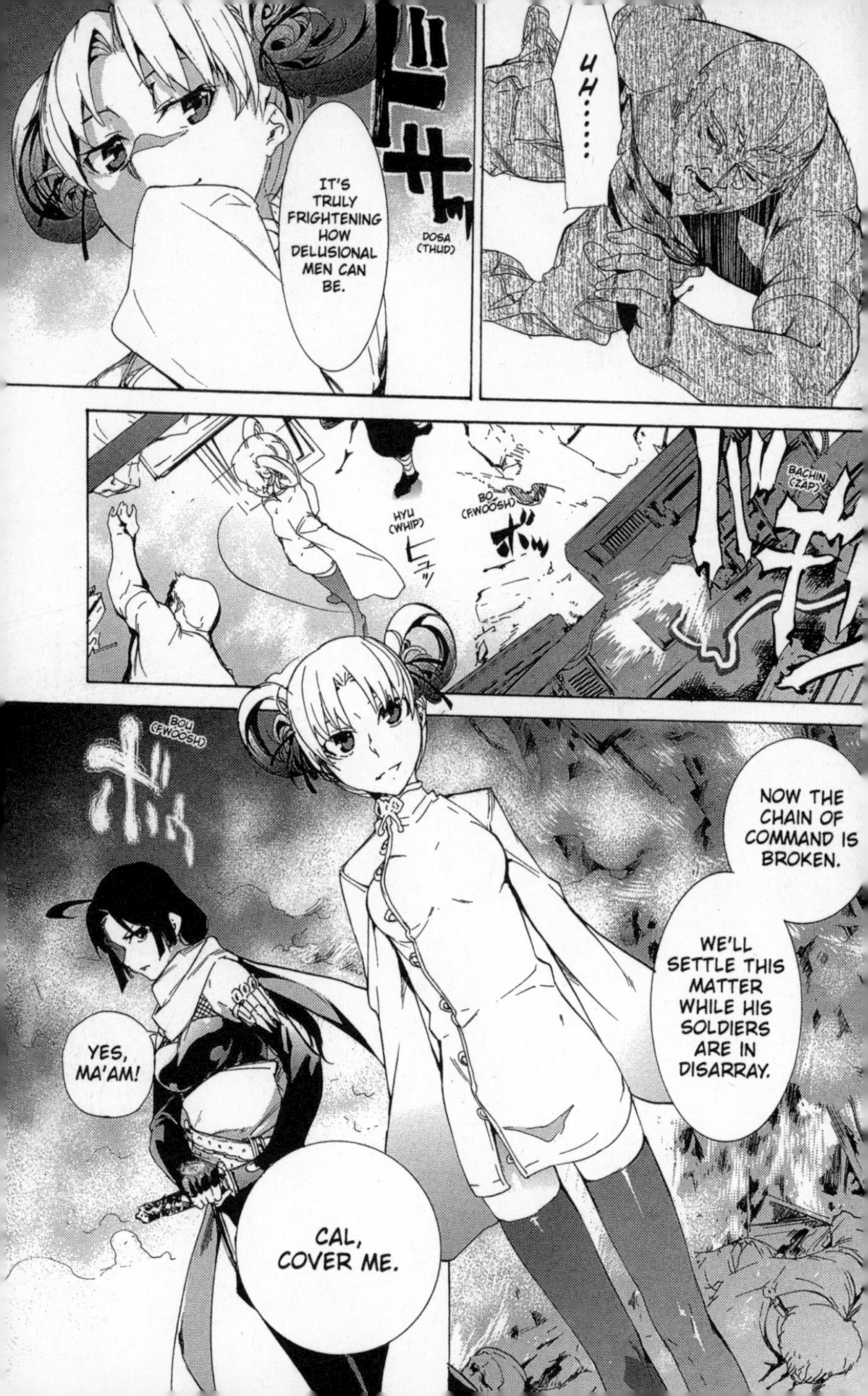
UH......
DOSA (THUD)
IT'S TRULY FRIGHTENING HOW DELUSIONAL MEN CAN BE.
BACHIN (ZAP)
BO (F.WOOSH)
HYU (WHIP)
BOU (F.WOOSH)
NOW THE CHAIN OF COMMAND IS BROKEN.
WE'LL SETTLE THIS MATTER WHILE HIS SOLDIERS ARE IN DISARRAY.
CAL, COVER ME.
YES, MA'AM!

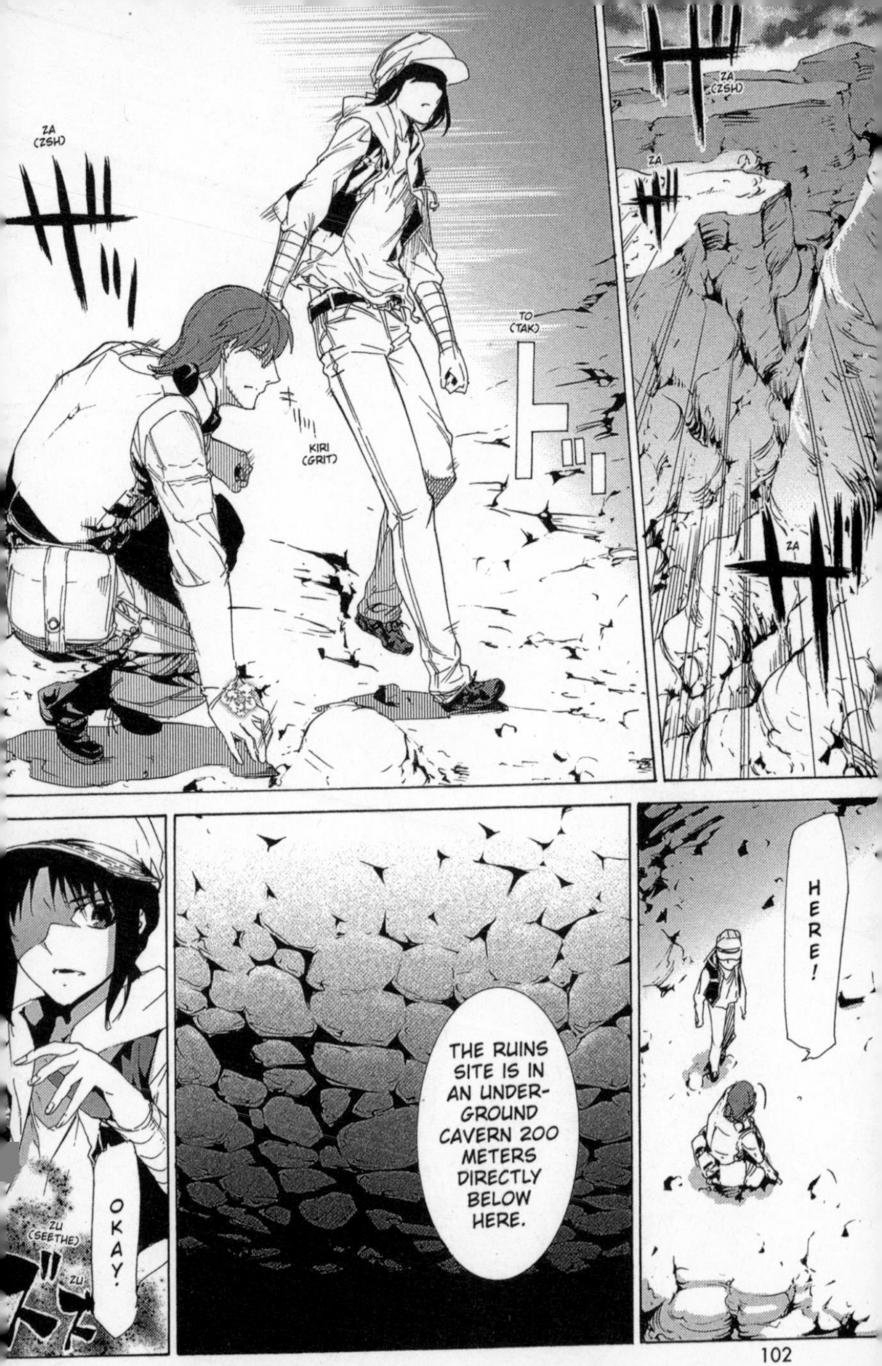
ZA
(ZSH)
ZA
ZA
ZA
(ZSH)
TO
(TAK)
KIRI
(GRIT)
HERE!
THE RUINS SITE IS IN AN UNDER-GROUND CAVERN 200 METERS DIRECTLY BELOW HERE.
OKAY.
ZU
(SEETHE)
ZU

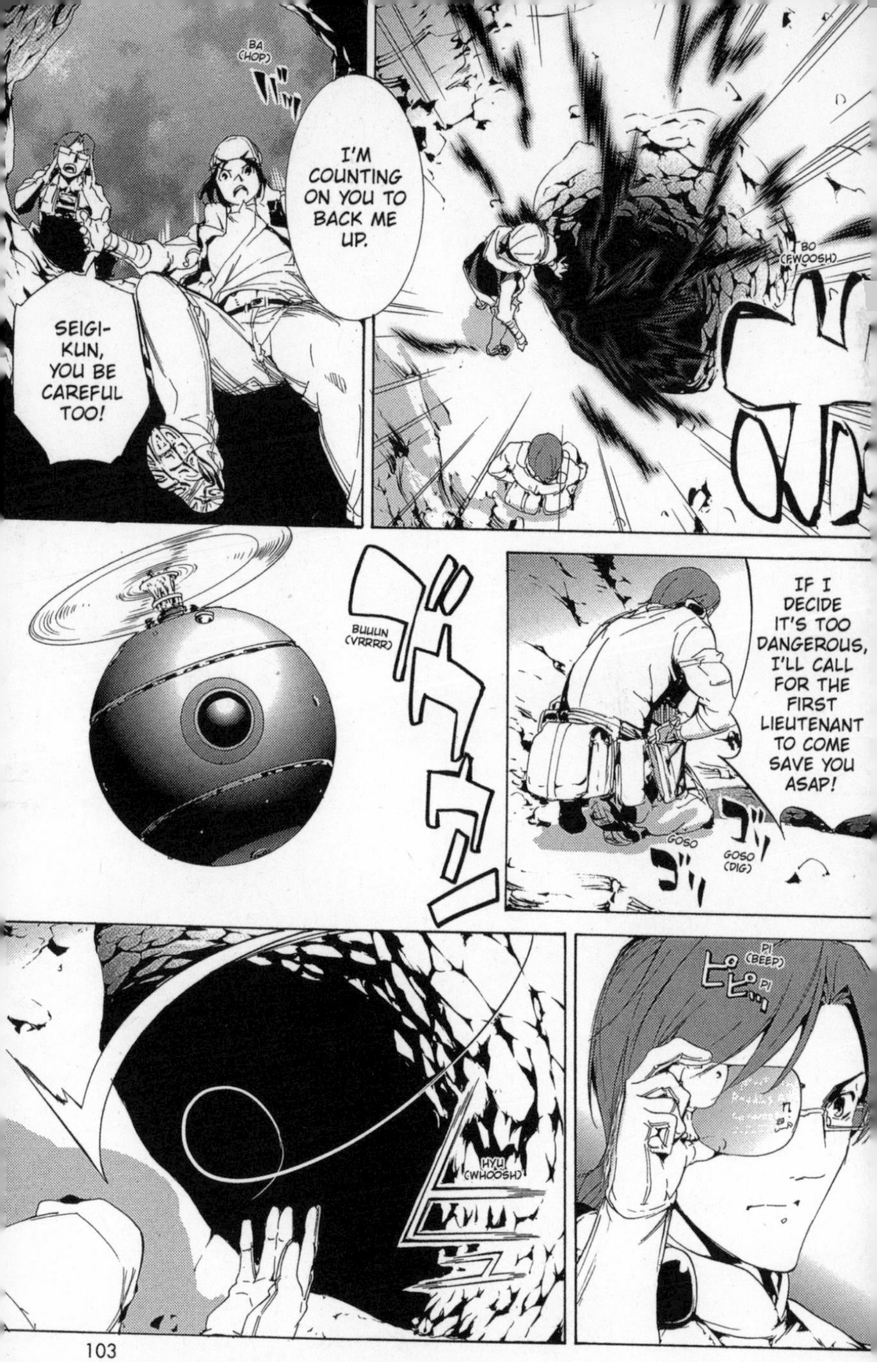
BO (FWOOSH)
BA (HOP)
I'M COUNTING ON YOU TO BACK ME UP.
SEIGI-KUN, YOU BE CAREFUL TOO!
IF I DECIDE IT'S TOO DANGEROUS, I'LL CALL FOR THE FIRST LIEUTENANT TO COME SAVE YOU ASAP!
GOSO
GOSO (DIG)
BUUUN (VRRRR)
PI (BEEP)
PI
HYU (WHOOSH)

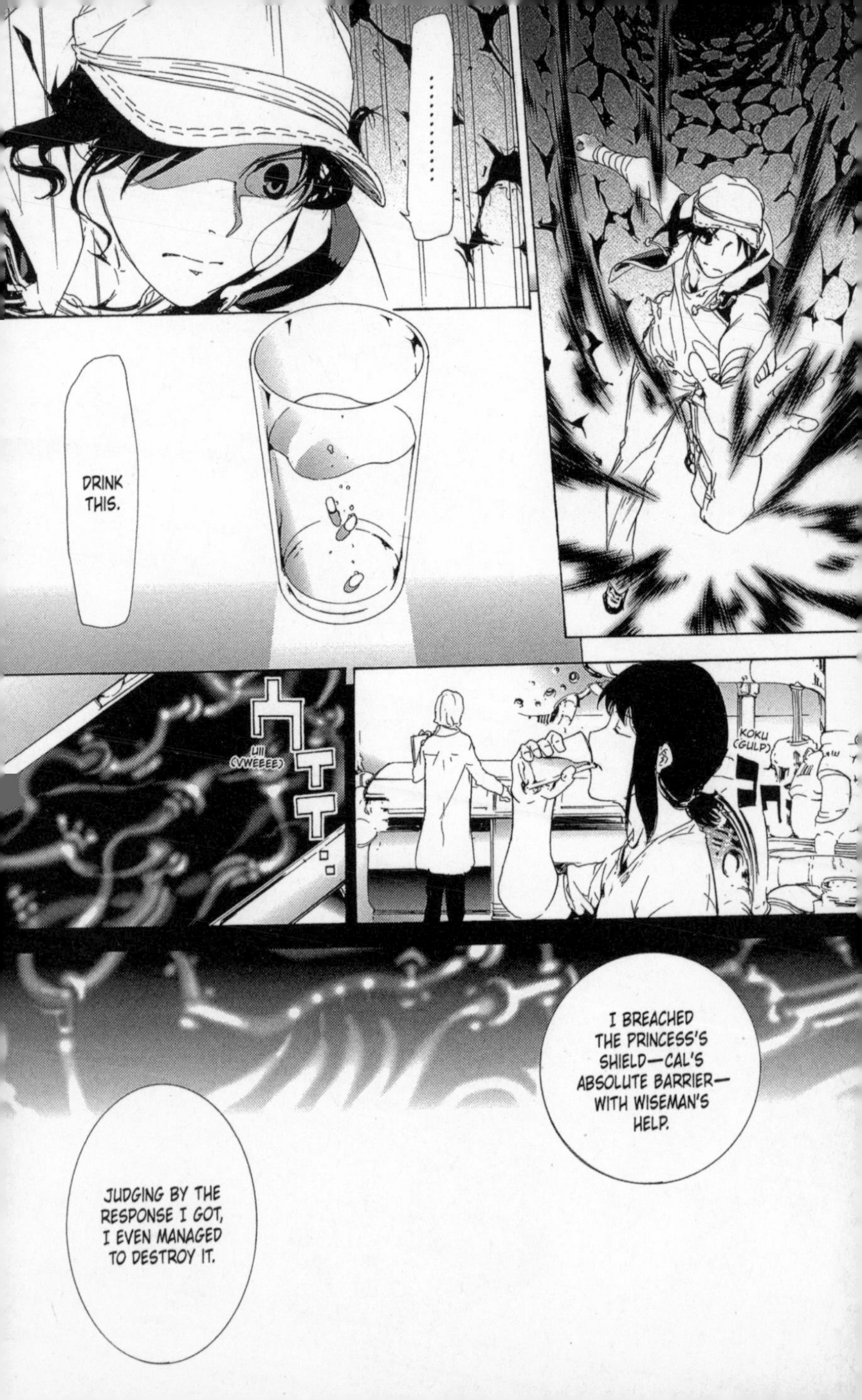
....
DRINK THIS.
KOKU (GULP)
LIII (VWEEEE)
I BREACHED THE PRINCESS'S SHIELD—CAL'S ABSOLUTE BARRIER—WITH WISEMAN'S HELP.
JUDGING BY THE RESPONSE I GOT, I EVEN MANAGED TO DESTROY IT.

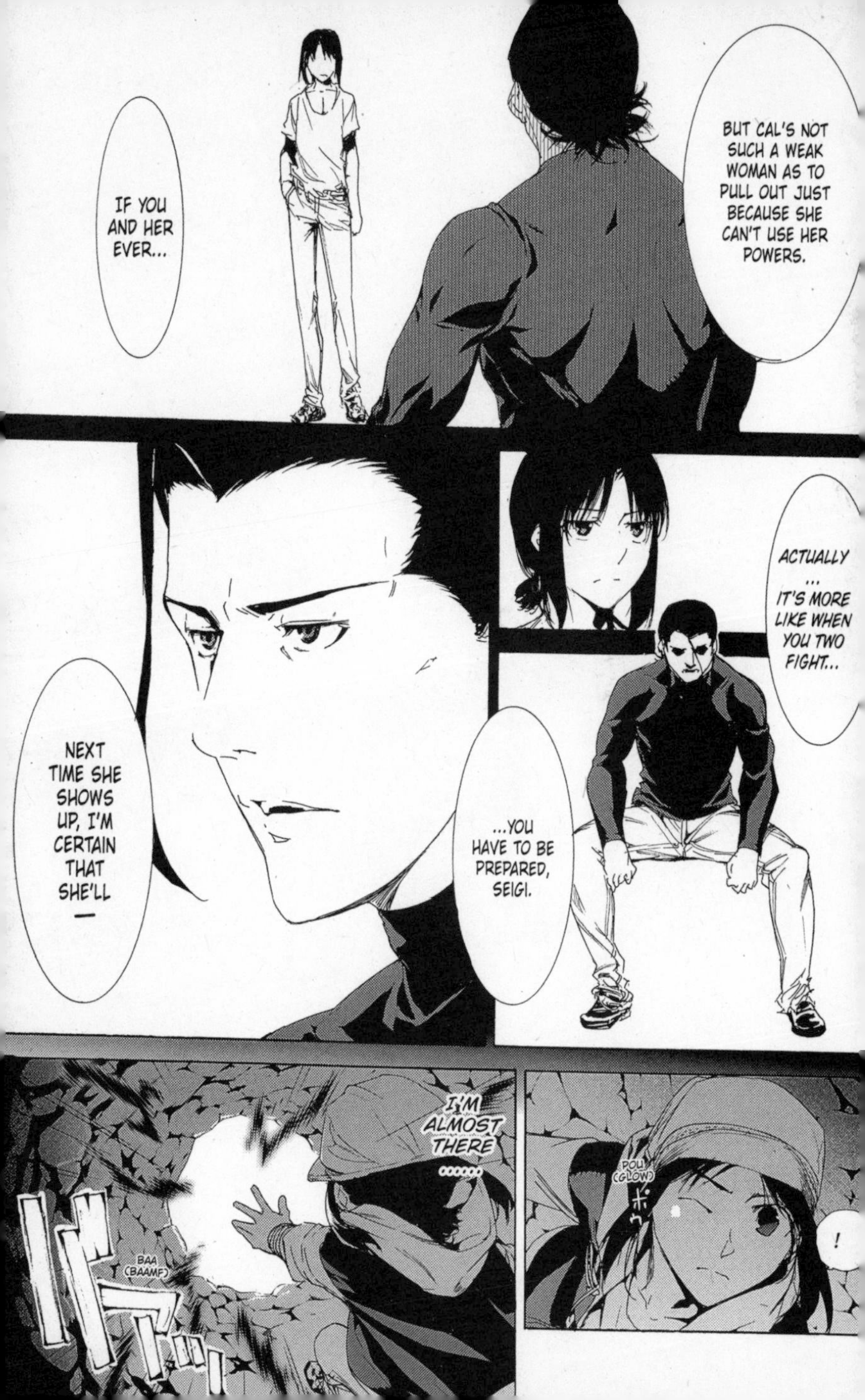
BUT CAL'S NOT SUCH A WEAK WOMAN AS TO PULL OUT JUST BECAUSE SHE CAN'T USE HER POWERS.
IF YOU AND HER EVER...
ACTUALLY ... IT'S MORE LIKE WHEN YOU TWO FIGHT...
...YOU HAVE TO BE PREPARED, SEIGI.
NEXT TIME SHE SHOWS UP, I'M CERTAIN THAT SHE'LL —
POU (GLOW)
!
I'M ALMOST THERE ......
BAA (BAAMF)

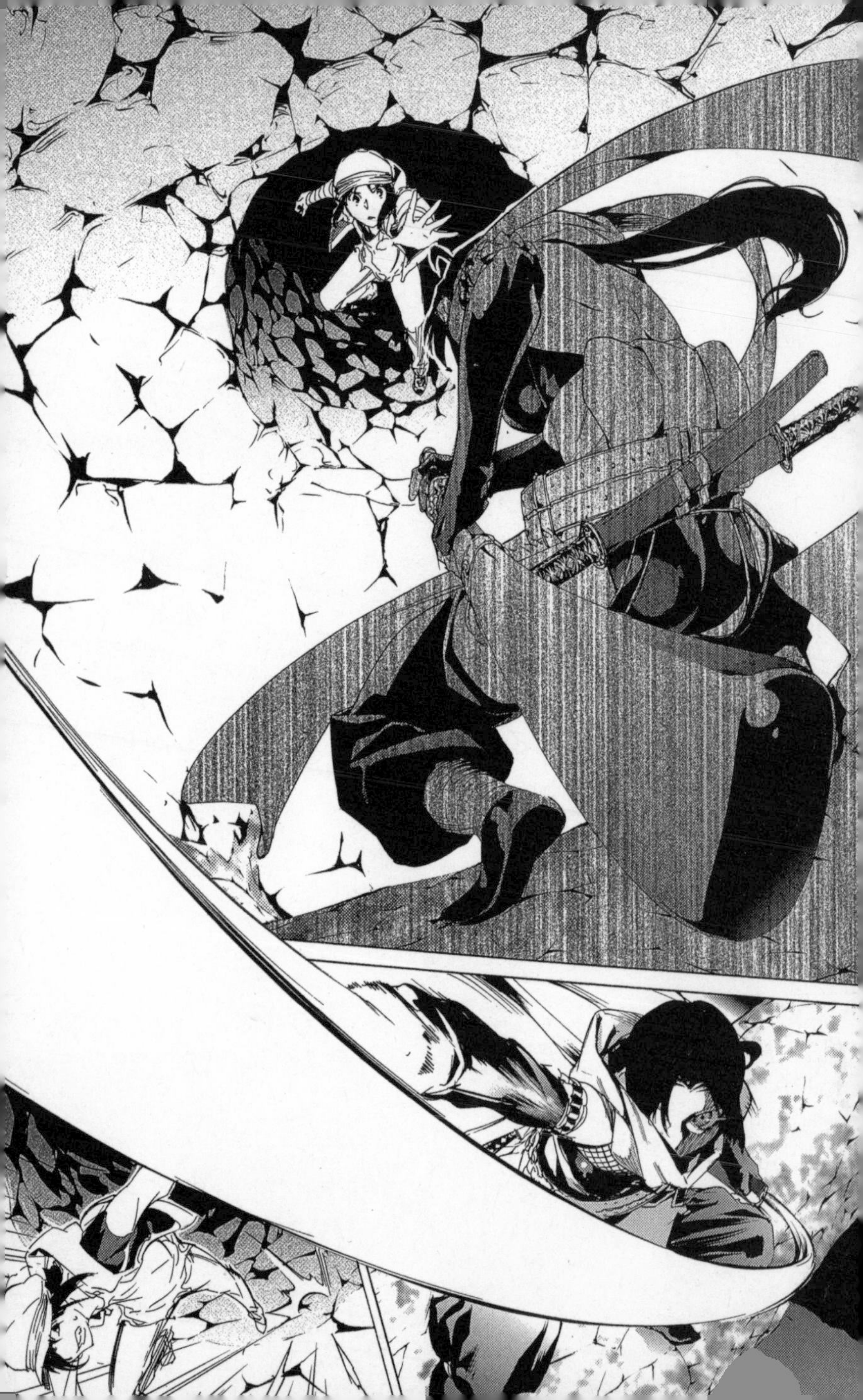

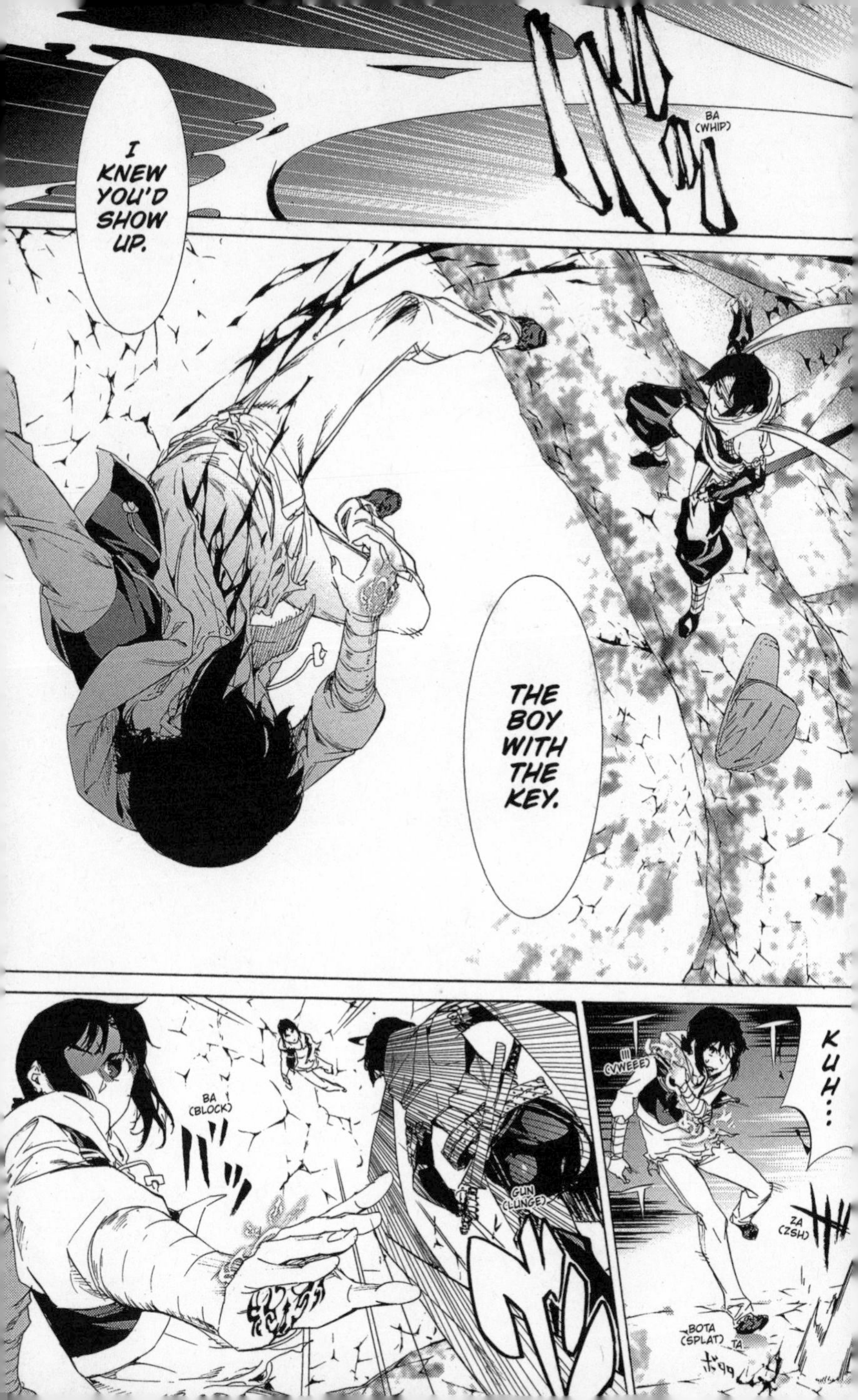
BA (WHIP)
I KNEW YOU'D SHOW UP.
THE BOY WITH THE KEY.
KUH...
(VWEEE)
ZA (ZSH)
BOTA (SPLAT)
TA
GUN (LUNGE)
BA (BLOCK)

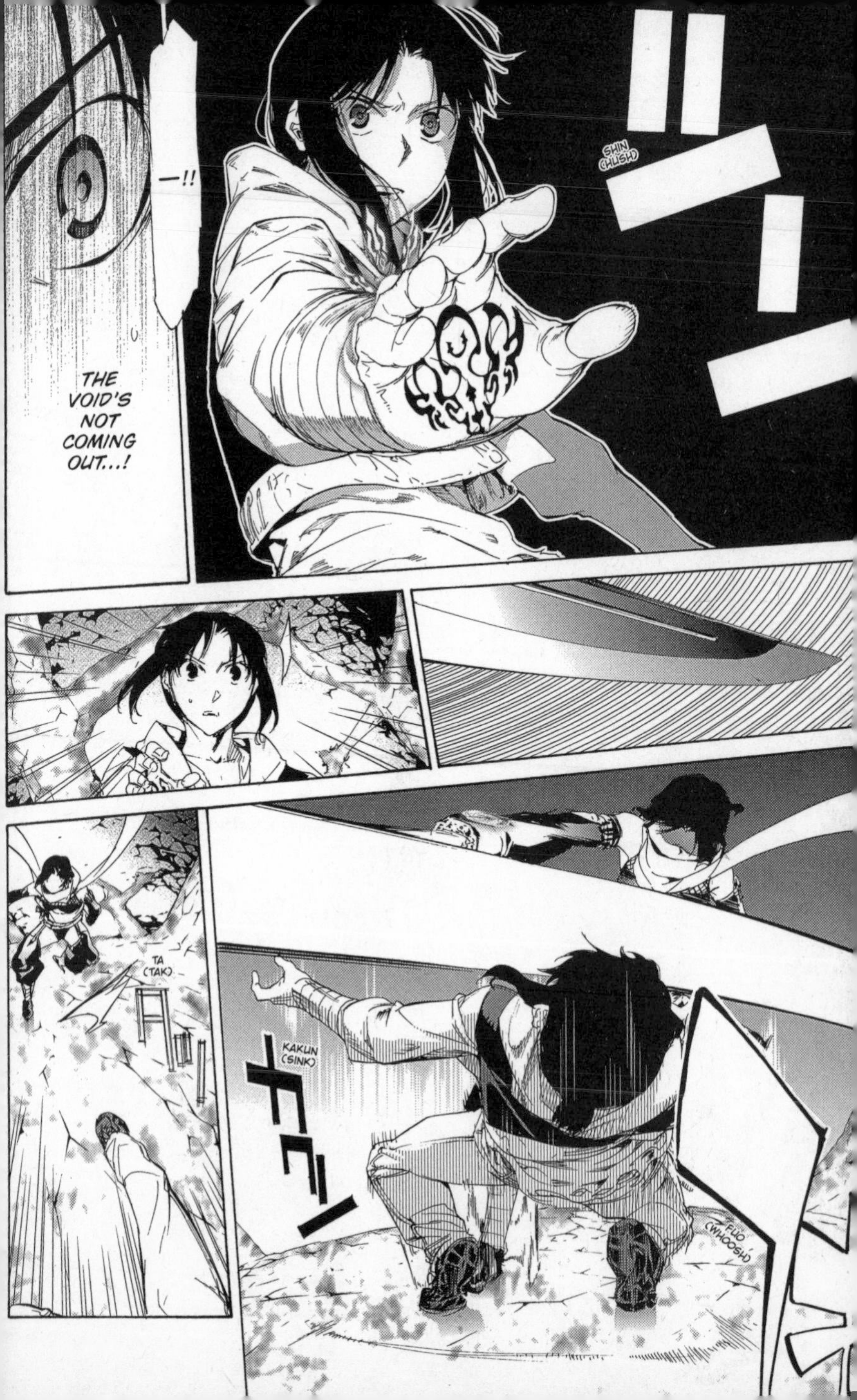
SHIN (HUSH)
—!!
THE VOID'S NOT COMING OUT...!
FUO (WHOOSH)
KAKUN (SINK)
TA (TAK)

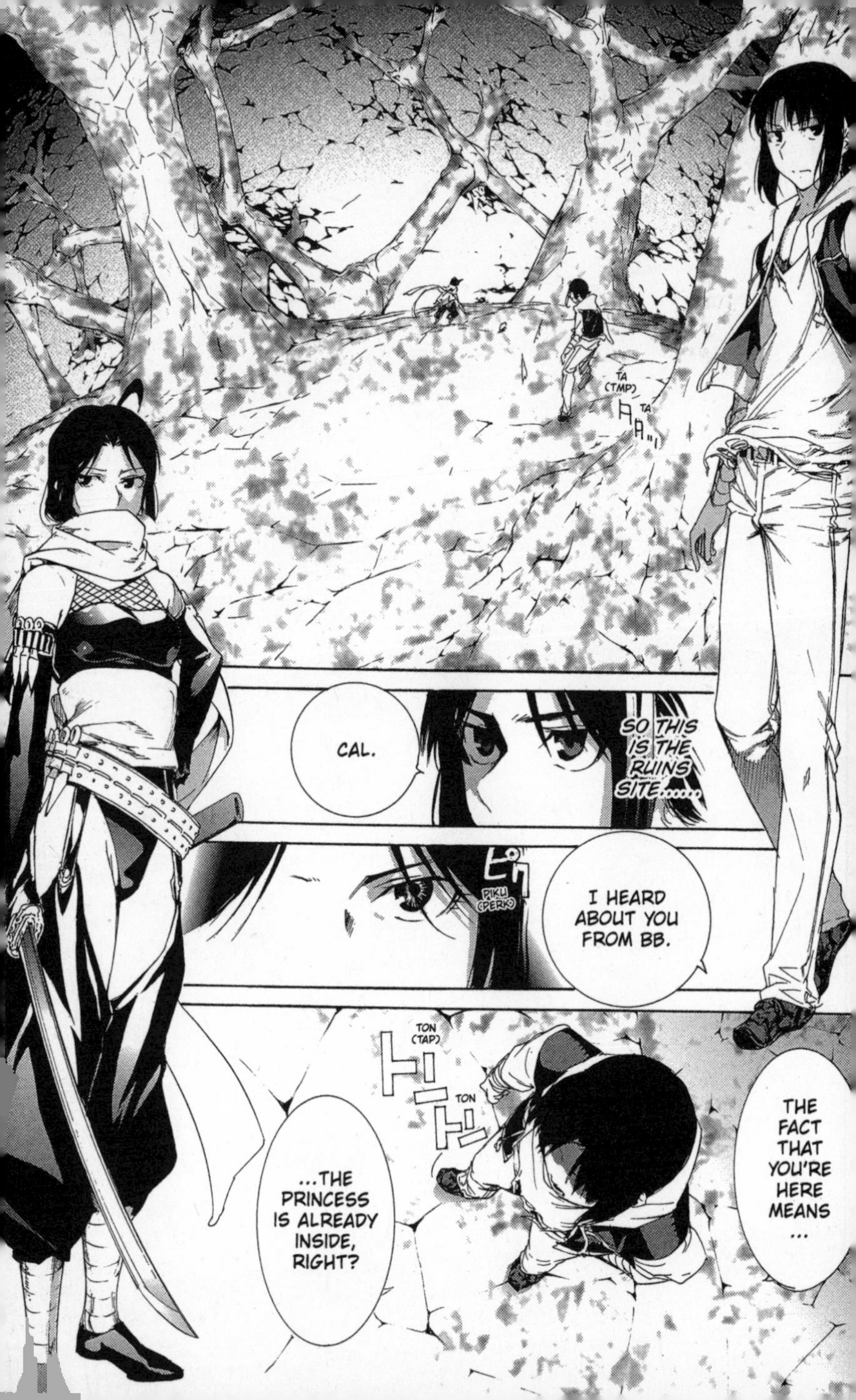
TA (TMP) TA
SO THIS IS THE RUINS SITE......
CAL.
I HEARD ABOUT YOU FROM BB.
PIKU (PERK)
THE FACT THAT YOU'RE HERE MEANS...
TON (TAP) TON
...THE PRINCESS IS ALREADY INSIDE, RIGHT?

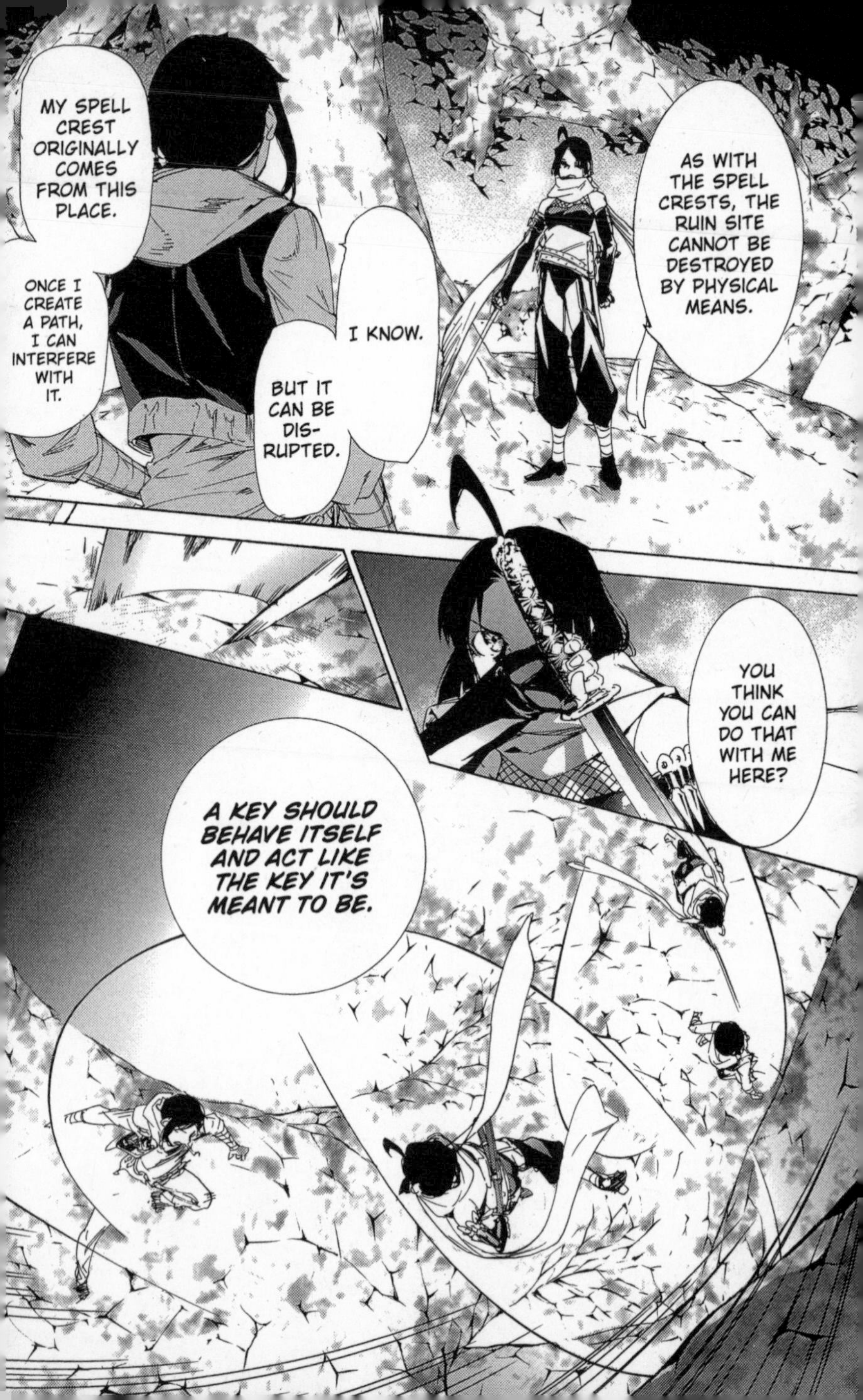
AS WITH THE SPELL CRESTS, THE RUIN SITE CANNOT BE DESTROYED BY PHYSICAL MEANS.
I KNOW.
BUT IT CAN BE DIS-RUPTED.
MY SPELL CREST ORIGINALLY COMES FROM THIS PLACE.
ONCE I CREATE A PATH, I CAN INTERFERE WITH IT.
YOU THINK YOU CAN DO THAT WITH ME HERE?
A KEY SHOULD BEHAVE ITSELF AND ACT LIKE THE KEY IT'S MEANT TO BE.

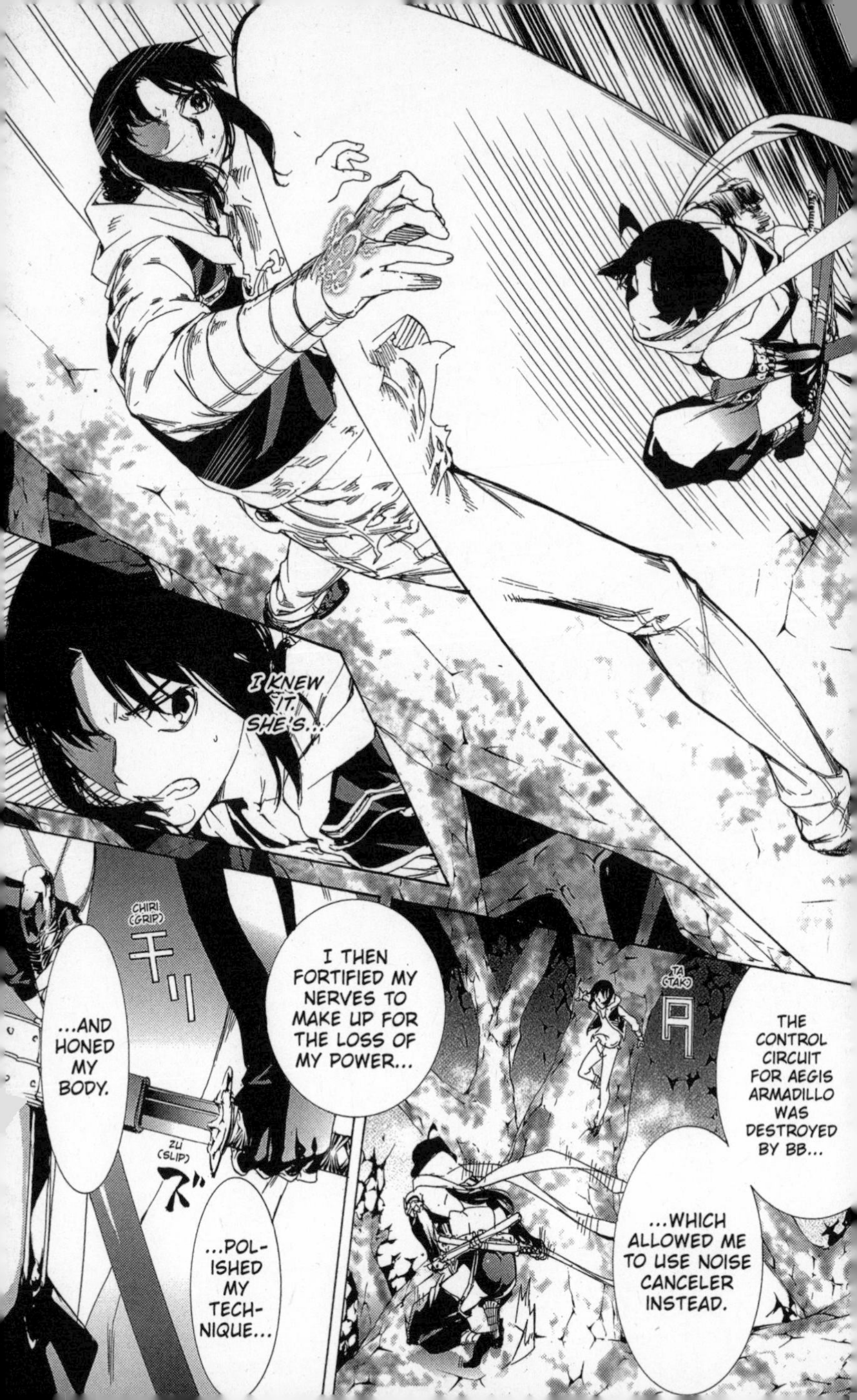
I KNEW IT. SHE'S...
TA (TAK)
THE CONTROL CIRCUIT FOR AEGIS ARMADILLO WAS DESTROYED BY BB...
...WHICH ALLOWED ME TO USE NOISE CANCELER INSTEAD.
CHIRI (GRIP)
I THEN FORTIFIED MY NERVES TO MAKE UP FOR THE LOSS OF MY POWER...
...POL-ISHED MY TECH-NIQUE...
ZU (SLIP)
...AND HONED MY BODY.

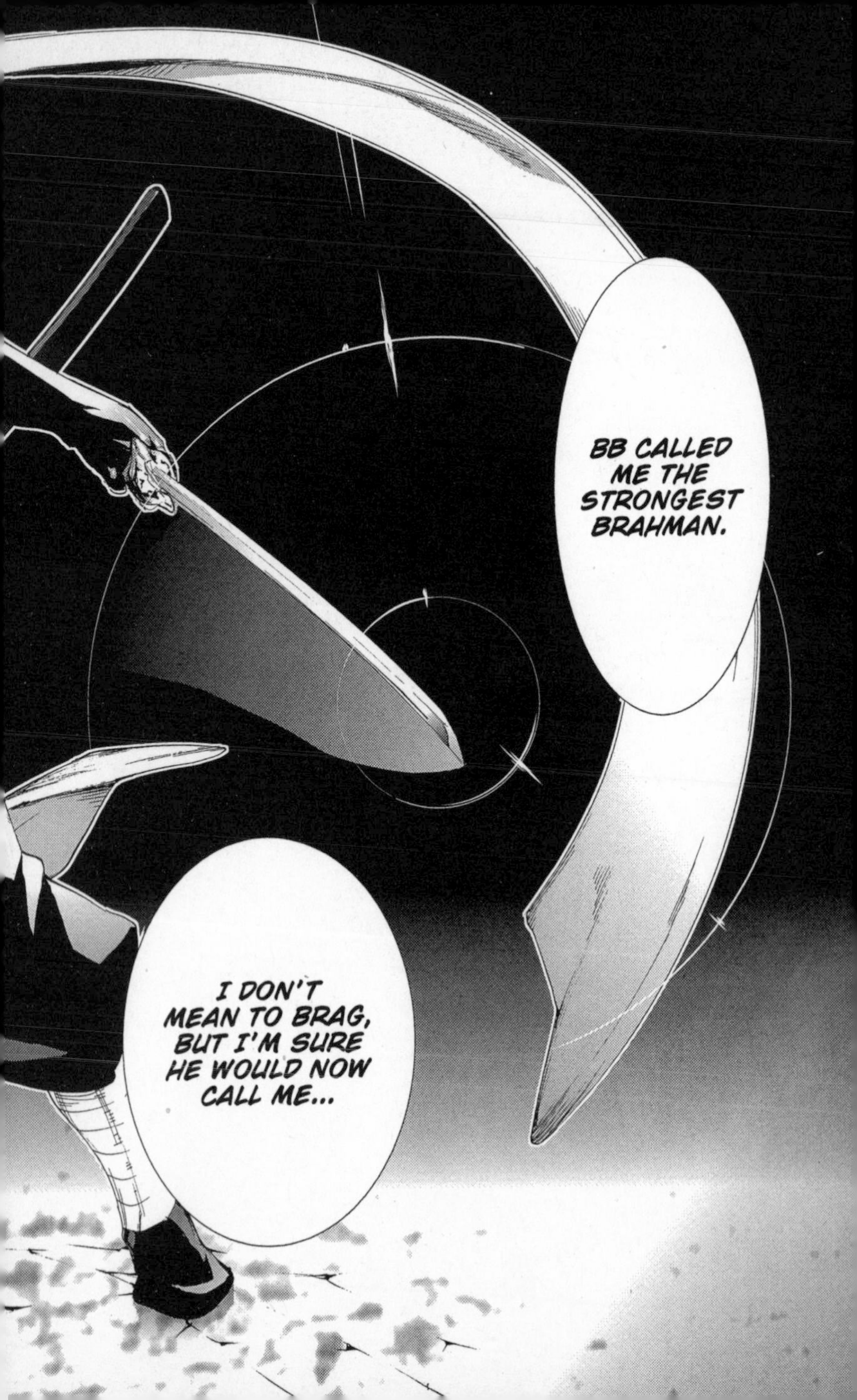
BB CALLED ME THE STRONGEST BRAHMAN.
I DON'T MEAN TO BRAG, BUT I'M SURE HE WOULD NOW CALL ME...

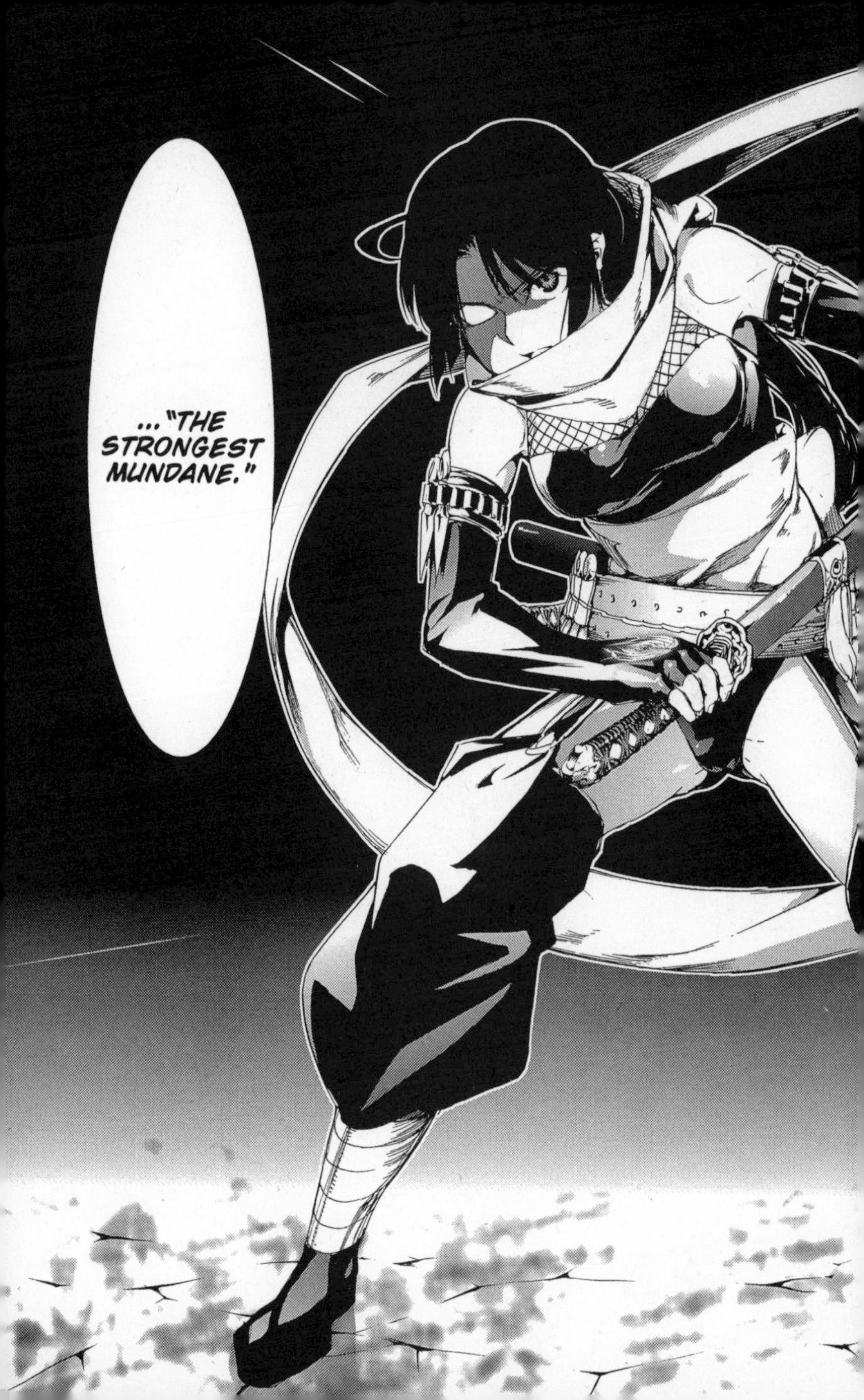
..."THE STRONGEST MUNDANE."

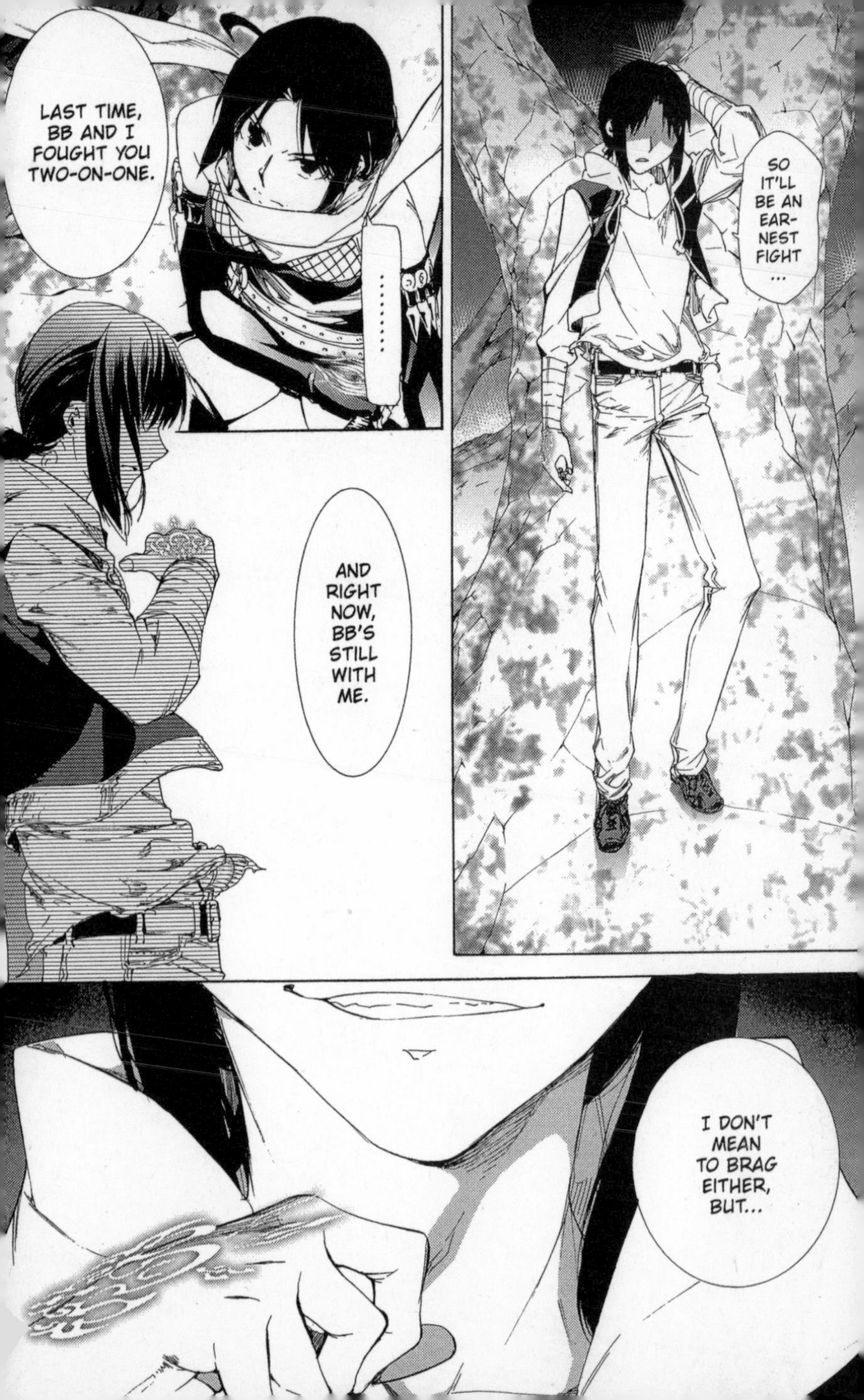
LAST TIME, BB AND I FOUGHT YOU TWO-ON-ONE.
......
AND RIGHT NOW, BB'S STILL WITH ME.
SO IT'LL BE AN EAR-NEST FIGHT ...
I DON'T MEAN TO BRAG EITHER, BUT...

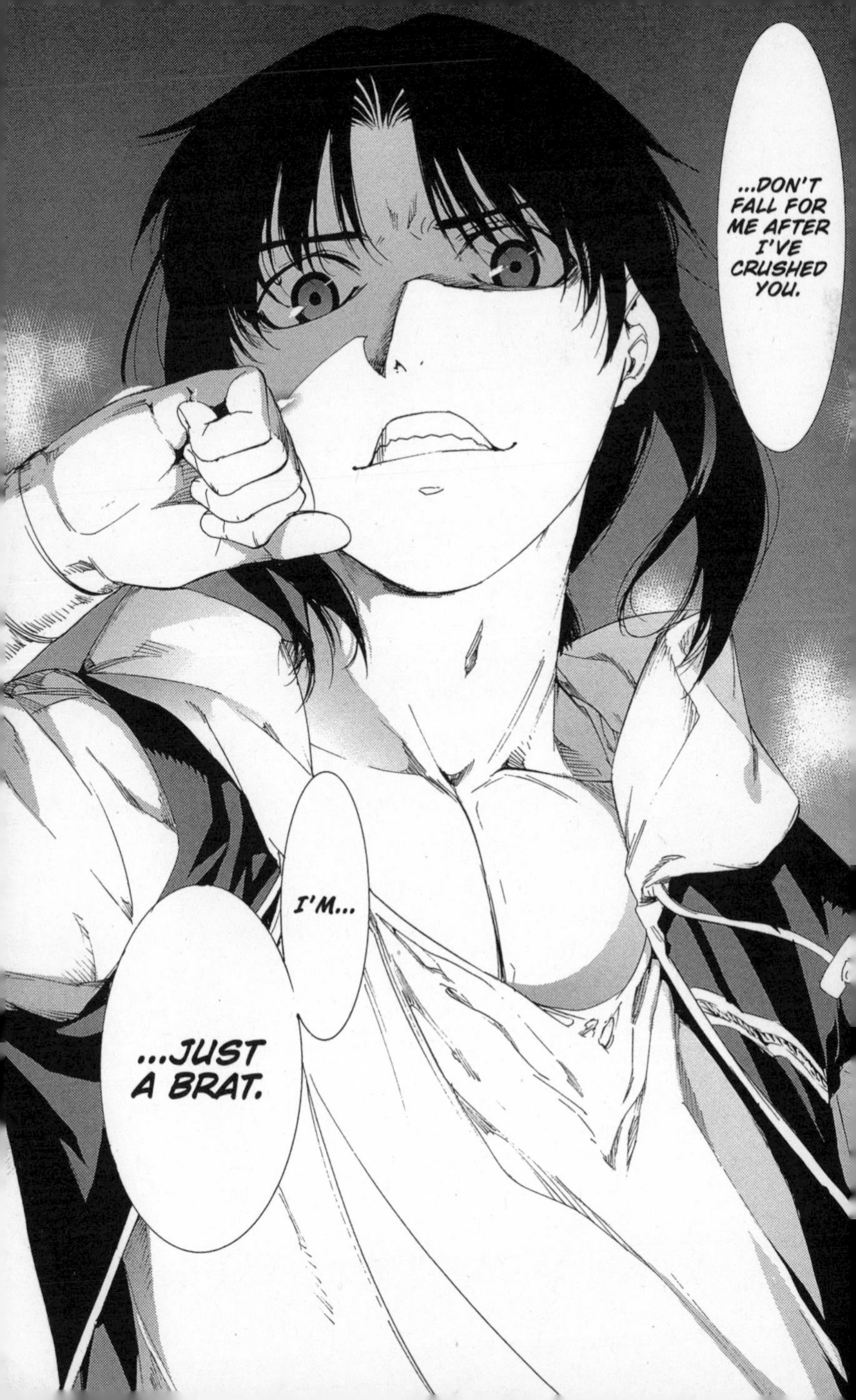
...DON'T FALL FOR ME AFTER I'VE CRUSHED YOU.
I'M...
...JUST A BRAT.

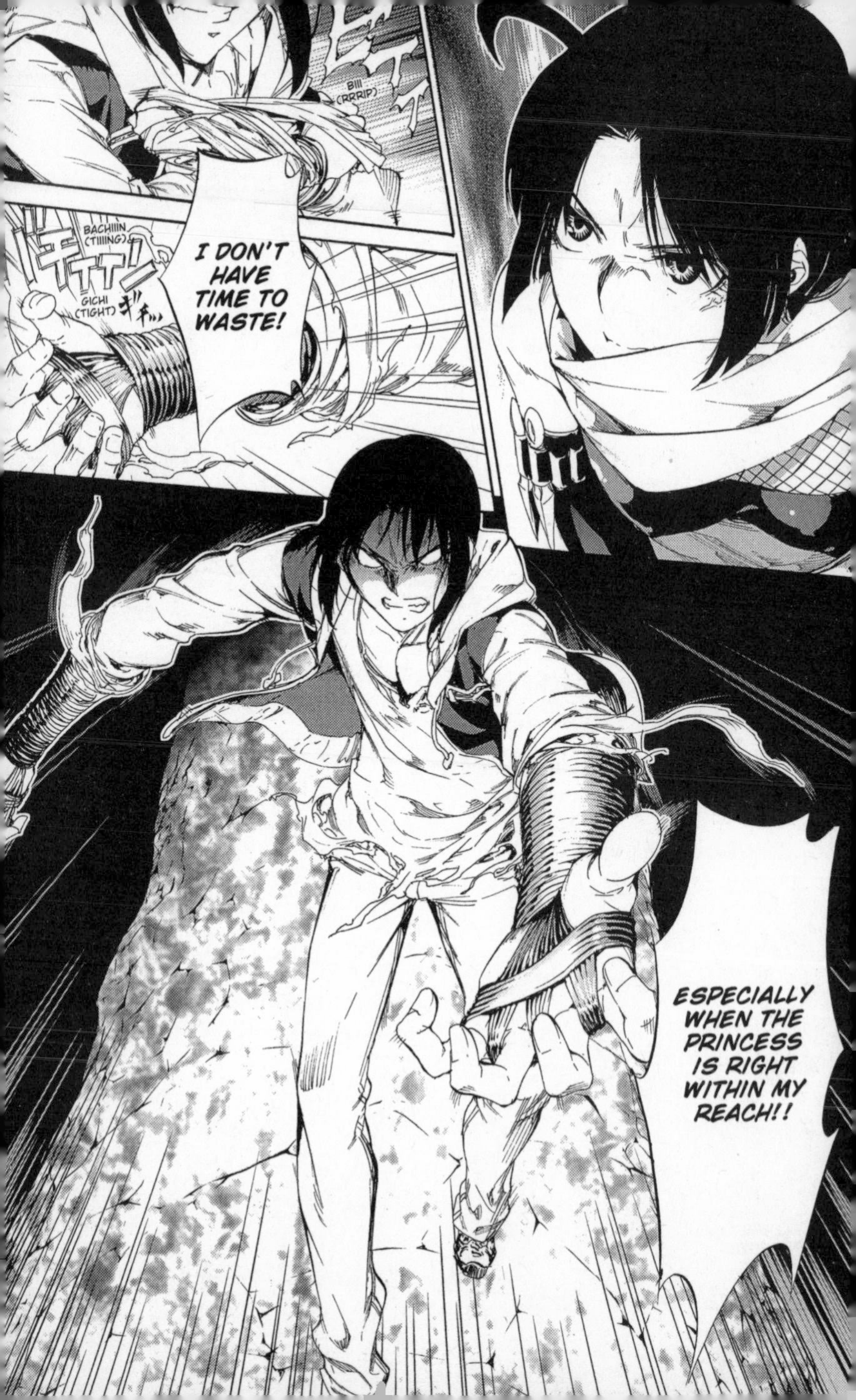
BIII (RRRIP)
I DON'T HAVE TIME TO WASTE!
BACHIIIN (TIIIING)
GICHI (TIGHT)
ESPECIALLY WHEN THE PRINCESS IS RIGHT WITHIN MY REACH!!

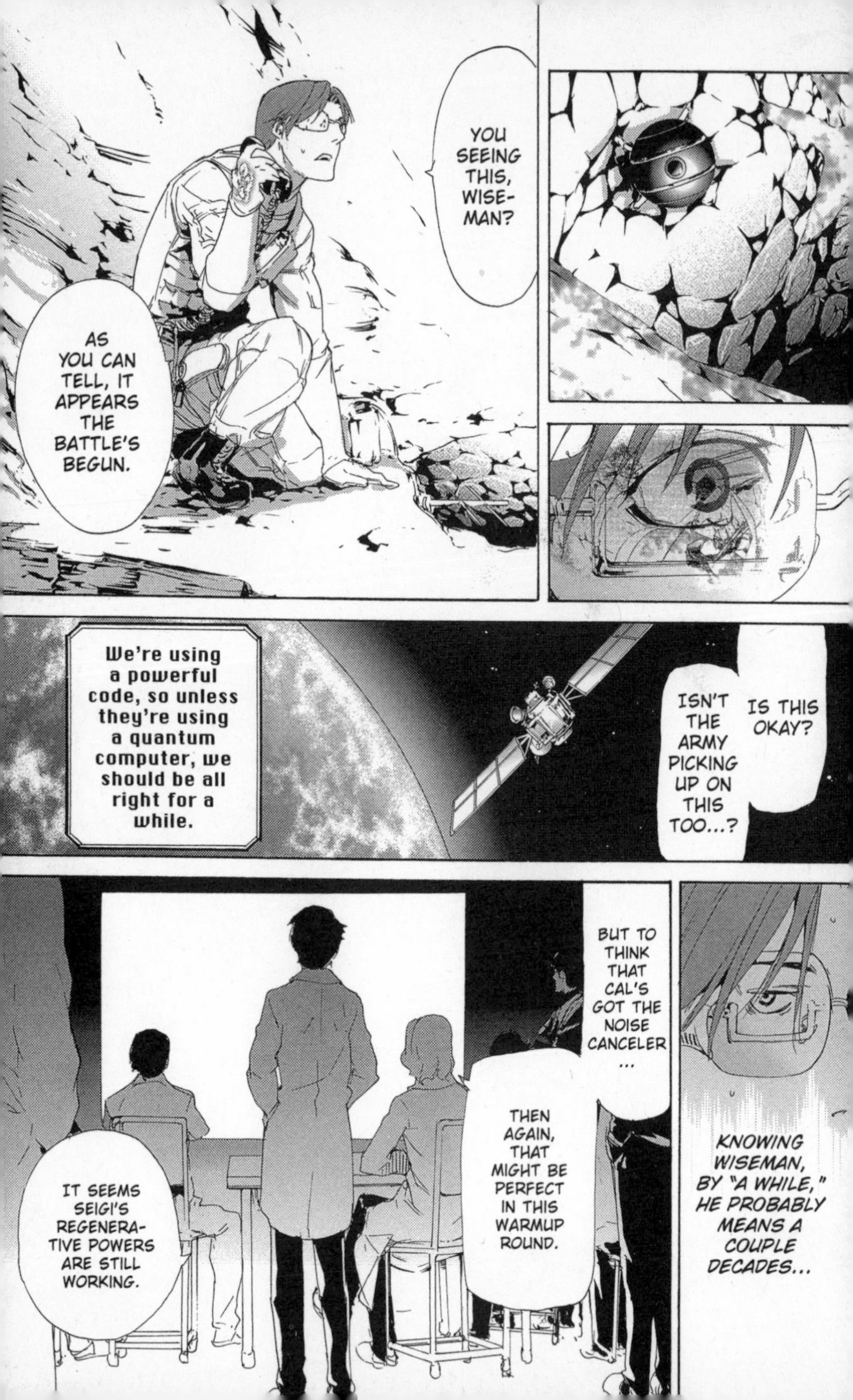
YOU SEEING THIS, WISE-MAN?
AS YOU CAN TELL, IT APPEARS THE BATTLE'S BEGUN.
IS THIS OKAY?
ISN'T THE ARMY PICKING UP ON THIS TOO...?
We're using a powerful code, so unless they're using a quantum computer, we should be all right for a while.
KNOWING WISEMAN, BY "A WHILE," HE PROBABLY MEANS A COUPLE DECADES...
BUT TO THINK THAT CAL'S GOT THE NOISE CANCELER ...
THEN AGAIN, THAT MIGHT BE PERFECT IN THIS WARMUP ROUND.
IT SEEMS SEIGI'S REGENERA-TIVE POWERS ARE STILL WORKING.

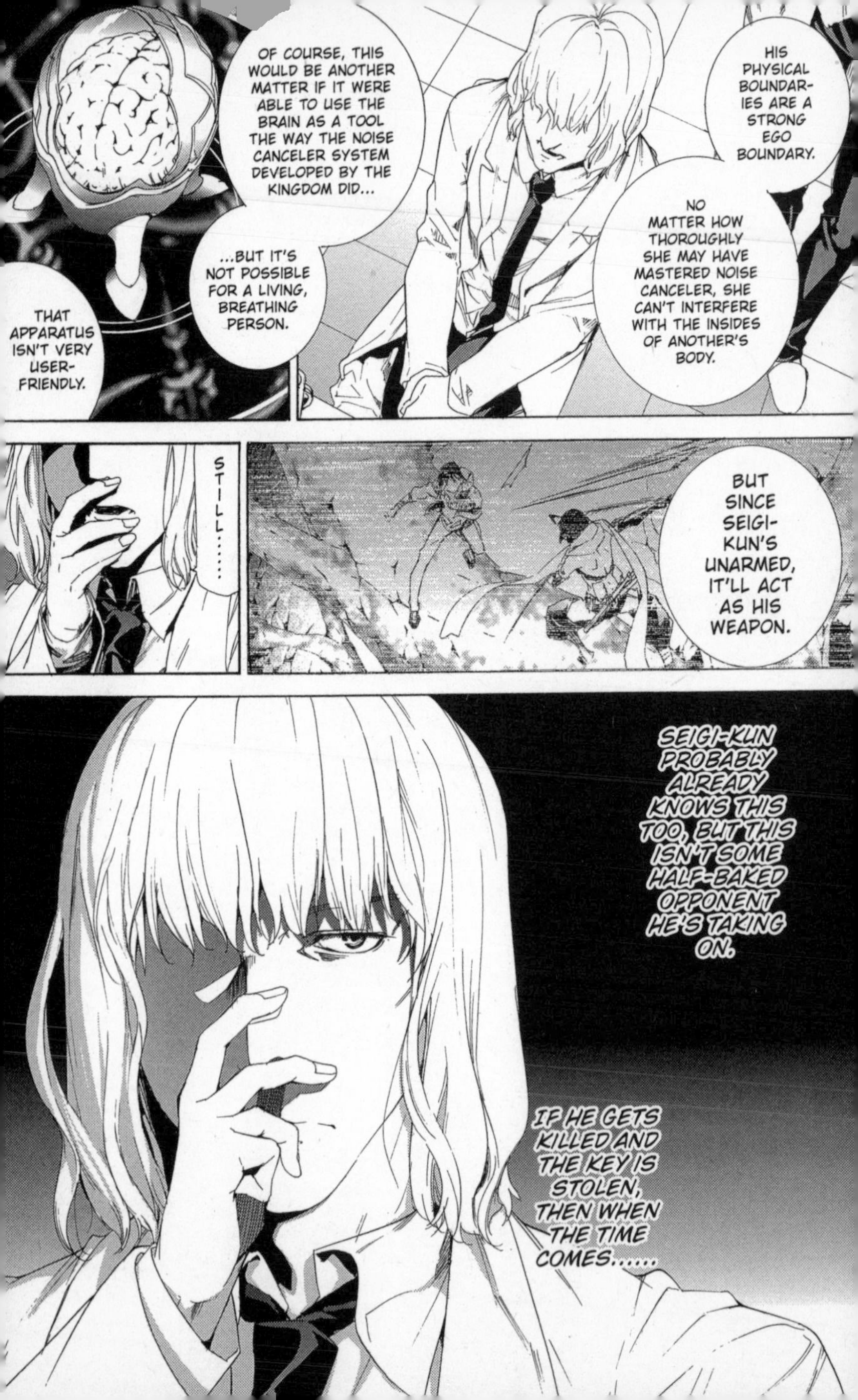
HIS PHYSICAL BOUNDARIES ARE A STRONG EGO BOUNDARY.
NO MATTER HOW THOROUGHLY SHE MAY HAVE MASTERED NOISE CANCELER, SHE CAN'T INTERFERE WITH THE INSIDES OF ANOTHER'S BODY.
OF COURSE, THIS WOULD BE ANOTHER MATTER IF IT WERE ABLE TO USE THE BRAIN AS A TOOL THE WAY THE NOISE CANCELER SYSTEM DEVELOPED BY THE KINGDOM DID...
...BUT IT'S NOT POSSIBLE FOR A LIVING, BREATHING PERSON.
THAT APPARATUS ISN'T VERY USER-FRIENDLY.
BUT SINCE SEIGI-KUN'S UNARMED, IT'LL ACT AS HIS WEAPON.
STILL......
SEIGI-KUN PROBABLY ALREADY KNOWS THIS TOO, BUT THIS ISN'T SOME HALF-BAKED OPPONENT HE'S TAKING ON.
IF HE GETS KILLED AND THE KEY IS STOLEN, THEN WHEN THE TIME COMES......

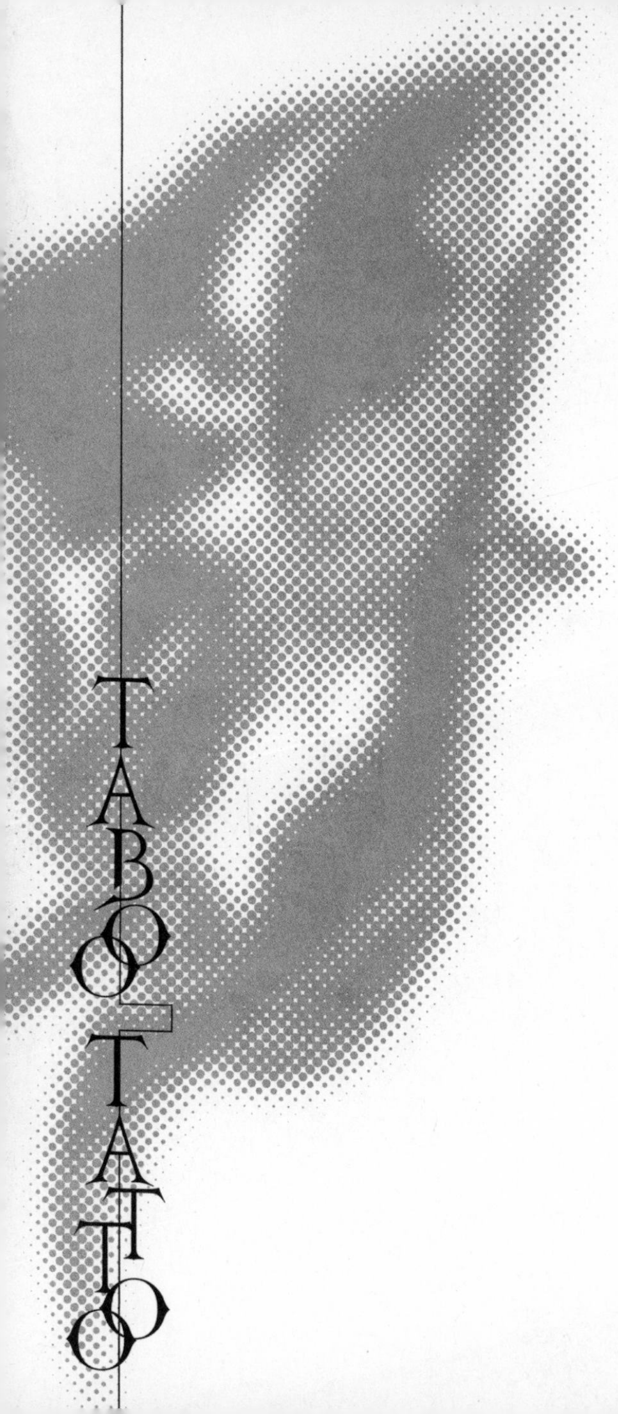

TABOO TATTOO

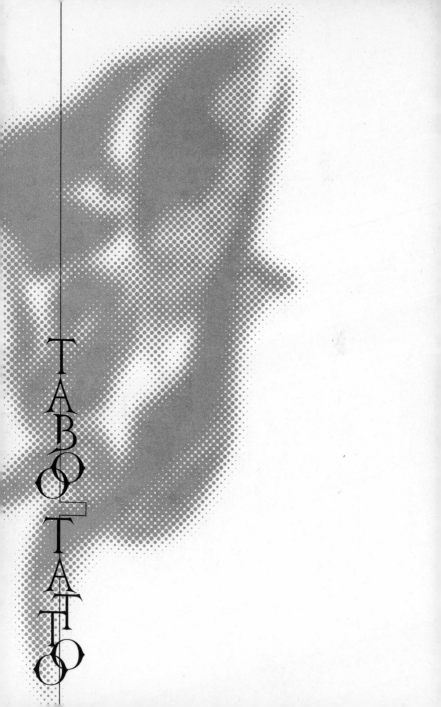

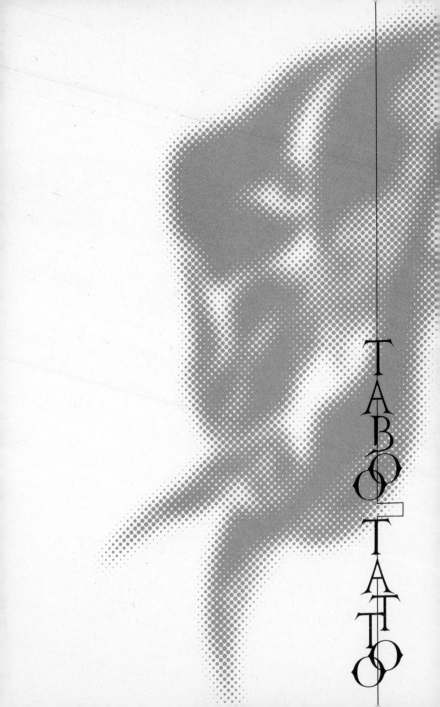

TABOO TATTOO

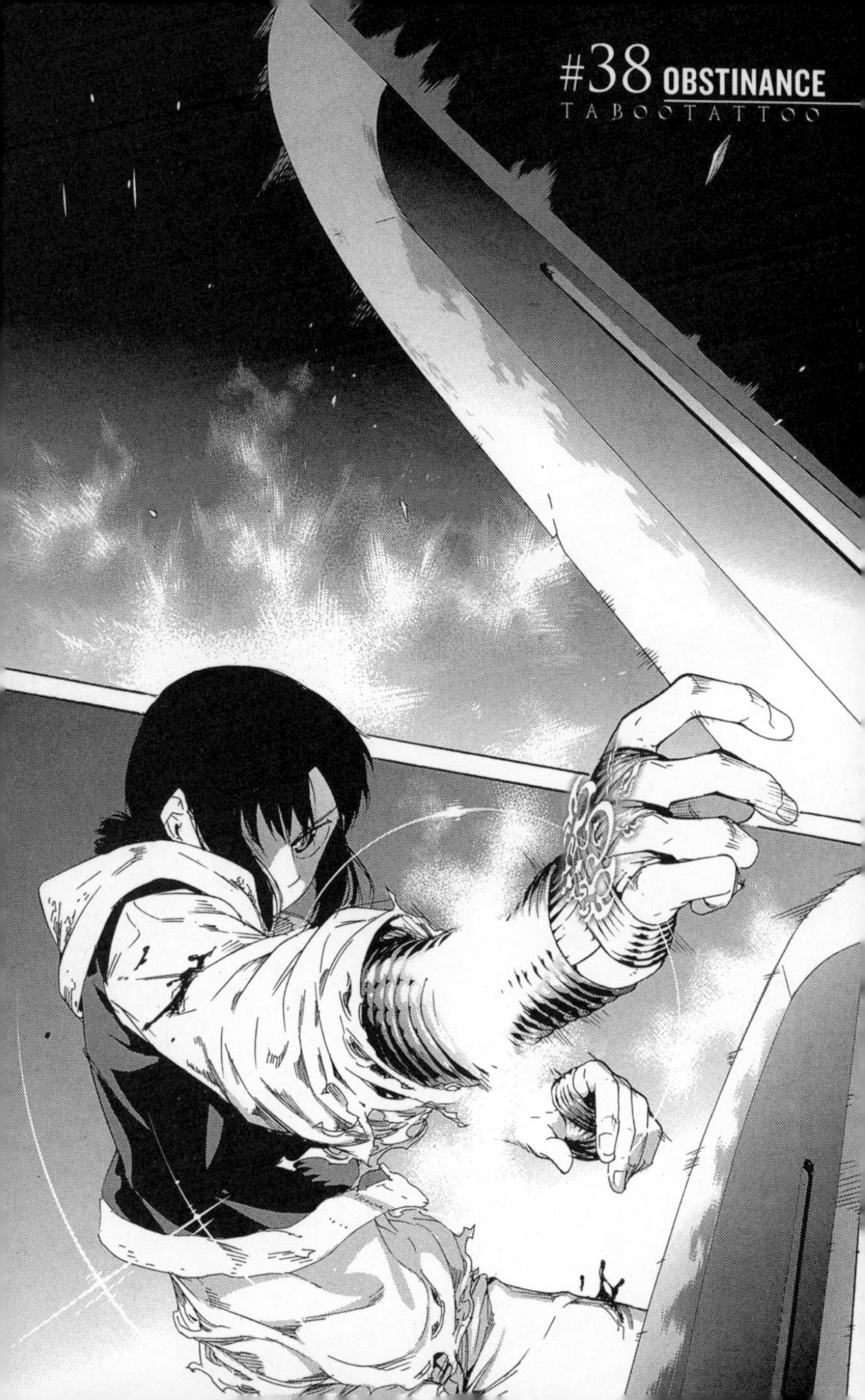
#38 OBSTINANCE
TABOOTATTOO

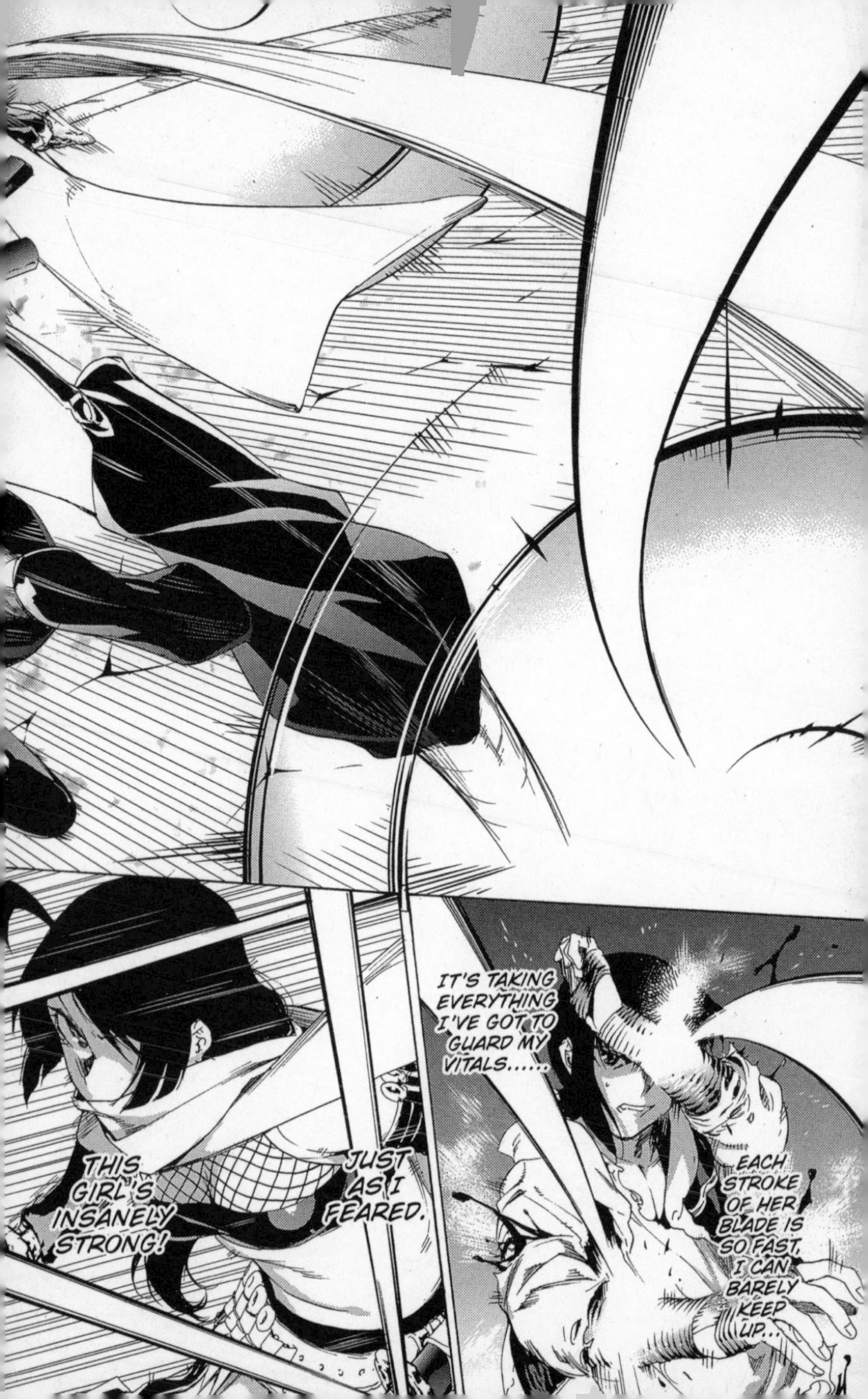
IT'S TAKING EVERYTHING I'VE GOT TO GUARD MY VITALS......
EACH STROKE OF HER BLADE IS SO FAST, I CAN BARELY KEEP UP...
JUST AS I FEARED.
THIS GIRL'S INSANELY STRONG!

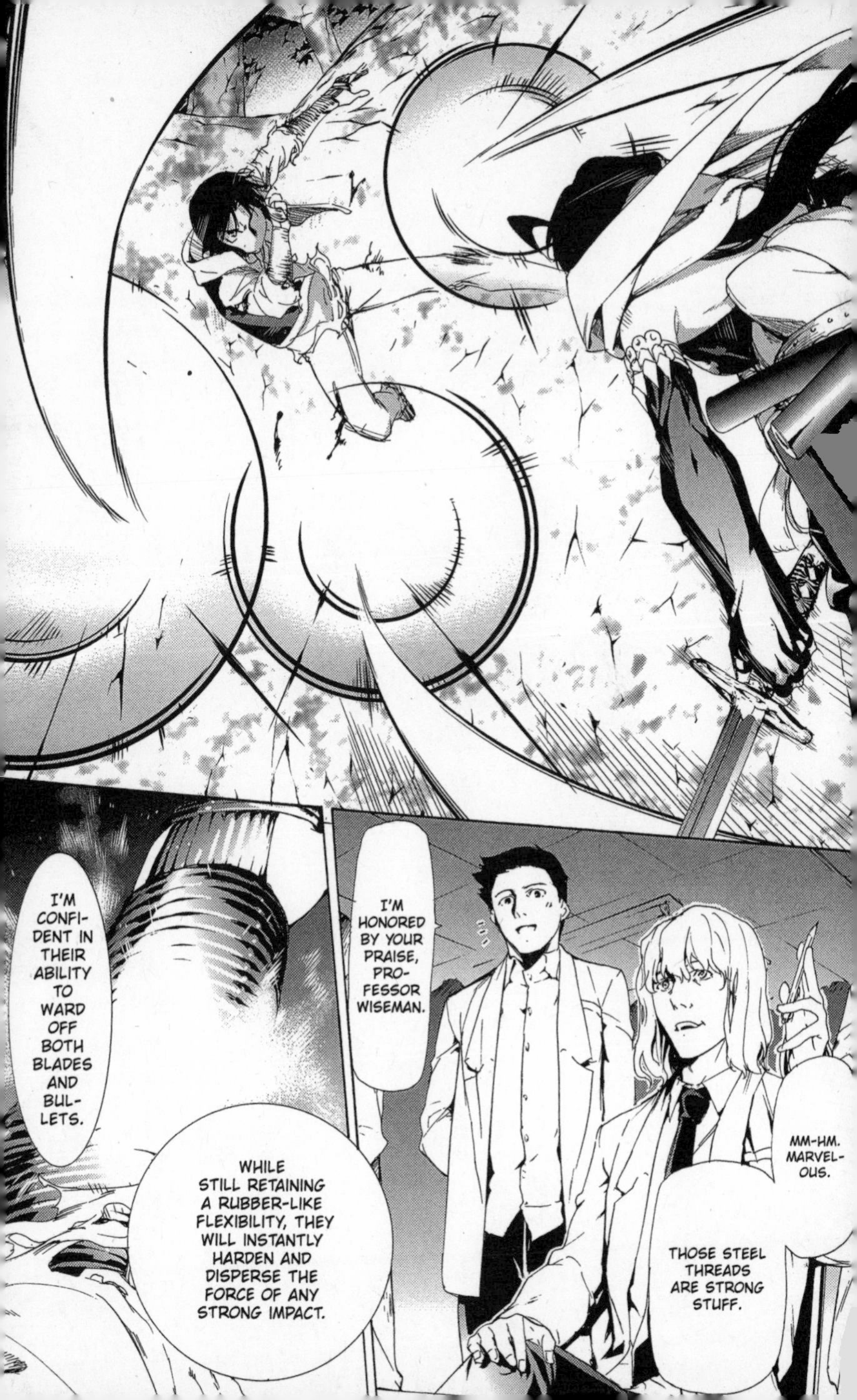
MM-HM. MARVELOUS.
THOSE STEEL THREADS ARE STRONG STUFF.
I'M HONORED BY YOUR PRAISE, PROFESSOR WISEMAN.
I'M CONFIDENT IN THEIR ABILITY TO WARD OFF BOTH BLADES AND BULLETS.
WHILE STILL RETAINING A RUBBER-LIKE FLEXIBILITY, THEY WILL INSTANTLY HARDEN AND DISPERSE THE FORCE OF ANY STRONG IMPACT.

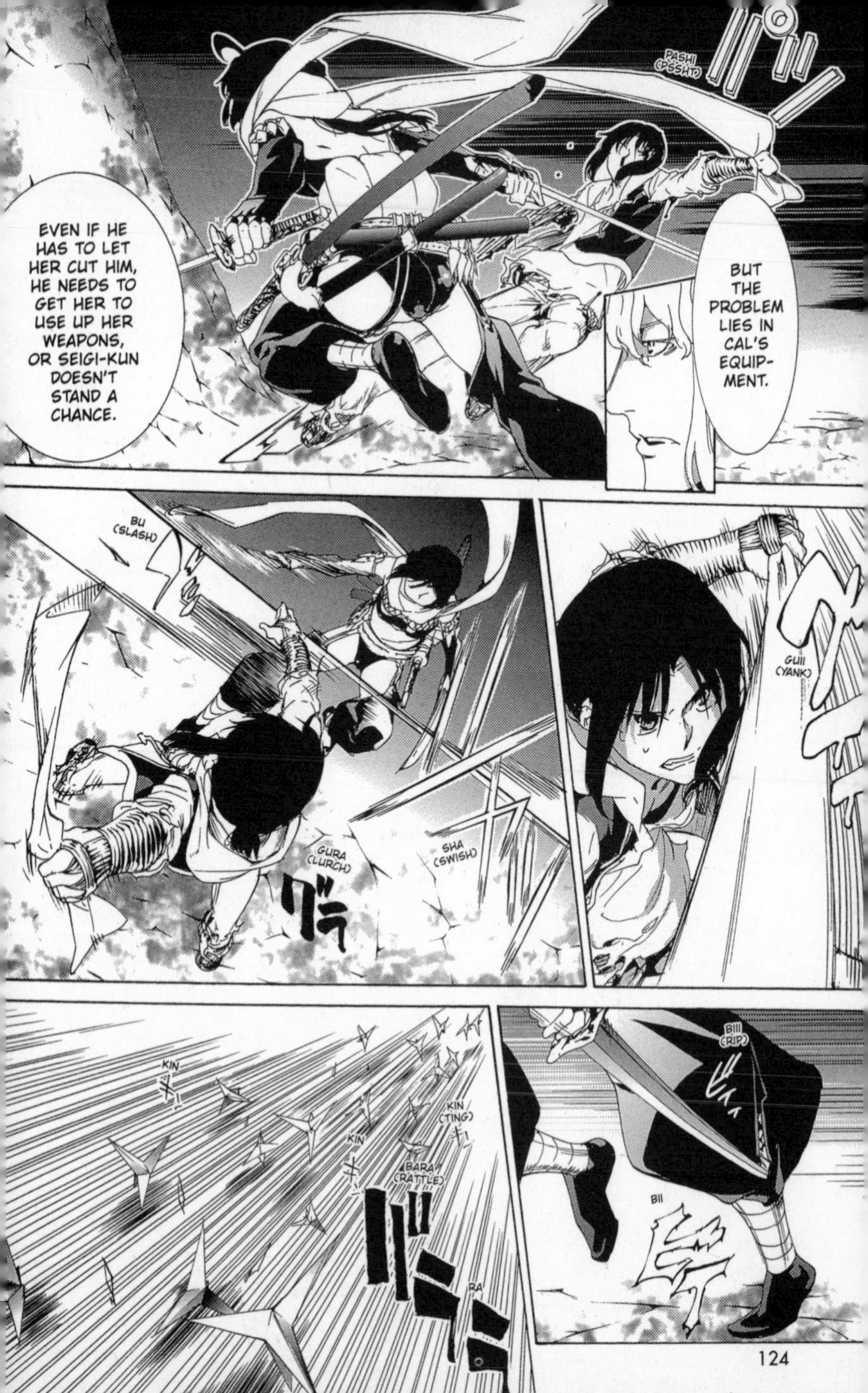
PASHI (PSSHT)
BUT THE PROBLEM LIES IN CAL'S EQUIPMENT.
EVEN IF HE HAS TO LET HER CUT HIM, HE NEEDS TO GET HER TO USE UP HER WEAPONS, OR SEIGI-KUN DOESN'T STAND A CHANCE.
GUII (YANK)
BU (SLASH)
SHA (SWISH)
GURA (LURCH)
BIII (RIP)
BII
KIN
KIN (TING)
KIN
BARA (RATTLE)
RA

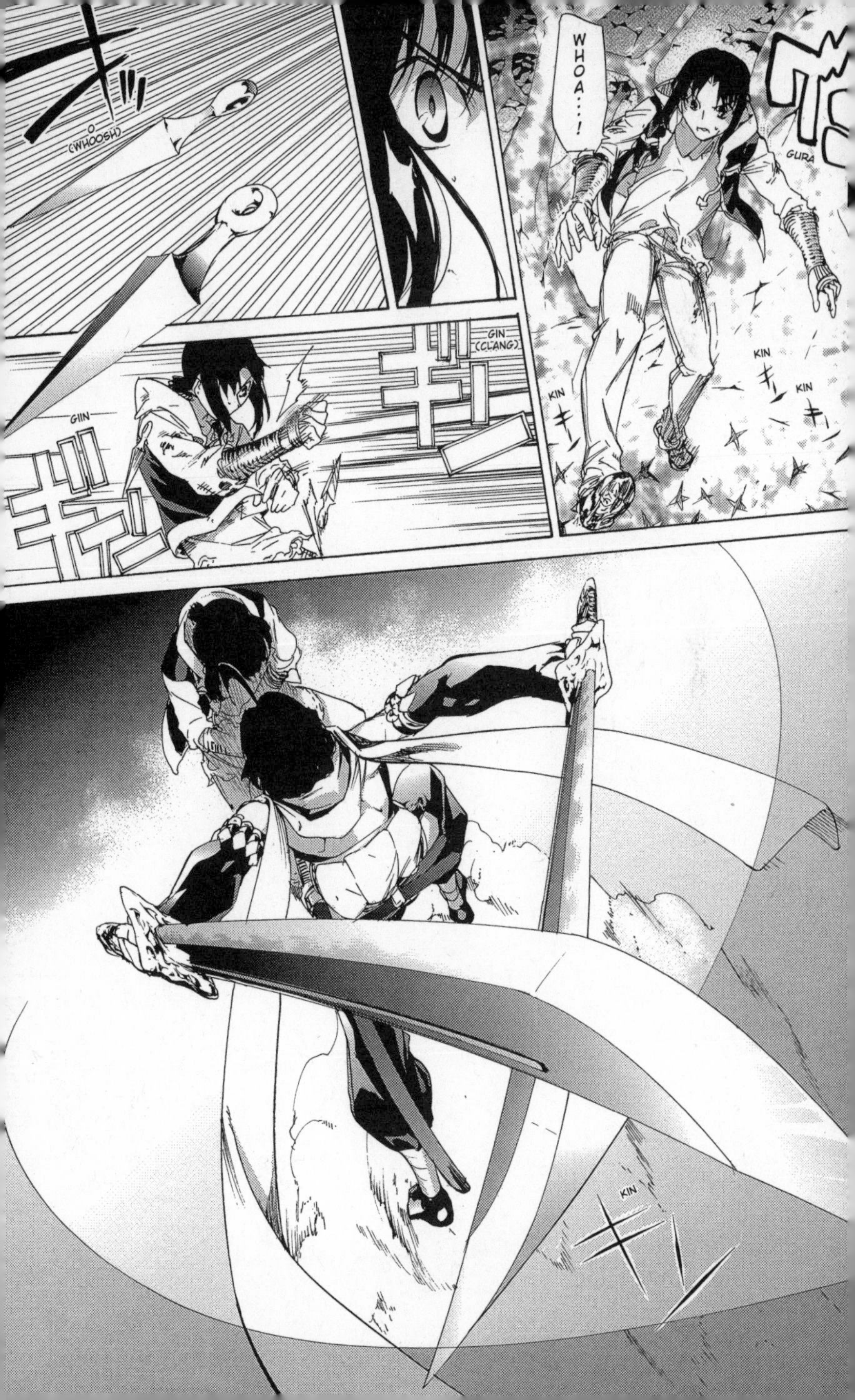
WHOA...!
GURA
KIN
KIN
KIN
O
(WHOOSH)
GIN
(CLANG)
GIIN
KIN

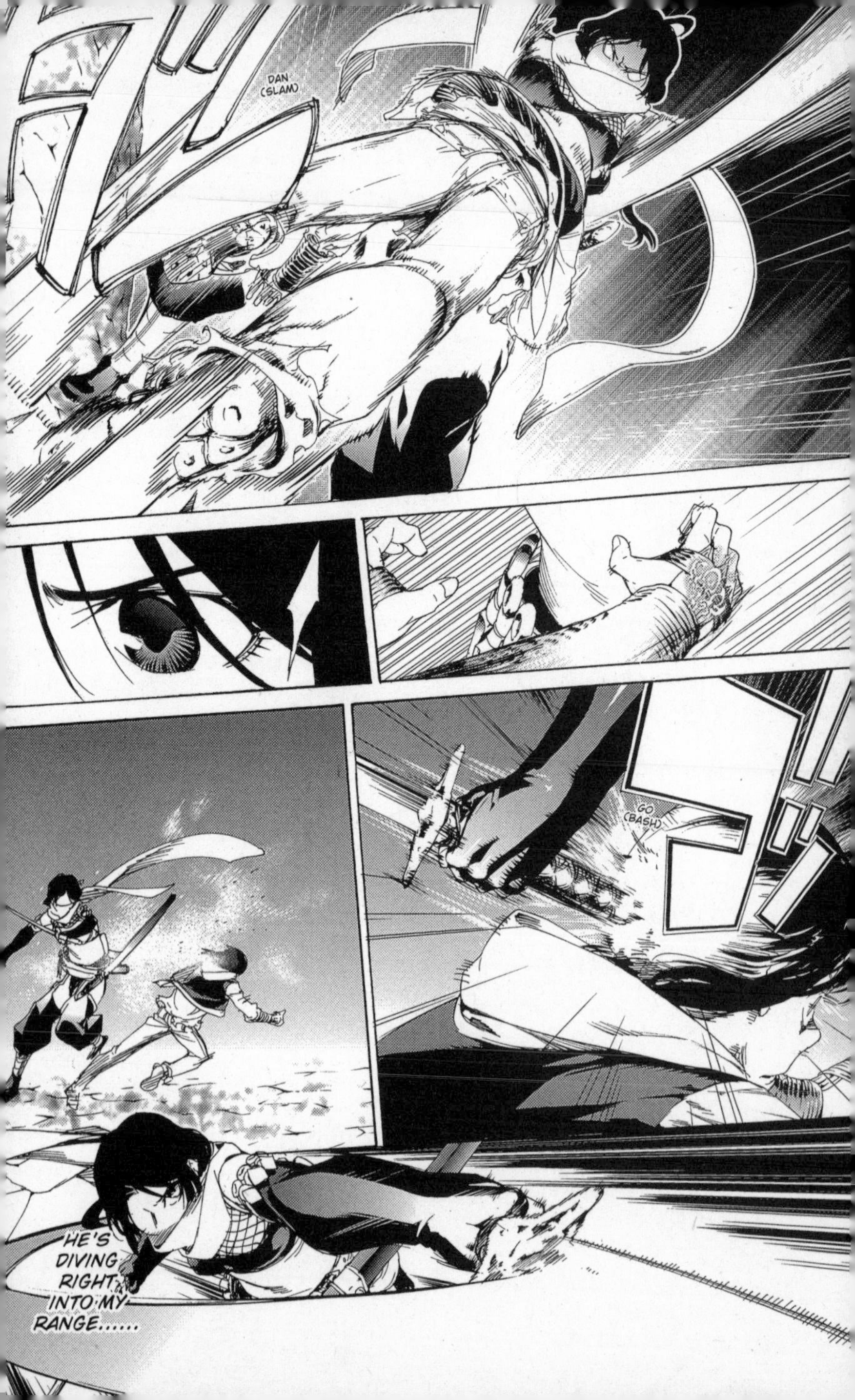
DAN (SLAM)
GO (BASH)
HE'S DIVING RIGHT INTO MY RANGE......

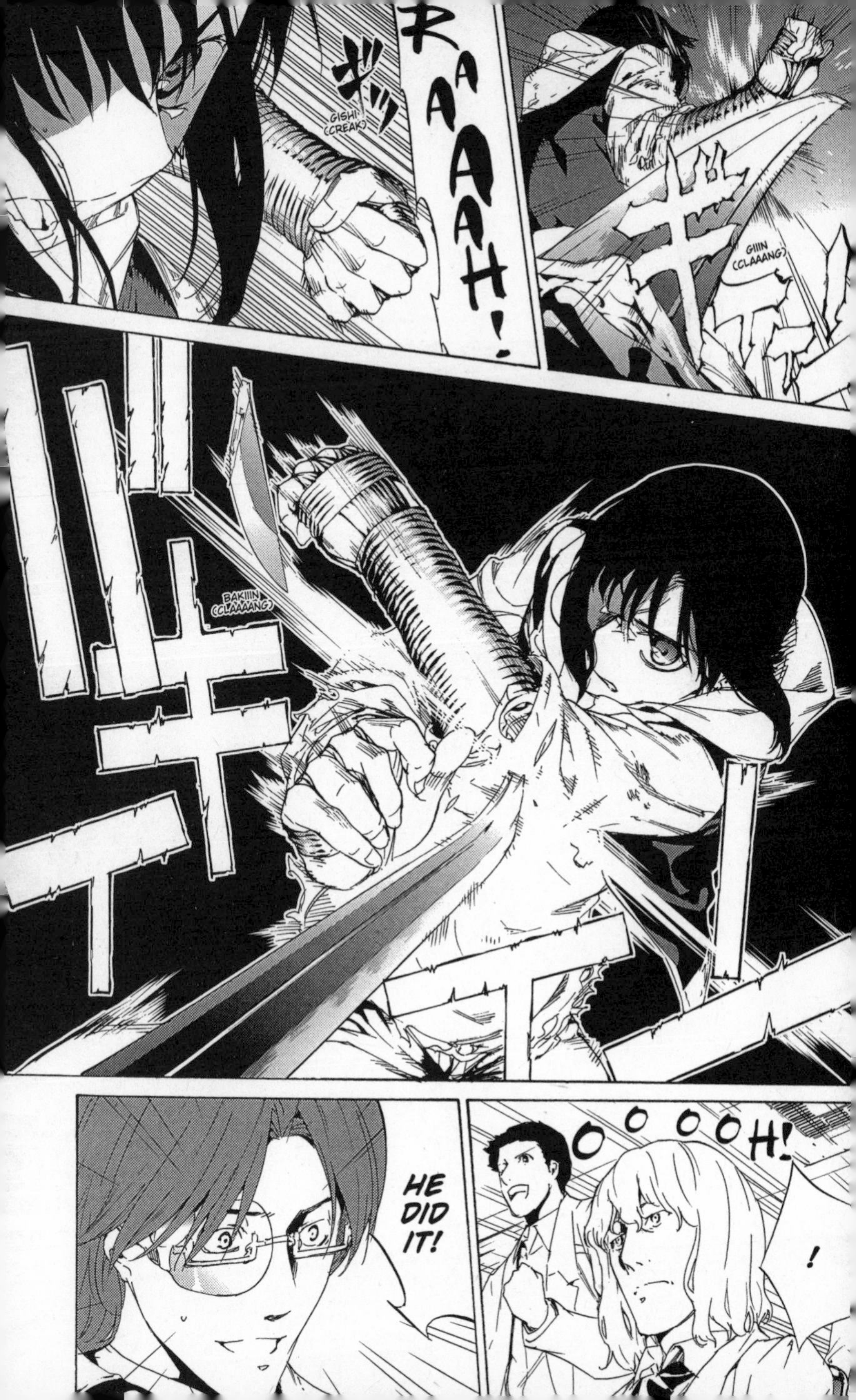
GIIIN (CLAAANG)
GISHI (CREAK)
RAAAAH!
BAKIIIN (CLAAAANG)
OOOOH!
!
HE DID IT!

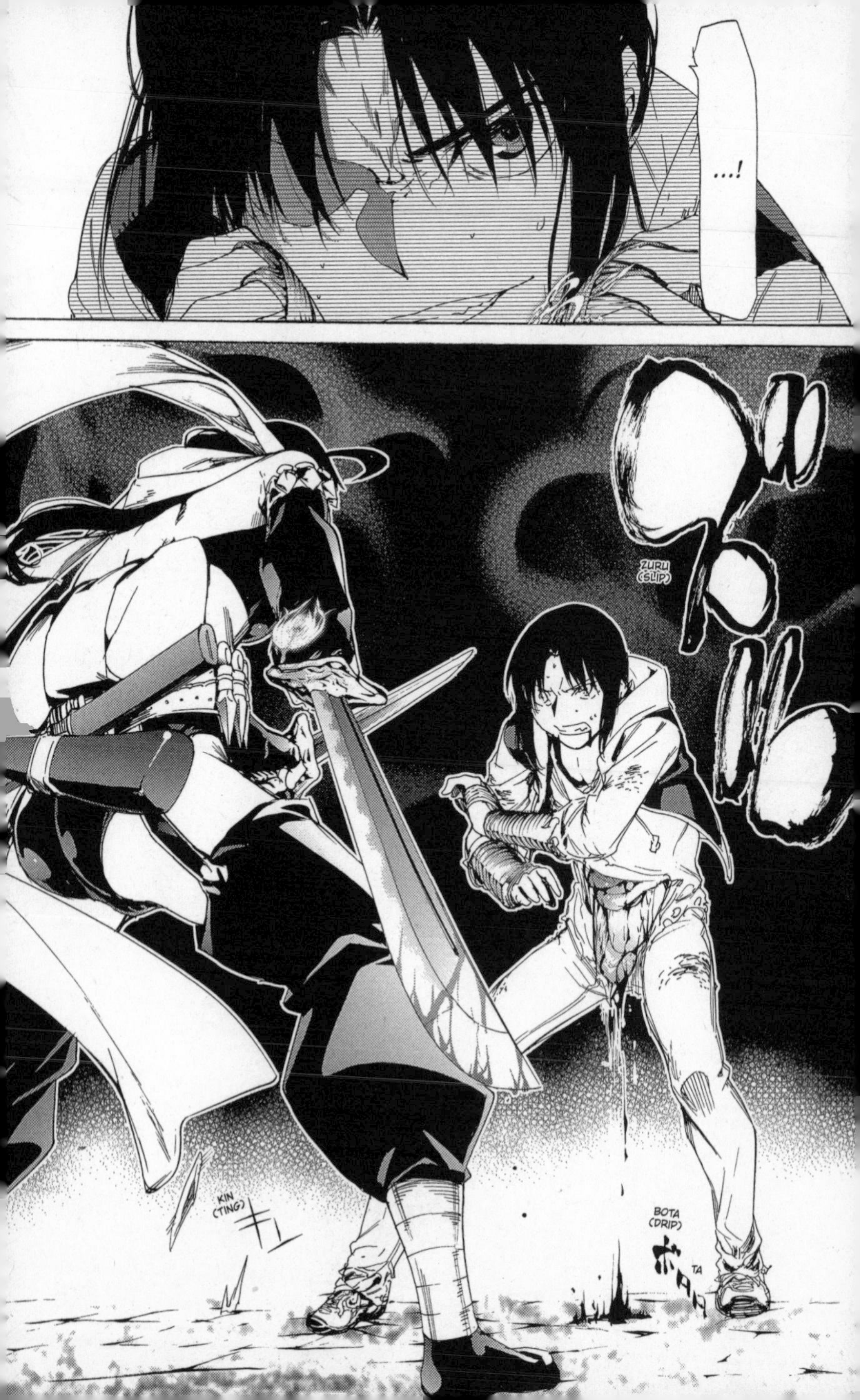
...!
ZURU (SLIP)
BOTA (DRIP)
TA
KIN (TING)

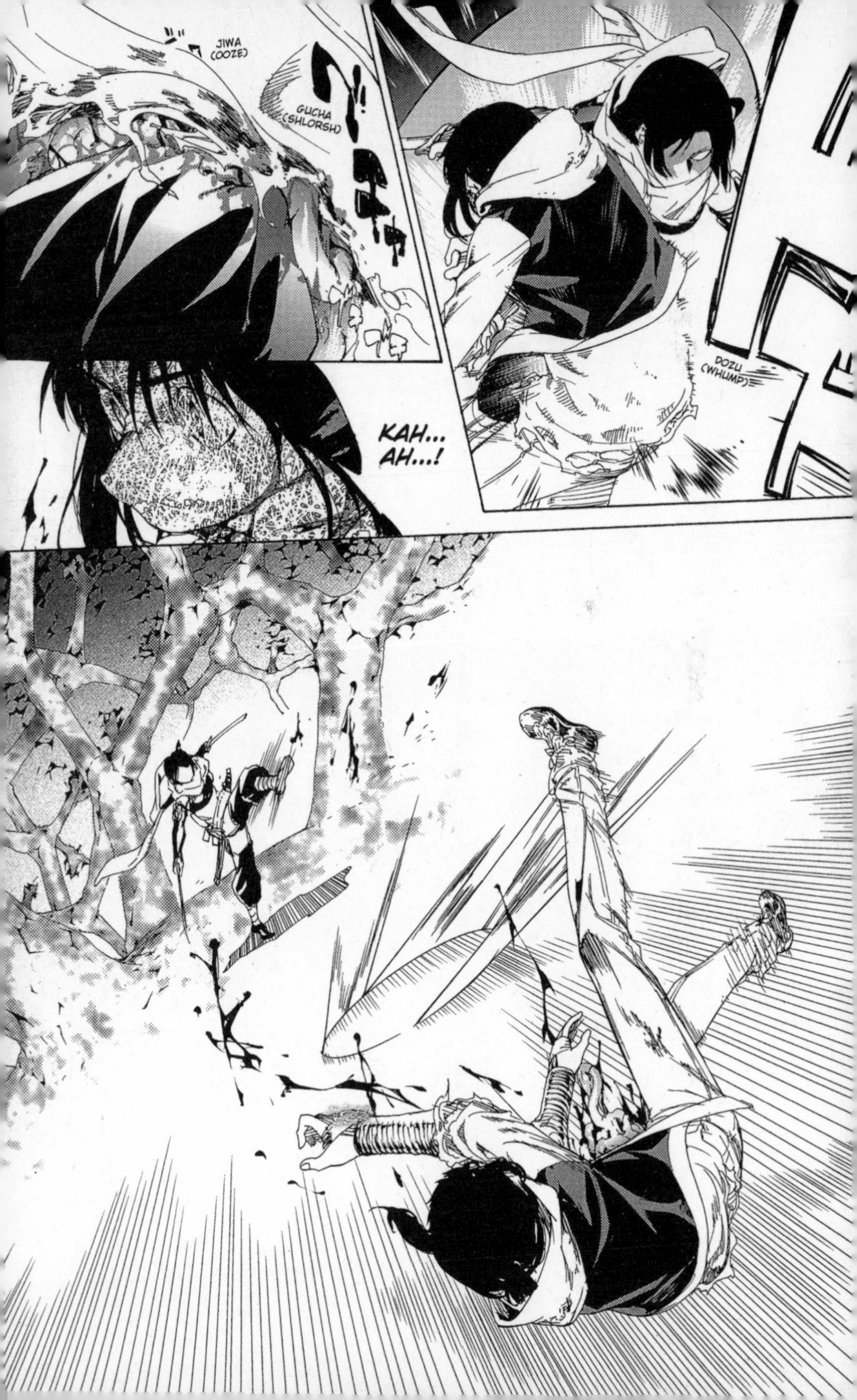
DOZU (WHUMP)
JIWA (OOZE)
GUCHA (SHLORSH)
KAH... AH...!

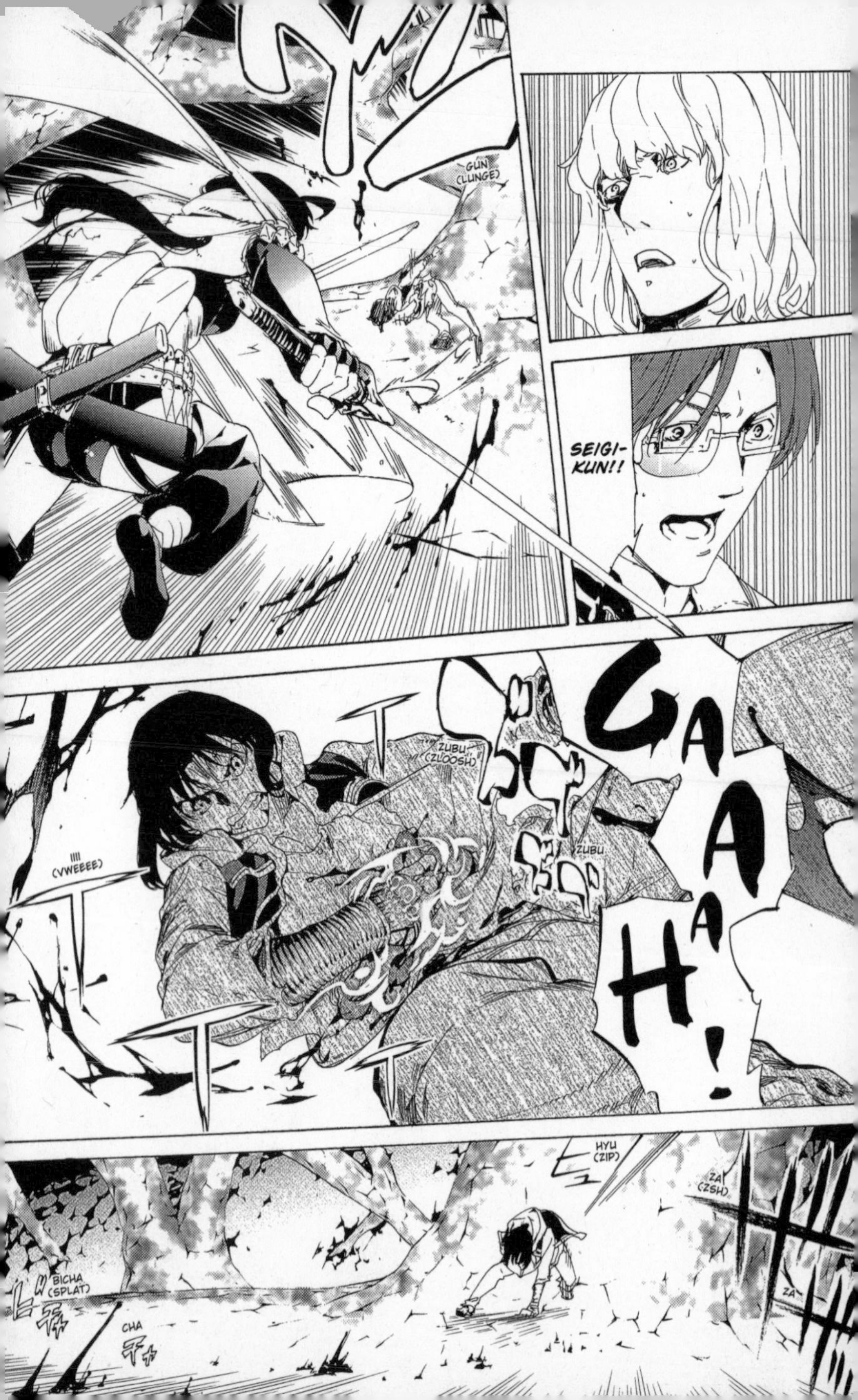

SEIGI-KUN!!
GUN (LUNGE)
GAAAH!
ZUBU (ZLOOSH)
ZUBU
IIII (VWEEEE)
HYU (ZIP)
ZA (ZSH)
ZA
BICHA (SPLAT)
CHA

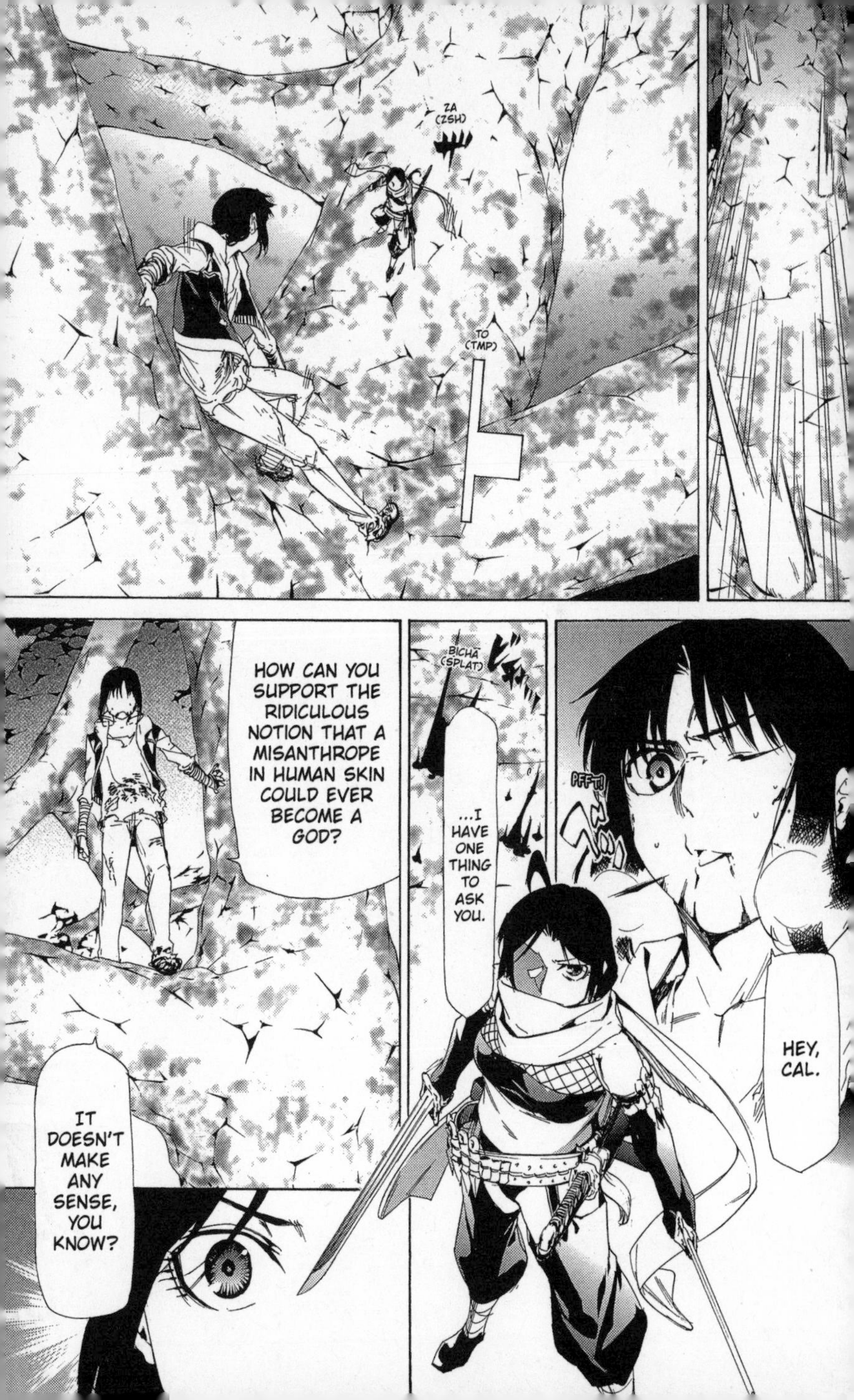
ZA (ZSH)
TO (TMP)
PFFT!!
HEY, CAL.
BICHA (SPLAT)
...I HAVE ONE THING TO ASK YOU.
HOW CAN YOU SUPPORT THE RIDICULOUS NOTION THAT A MISANTHROPE IN HUMAN SKIN COULD EVER BECOME A GOD?
IT DOESN'T MAKE ANY SENSE, YOU KNOW?

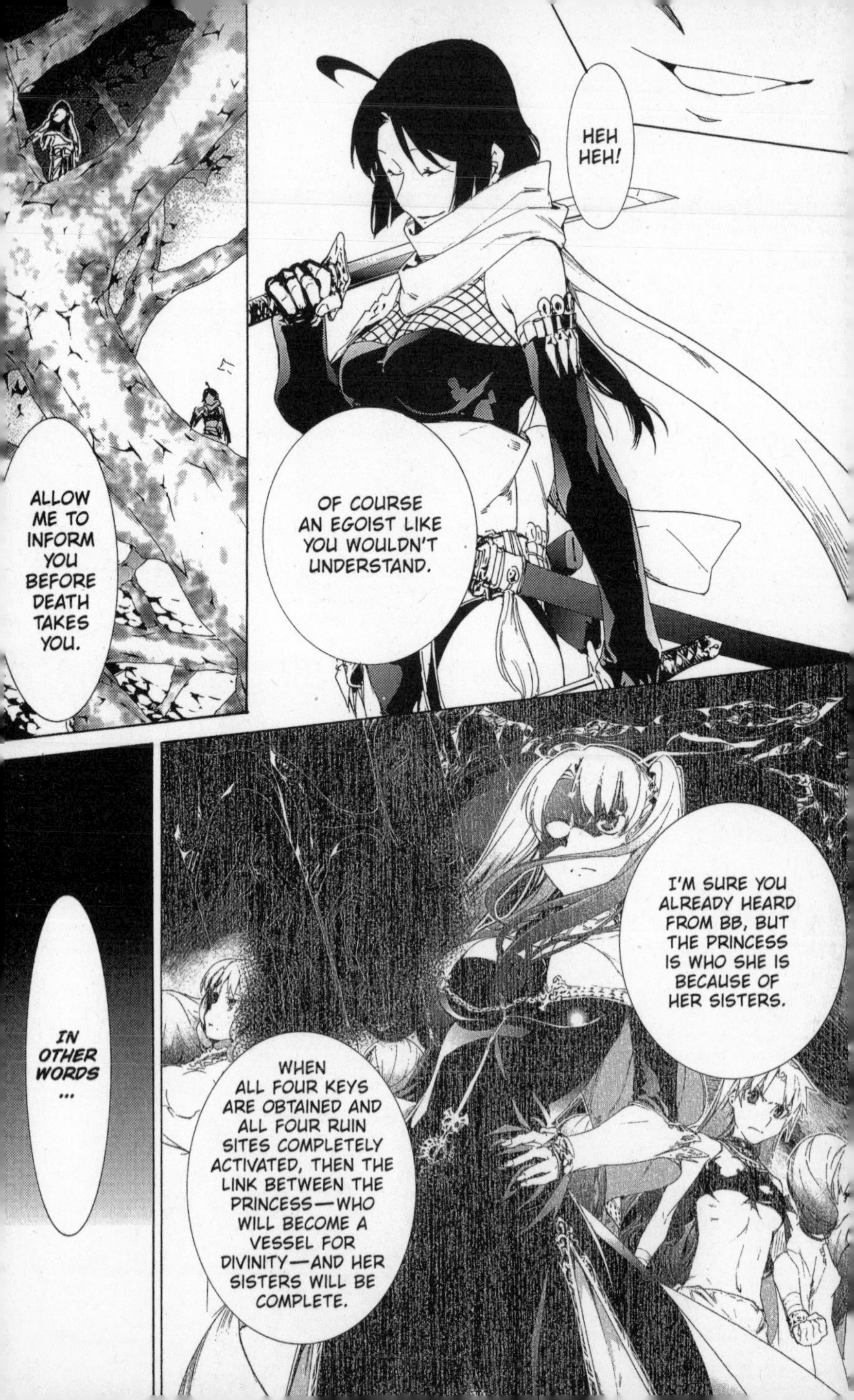
HEH HEH!
OF COURSE AN EGOIST LIKE YOU WOULDN'T UNDERSTAND.
ALLOW ME TO INFORM YOU BEFORE DEATH TAKES YOU.
I'M SURE YOU ALREADY HEARD FROM BB, BUT THE PRINCESS IS WHO SHE IS BECAUSE OF HER SISTERS.
WHEN ALL FOUR KEYS ARE OBTAINED AND ALL FOUR RUIN SITES COMPLETELY ACTIVATED, THEN THE LINK BETWEEN THE PRINCESS—WHO WILL BECOME A VESSEL FOR DIVINITY—AND HER SISTERS WILL BE COMPLETE.
IN OTHER WORDS...

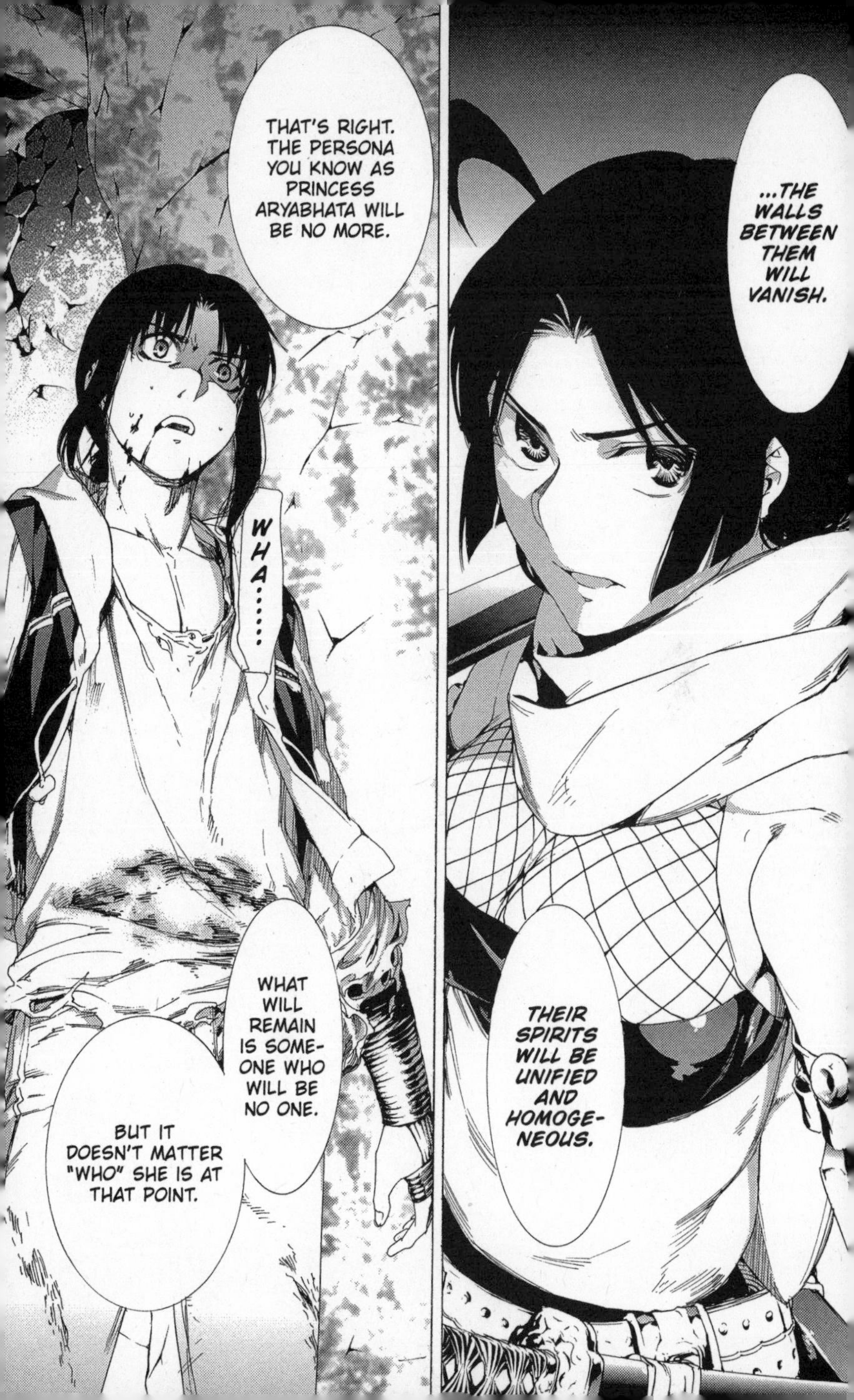
...THE WALLS BETWEEN THEM WILL VANISH.
THEIR SPIRITS WILL BE UNIFIED AND HOMOGENEOUS.
THAT'S RIGHT. THE PERSONA YOU KNOW AS PRINCESS ARYABHATA WILL BE NO MORE.
WHA......
WHAT WILL REMAIN IS SOMEONE WHO WILL BE NO ONE.
BUT IT DOESN'T MATTER "WHO" SHE IS AT THAT POINT.

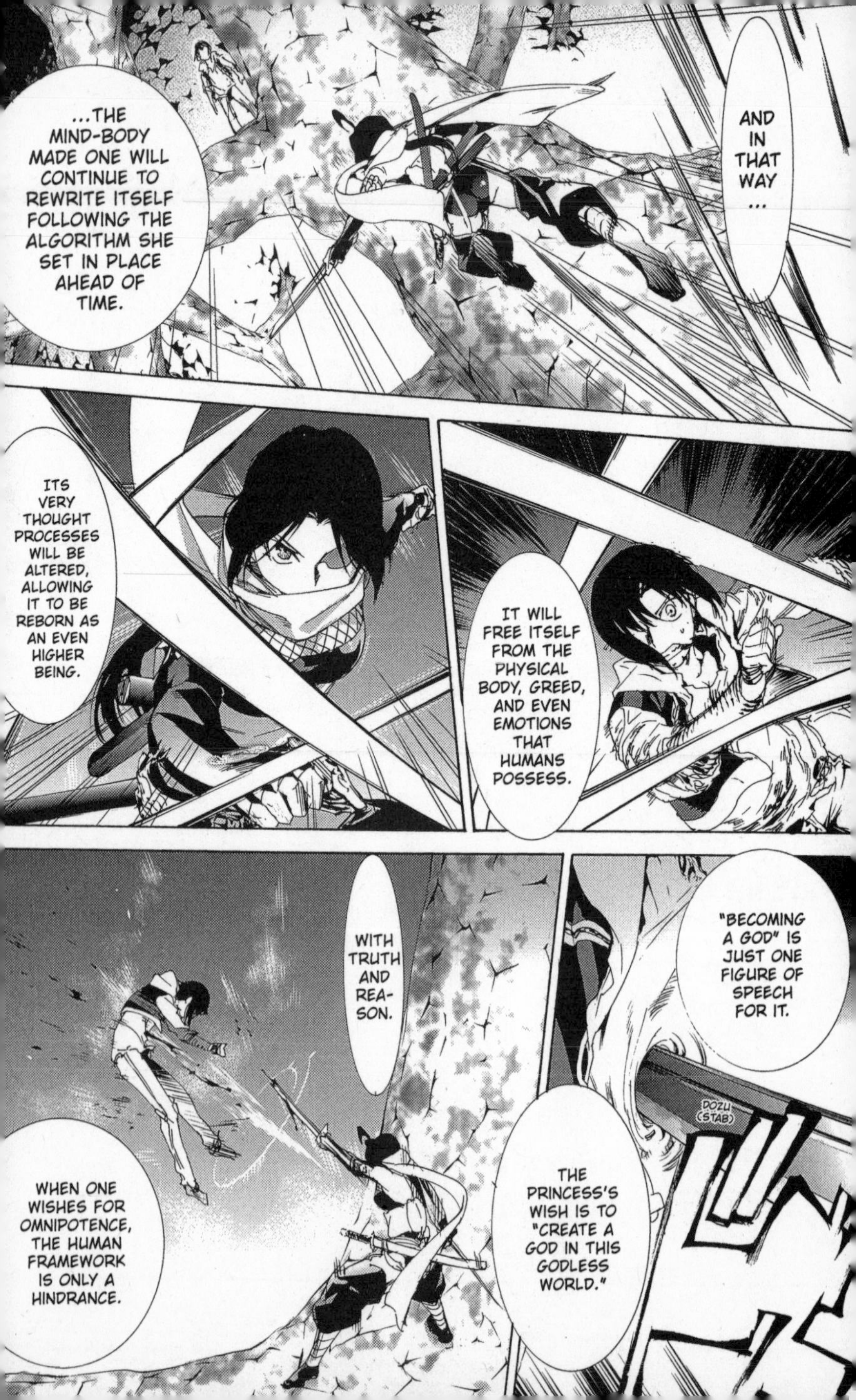

AND IN THAT WAY...
...THE MIND-BODY MADE ONE WILL CONTINUE TO REWRITE ITSELF FOLLOWING THE ALGORITHM SHE SET IN PLACE AHEAD OF TIME.
IT WILL FREE ITSELF FROM THE PHYSICAL BODY, GREED, AND EVEN EMOTIONS THAT HUMANS POSSESS.
ITS VERY THOUGHT PROCESSES WILL BE ALTERED, ALLOWING IT TO BE REBORN AS AN EVEN HIGHER BEING.
"BECOMING A GOD" IS JUST ONE FIGURE OF SPEECH FOR IT.
DOZU (STAB)
THE PRINCESS'S WISH IS TO "CREATE A GOD IN THIS GODLESS WORLD."
WITH TRUTH AND REA-SON.
WHEN ONE WISHES FOR OMNIPOTENCE, THE HUMAN FRAMEWORK IS ONLY A HINDRANCE.

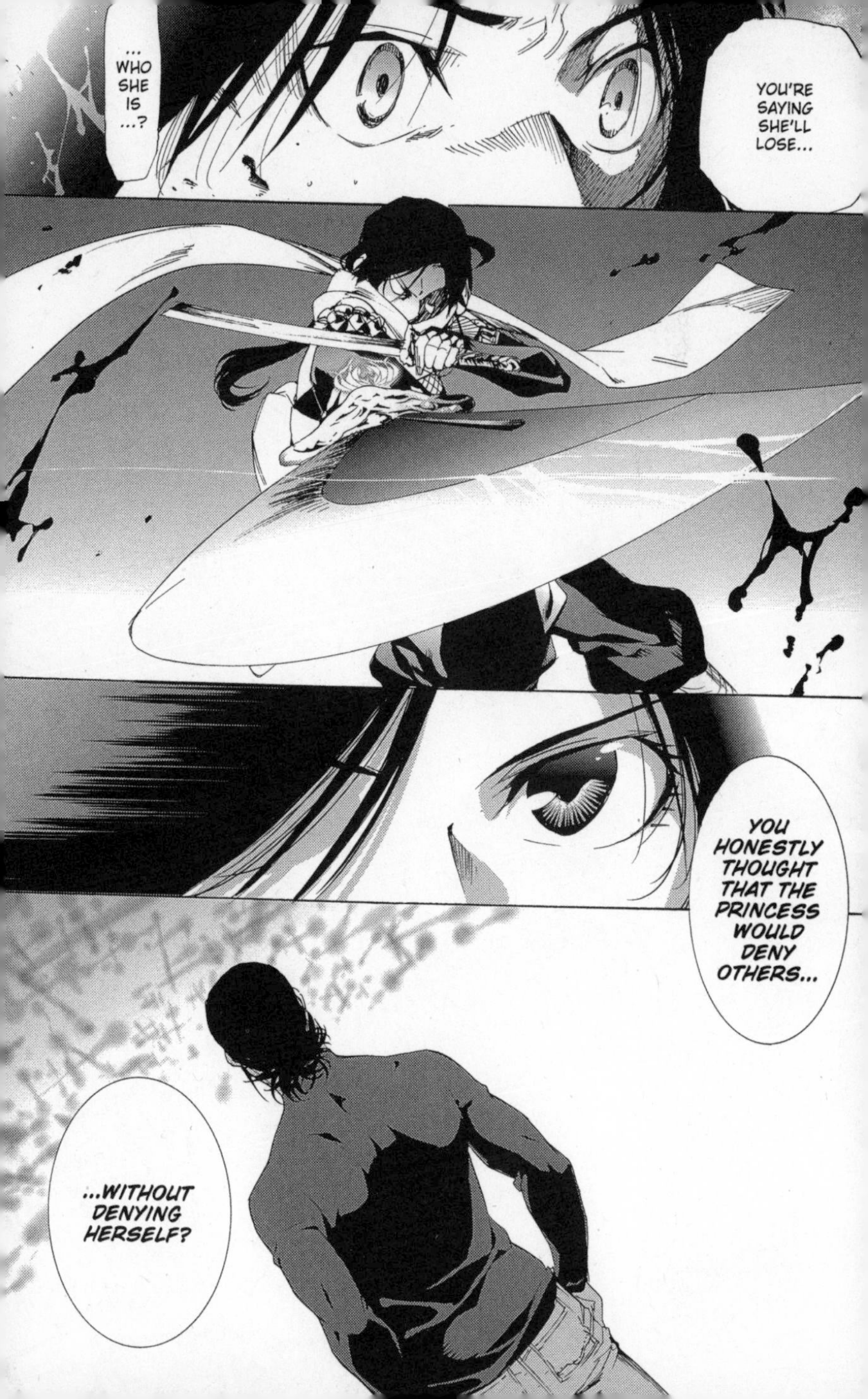
YOU'RE SAYING SHE'LL LOSE...
...WHO SHE IS...?
YOU HONESTLY THOUGHT THAT THE PRINCESS WOULD DENY OTHERS...
...WITHOUT DENYING HERSELF?

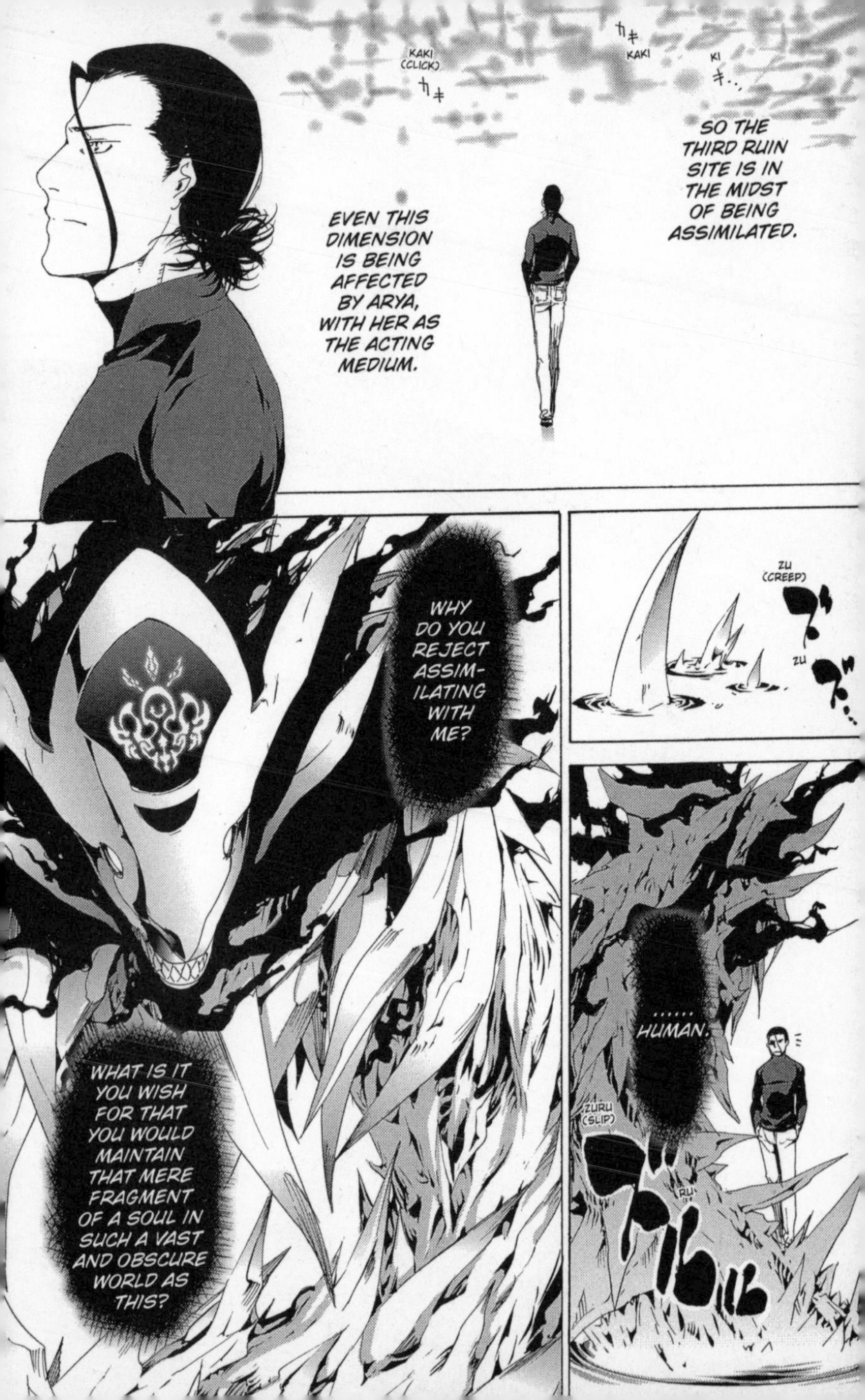

キ…
KI
カキ
KAKI
カキ
KAKI (CLICK)
SO THE THIRD RUIN SITE IS IN THE MIDST OF BEING ASSIMILATED.
EVEN THIS DIMENSION IS BEING AFFECTED BY ARYA, WITH HER AS THE ACTING MEDIUM.
ZU (CREEP)
ZU
......HUMAN.
ZURU (SLIP)
RU
WHY DO YOU REJECT ASSIM-ILATING WITH ME?
WHAT IS IT YOU WISH FOR THAT YOU WOULD MAINTAIN THAT MERE FRAGMENT OF A SOUL IN SUCH A VAST AND OBSCURE WORLD AS THIS?

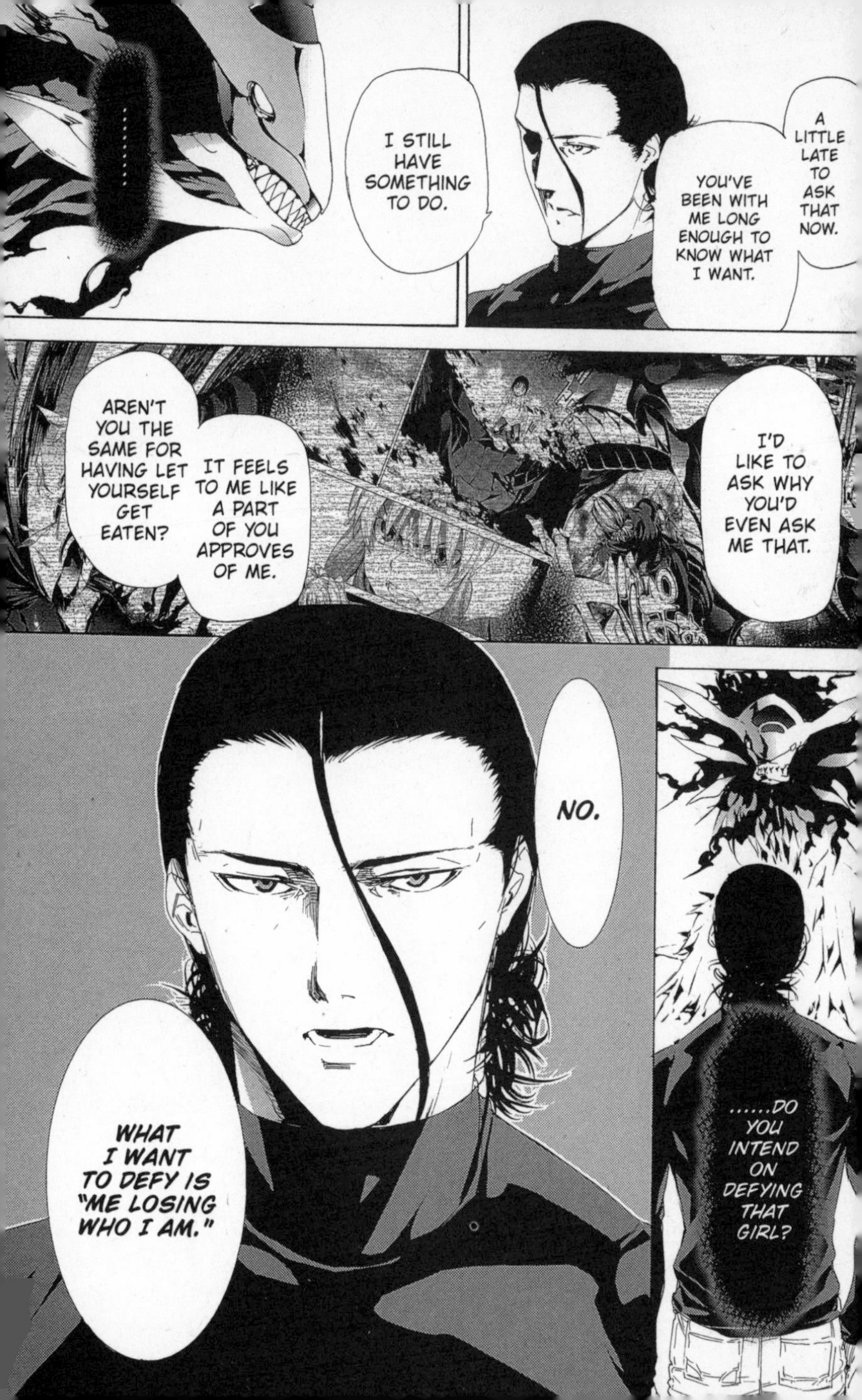
A LITTLE LATE TO ASK THAT NOW.
YOU'VE BEEN WITH ME LONG ENOUGH TO KNOW WHAT I WANT.
I STILL HAVE SOMETHING TO DO.
......
I'D LIKE TO ASK WHY YOU'D EVEN ASK ME THAT.
IT FEELS TO ME LIKE A PART OF YOU APPROVES OF ME.
AREN'T YOU THE SAME FOR HAVING LET YOURSELF GET EATEN?
......DO YOU INTEND ON DEFYING THAT GIRL?
NO.
WHAT I WANT TO DEFY IS "ME LOSING WHO I AM."

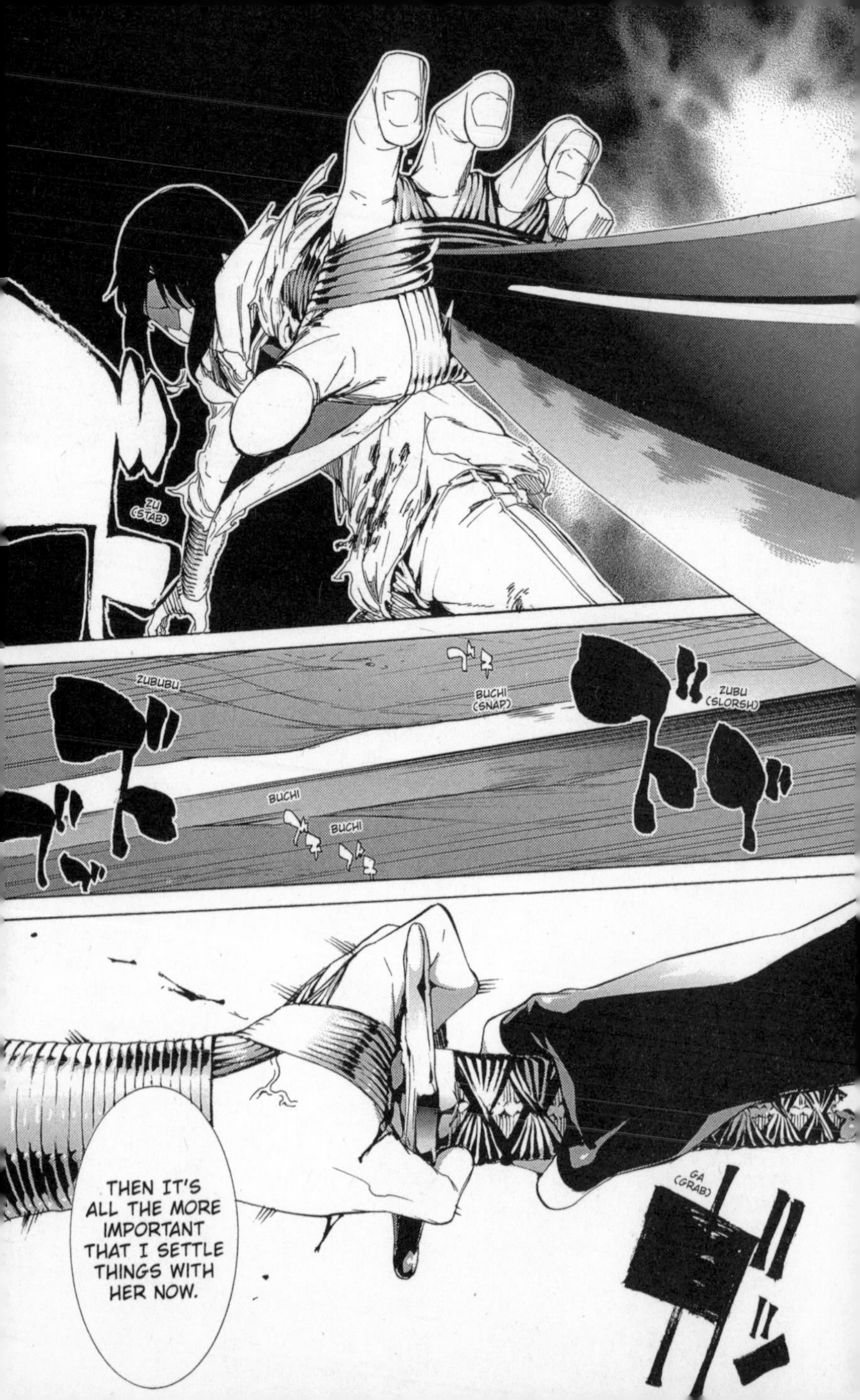
ZU (STAB)
ZUBU (SLORSH)
BUCHI (SNAP)
BUCHI
BUCHI
ZUBUBU
GA (GRAB)
THEN IT'S ALL THE MORE IMPORTANT THAT I SETTLE THINGS WITH HER NOW.

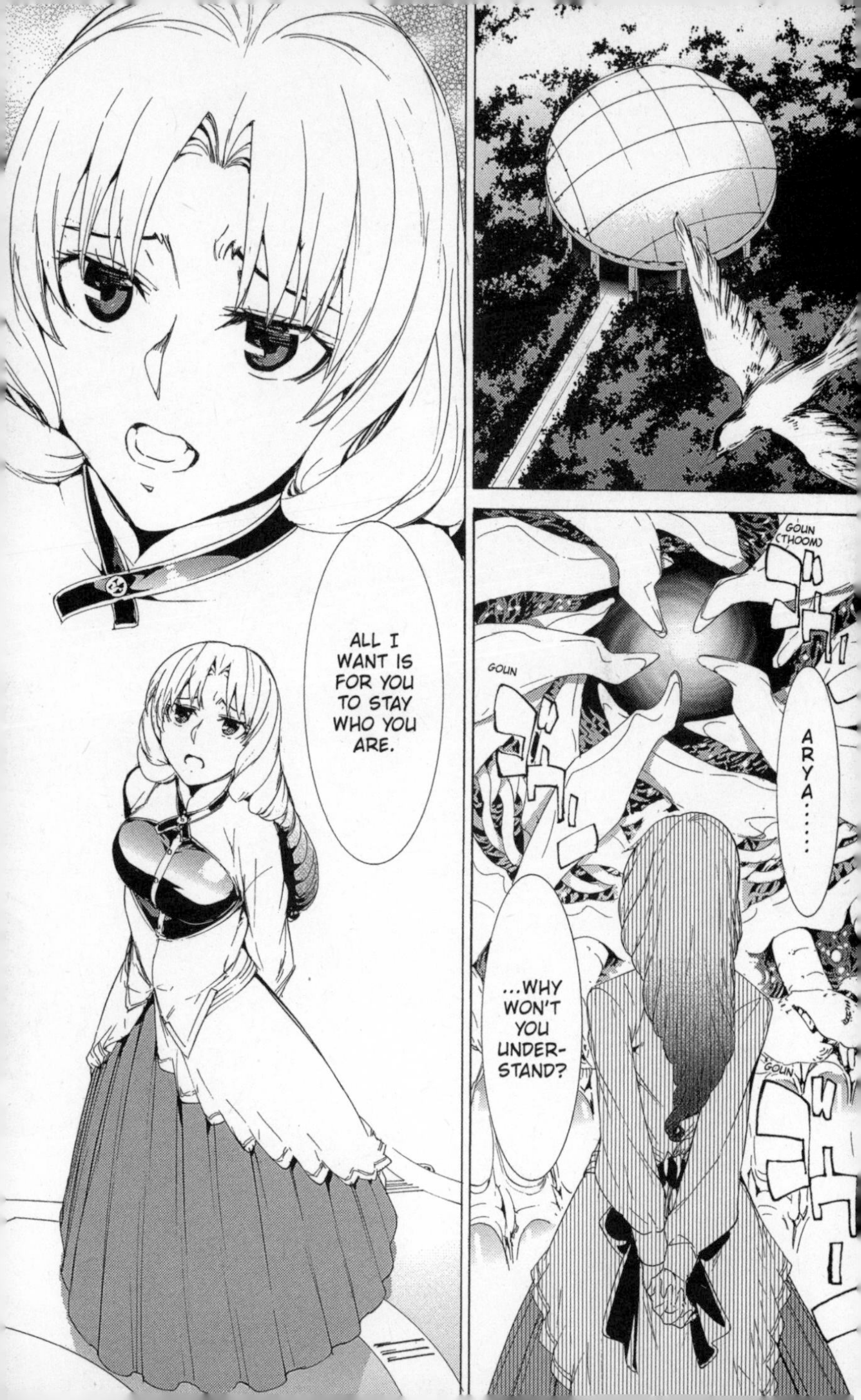
GOUN (THOOM)
ARYA......
GOUN
...WHY WON'T YOU UNDER-STAND?
GOUN
ALL I WANT IS FOR YOU TO STAY WHO YOU ARE.

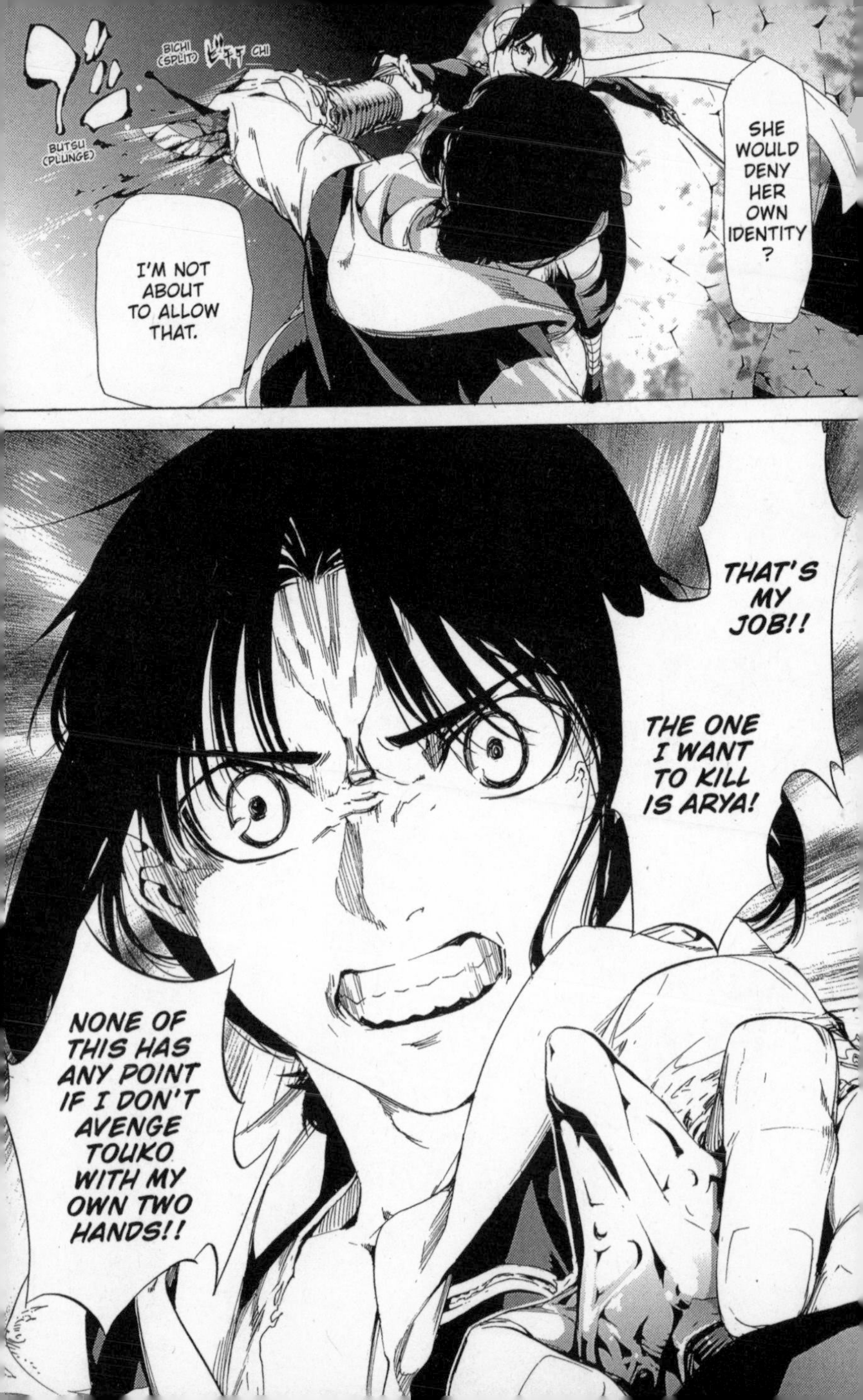
SHE WOULD DENY HER OWN IDENTITY?
BICHI (SPLIT) CHI
BUTSU (PLUNGE)
I'M NOT ABOUT TO ALLOW THAT.
THAT'S MY JOB!!
THE ONE I WANT TO KILL IS ARYA!
NONE OF THIS HAS ANY POINT IF I DON'T AVENGE TOUKO WITH MY OWN TWO HANDS!!

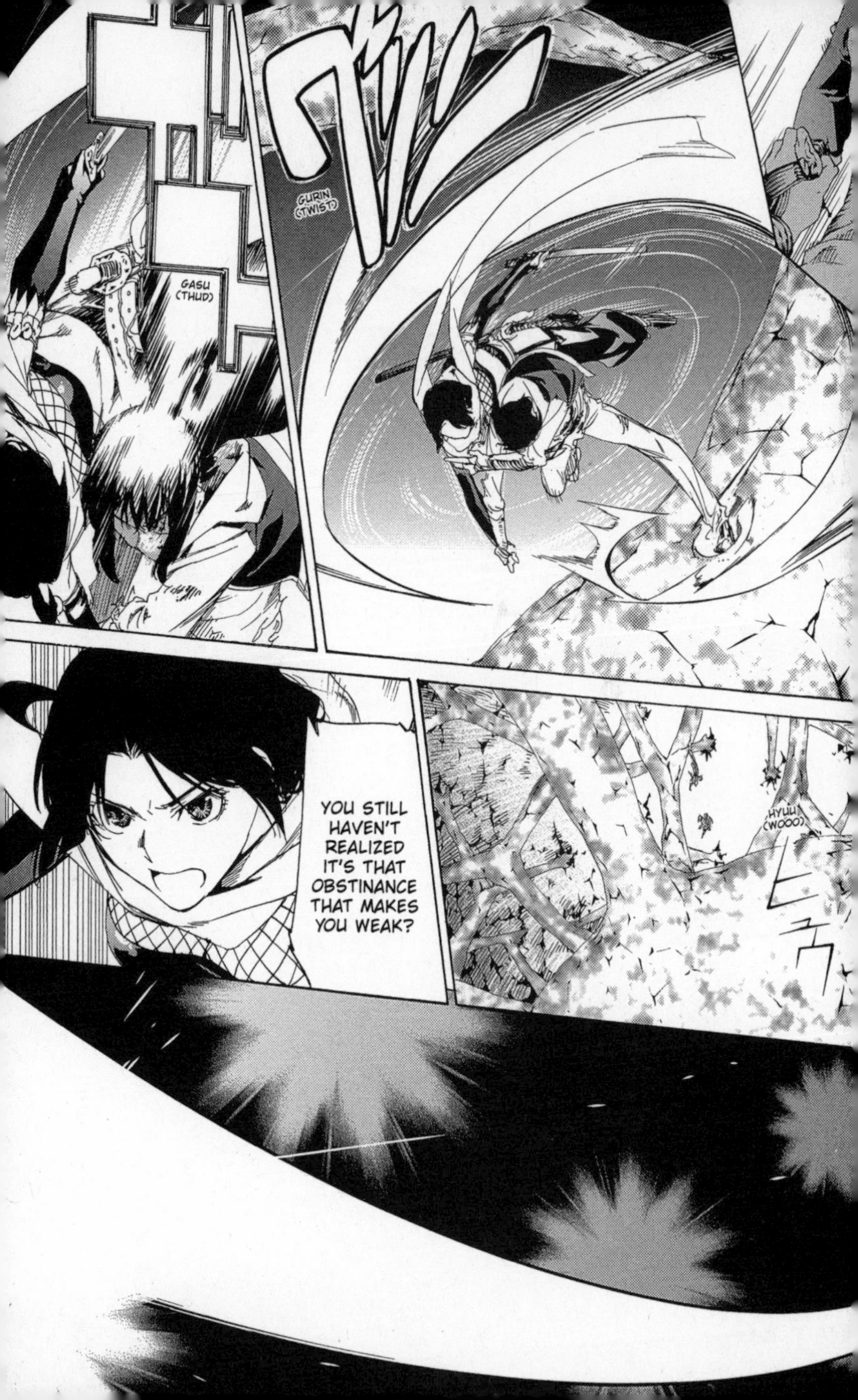
GURIN (TWIST)
GASU (THUD)
HYUU (WOOO)
YOU STILL HAVEN'T REALIZED IT'S THAT OBSTINANCE THAT MAKES YOU WEAK?

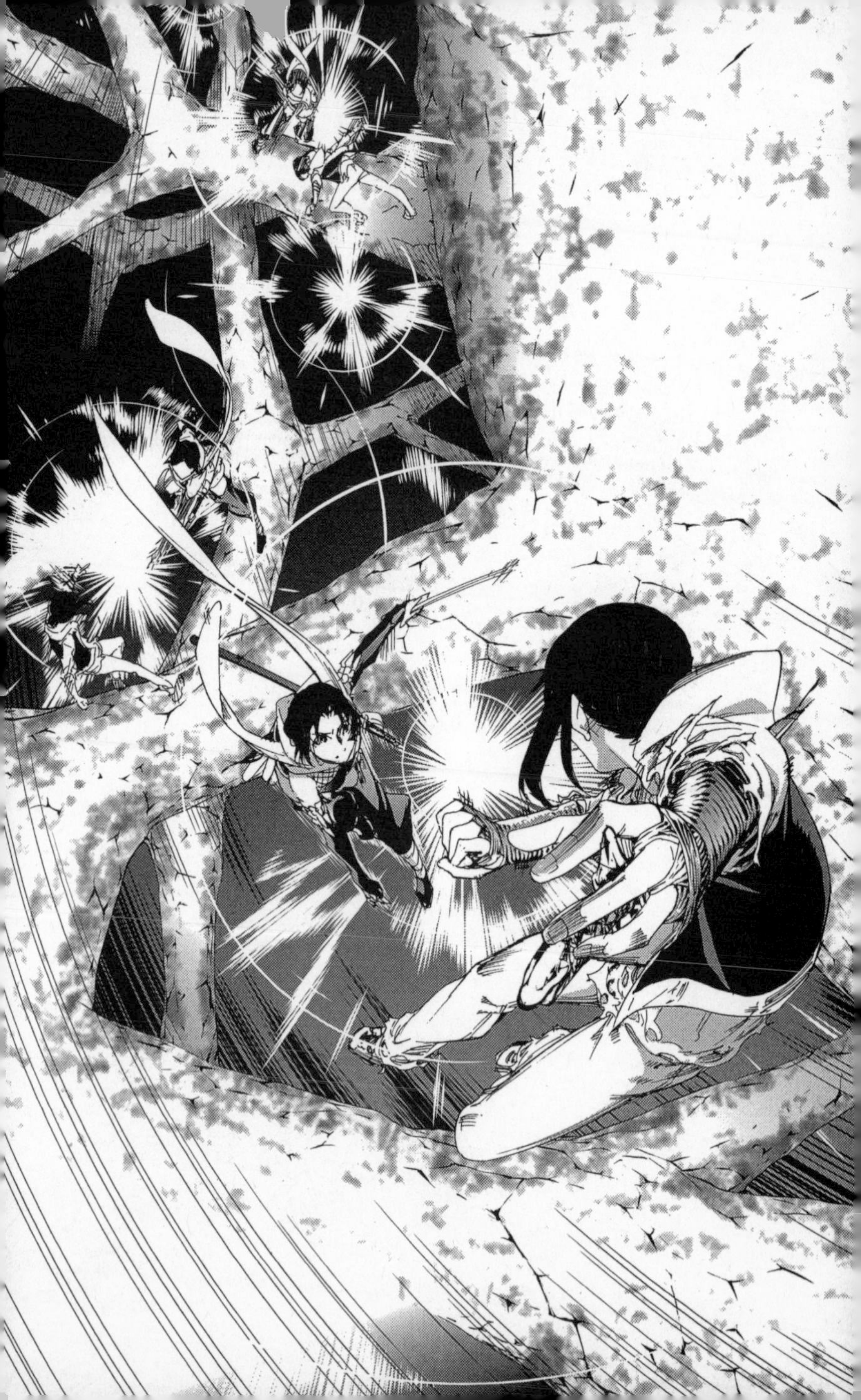

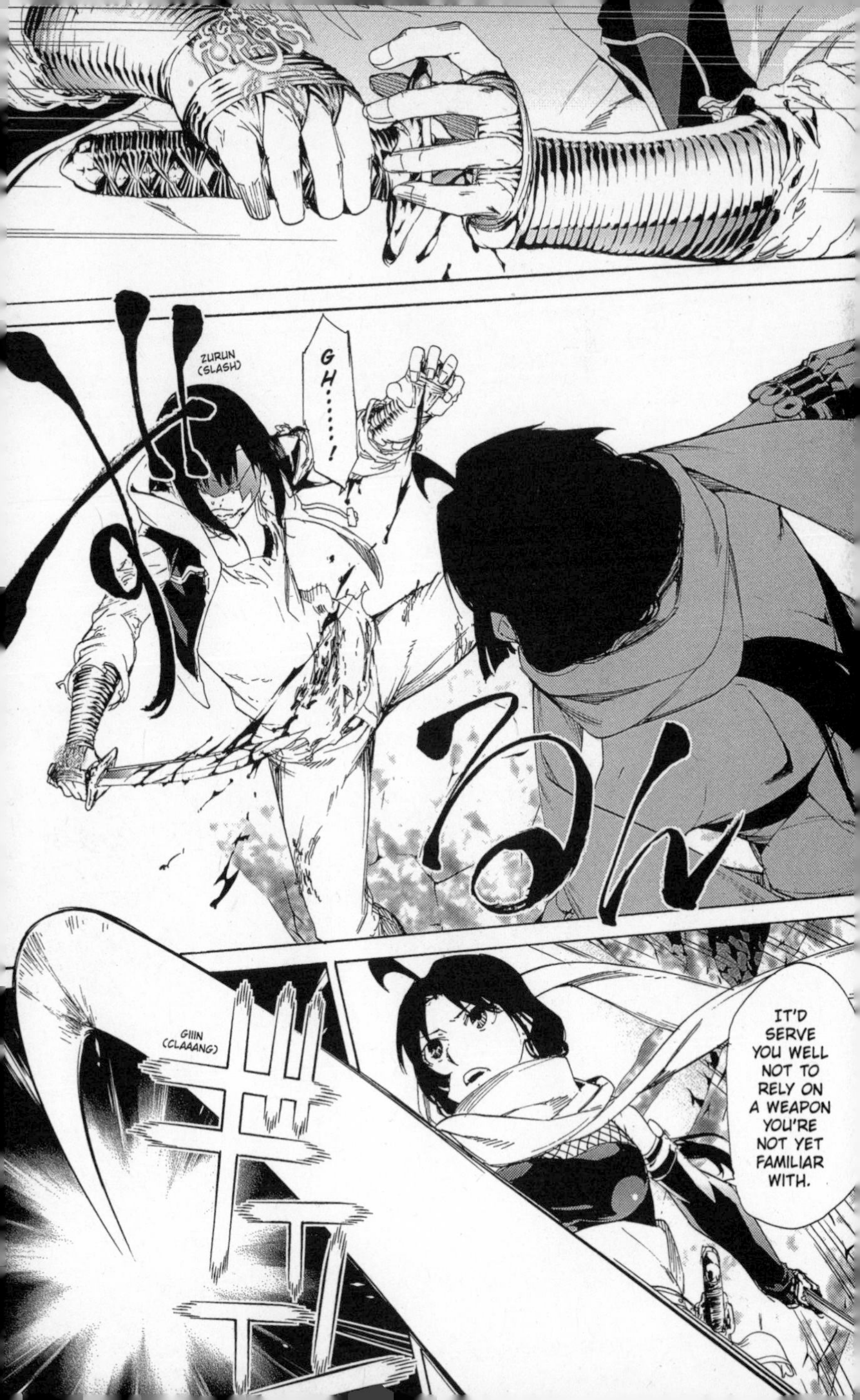
GH.....!
ZURUN (SLASH)
IT'D SERVE YOU WELL NOT TO RELY ON A WEAPON YOU'RE NOT YET FAMILIAR WITH.
GIIIN (CLAAANG)

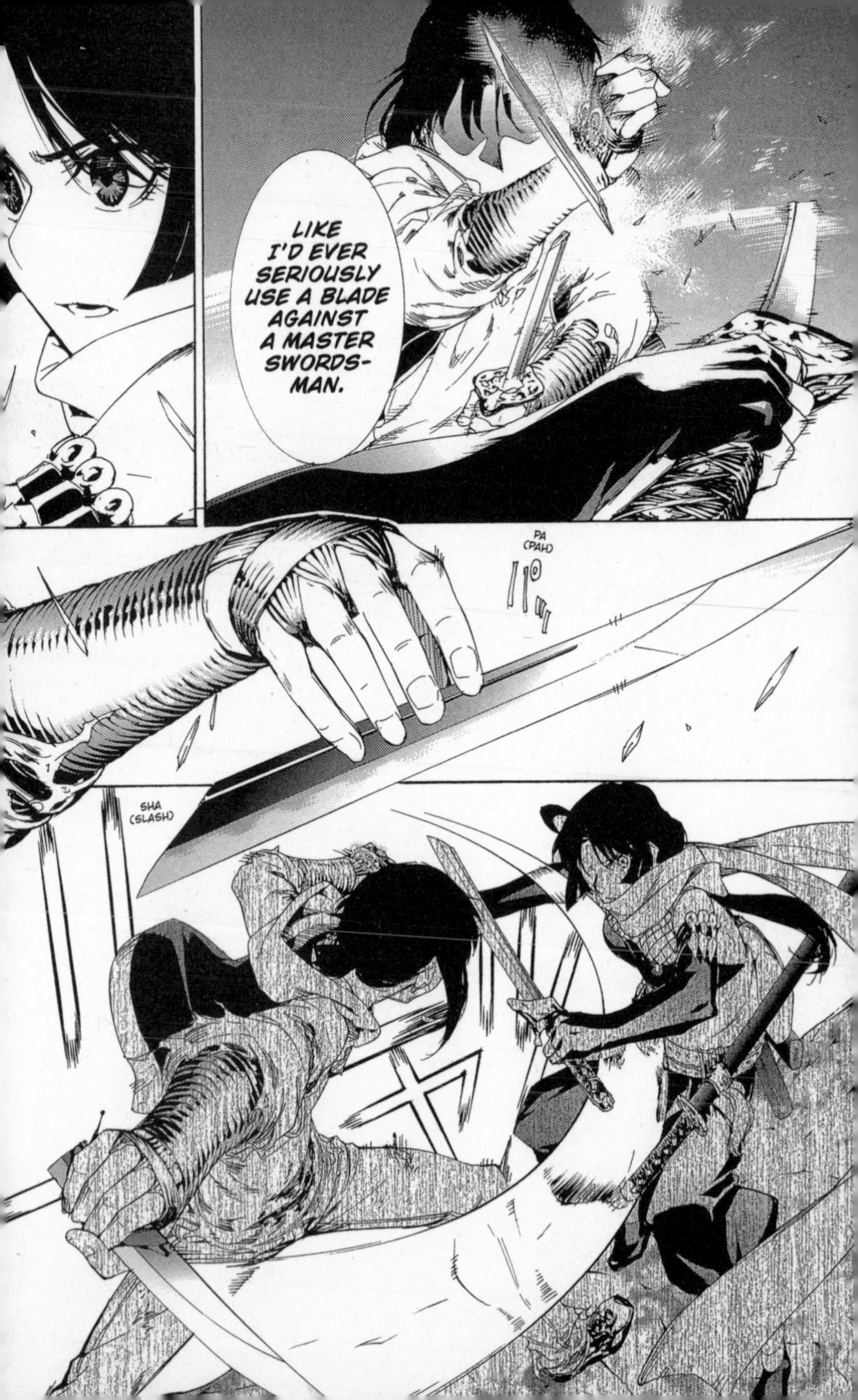
LIKE I'D EVER SERIOUSLY USE A BLADE AGAINST A MASTER SWORDS-MAN.
PA (PAH)
SHA (SLASH)

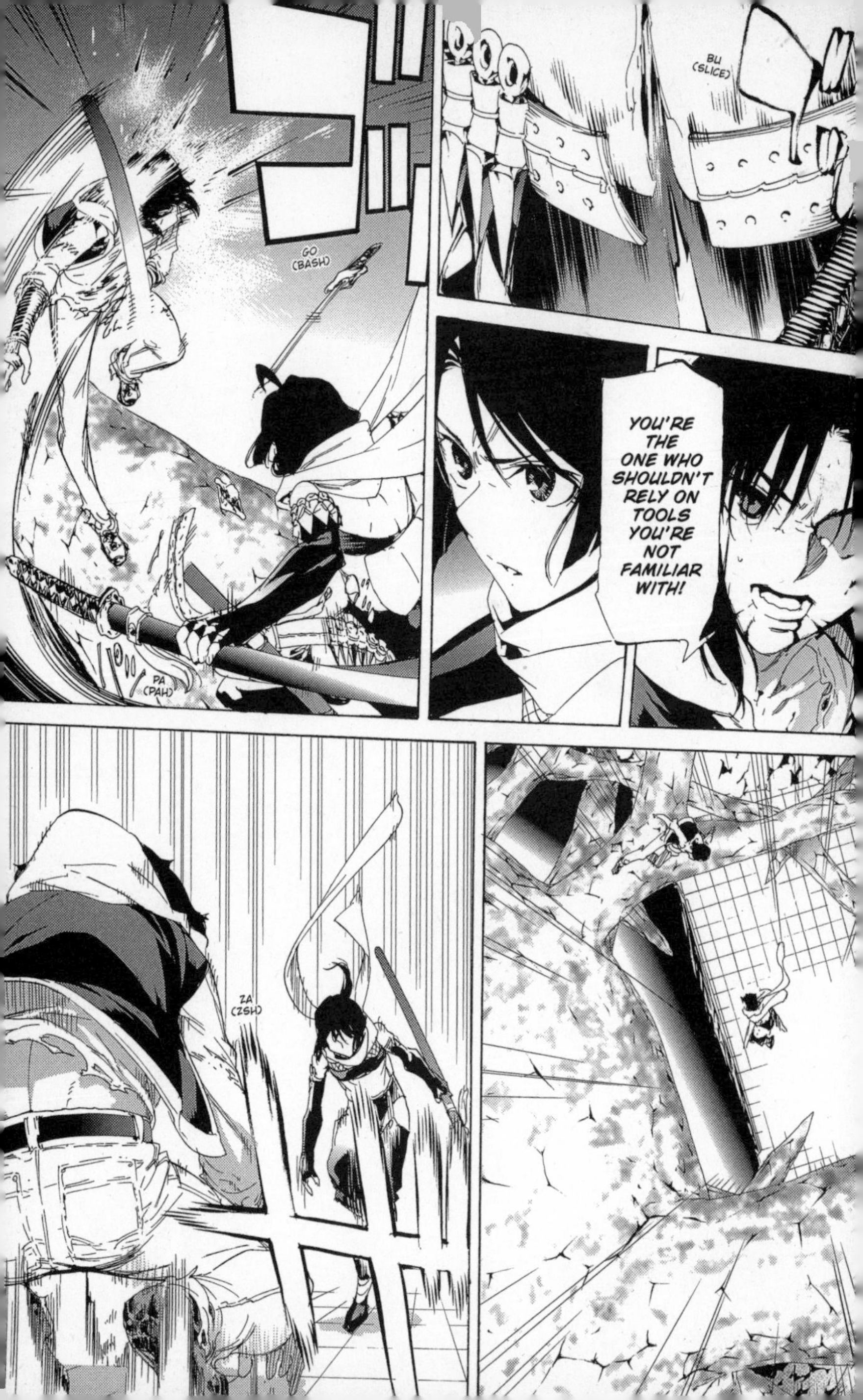
BU
(SLICE)
YOU'RE THE ONE WHO SHOULDN'T RELY ON TOOLS YOU'RE NOT FAMILIAR WITH!
GO
(BASH)
PA
(PAH)
ZA
(ZSH)

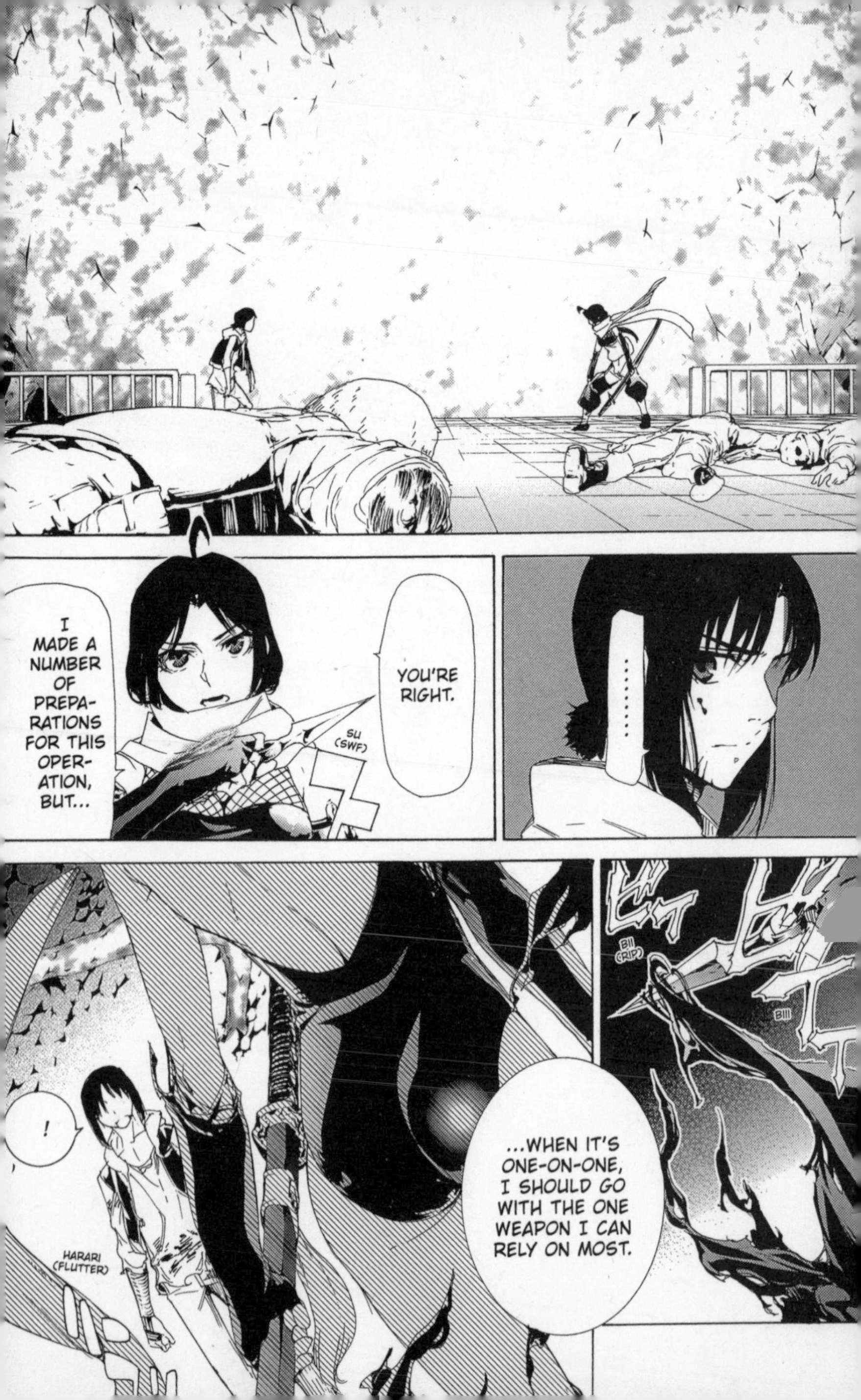
......
YOU'RE RIGHT.
SU (SWF)
I MADE A NUMBER OF PREPARATIONS FOR THIS OPERATION, BUT...
BII (RIP)
BIII
...WHEN IT'S ONE-ON-ONE, I SHOULD GO WITH THE ONE WEAPON I CAN RELY ON MOST.
!
HARARI (FLUTTER)

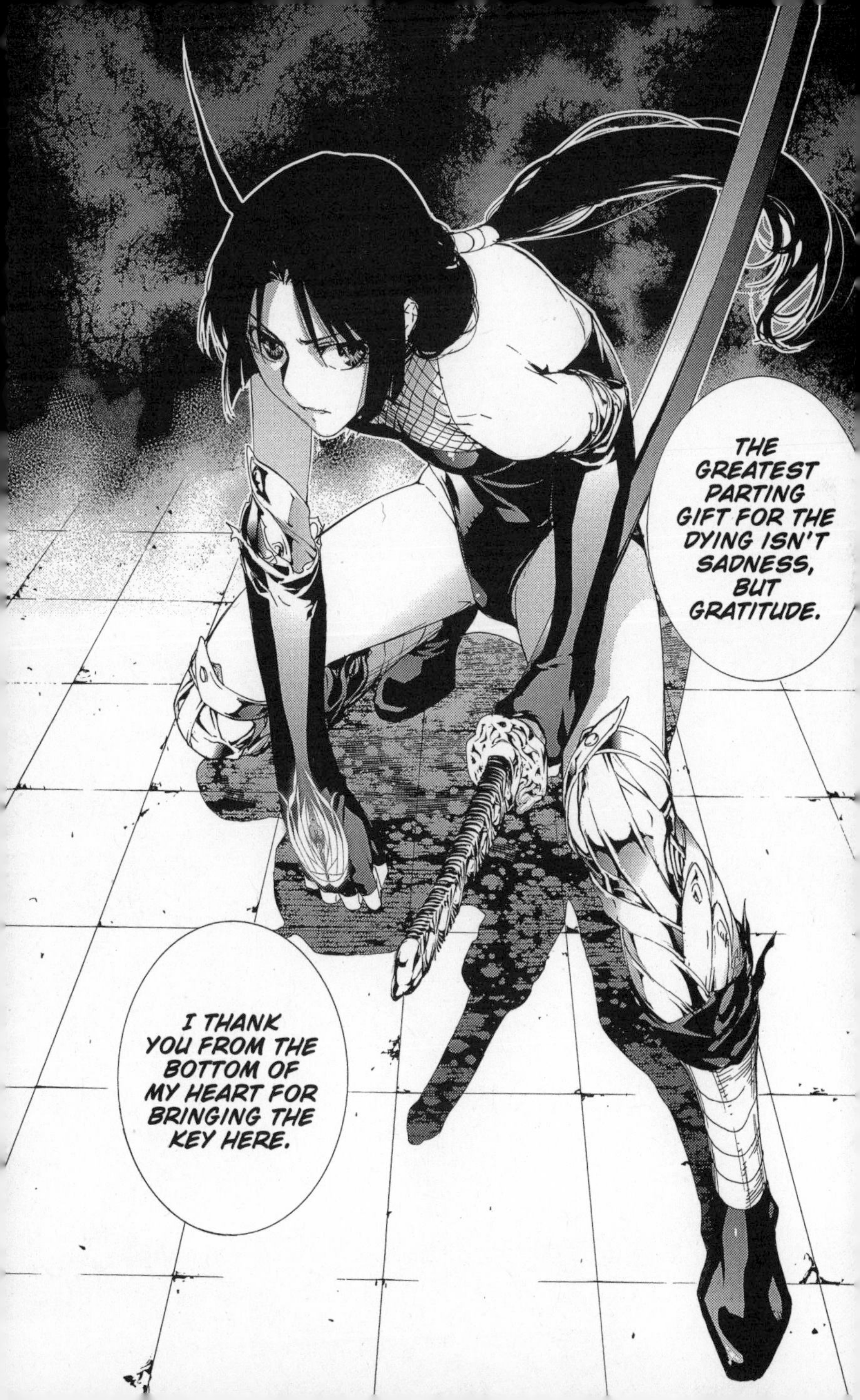
THE GREATEST PARTING GIFT FOR THE DYING ISN'T SADNESS, BUT GRATITUDE.
I THANK YOU FROM THE BOTTOM OF MY HEART FOR BRINGING THE KEY HERE.

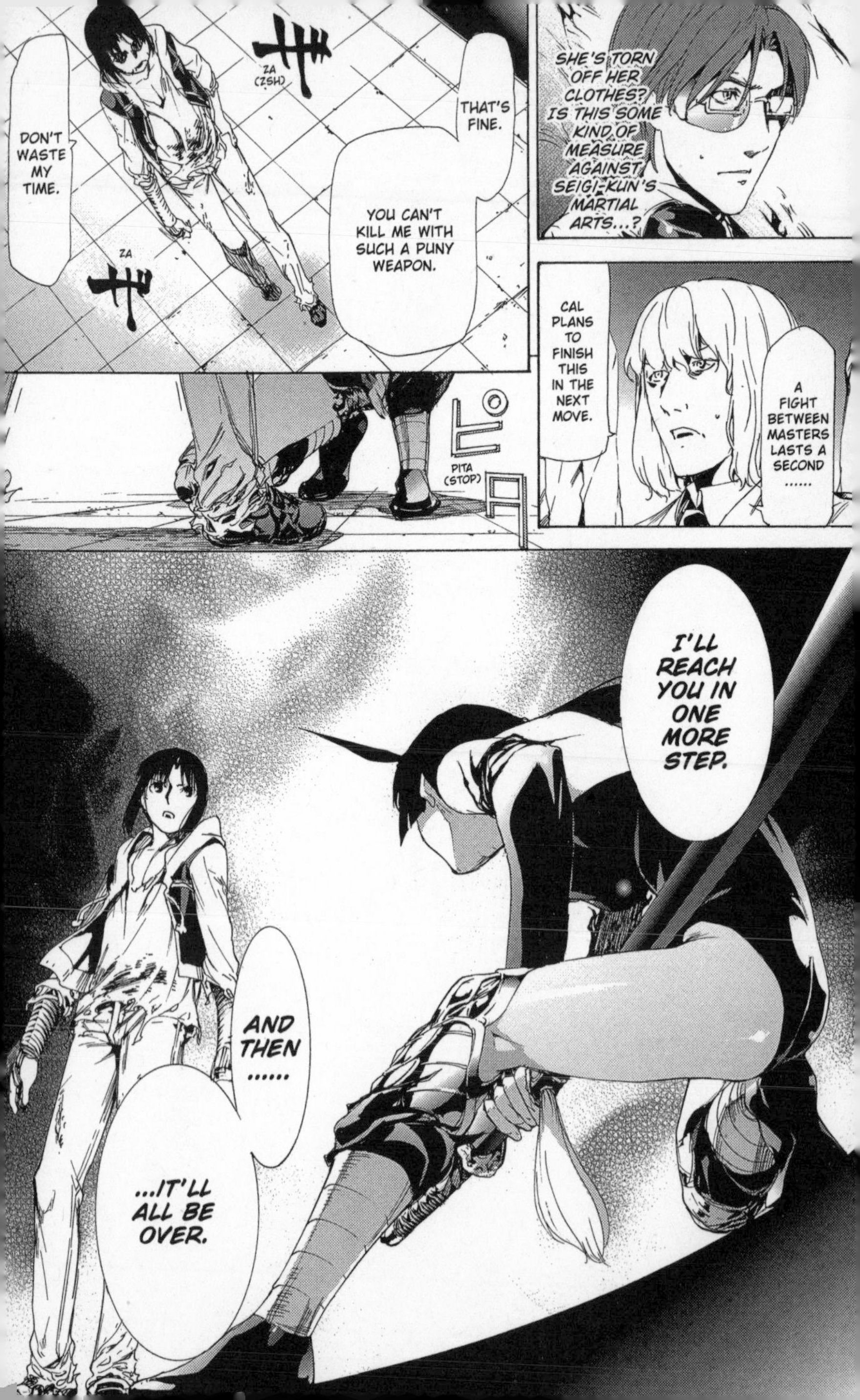
SHE'S TORN OFF HER CLOTHES? IS THIS SOME KIND OF MEASURE AGAINST SEIGI-KUN'S MARTIAL ARTS...?
THAT'S FINE.
YOU CAN'T KILL ME WITH SUCH A PUNY WEAPON.
ZA (ZSH)
DON'T WASTE MY TIME.
ZA
A FIGHT BETWEEN MASTERS LASTS A SECOND......
CAL PLANS TO FINISH THIS IN THE NEXT MOVE.
PITA (STOP)
I'LL REACH YOU IN ONE MORE STEP.
AND THEN......
...IT'LL ALL BE OVER.

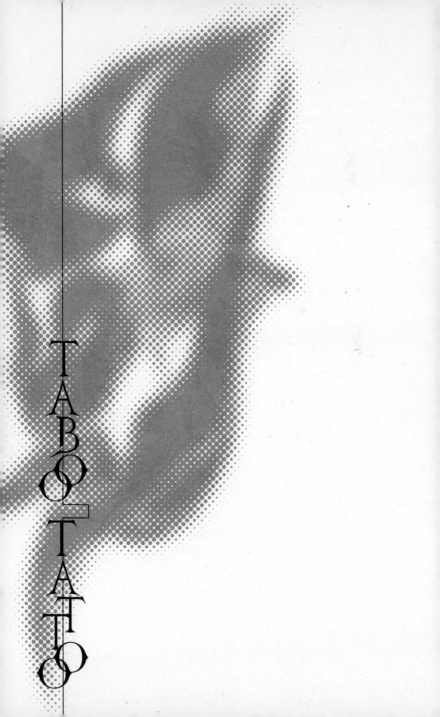

TABOO TATTOO

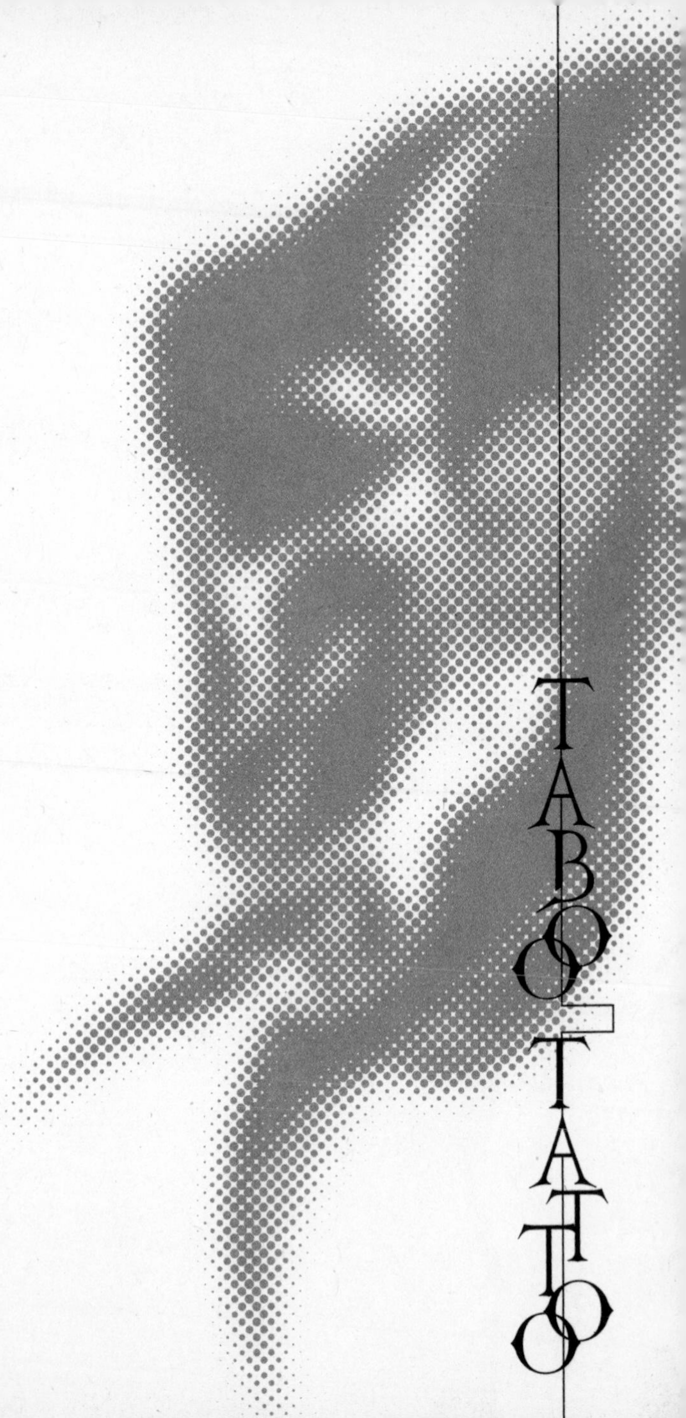
TABOO TATTOO

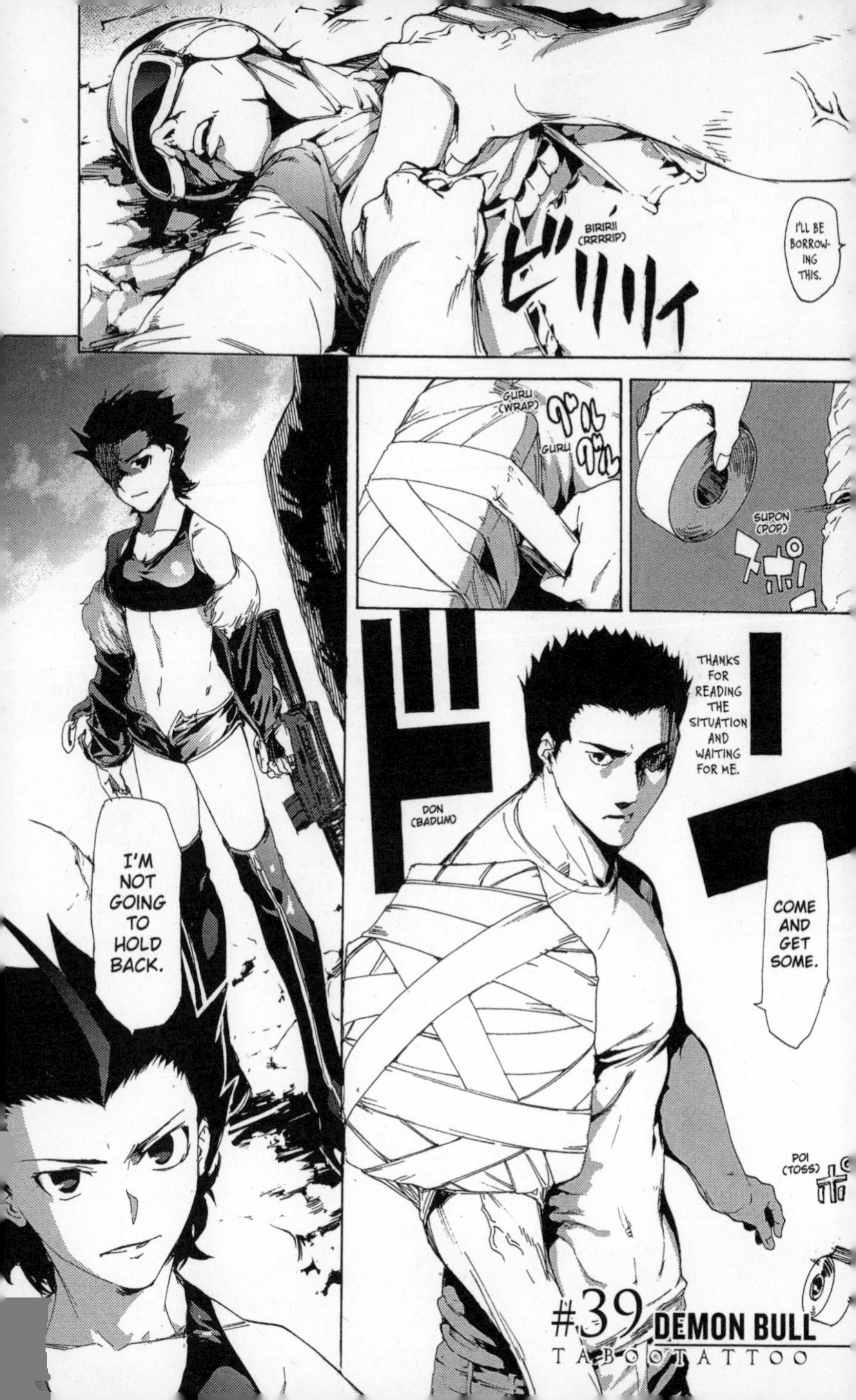
I'LL BE BORROWING THIS.
BIRIRII (RRRRIP)
SUPON (POP)
GURU (WRAP)
GURU
THANKS FOR READING THE SITUATION AND WAITING FOR ME.
DON (BADUM)
COME AND GET SOME.
POI (TOSS)
#39 DEMON BULL
TABOO TATTOO
I'M NOT GOING TO HOLD BACK.

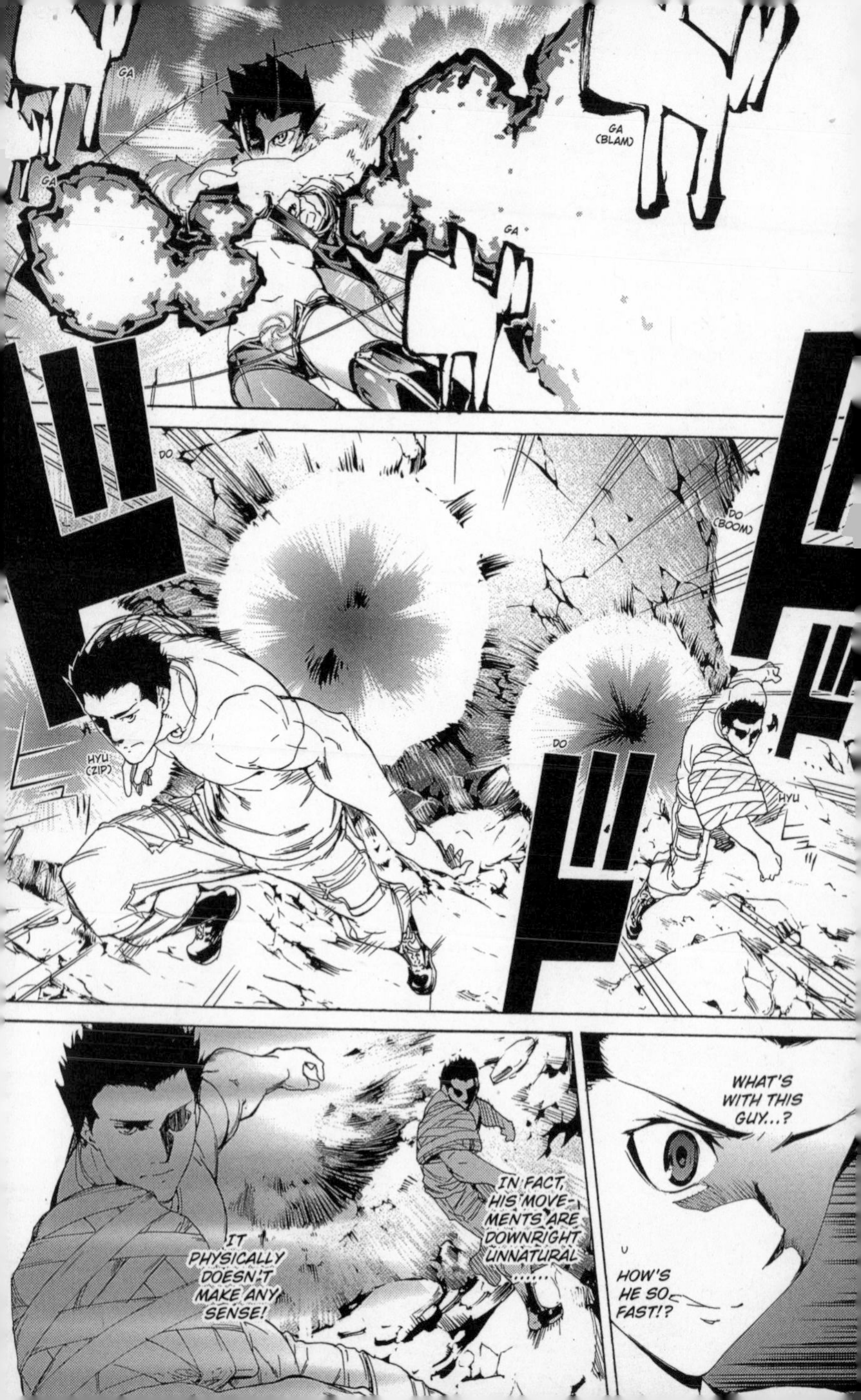
GA (BLAM)
GA
GA
GA
DO (BOOM)
HYU
DO
DO
HYU (ZIP)
WHAT'S WITH THIS GUY...?
U
HOW'S HE SO FAST!?
IN FACT, HIS MOVE-MENTS ARE DOWNRIGHT UNNATURAL......
IT PHYSICALLY DOESN'T MAKE ANY SENSE!

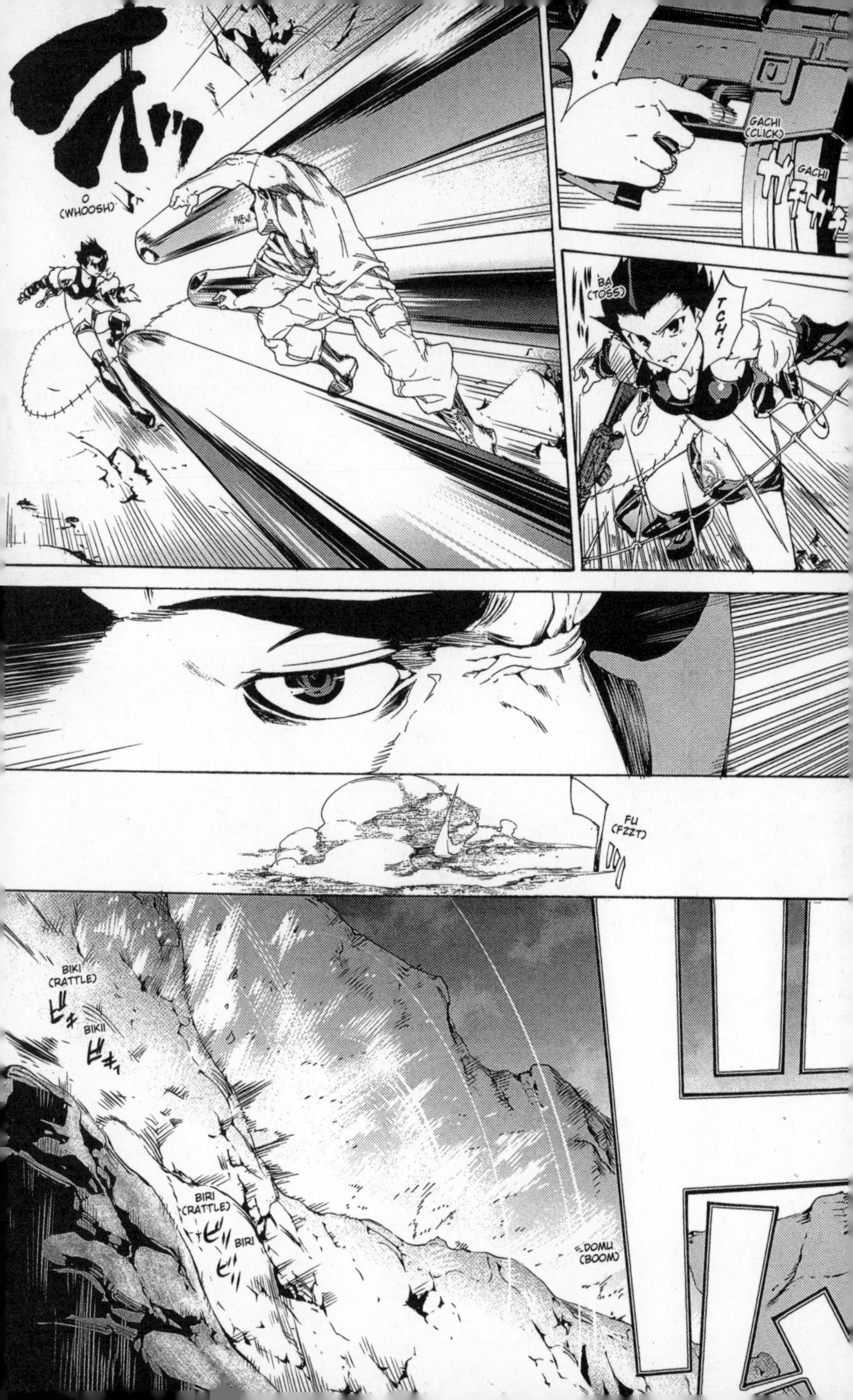
!
GACHI
(CLICK)
GACHI
BA
(TOSS)
TCHI!
O
(WHOOSH)
PHEW!
FU
(FZZT)
DOMU
(BOOM)
BIKI
(RATTLE)
BIKII
BIRI
(RATTLE)
BIRI

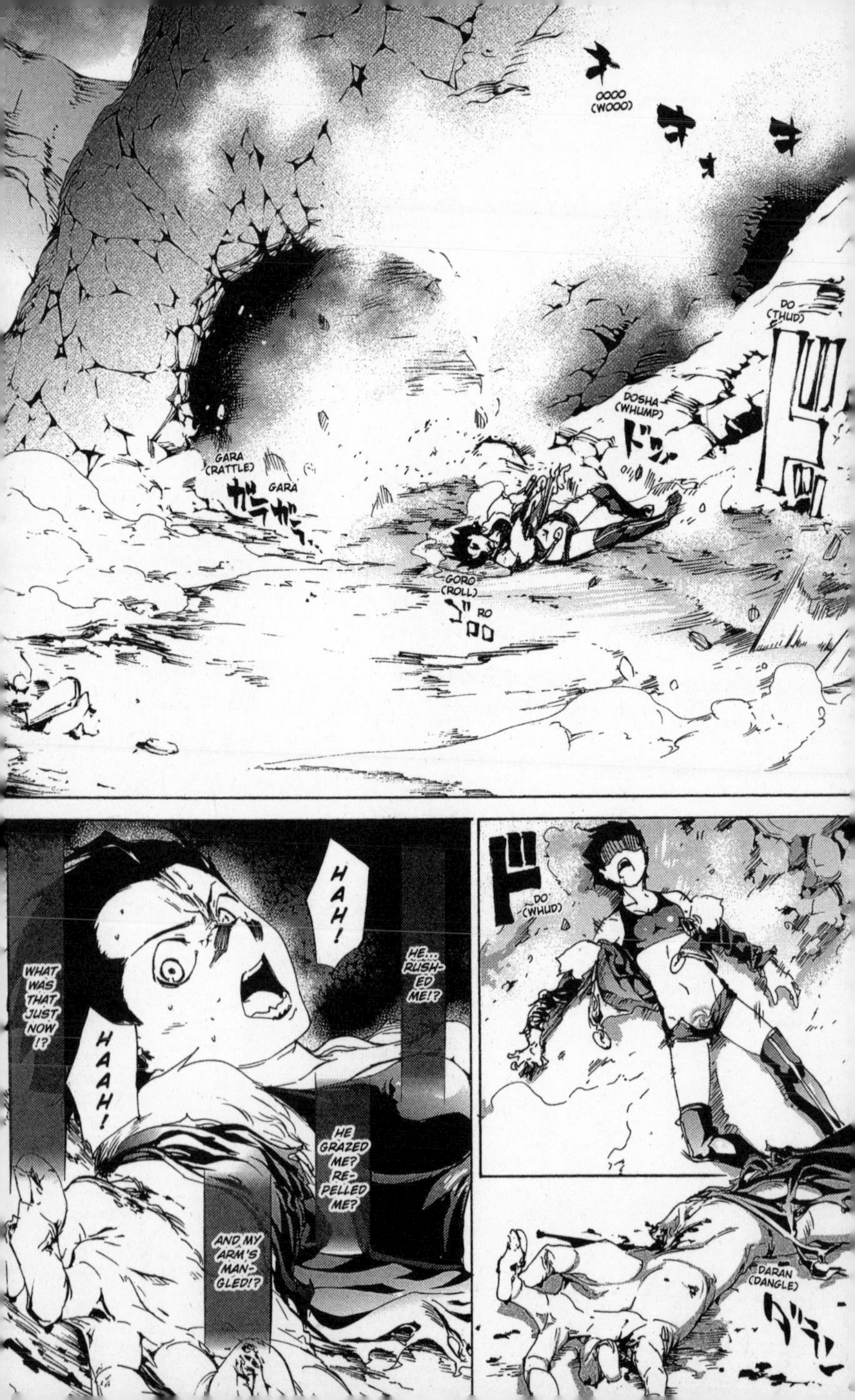

OOOO (WOOO)
DO (THUD)
DOSHA (WHUMP)
GARA (RATTLE) GARA
GORO (ROLL) RO
DO (WHUD)
HAH!
HE... RUSH-ED ME!?
WHAT WAS THAT JUST NOW !?
HAAAH!
HE GRAZED ME? RE-PELLED ME?
AND MY ARM'S MAN-GLED!?
DARAN (DANGLE)

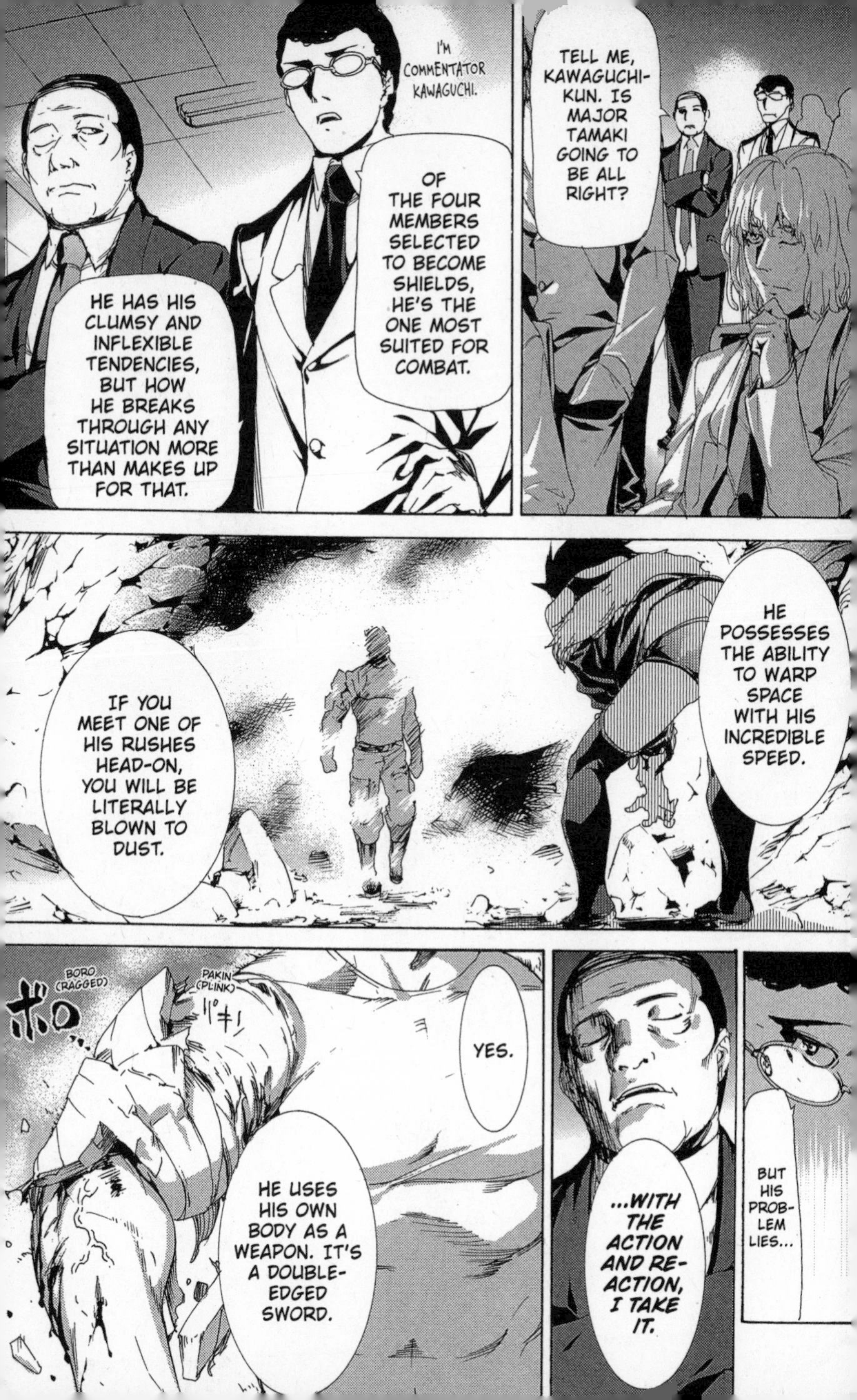
TELL ME, KAWAGUCHI-KUN. IS MAJOR TAMAKI GOING TO BE ALL RIGHT?
I'M COMMENTATOR KAWAGUCHI.
OF THE FOUR MEMBERS SELECTED TO BECOME SHIELDS, HE'S THE ONE MOST SUITED FOR COMBAT.
HE HAS HIS CLUMSY AND INFLEXIBLE TENDENCIES, BUT HOW HE BREAKS THROUGH ANY SITUATION MORE THAN MAKES UP FOR THAT.
HE POSSESSES THE ABILITY TO WARP SPACE WITH HIS INCREDIBLE SPEED.
IF YOU MEET ONE OF HIS RUSHES HEAD-ON, YOU WILL BE LITERALLY BLOWN TO DUST.
BUT HIS PROB-LEM LIES...
...WITH THE ACTION AND RE-ACTION, I TAKE IT.
YES.
PAKIN (PLINK)
BORO (RAGGED)
ボロ
HE USES HIS OWN BODY AS A WEAPON. IT'S A DOUBLE-EDGED SWORD.

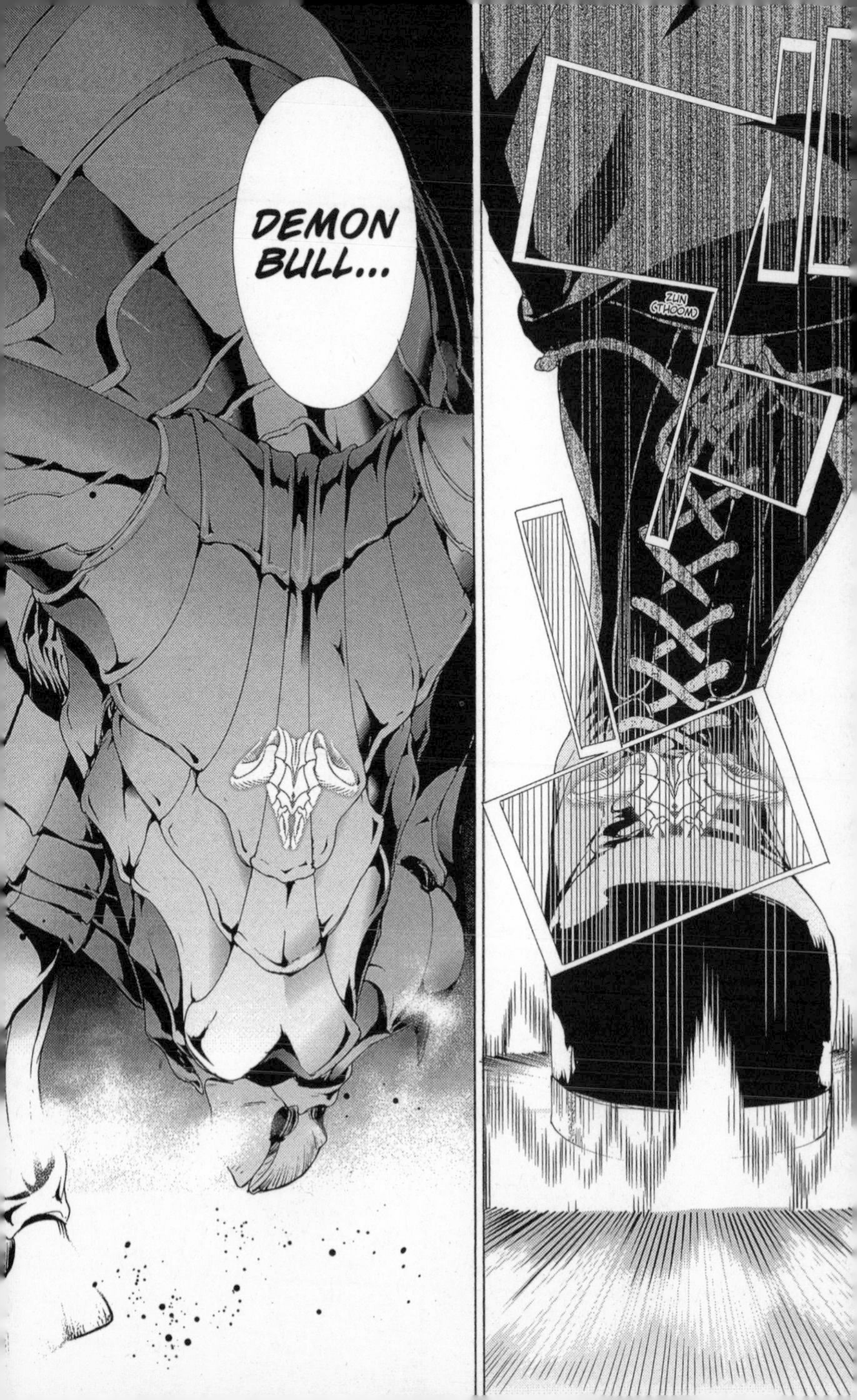
ZUN (THOOM)
DEMON BULL...

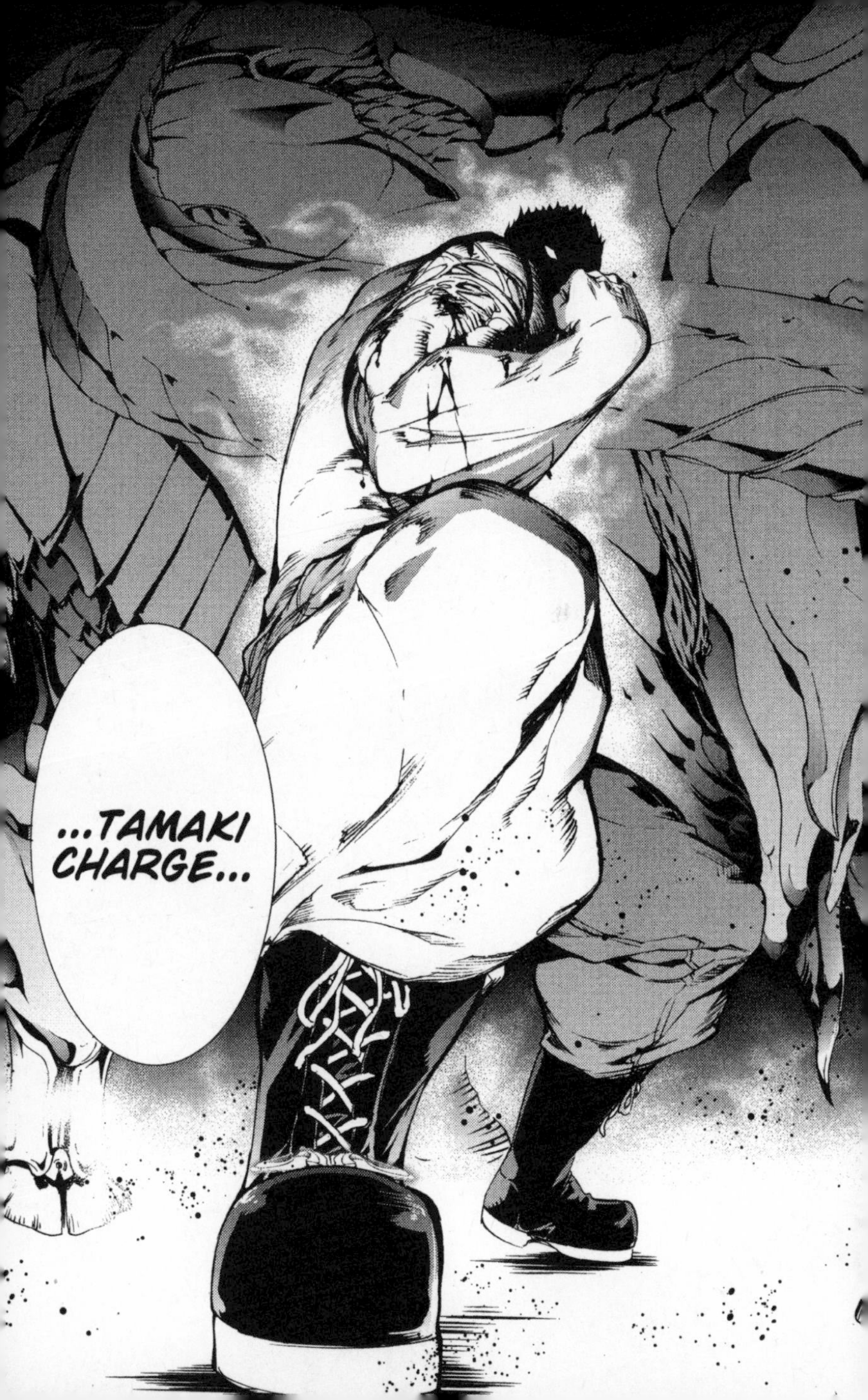
...TAMAKI CHARGE...

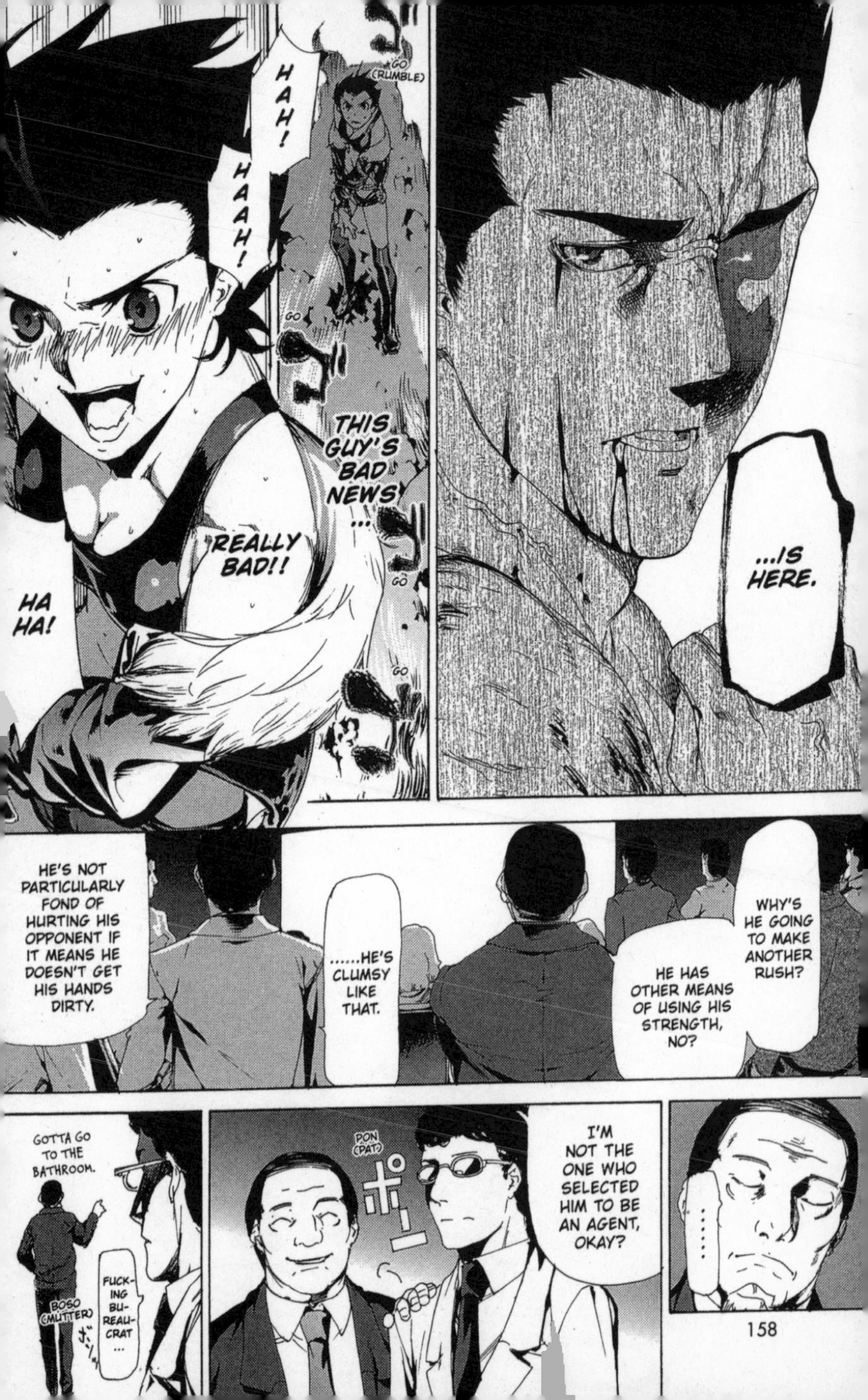
...IS HERE.
HAH!
HAAAH!
GO (RUMBLE)
GO
GO
GO
THIS GUY'S BAD NEWS...
REALLY BAD!!
HA HA!
WHY'S HE GOING TO MAKE ANOTHER RUSH?
HE HAS OTHER MEANS OF USING HIS STRENGTH, NO?
......HE'S CLUMSY LIKE THAT.
HE'S NOT PARTICULARLY FOND OF HURTING HIS OPPONENT IF IT MEANS HE DOESN'T GET HIS HANDS DIRTY.
......
I'M NOT THE ONE WHO SELECTED HIM TO BE AN AGENT, OKAY?
PON (PAT)
GOTTA GO TO THE BATHROOM.
FUCKING BUREAUCRAT...
BOSO (MUTTER)

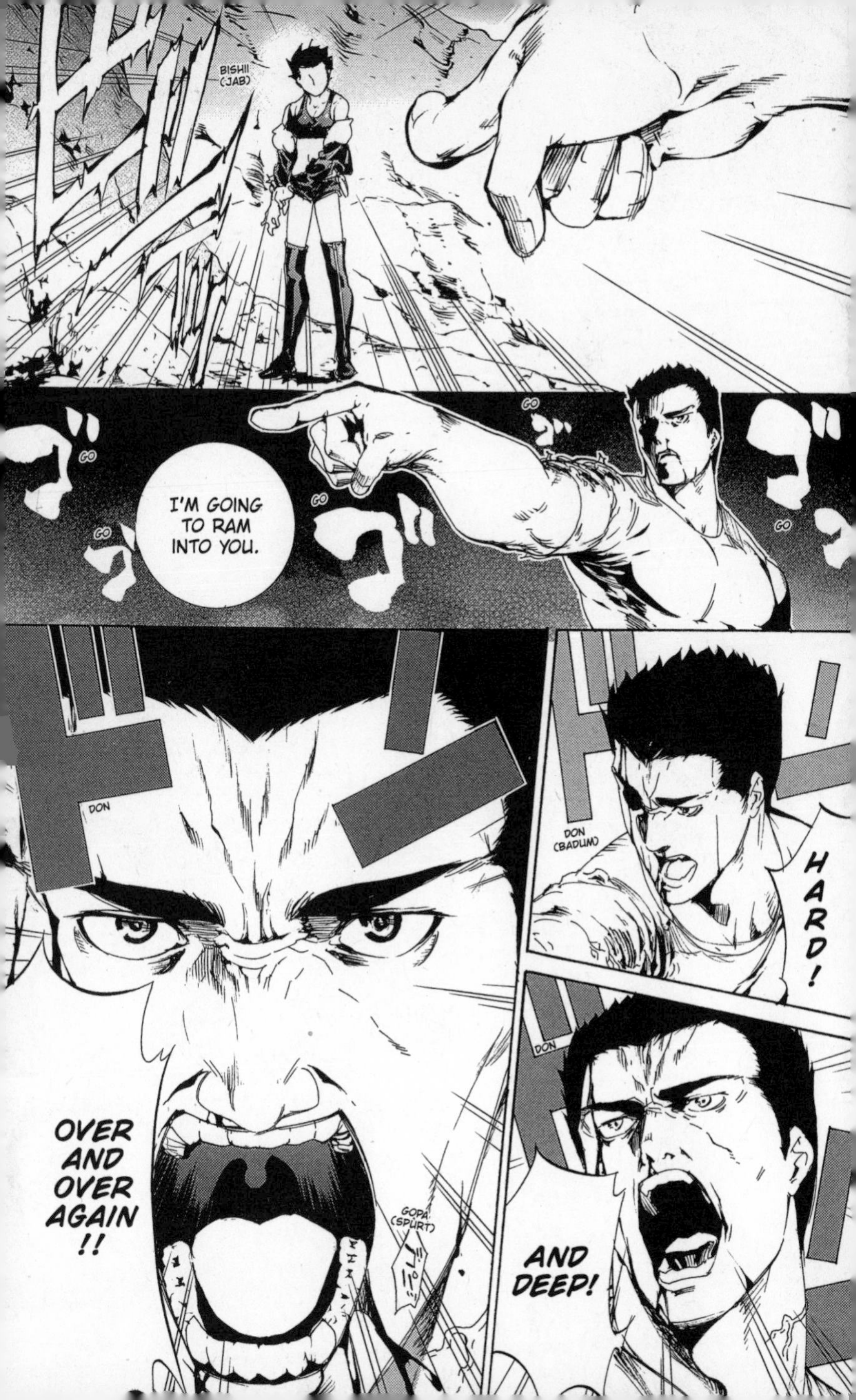
BISHI! (JAB)
GO
I'M GOING TO RAM INTO YOU.
GO
GO
GO
GO
DON (BADUM)
HARD!
DON
AND DEEP!
DON
OVER AND OVER AGAIN!!
GOPA (SPURT)

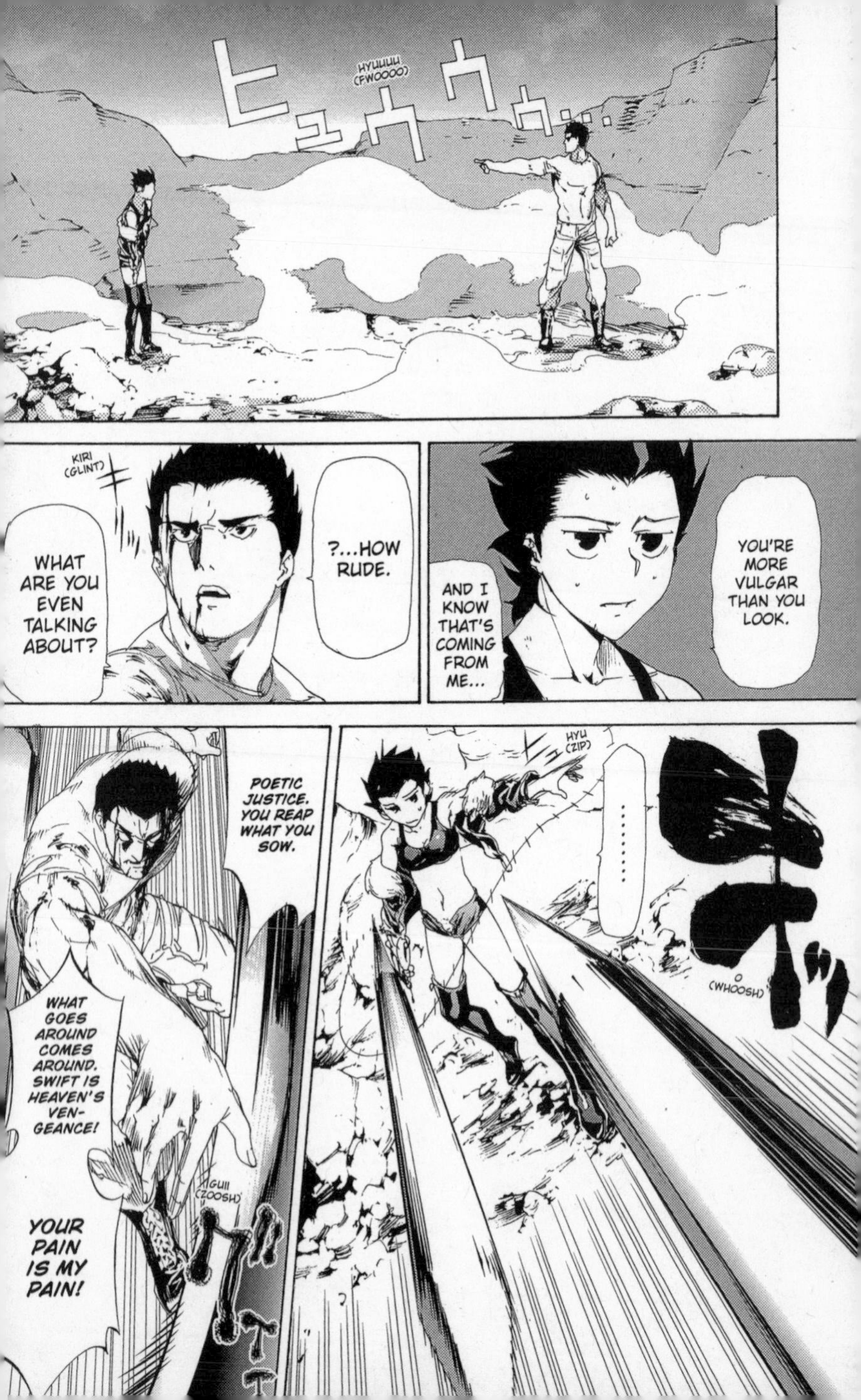
ヒュウウゥ...
HYUUUU (FWOOOO)
YOU'RE MORE VULGAR THAN YOU LOOK.
AND I KNOW THAT'S COMING FROM ME...
KIRI (GLINT)
?...HOW RUDE.
WHAT ARE YOU EVEN TALKING ABOUT?
HYU (ZIP)
......
O (WHOOSH)
POETIC JUSTICE. YOU REAP WHAT YOU SOW.
WHAT GOES AROUND COMES AROUND. SWIFT IS HEAVEN'S VEN-GEANCE!
GUII (ZOOSH)
YOUR PAIN IS MY PAIN!

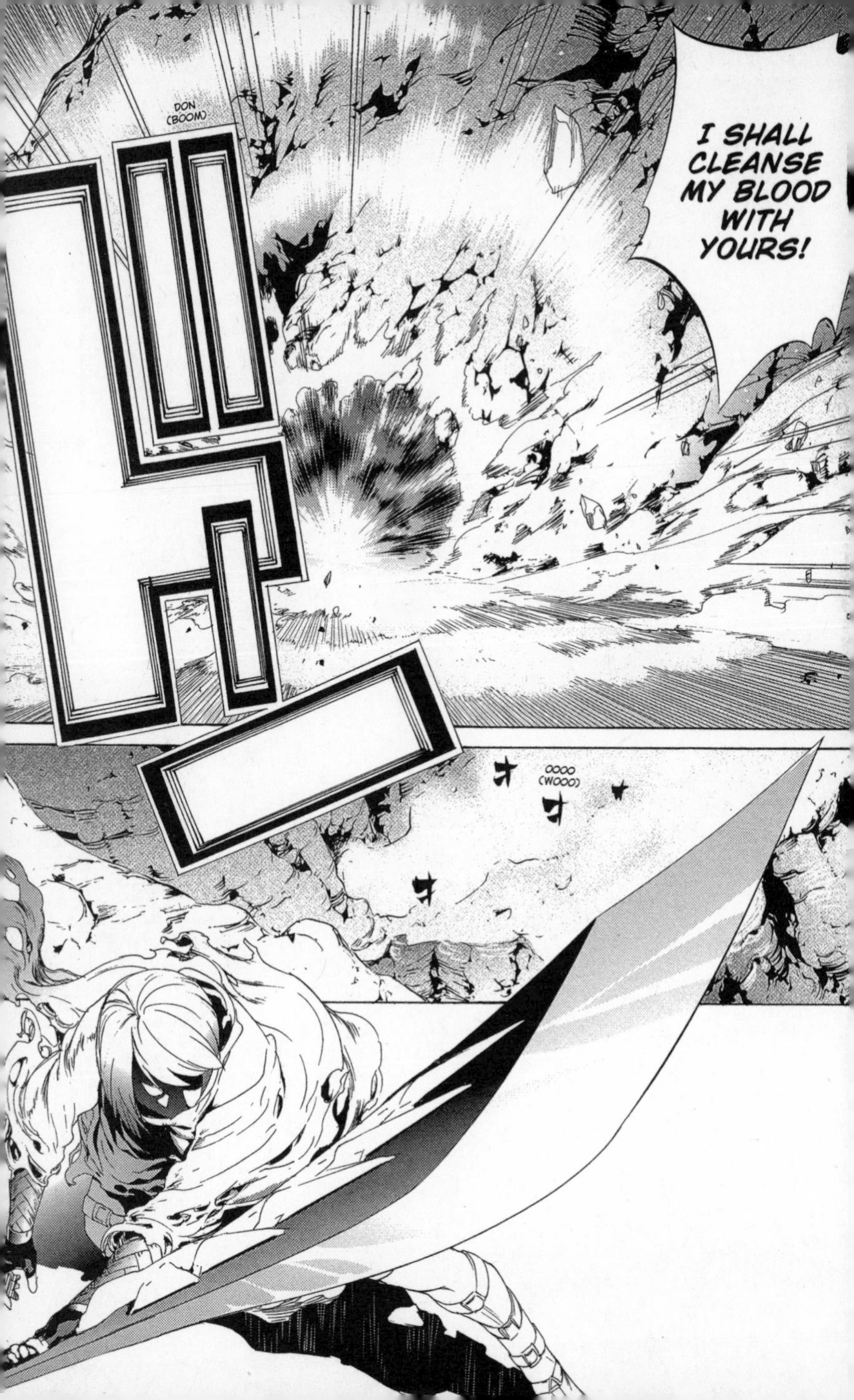
I SHALL CLEANSE MY BLOOD WITH YOURS!
DON (BOOM)
OOOO (WOOO)

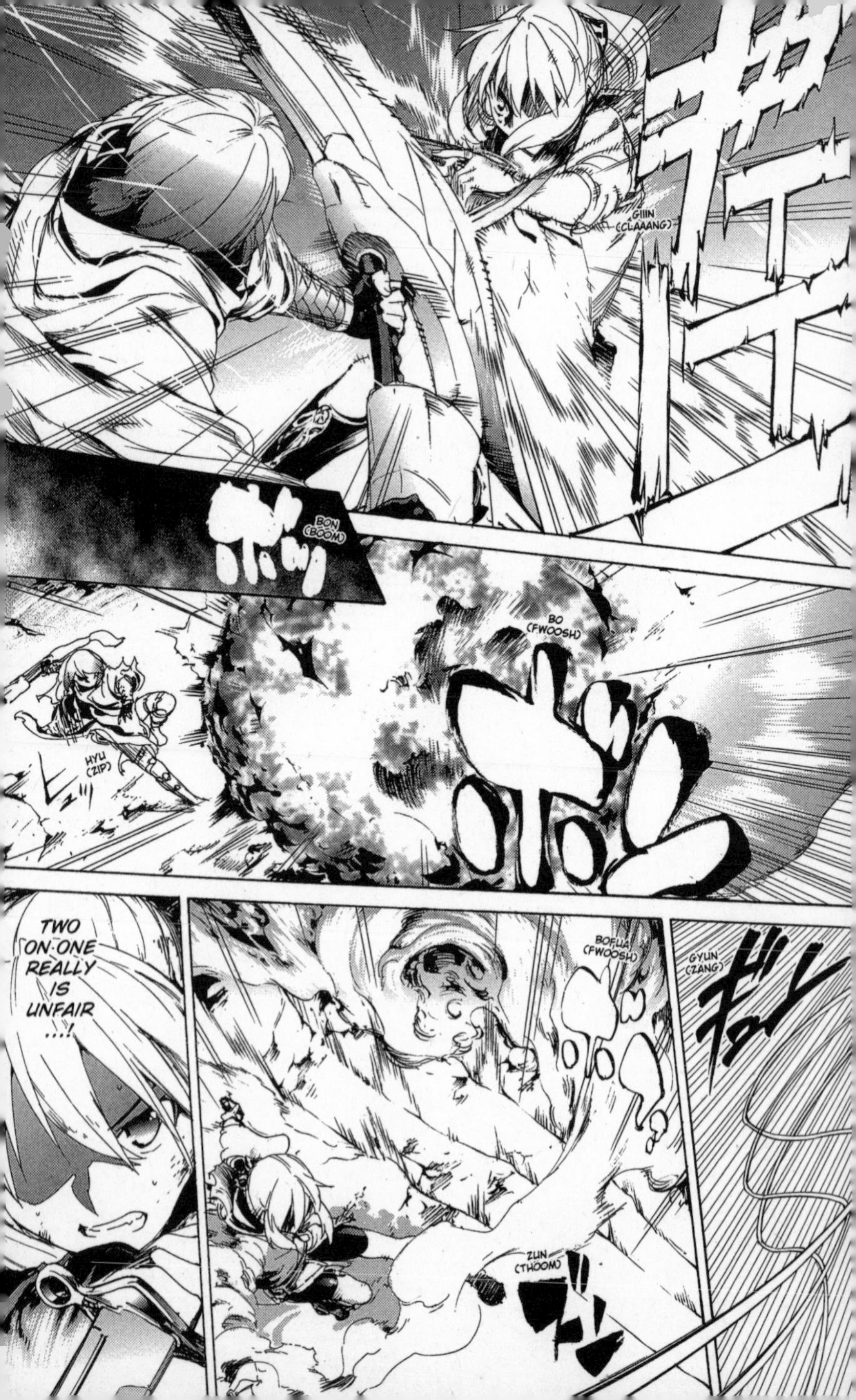
GIIIN
(CLAAANG)
BON
(BOOM)
BO
(FWOOSH)
HYU
(ZIP)
GYUN
(ZANG)
BOFUA
(FWOOSH)
ZUN
(THOOM)
TWO ON-ONE REALLY IS UNFAIR ...!

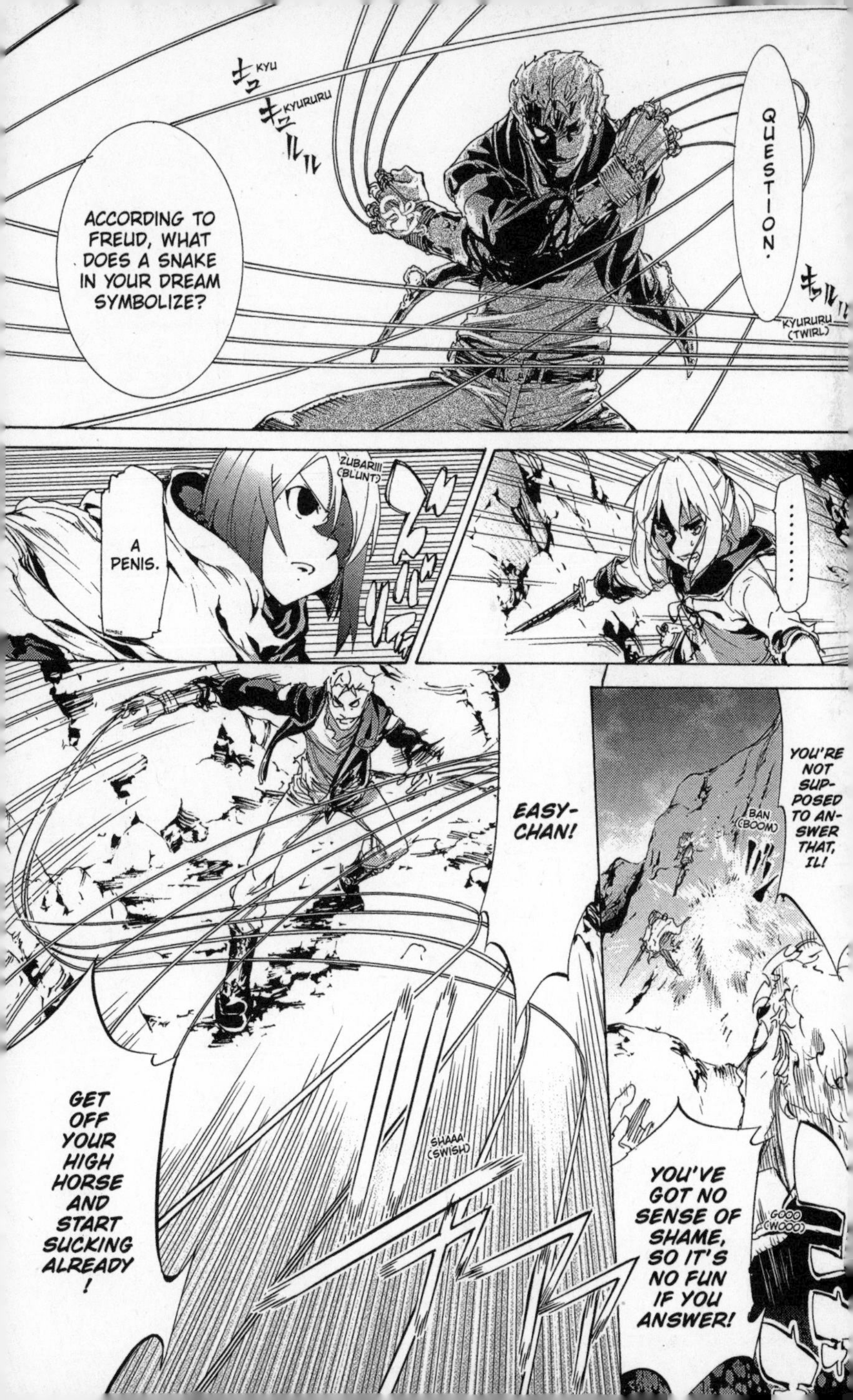
QUESTION.
KYURURU (TWIRL)
KYU
KYURURU
ACCORDING TO FREUD, WHAT DOES A SNAKE IN YOUR DREAM SYMBOLIZE?
......
ZUBARIII (BLUNT)
A PENIS.
YOU'RE NOT SUPPOSED TO ANSWER THAT, IL!
BAN (BOOM)
GOOO (WOOO)
YOU'VE GOT NO SENSE OF SHAME, SO IT'S NO FUN IF YOU ANSWER!
EASY-CHAN!
SHAAA (SWISH)
GET OFF YOUR HIGH HORSE AND START SUCKING ALREADY!

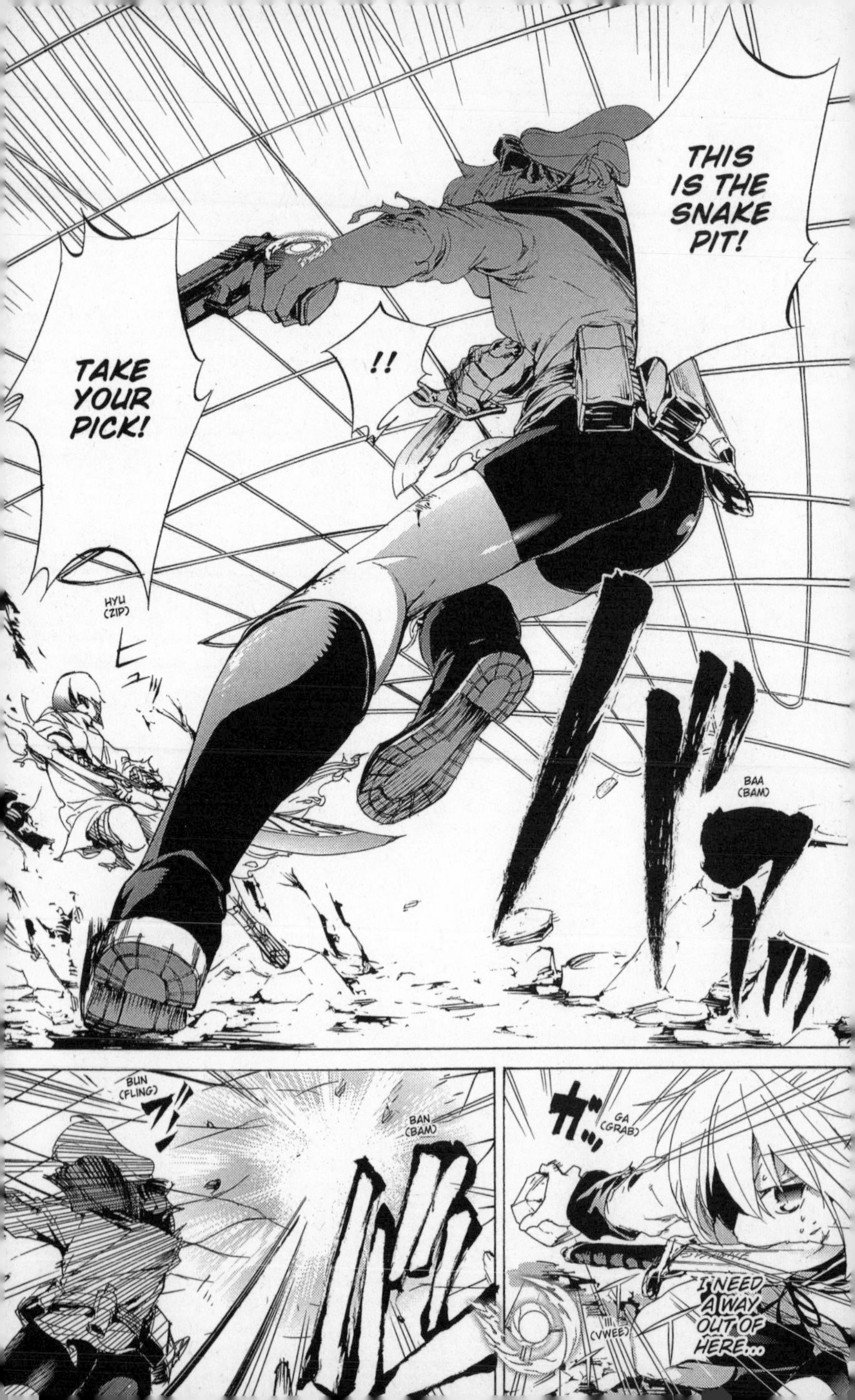
THIS IS THE SNAKE PIT!
!!
TAKE YOUR PICK!
HYU (ZIP)
BAA (BAM)
GA (GRAB)
I NEED A WAY OUT OF HERE...
(VWEE)
BUN (FLING)
BAN (BAM)

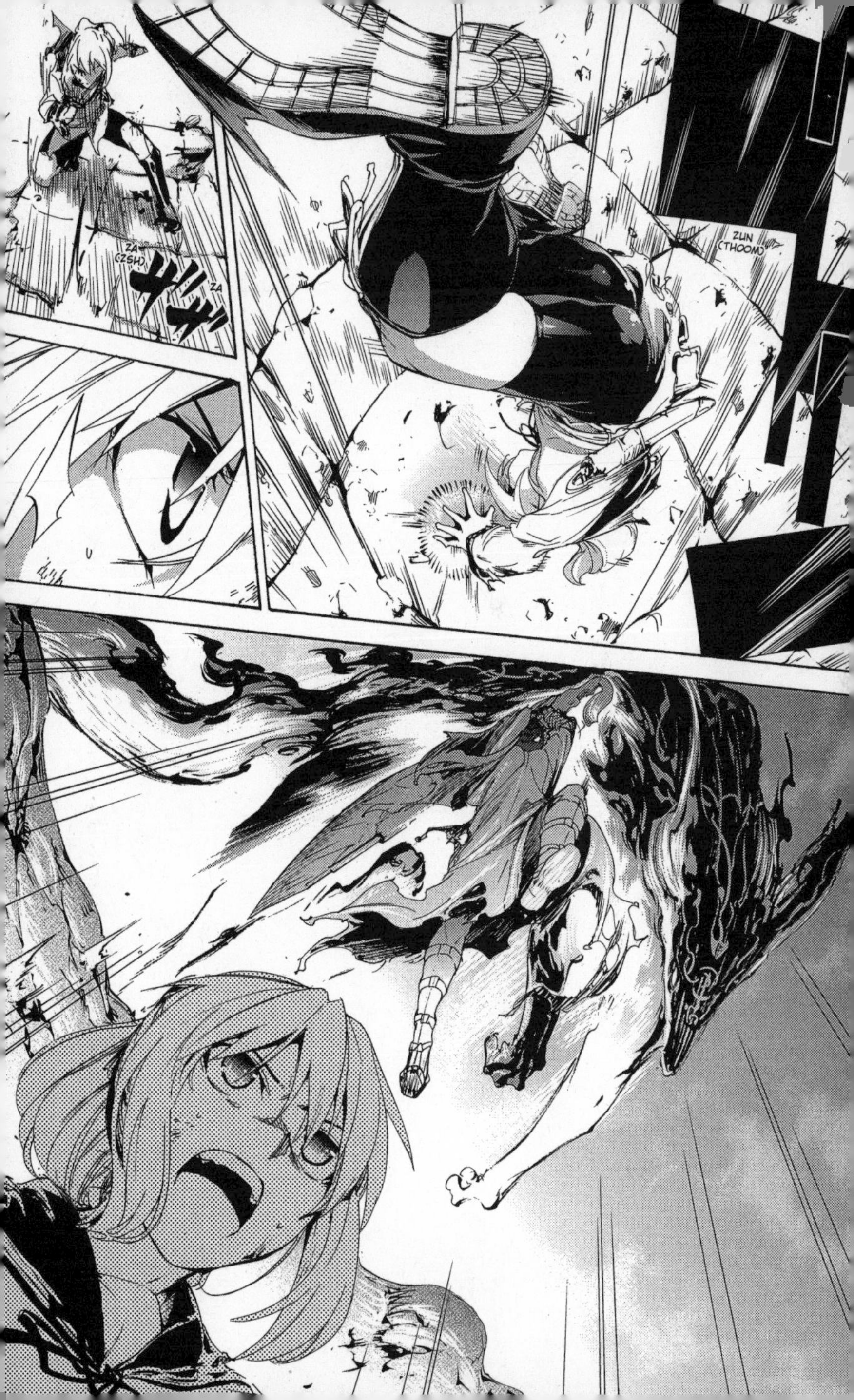
ZUN (THOOM)
ZA (ZSH) ZA

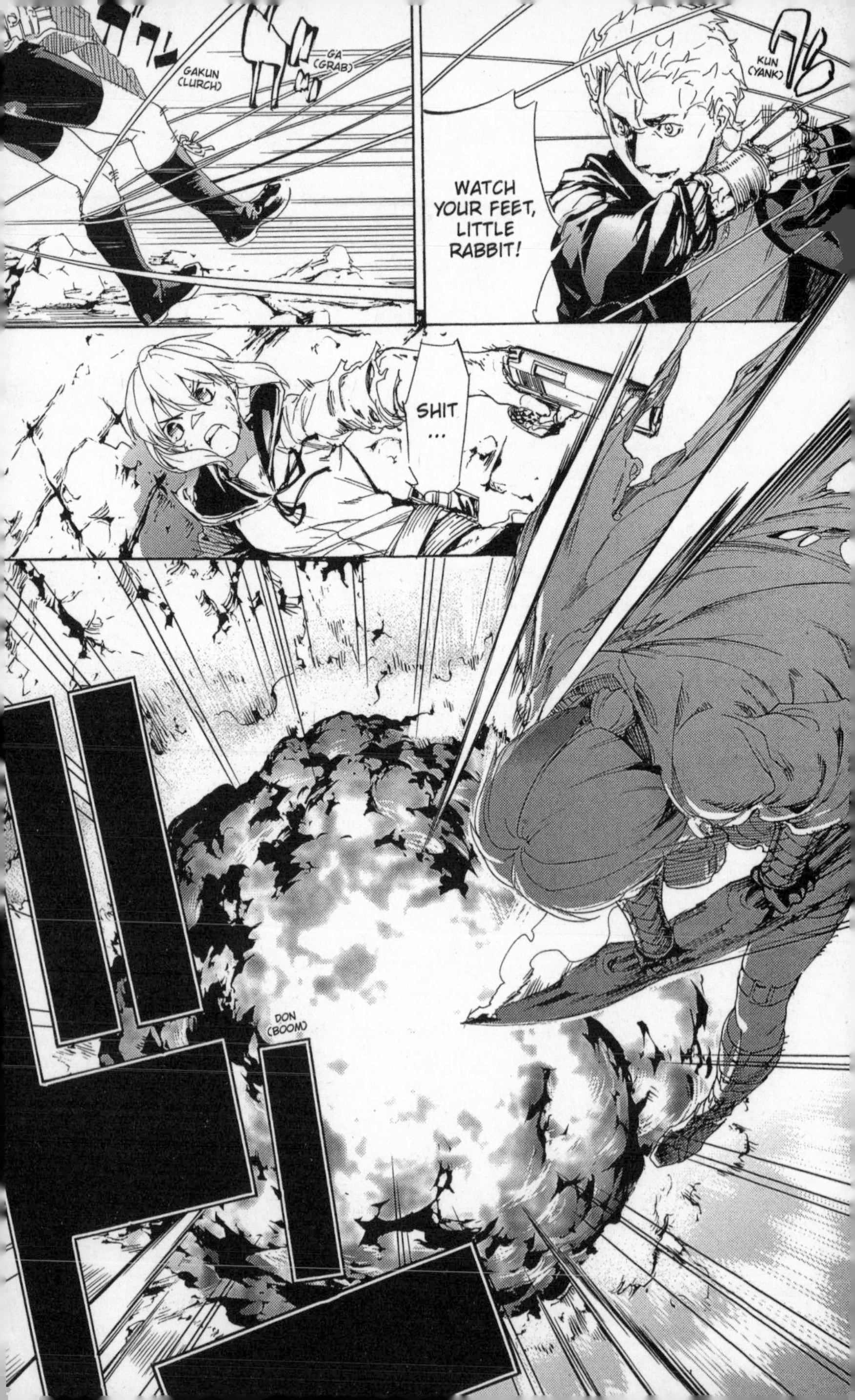
KUN (YANK)
WATCH YOUR FEET, LITTLE RABBIT!
GA (GRAB)
GAKUN (LURCH)
SHIT ...
DON (BOOM)

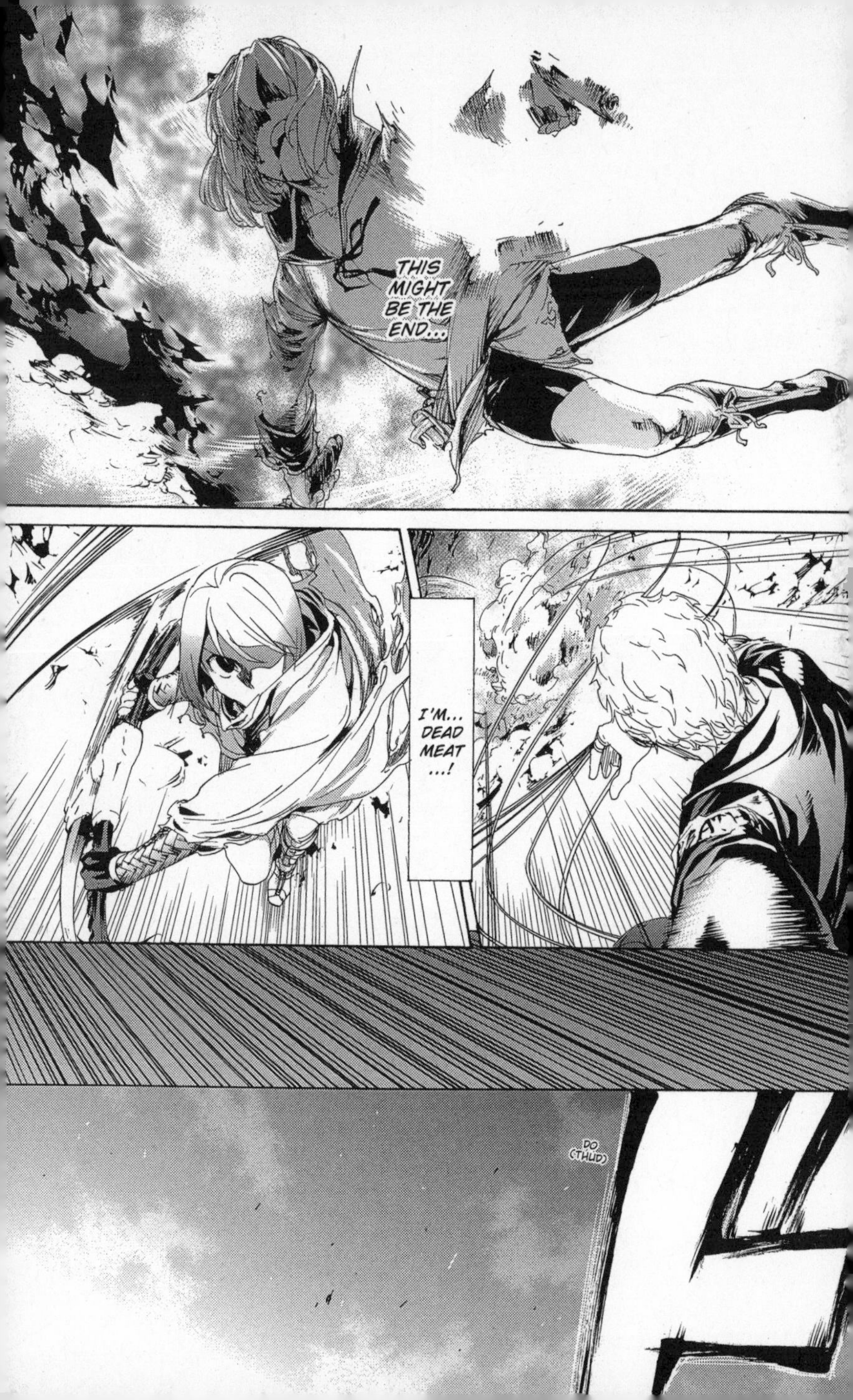
THIS MIGHT BE THE END...
I'M... DEAD MEAT ...!
DO (THUD)

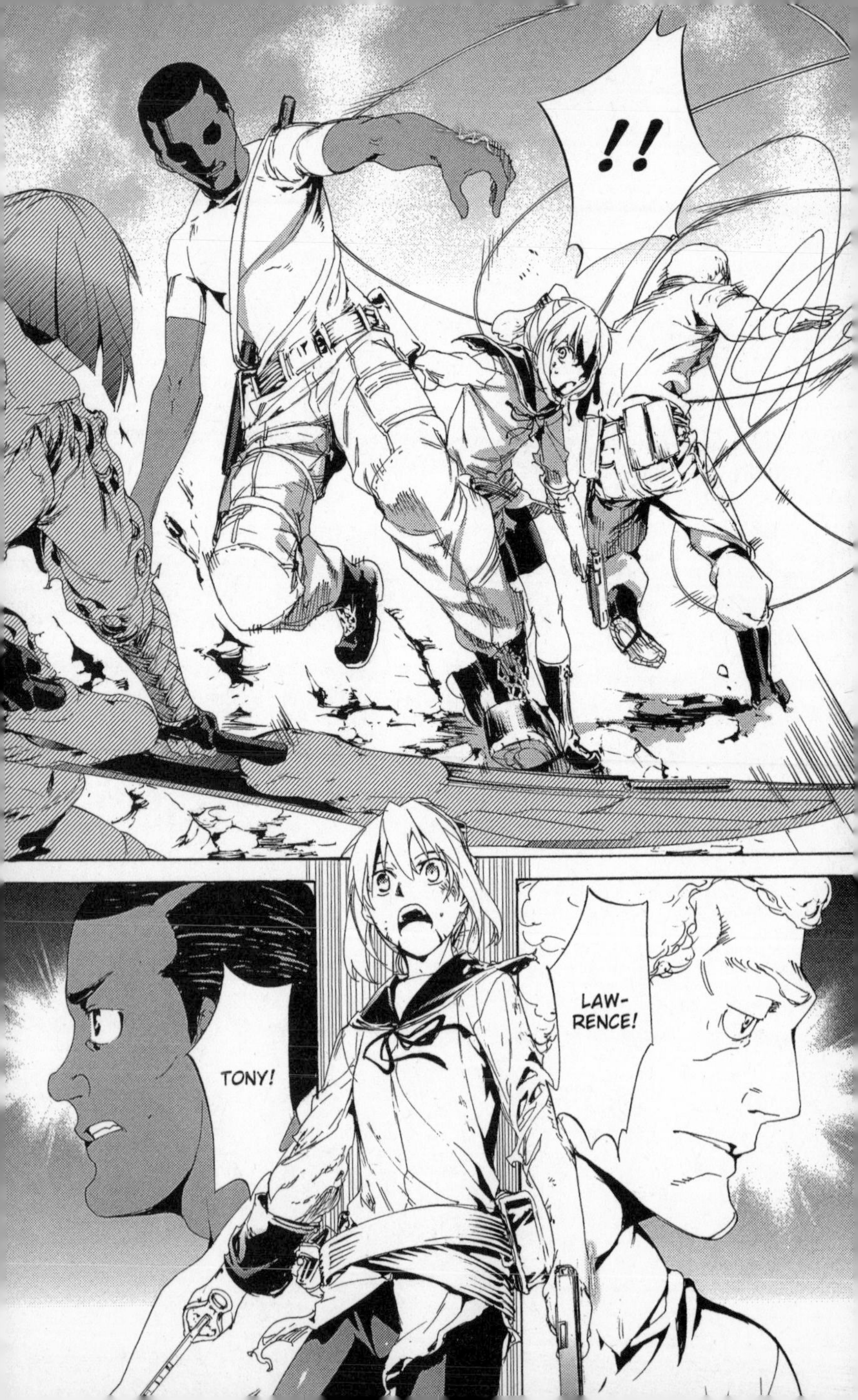
!!
LAW-
RENCE!
TONY!

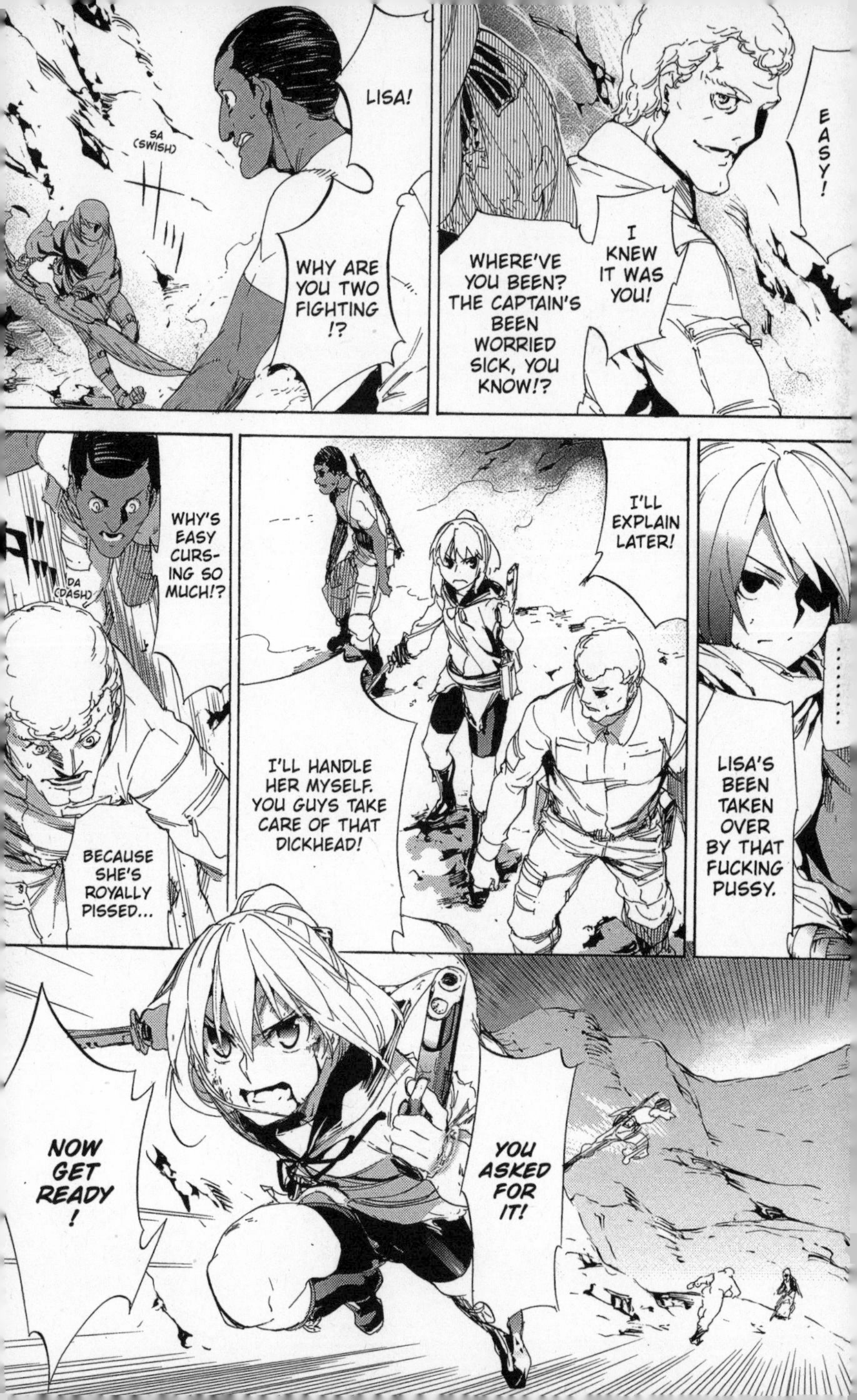
EASY!
I KNEW IT WAS YOU!
WHERE'VE YOU BEEN? THE CAPTAIN'S BEEN WORRIED SICK, YOU KNOW!?
LISA!
SA (SWISH)
WHY ARE YOU TWO FIGHTING!?
LISA'S BEEN TAKEN OVER BY THAT FUCKING PUSSY.
I'LL EXPLAIN LATER!
I'LL HANDLE HER MYSELF. YOU GUYS TAKE CARE OF THAT DICKHEAD!
WHY'S EASY CURSING SO MUCH!?
DA (DASH)
BECAUSE SHE'S ROYALLY PISSED...
YOU ASKED FOR IT!
NOW GET READY!

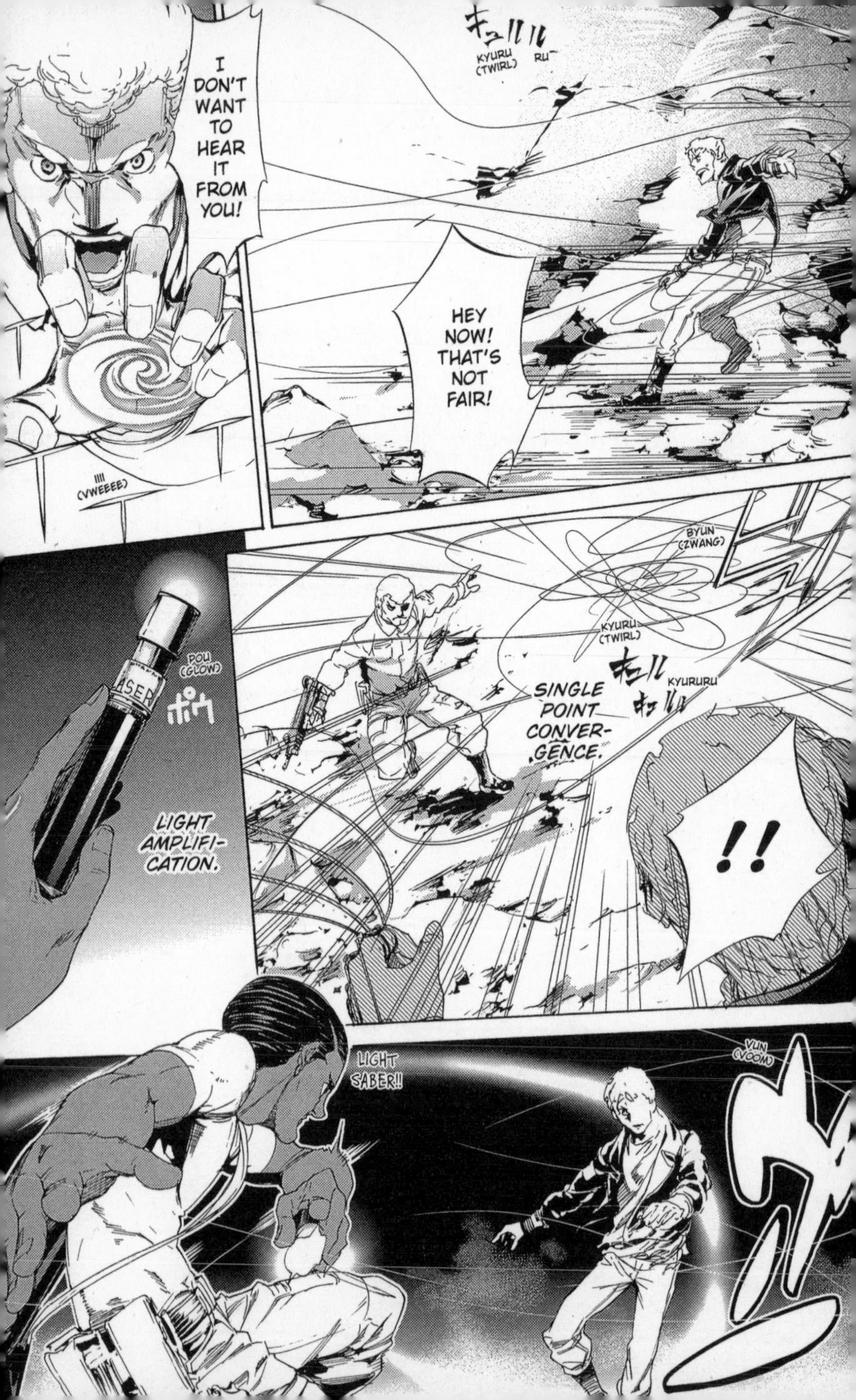
キュルル
KYURU (TWIRL) RU
HEY NOW! THAT'S NOT FAIR!
I DON'T WANT TO HEAR IT FROM YOU!
IIII (VWEEEE)
BYUN (ZWANG)
KYURU (TWIRL)
キュル キュルル
KYURURU
SINGLE POINT CONVER-GENCE.
!!
LASER
POU (GLOW)
ポウ
LIGHT AMPLIFI-CATION.
VUN (VOOM)
LIGHT SABER!!

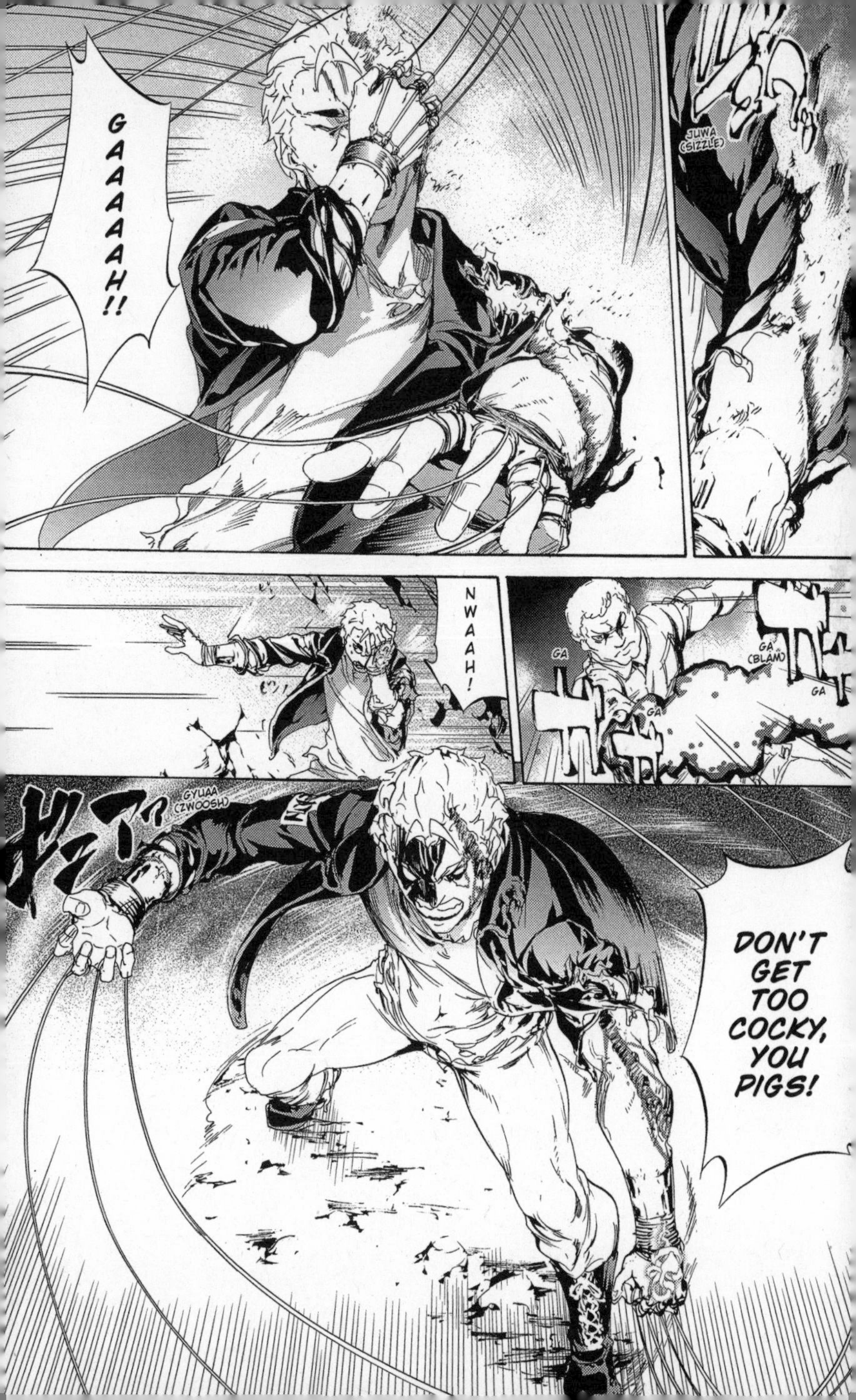
JUWA (SIZZLE)
GAAAAAAH!!
GA
GA (BLAM)
GA
GA
NWAAAH!
GYUAA (ZWOOSH)
DON'T GET TOO COCKY, YOU PIGS!

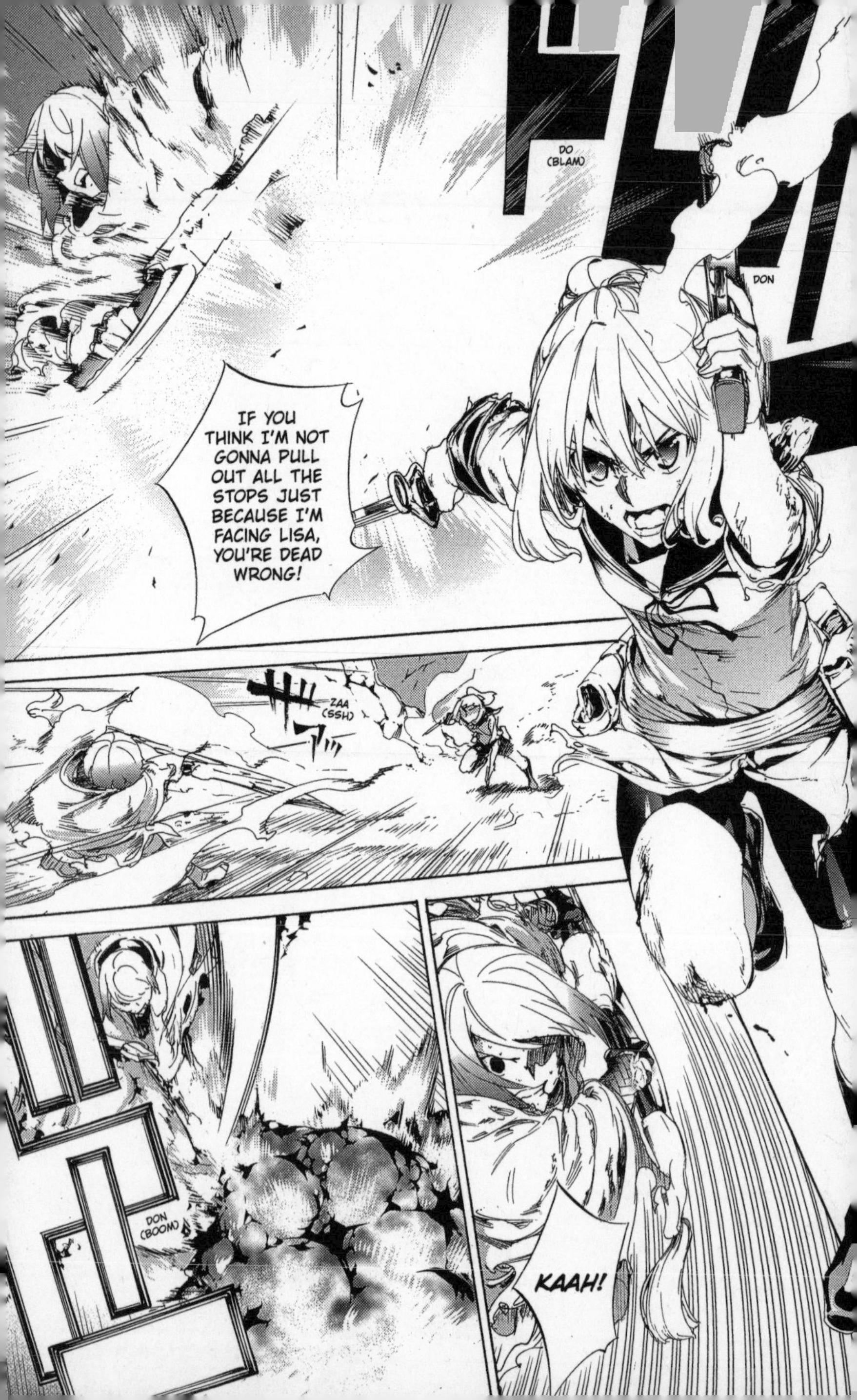
DO (BLAM)
DON
IF YOU THINK I'M NOT GONNA PULL OUT ALL THE STOPS JUST BECAUSE I'M FACING LISA, YOU'RE DEAD WRONG!
ZAA (SSH)
KAAH!
DON (BOOM)

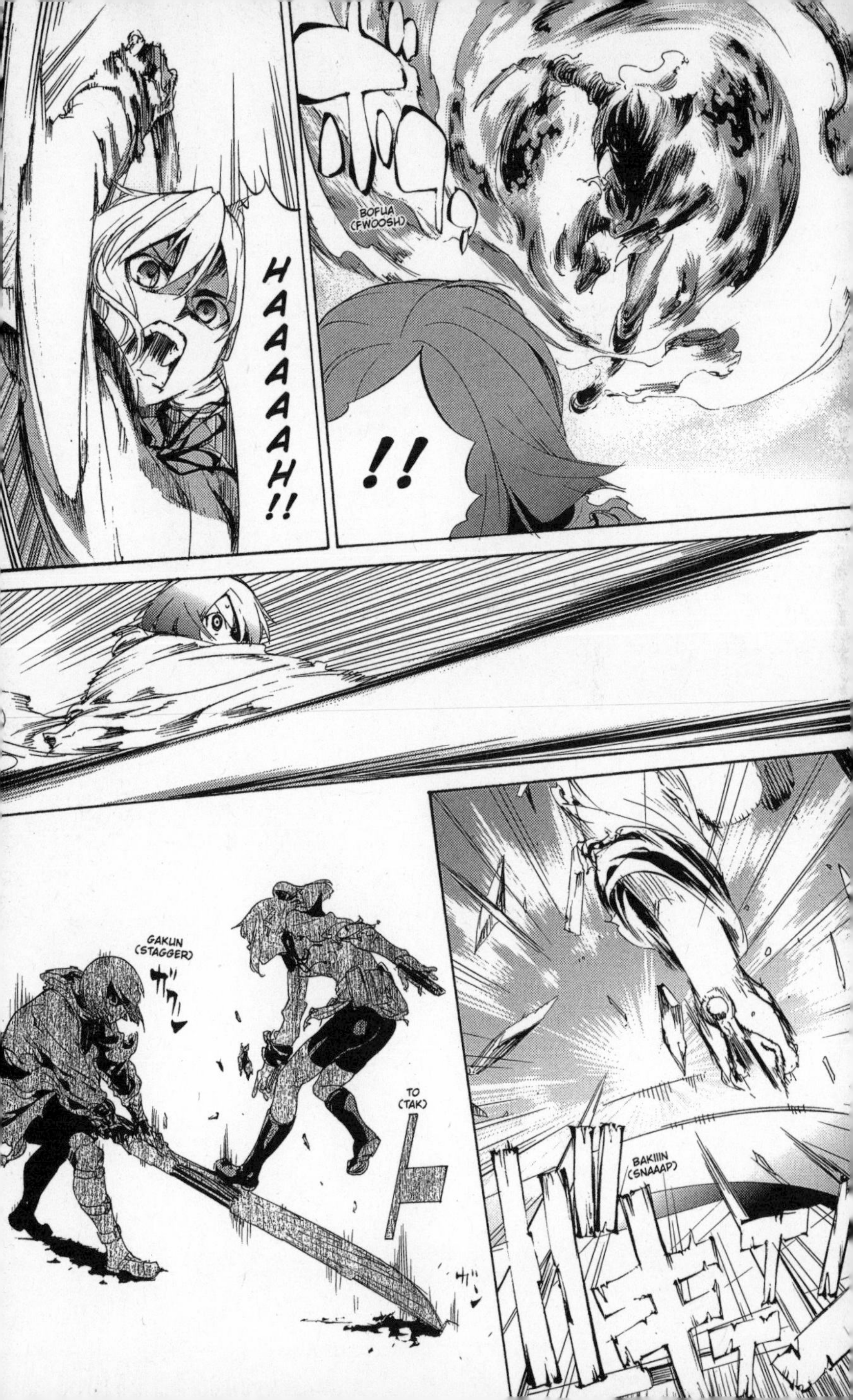
BOFUA (FWOOSH)
!!
HAAAAAAH!!
BAKIIN (SNAAAP)
GAKUN (STAGGER)
TO (TAK)

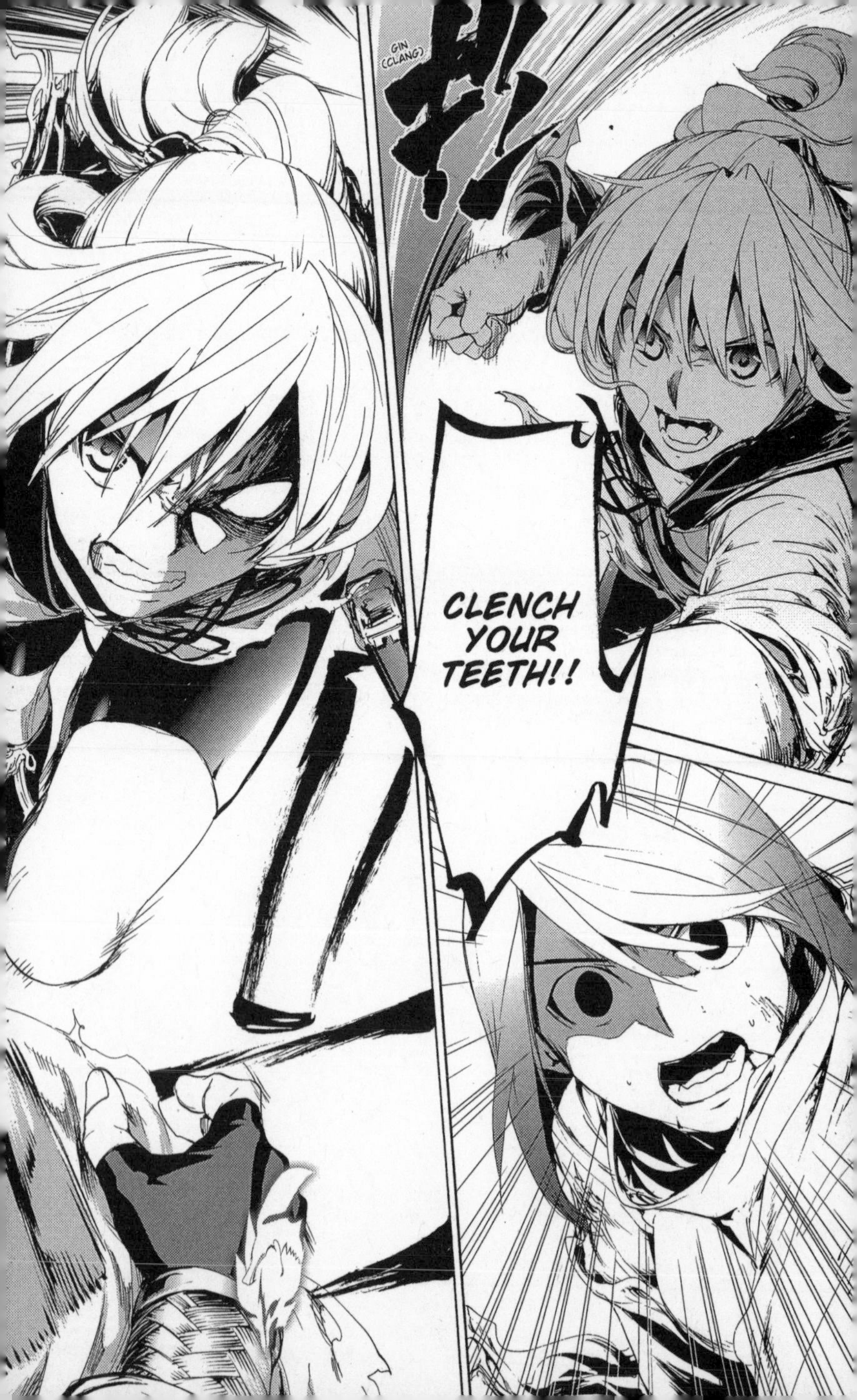
GIN
(CLANG)
CLENCH YOUR TEETH!!

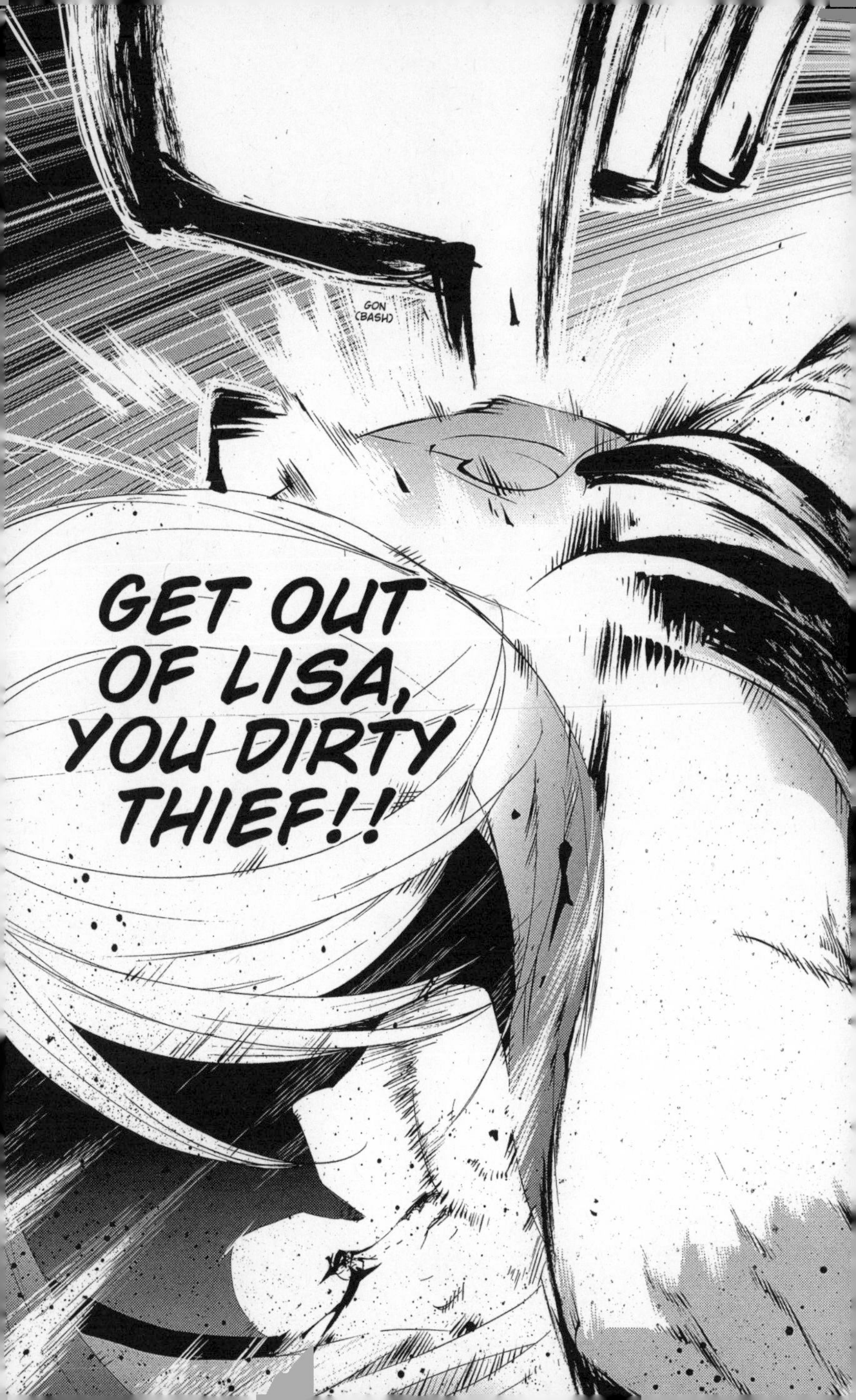
GON
(BASH)
GET OUT OF LISA, YOU DIRTY THIEF!!

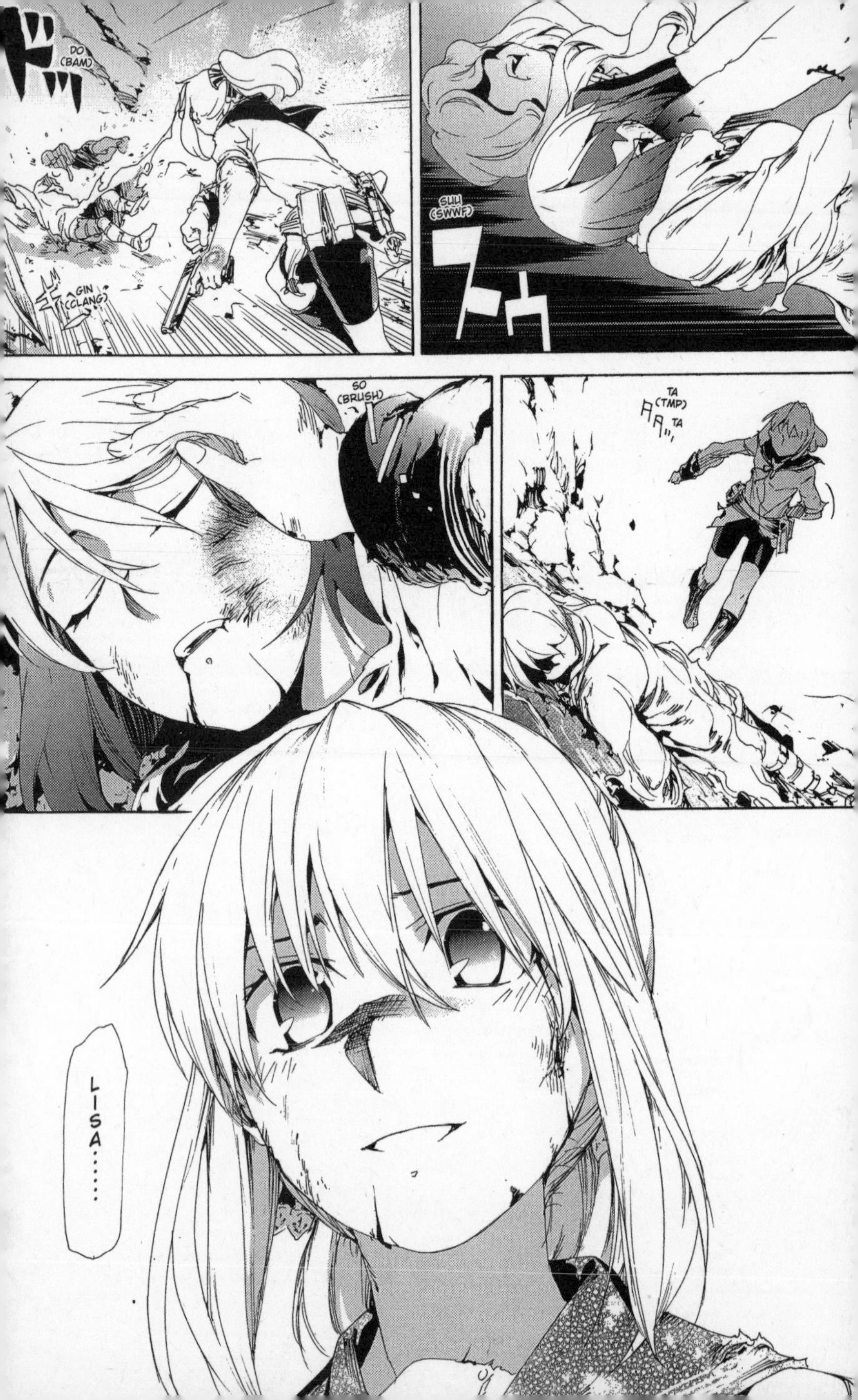
SUU
(SWWF)
DO
(BAM)
GIN
(CLANG)
TA
(TMP)
TA
SO
(BRUSH)
LISA……

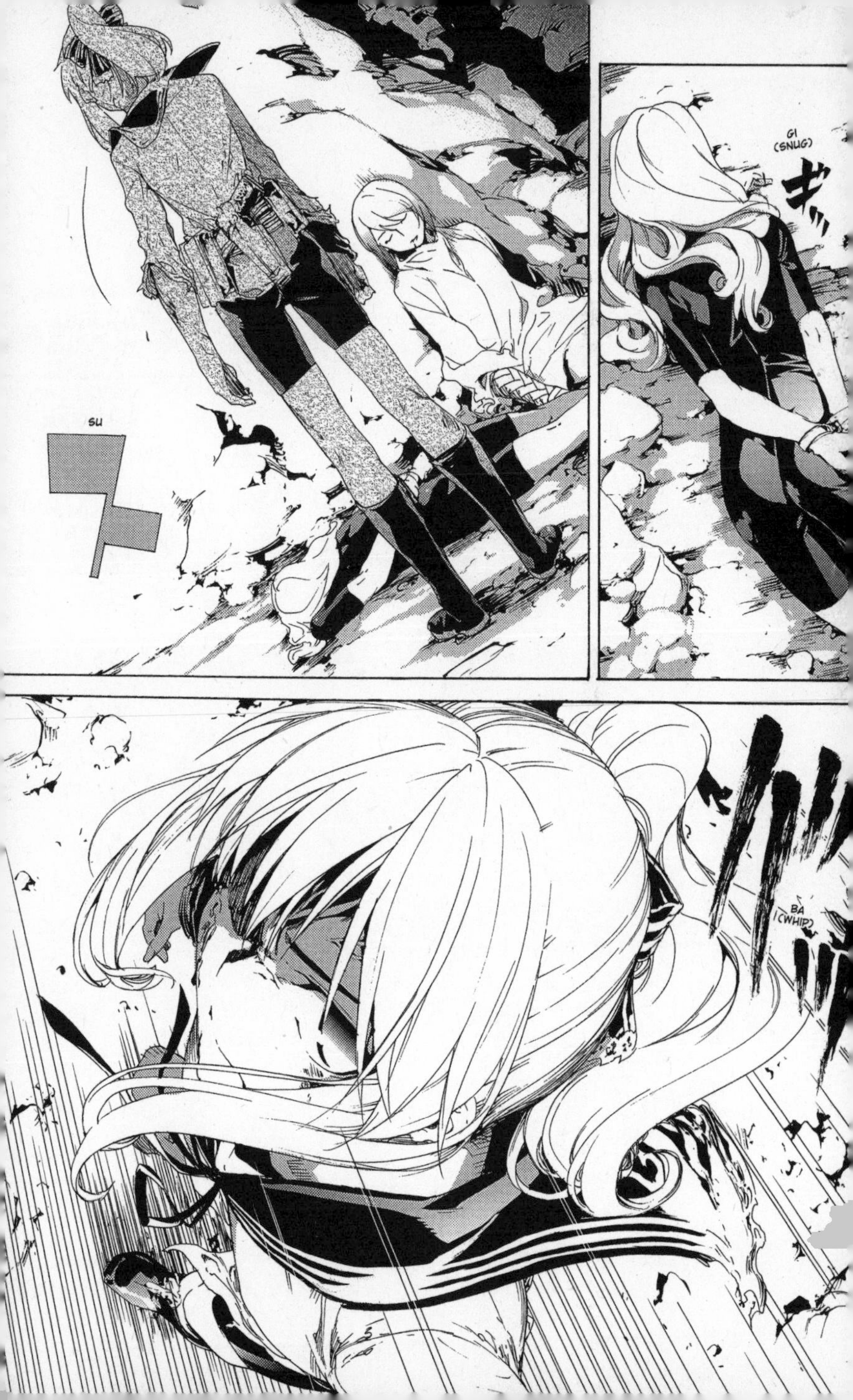
GI
(SNUG)
SU
BA
(WHIP)

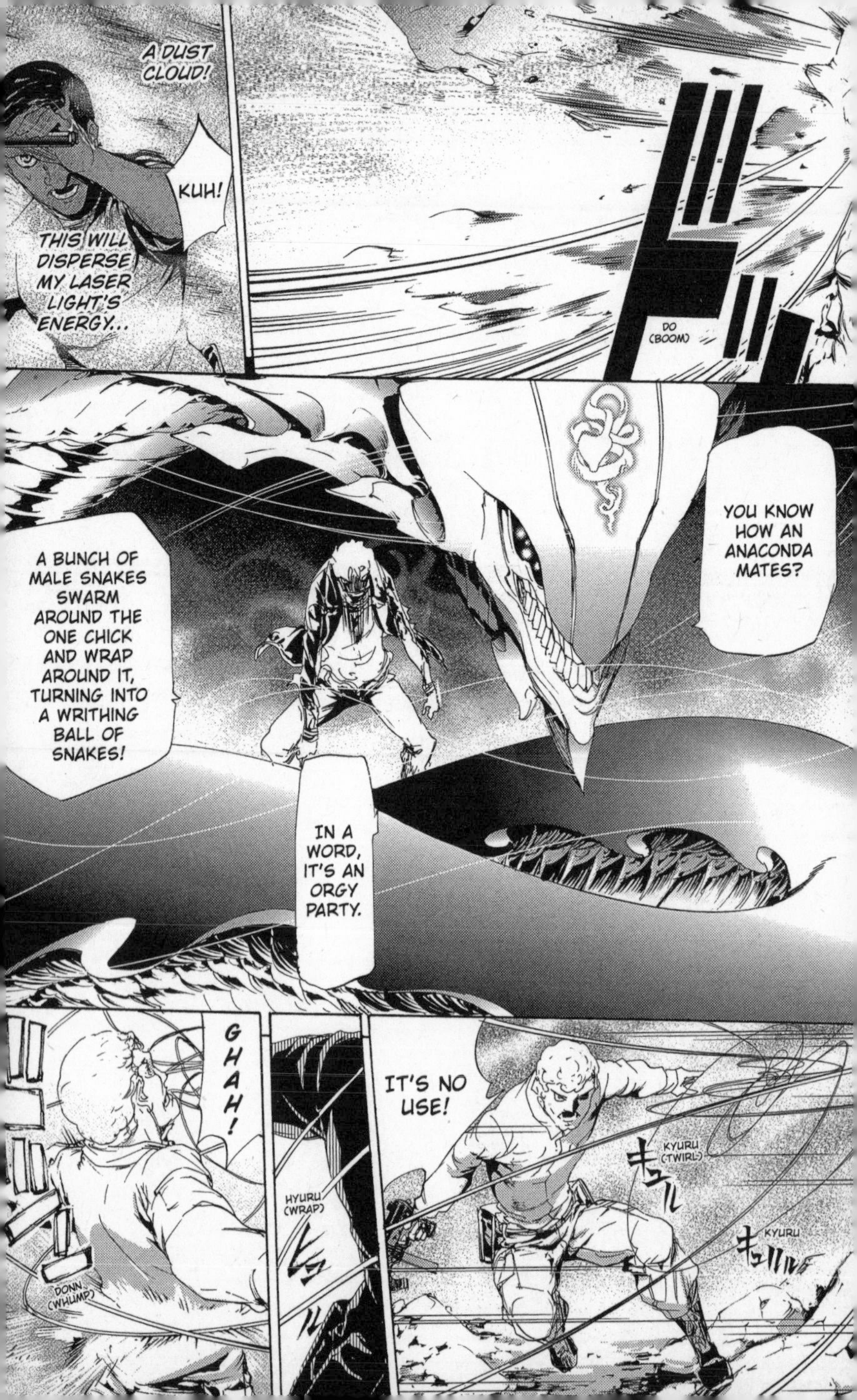
DO (BOOM)
A DUST CLOUD!
KUH!
THIS WILL DISPERSE MY LASER LIGHT'S ENERGY...
YOU KNOW HOW AN ANACONDA MATES?
A BUNCH OF MALE SNAKES SWARM AROUND THE ONE CHICK AND WRAP AROUND IT, TURNING INTO A WRITHING BALL OF SNAKES!
IN A WORD, IT'S AN ORGY PARTY.
IT'S NO USE!
KYURU (TWIRL)
KYURU
HYURU (WRAP)
GHAH!
DONN (WHUMP)

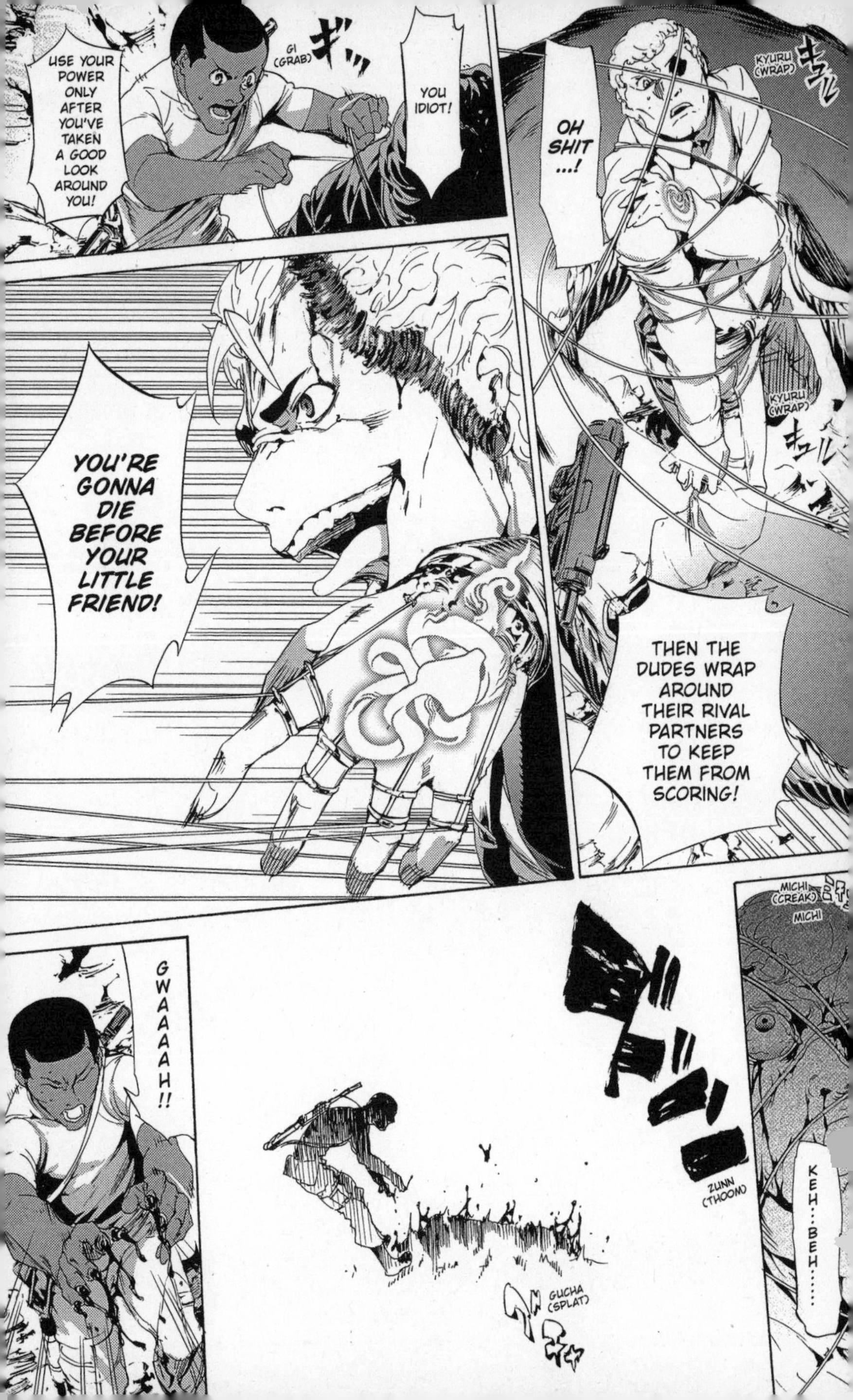

KYURU (WRAP)
OH SHIT ...!
KYURU (WRAP)
THEN THE DUDES WRAP AROUND THEIR RIVAL PARTNERS TO KEEP THEM FROM SCORING!
GI (GRAB)
YOU IDIOT!
USE YOUR POWER ONLY AFTER YOU'VE TAKEN A GOOD LOOK AROUND YOU!
YOU'RE GONNA DIE BEFORE YOUR LITTLE FRIEND!
MICHI (CREAK)
MICHI
KEH...BEH......
ZUNN (THOOM)
GUCHA (SPLAT)
GWAAAAAH!!

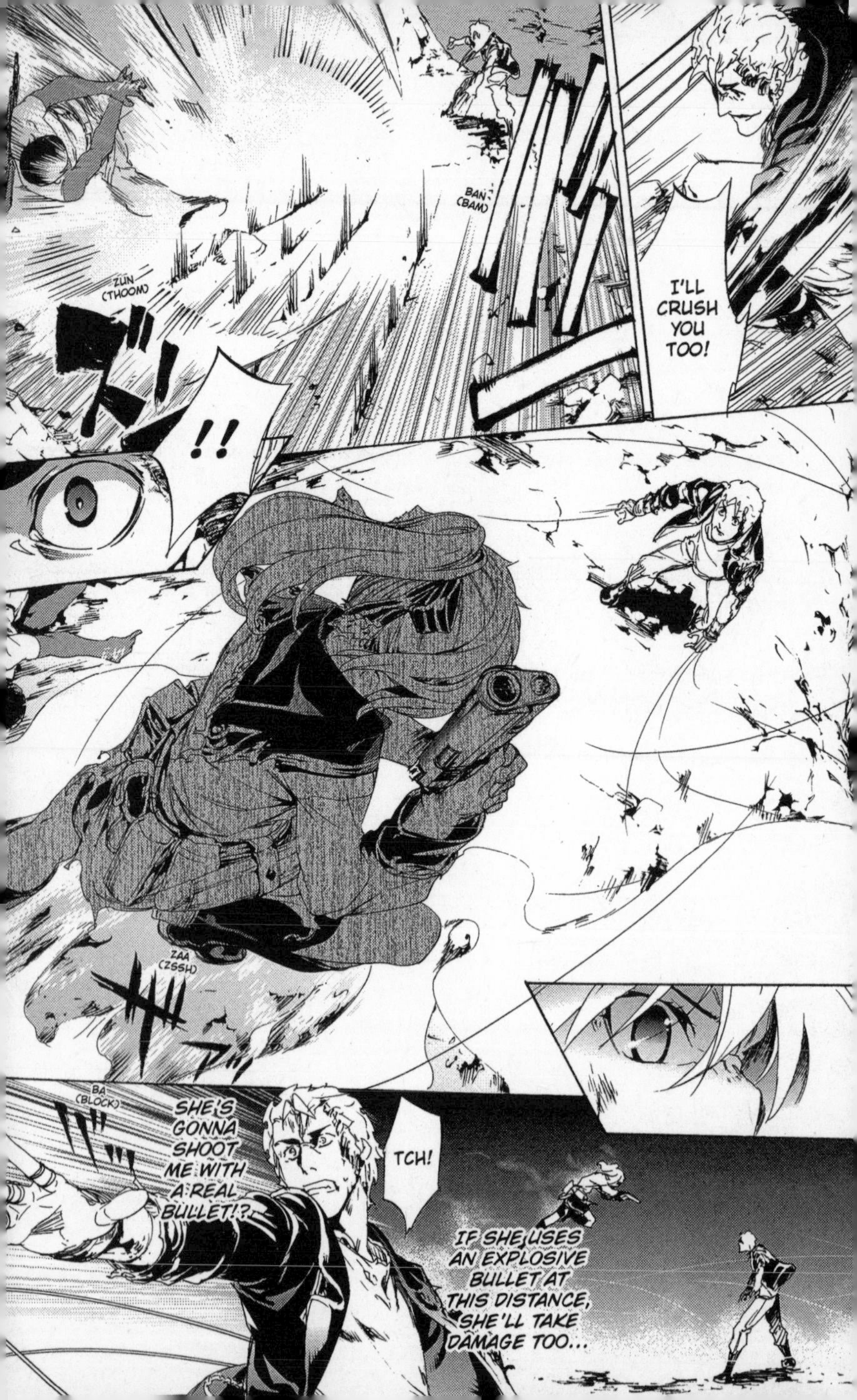
I'LL CRUSH YOU TOO!
BAN (BAM)
ZUN (THOOM)
!!
ZAA (ZSSH)
TCH!
SHE'S GONNA SHOOT ME WITH A REAL BULLET!?
BA (BLOCK)
IF SHE USES AN EXPLOSIVE BULLET AT THIS DISTANCE, SHE'LL TAKE DAMAGE TOO...

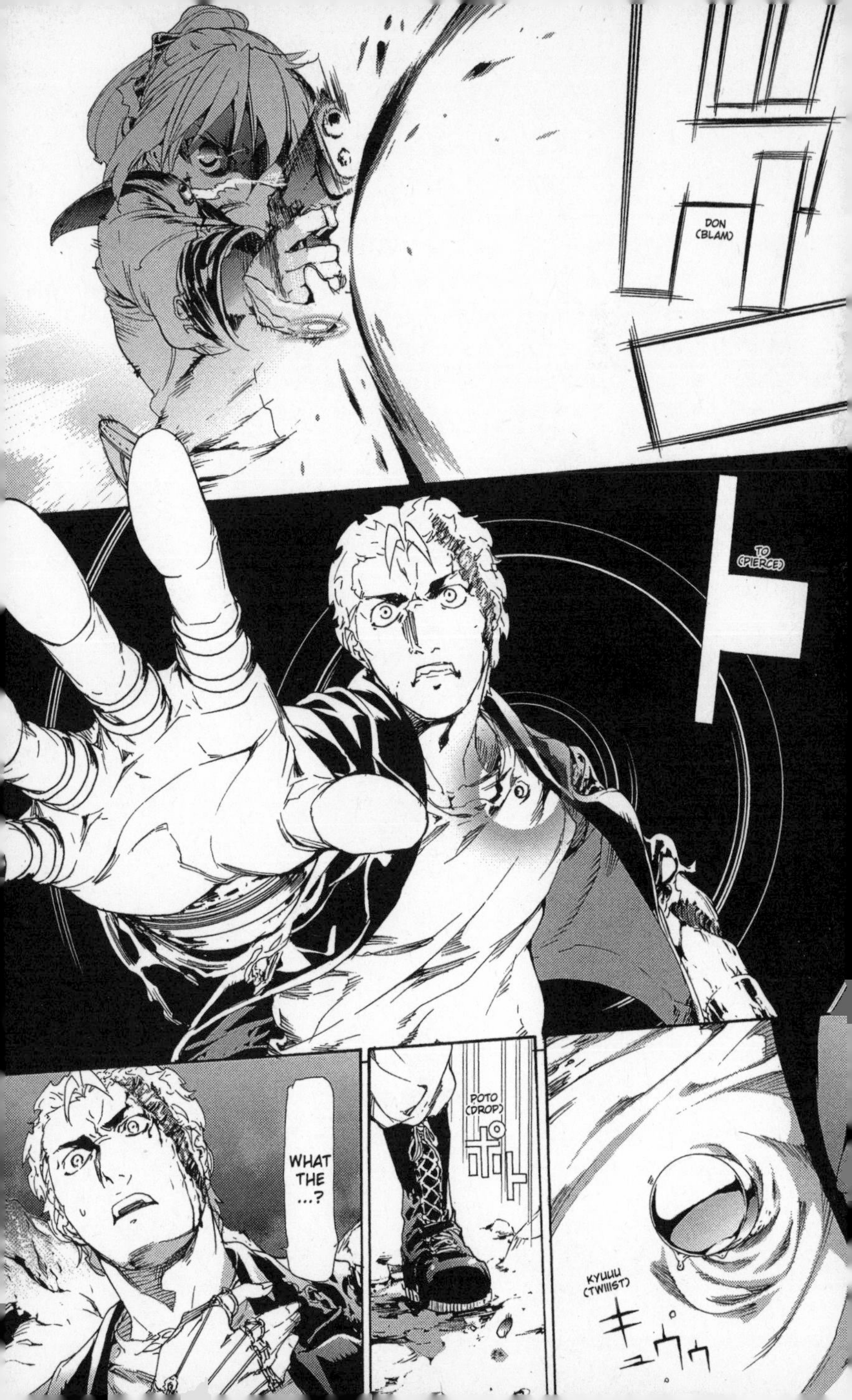
DON (BLAM)
TO (PIERCE)
KYUUU (TWIIIST)
POTO (DROP)
WHAT THE ...?

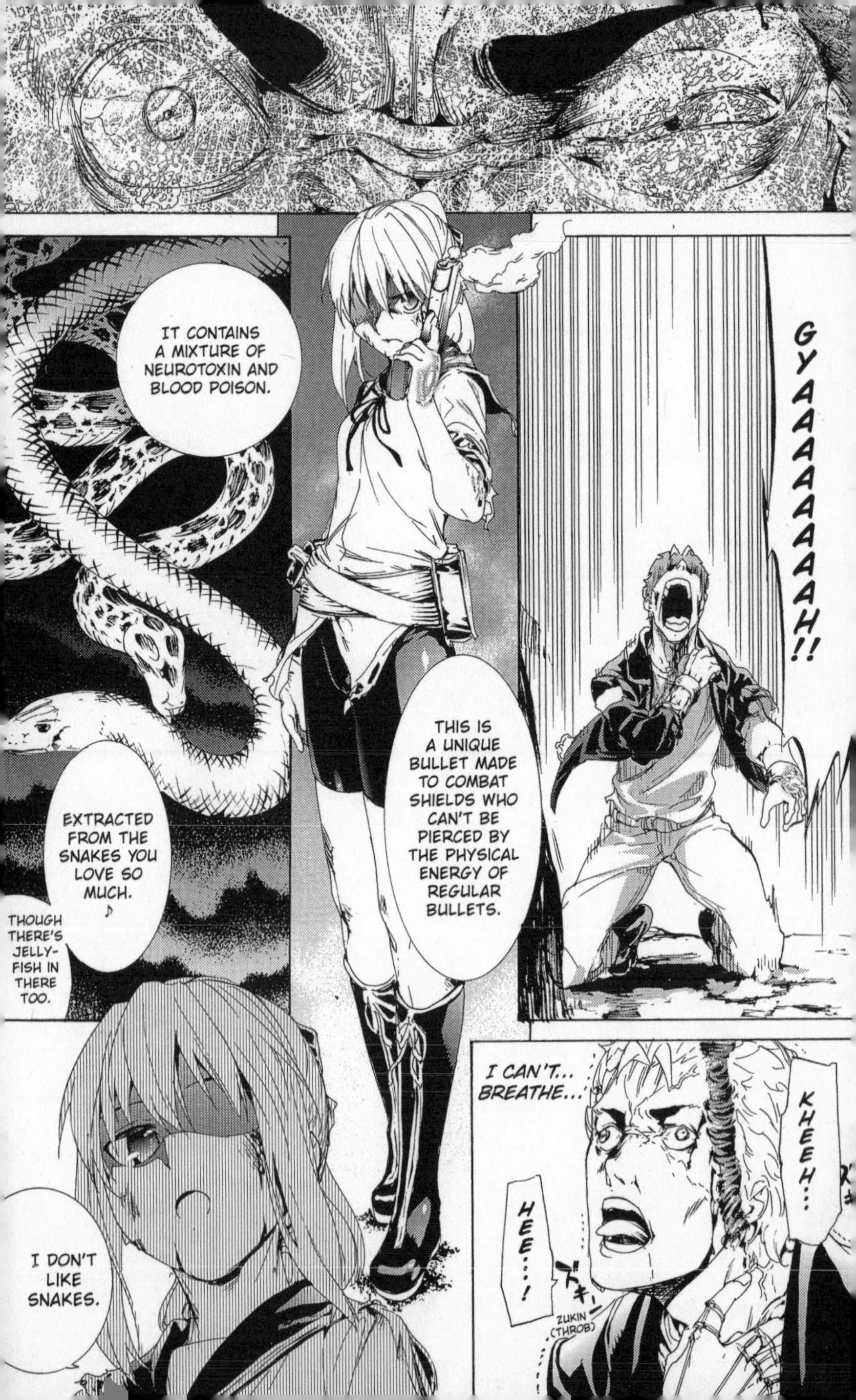
GYAAAAAAAAAAH!!
THIS IS A UNIQUE BULLET MADE TO COMBAT SHIELDS WHO CAN'T BE PIERCED BY THE PHYSICAL ENERGY OF REGULAR BULLETS.
IT CONTAINS A MIXTURE OF NEUROTOXIN AND BLOOD POISON.
EXTRACTED FROM THE SNAKES YOU LOVE SO MUCH. ♪
THOUGH THERE'S JELLY-FISH IN THERE TOO.
I CAN'T... BREATHE...
KHEEH...
HEE...!
ZUKIN (THROB)
I DON'T LIKE SNAKES.

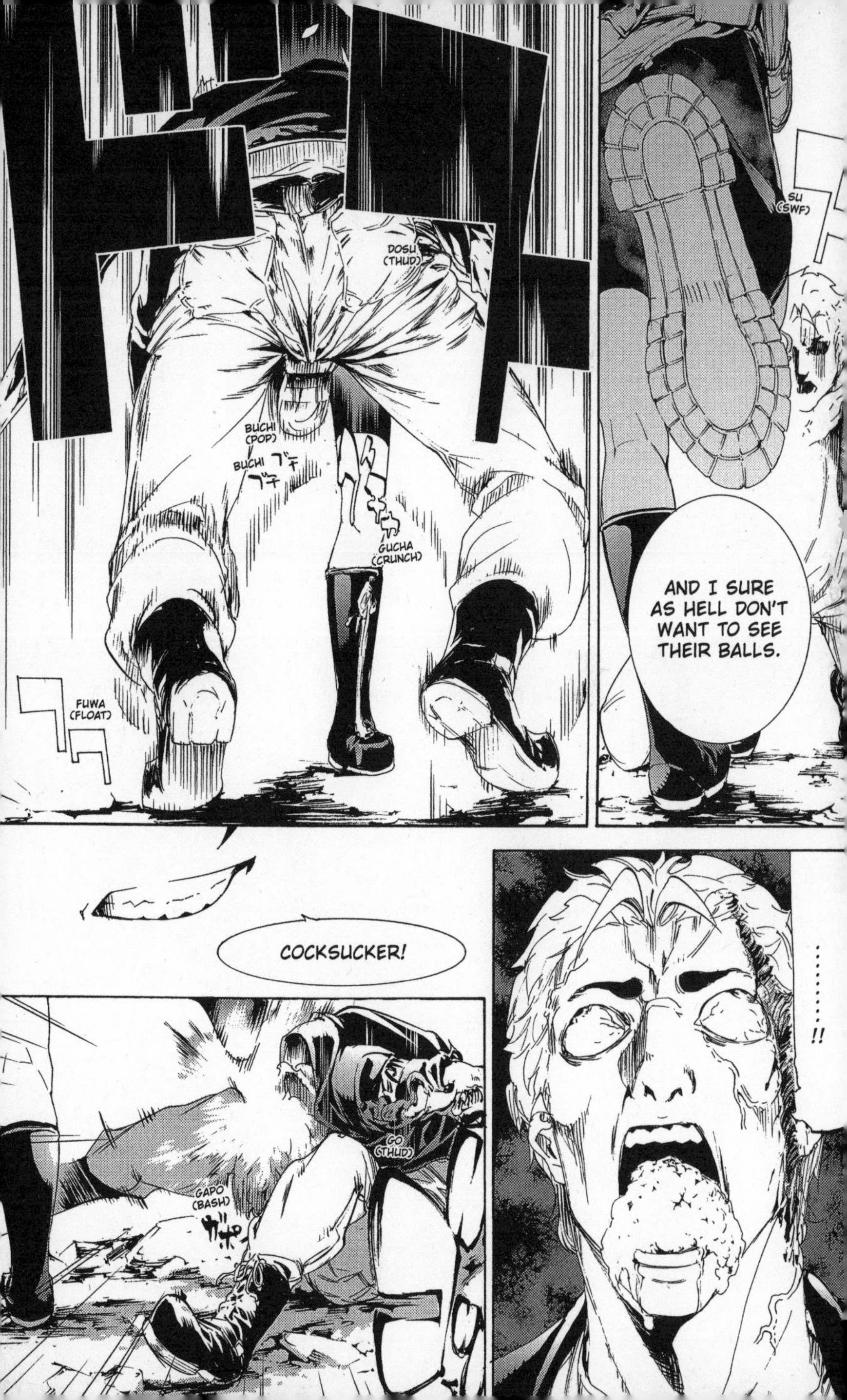
SU (SWF)
AND I SURE AS HELL DON'T WANT TO SEE THEIR BALLS.
DOSU (THUD)
BUCHI (POP)
BUCHI
GUCHA (CRUNCH)
FUWA (FLOAT)
......!!
COCKSUCKER!
GO (THUD)
GAPO (BASH)

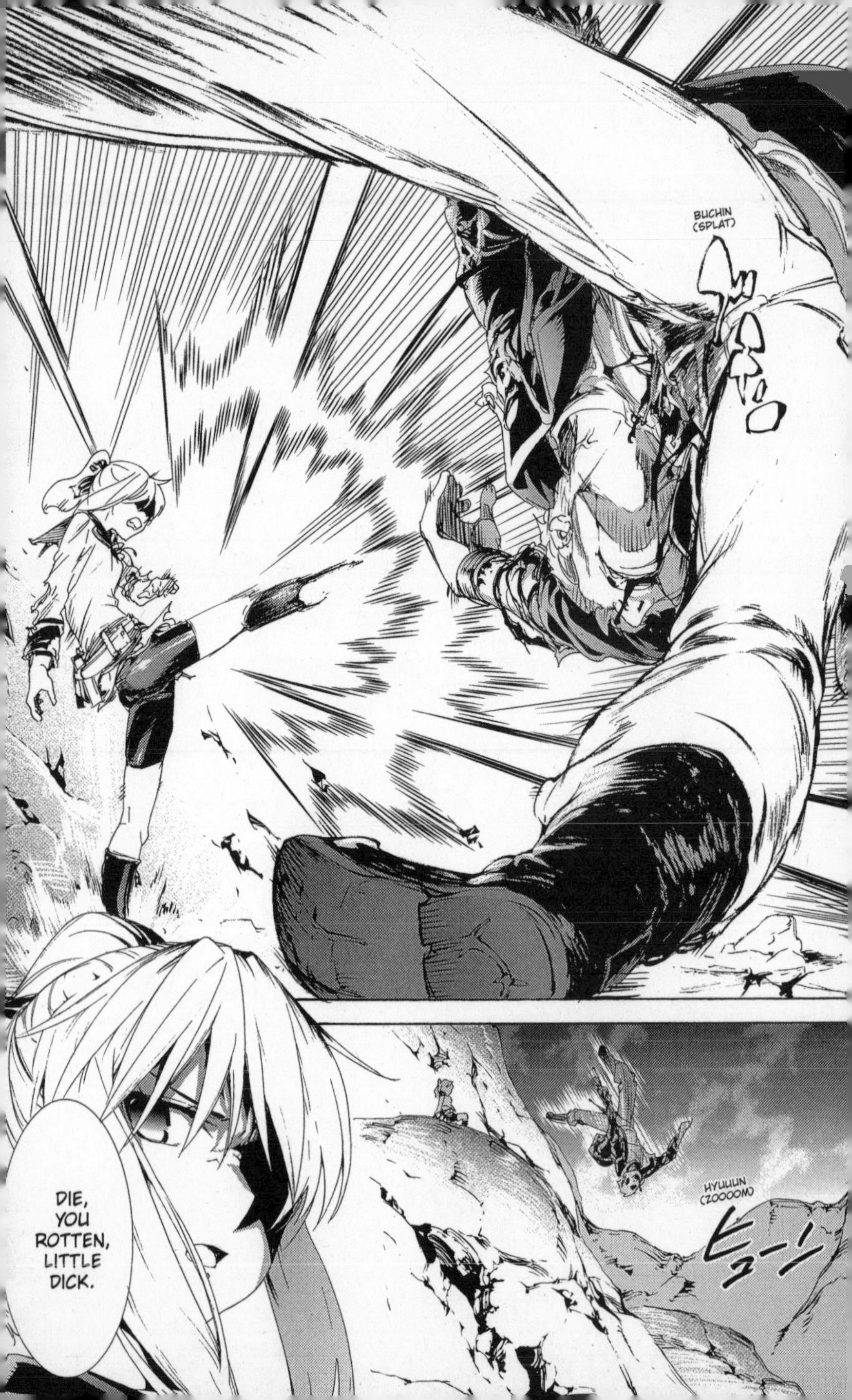
BUCHIN
(SPLAT)
HYUUUN
(ZOOOOM)
DIE, YOU ROTTEN, LITTLE DICK.

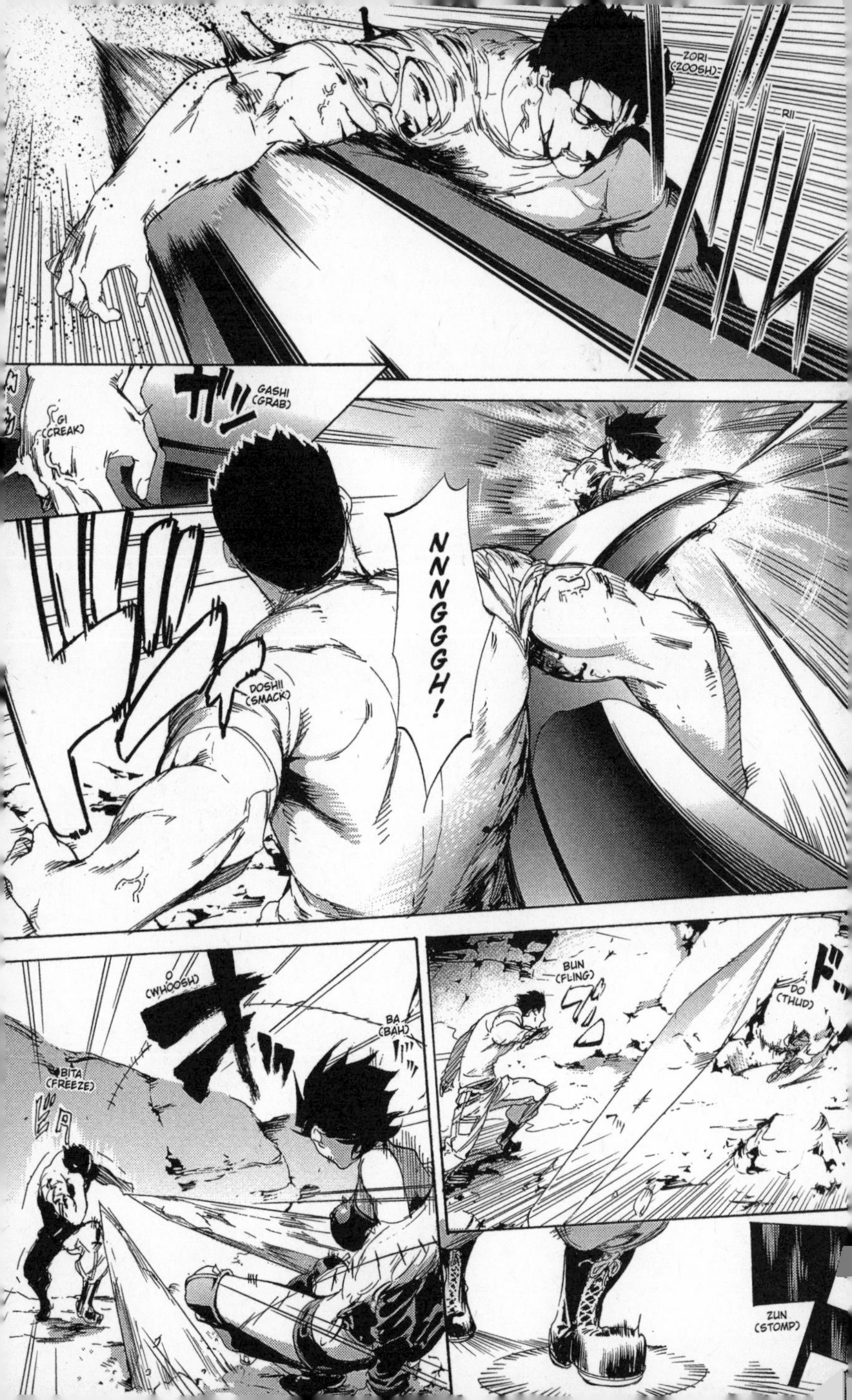
ZORI (ZOOSH)
RII
NNNGGGH!
DOSHI (SMACK)
GASHI (GRAB)
GI (CREAK)
DO (THUD)
BUN (FLING)
BA (BAH)
O (WHOOSH)
BITA (FREEZE)
ZUN (STOMP)

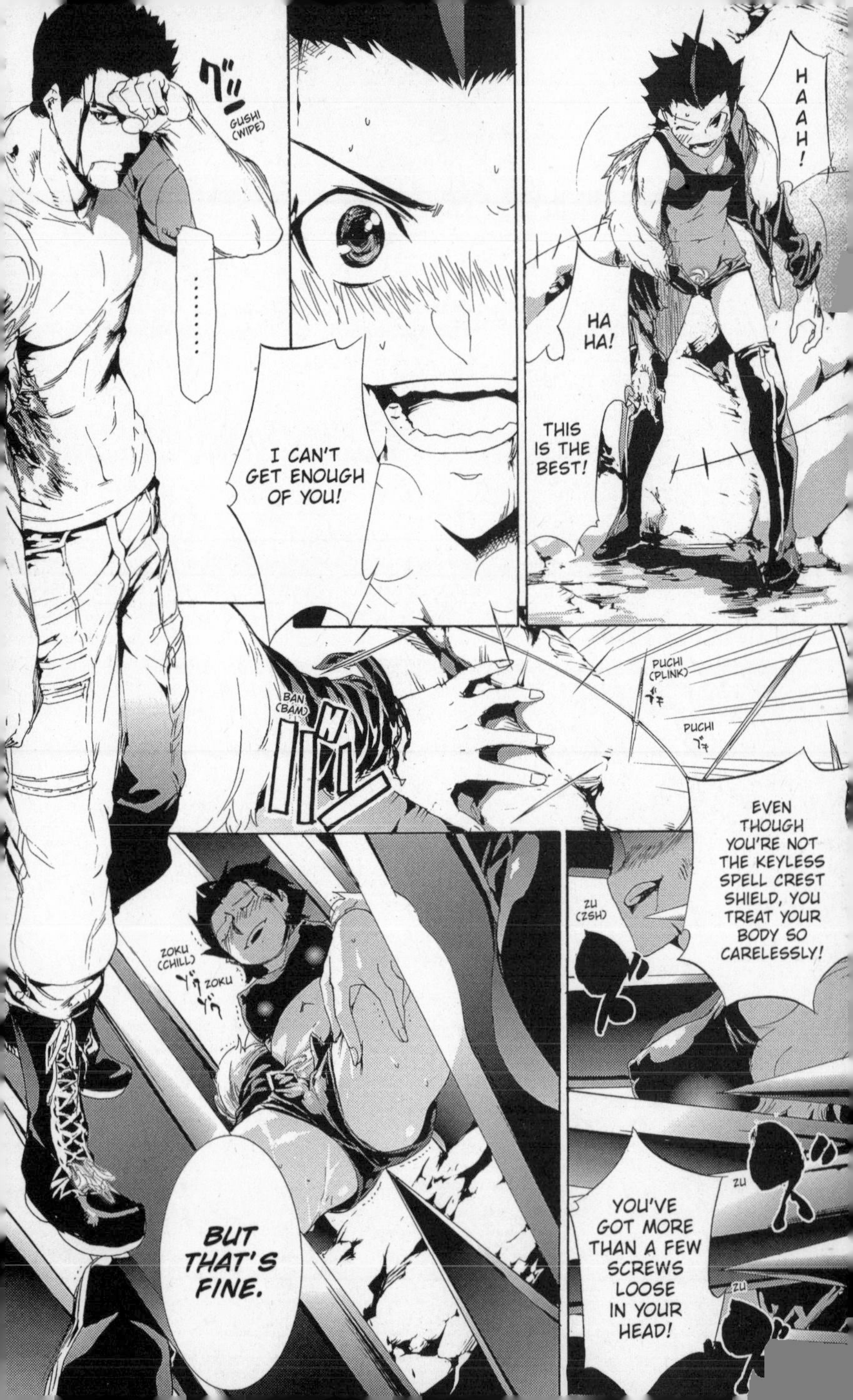
HAAAH!
HA HA!
THIS IS THE BEST!
I CAN'T GET ENOUGH OF YOU!
PUCHI (PLINK)
PUCHI
BAN (BAM)
EVEN THOUGH YOU'RE NOT THE KEYLESS SPELL CREST SHIELD, YOU TREAT YOUR BODY SO CARELESSLY!
ZU (ZSH)
ZU
ZU
YOU'VE GOT MORE THAN A FEW SCREWS LOOSE IN YOUR HEAD!
ZOKU (CHILL)
ZOKU
BUT THAT'S FINE.
GUSHI (WIPE)
......

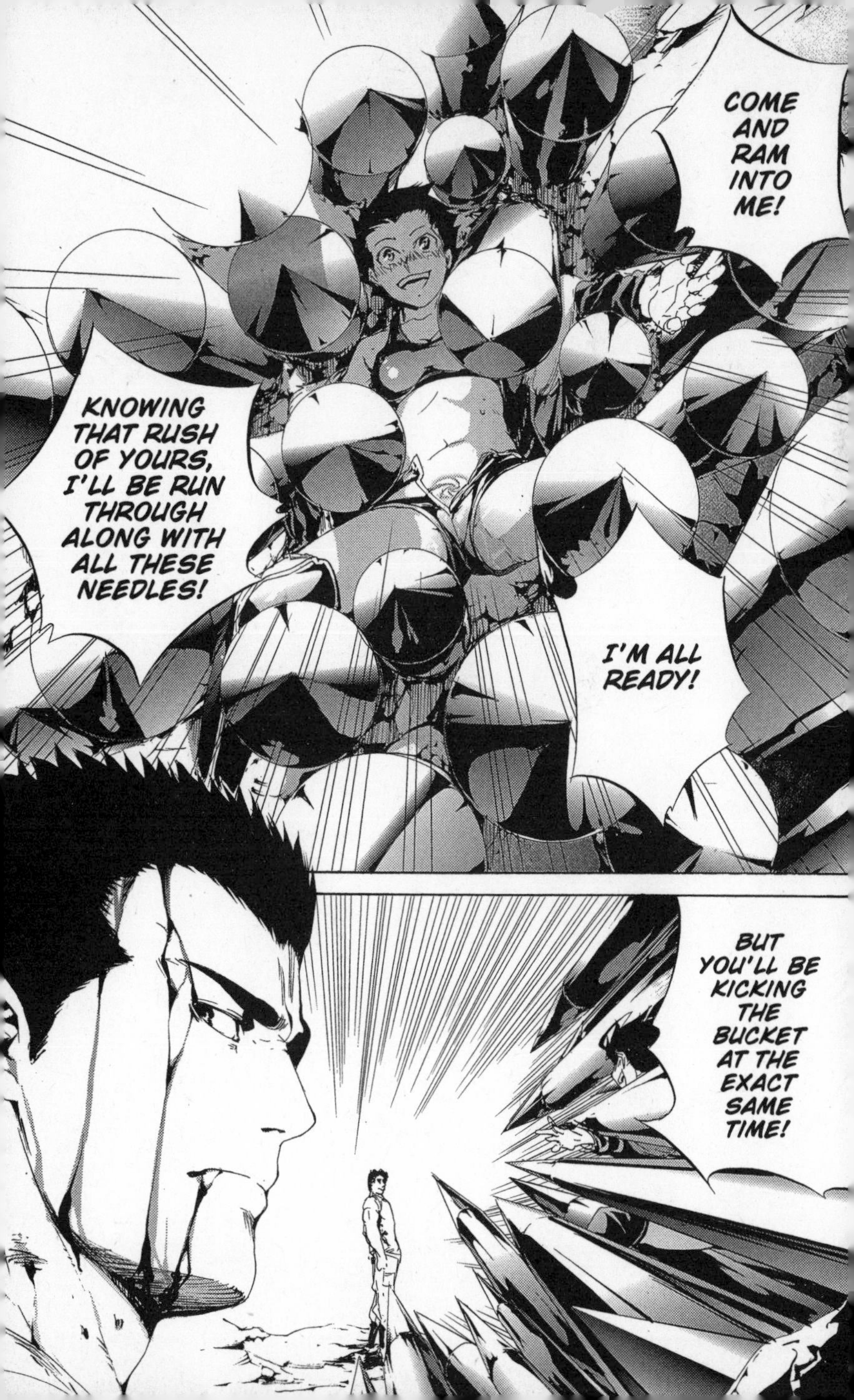
COME AND RAM INTO ME!
KNOWING THAT RUSH OF YOURS, I'LL BE RUN THROUGH ALONG WITH ALL THESE NEEDLES!
I'M ALL READY!
BUT YOU'LL BE KICKING THE BUCKET AT THE EXACT SAME TIME!

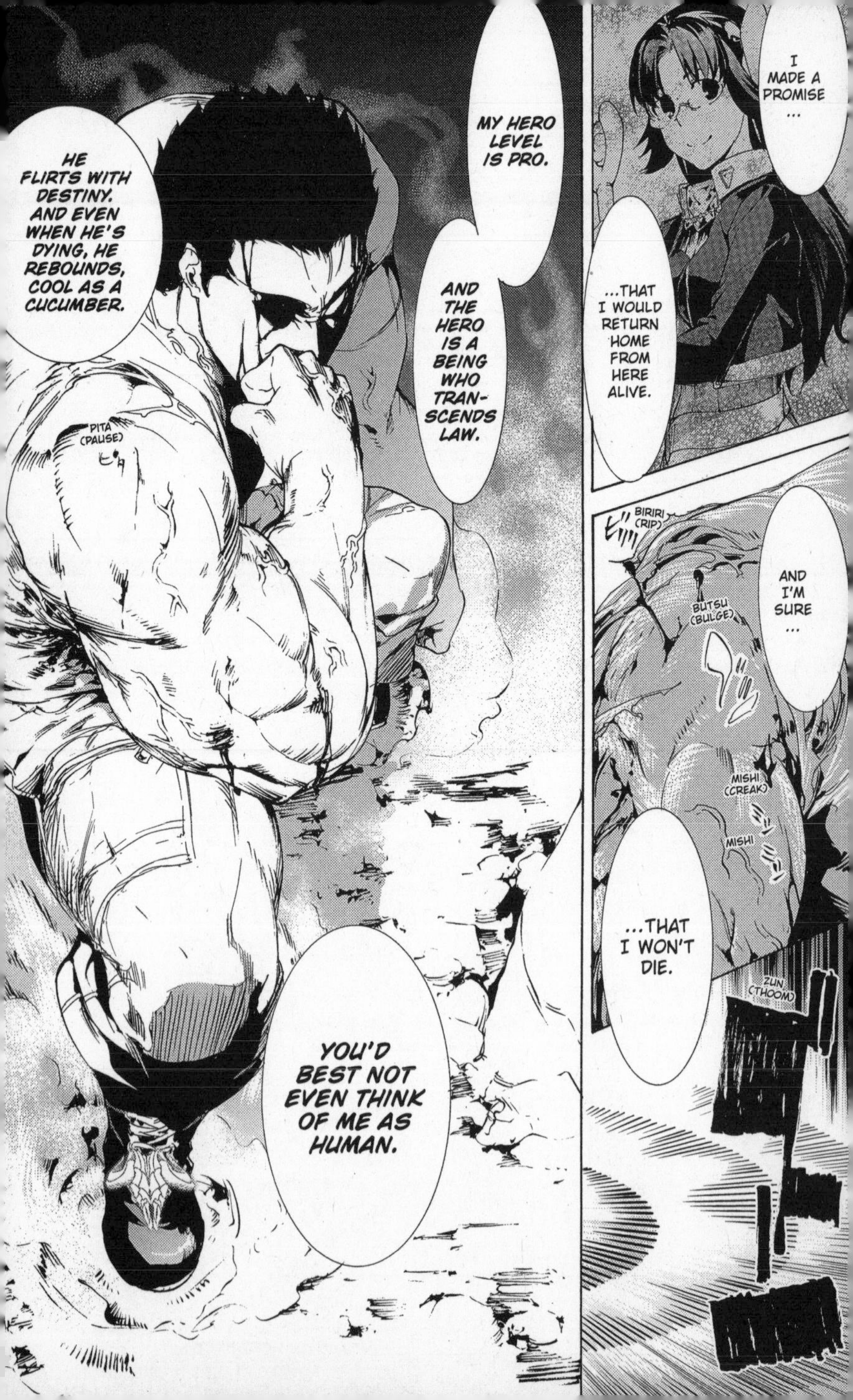
I MADE A PROMISE ...
...THAT I WOULD RETURN HOME FROM HERE ALIVE.
BIRIRI (RIP)
AND I'M SURE ...
BUTSU (BULGE)
MISHI (CREAK)
MISHI
...THAT I WON'T DIE.
ZUN (THOOM)
MY HERO LEVEL IS PRO.
AND THE HERO IS A BEING WHO TRAN-SCENDS LAW.
HE FLIRTS WITH DESTINY. AND EVEN WHEN HE'S DYING, HE REBOUNDS, COOL AS A CUCUMBER.
PITA (PAUSE)
YOU'D BEST NOT EVEN THINK OF ME AS HUMAN.

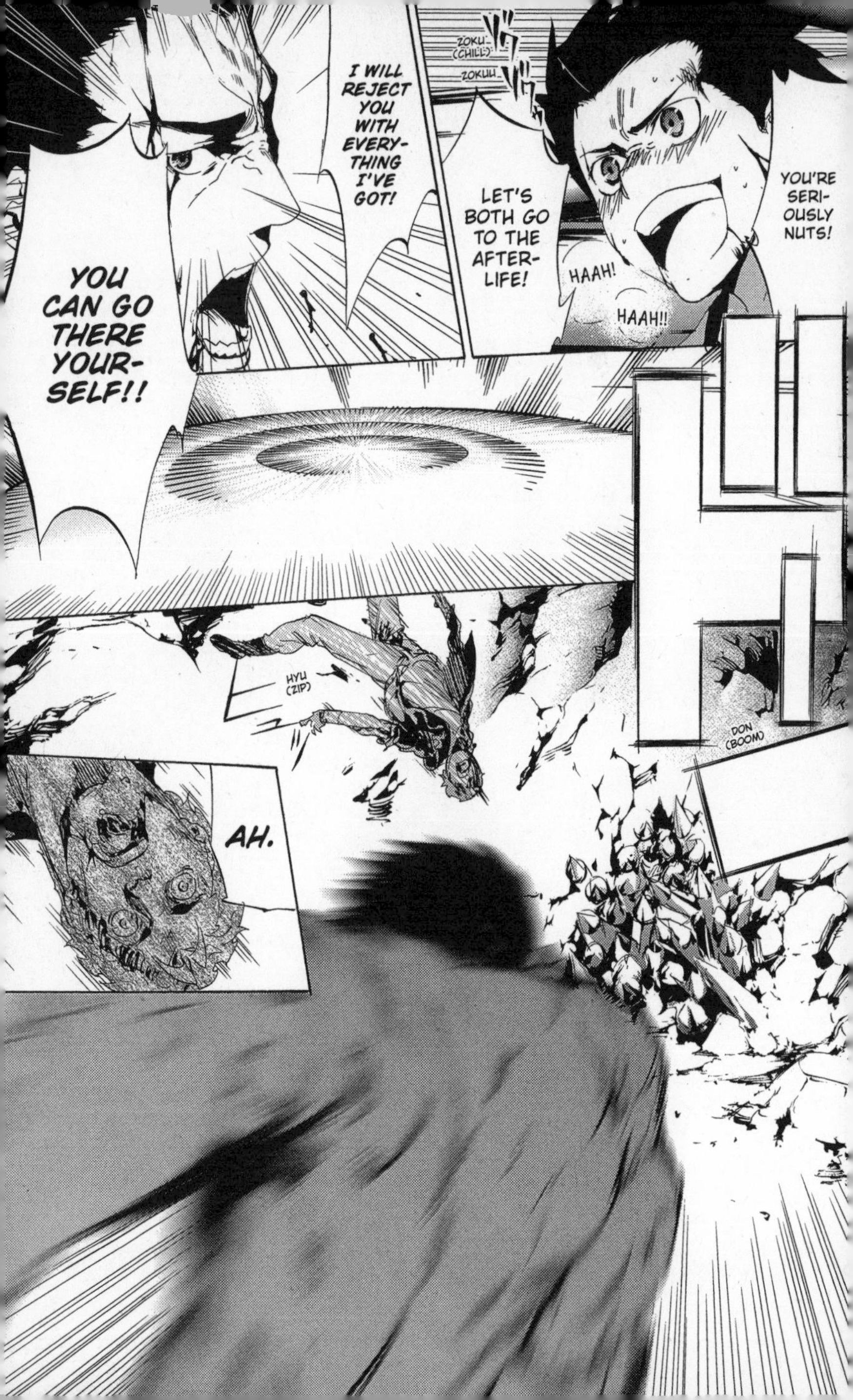
ZOKU (CHILL)
ZOKUU
YOU'RE SERIOUSLY NUTS!
LET'S BOTH GO TO THE AFTERLIFE!
HAAH!
HAAH!!
I WILL REJECT YOU WITH EVERYTHING I'VE GOT!
YOU CAN GO THERE YOURSELF!!
DON (BOOM)
HYU (ZIP)
AH.

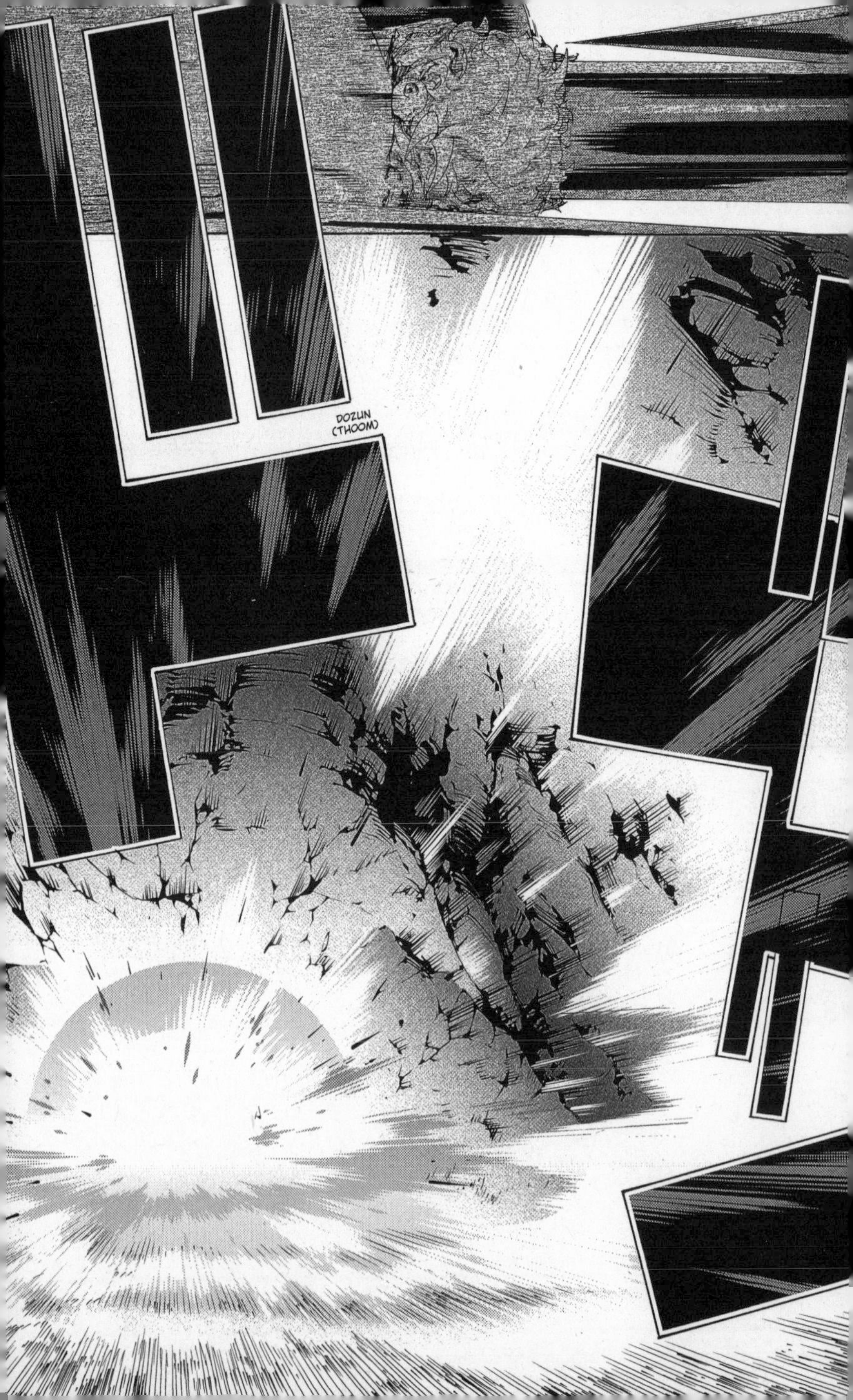
DOZUN
(THOOM)

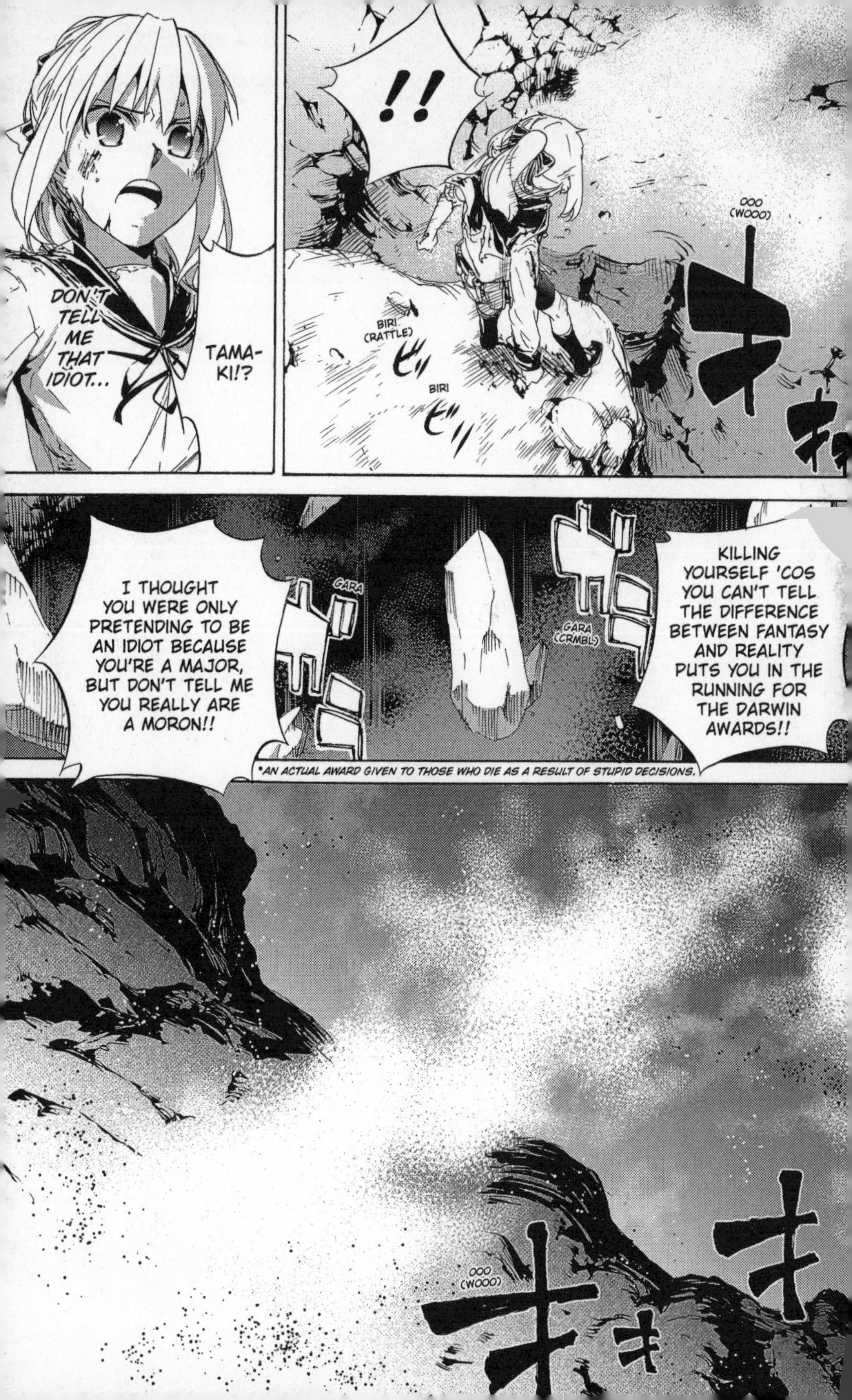
!!
OOO (WOOO)
BIRI (RATTLE)
BIRI
TAMA-KI!?
DON'T TELL ME THAT IDIOT...
KILLING YOURSELF 'COS YOU CAN'T TELL THE DIFFERENCE BETWEEN FANTASY AND REALITY PUTS YOU IN THE RUNNING FOR THE DARWIN AWARDS!!
GARA (CRMBL)
GARA
I THOUGHT YOU WERE ONLY PRETENDING TO BE AN IDIOT BECAUSE YOU'RE A MAJOR, BUT DON'T TELL ME YOU REALLY ARE A MORON!!
*AN ACTUAL AWARD GIVEN TO THOSE WHO DIE AS A RESULT OF STUPID DECISIONS.
OOO (WOOO)

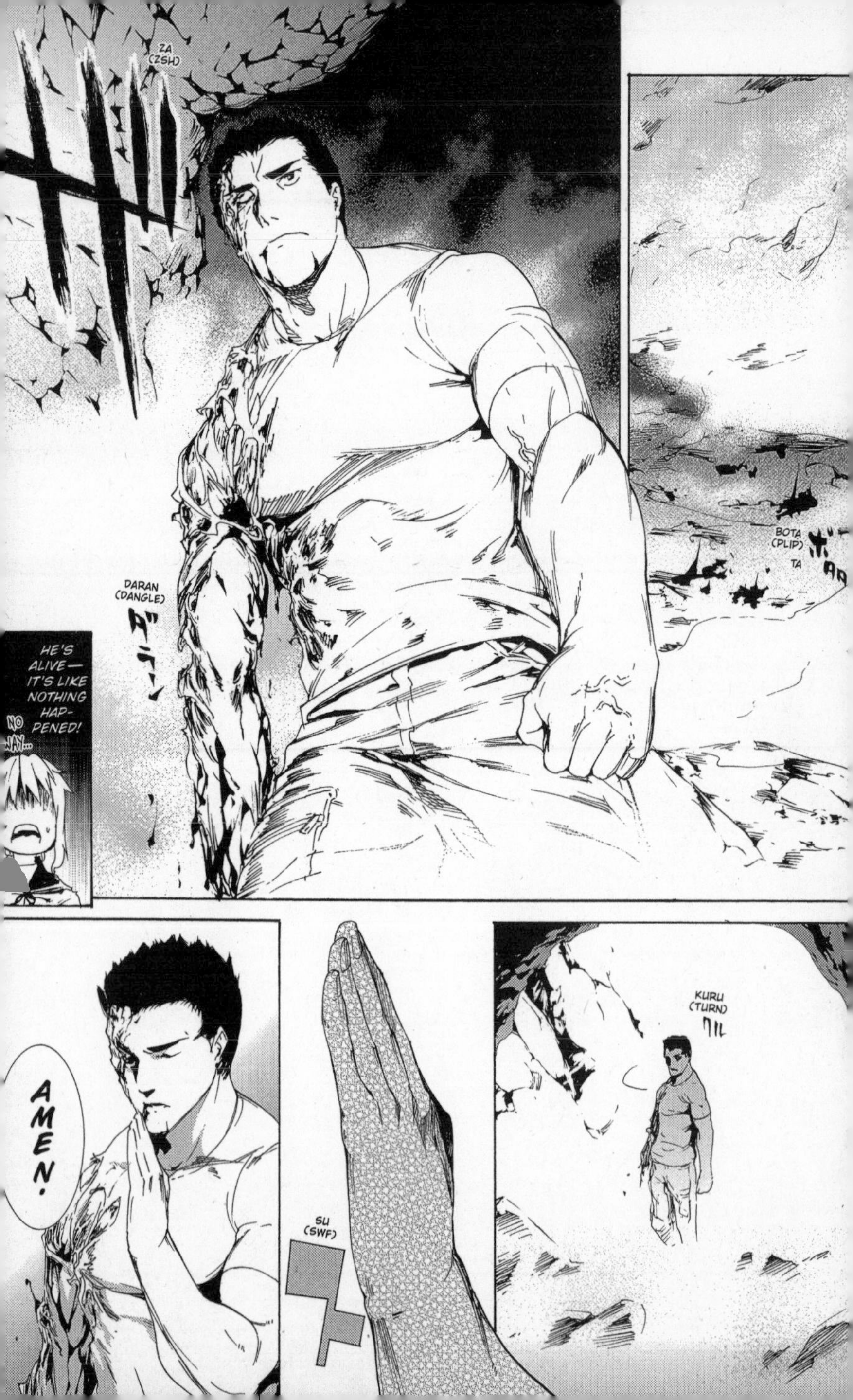
BOTA (PLIP) TA
ZA (ZSH)
DARAN (DANGLE)
HE'S ALIVE—IT'S LIKE NOTHING HAPPENED!
NO WAY...
KURU (TURN)
SU (SWF)
AMEN.

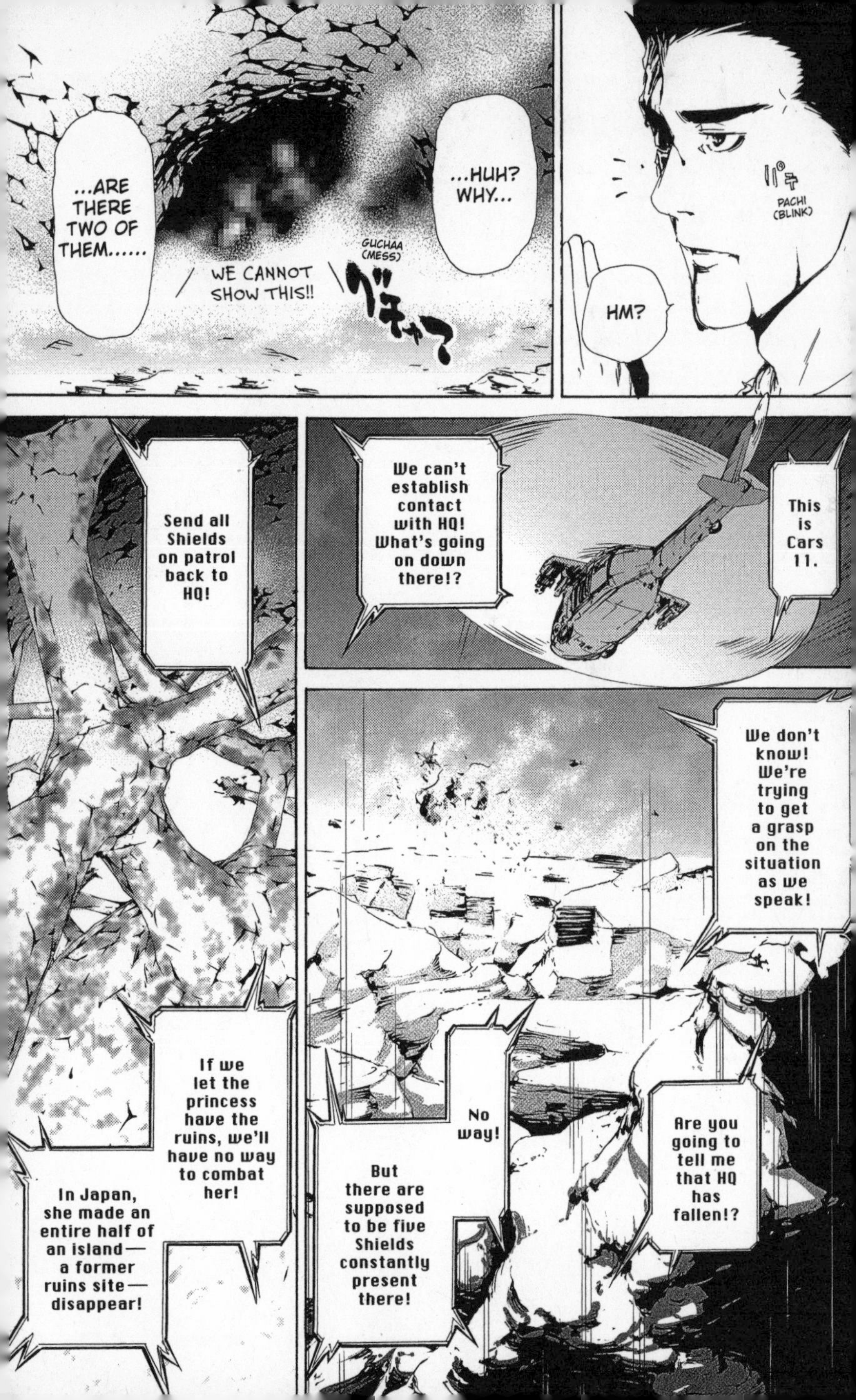
PACHI (BLINK)
HM?
...HUH? WHY...
GUCHAA (MESS)
WE CANNOT SHOW THIS!!
...ARE THERE TWO OF THEM......
This is Cars 11.
We can't establish contact with HQ! What's going on down there!?
We don't know! We're trying to get a grasp on the situation as we speak!
Are you going to tell me that HQ has fallen!?
No way!
But there are supposed to be five Shields constantly present there!
Send all Shields on patrol back to HQ!
If we let the princess have the ruins, we'll have no way to combat her!
In Japan, she made an entire half of an island—a former ruins site—disappear!

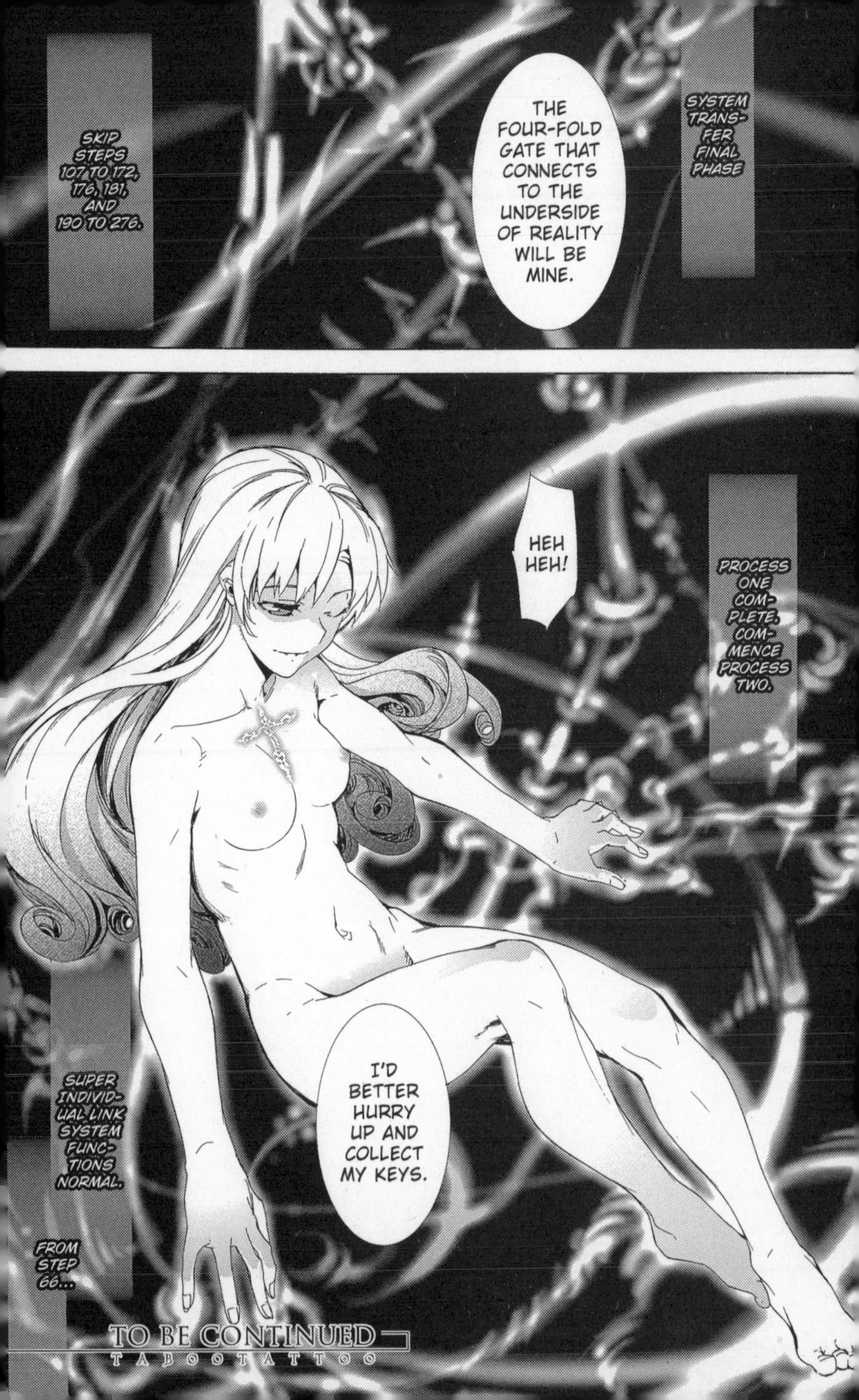
SYSTEM TRANSFER FINAL PHASE
THE FOUR-FOLD GATE THAT CONNECTS TO THE UNDERSIDE OF REALITY WILL BE MINE.
SKIP STEPS 107 TO 172, 176, 181, AND 190 TO 276.
PROCESS ONE COMPLETE. COMMENCE PROCESS TWO.
HEH HEH!
I'D BETTER HURRY UP AND COLLECT MY KEYS.
SUPER INDIVIDUAL LINK SYSTEM FUNCTIONS NORMAL.
FROM STEP 66...
TO BE CONTINUED
TABOO TATTOO

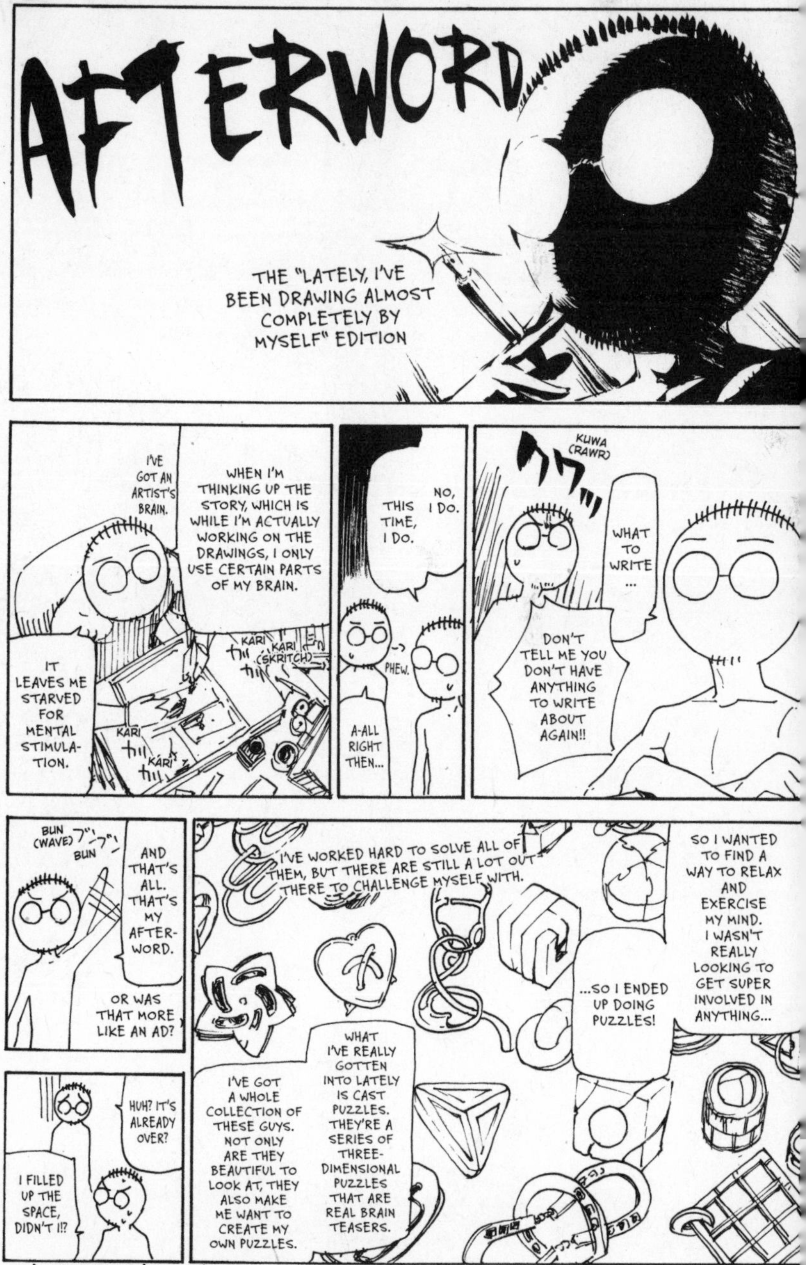
AFTERWORD
THE "LATELY, I'VE BEEN DRAWING ALMOST COMPLETELY BY MYSELF" EDITION
KUWA (RAWR)
WHAT TO WRITE...
DON'T TELL ME YOU DON'T HAVE ANYTHING TO WRITE ABOUT AGAIN!!
NO, I DO.
THIS TIME, I DO.
PHEW.
A-ALL RIGHT THEN...
I'VE GOT AN ARTIST'S BRAIN.
WHEN I'M THINKING UP THE STORY, WHICH IS WHILE I'M ACTUALLY WORKING ON THE DRAWINGS, I ONLY USE CERTAIN PARTS OF MY BRAIN.
KARI KARI (SKRITCH)
IT LEAVES ME STARVED FOR MENTAL STIMULA-TION.
KARI KARI
SO I WANTED TO FIND A WAY TO RELAX AND EXERCISE MY MIND. I WASN'T REALLY LOOKING TO GET SUPER INVOLVED IN ANYTHING...
...SO I ENDED UP DOING PUZZLES!
WHAT I'VE REALLY GOTTEN INTO LATELY IS CAST PUZZLES. THEY'RE A SERIES OF THREE-DIMENSIONAL PUZZLES THAT ARE REAL BRAIN TEASERS.
I'VE GOT A WHOLE COLLECTION OF THESE GUYS. NOT ONLY ARE THEY BEAUTIFUL TO LOOK AT, THEY ALSO MAKE ME WANT TO CREATE MY OWN PUZZLES.
I'VE WORKED HARD TO SOLVE ALL OF THEM, BUT THERE ARE STILL A LOT OUT THERE TO CHALLENGE MYSELF WITH.
AND THAT'S ALL. THAT'S MY AFTER-WORD.
BUN BUN (WAVE)
OR WAS THAT MORE LIKE AN AD?
HUH? IT'S ALREADY OVER?
I FILLED UP THE SPACE, DIDN'T I!?

⇨ SPECIAL THANKS! RIKU NATSUME #34, 35

TABOO TATTOO

by SHINJIRO

Translation: Christine Dashiell • Lettering: Phil Christie

TABOO TATTOO
© Shinjiro 2013
First published in Japan in 2013 by KADOKAWA CORPORATION. English translation rights reserved by Yen Press, LLC under the license from KADOKAWA CORPORATION, Tokyo through TUTTLE-MORI AGENCY, Inc., Tokyo.

English translation © 2017 by Yen Press, LLC

Yen Press
1290 Avenue of the Americas
New York, NY 10104

Visit us at yenpress.com
facebook.com/yenpress
twitter.com/yenpress
yenpress.tumblr.com
instagram.com/yenpress

First Yen Press Edition: July 2017

Yen Press is an imprint of Yen Press, LLC.
The Yen Press name and logo are trademarks of Yen Press, LLC.

The publisher is not responsible for websites (or their content) that are not owned by the publisher.

Library of Congress Control Number: 2015952591

ISBNs: 978-0-316-31065-9 (paperback)
978-0-316-31067-3 (ebook)

10 9 8 7 6 5 4 3 2 1

BVG

Printed in the United States of America